Purchased with the
Ellen & Peter Cantoni
Endowment

The World's Best Movies...

To Make Sure You Have Seen Before Your Popcorn Runs Out

EDITOR
Curt Gathje

COORDINATOR
Larry Cohn

Published and distributed by
Zagat Survey, LLC
4 Columbus Circle
New York, NY 10019
T: 212.977.6000
E: movies@zagat.com
www.zagat.com

ACKNOWLEDGMENTS

We thank the Arizona Film Society, DC Independent Film Festival, MSC Film Society, Olympia Film Society, Peachtree Film Society, University Film Society, Yale Film Society, Carol Bialkowski, Jason Briker, Kimberly Butler, Ed Dwyer, Gwen Hyman, Bob Laurie, David Margolick, Joshua Mooney, Pia Nordlinger, Maura O'Connell, Bernard Onken, Jane Rosenthal and Bill Wolf, as well as the following members of our staff: Josh Rogers (senior associate editor), Brian Albert, Jane Chang, Sandy Cheng, Reni Chin, Jeff Freier, Michelle Golden, Matthew Hamm, Natalie Lebert, Mike Liao, Becky Ruthenburg, Art Yaghci, Sharon Yates and Kyle Zolner.

The reviews in this guide are based on public opinion surveys. The ratings reflect the average scores given by the survey participants who voted on each film. The text is based on quotes from, or paraphrasings of, the surveyors' comments. Factual information was correct to the best of our knowledge when published in this guide.

DECATUR PUBLIC LIBRARY
MAR 15 2011
DECATUR, ILLINOIS

Our guides are printed using environmentally preferable inks containing 20%, by weight, renewable resources on papers sourced from well-managed forests. Deluxe editions are covered with Skivertex Recover® Double containing a minimum of 30% post-consumer waste fiber.

Certified Chain of Custody
Promoting Sustainable Forest Management
www.sfiprogram.org

PWC-SFICOC-260

ENVIROINK™

The inks used to print the body of this publication contain a minimum of 20%, by weight, renewable resources.

© 2010 Zagat Survey, LLC

ISBN-13: 978-1-60478-323-0
ISBN-10: 1-60478-323-0
Printed in the United States of America

Contents

Ratings & Symbols 4
About This Survey 5
Top Ratings:
- Overall Quality 6
- Acting 17
- Story 26
- Production Values 27
- Foreign Language Films 28

MOVIE DIRECTORY

Names, Release Dates, Directors, Cast, Running Times, MPAA Classifications, Ratings & Reviews 29

INDEXES

Years:
1910s/1920s 212
1930s 212
1940s 212
1950s 214
1960s 215
1970s 216
1980s 218
1990s 219
2000s 220

Genres/Special Features:
Action/Adventure 223
Americana 223
Animated 224
Biographies 224
Black Comedies 225
Blockbusters 225
Buddy Films 225
Camp Classics 226
Capers 226
Chick Flicks 226
Children/Family 226
City Settings 226
- LA 226
- London 227
- New York 227
- Paris 227
- Rome 227
- San Francisco 227

Comedies 228
Comic Book Adaptations 228
Coming of Age 229
Crime 229
Cult Films 229
Date Flicks 230
Dramas 230
Dramedies 231
DVD Not Available 232
End of the World 232
Epics 232
Fantasy 232
Film Noir 233
Food-Themed 233
Foreign Films 233
Gay-Themed 236
High School 236
Horror 236
Indies 236
James Bond 237
Literary Adaptations 237
Martial Arts 238
Movies About Movies 238
Musicals 238
Occupations 239
- Doctors 239
- Journalists 239
- Lawyers 239
- Politicians 239
- Prostitutes 239
- Spies 240
- Teachers 240

Office Politics 240
Oscar Winners 240
Religion 245
Road Movies 245
Rock 'n' Roll 245
Romance 245
Sci-Fi 246
Screwball Comedies 247
Silent 247
Soundtracks 247
Sports 249
Stage Adaptations 249
Swashbucklers 250
Thrillers 250
War 251
Weddings 252
Westerns 252

Ratings & Symbols

	Name	Symbols	Zagat Ratings: OVERALL	ACTING	STORY	PROD.
Title, Director, Cast, Running Time	**Tim & Nina Uncut**	◑	25	19	25	12

2001 | Directed by Quentin Tarantino | With Brad Pitt, Angelina Jolie | 90 minutes | Rated PG

Review, surveyor comments in quotes

Tim and Nina's "courtship in Paris" is the "ooh-la-la" subject of this chop-socky/docudrama hybrid (think *Breathless* meets *Rush Hour*) that "inspires" the insipid but is "boring as heck" for everyone else; all applaud Pitt's "butch but tender" take on Tim as a "young buck", while Jolie is "so adorable" as "Nina in love" that many "want to adopt *her*"; P.S. the interminable cinéma-vérité "dinner scenes in bed" aren't for the squeamish, and Angie is rumored to have gotten pregnant during the mashed-potatoes course.

Ratings

Overall Quality, Acting, Story and **Production Values** are rated on the Zagat 0 to 30 scale.

- 0 - 9 poor to fair
- 10 - 15 fair to good
- 16 - 19 good to very good
- 20 - 25 very good to excellent
- 26 - 30 extraordinary to perfection

Symbols

- ✉ Oscar winner for Best Picture, Actor, Actress, Director, Screenplay, Foreign Language Film
- ◑ filmed in black & white
- 🅵 foreign language film
- ∅ not yet on DVD

About This Survey

This **World's Best Movies** guide covers the top 1,000 movies of all time, ranging from box-office blockbusters to foreign-language standouts to cult favorites. We have been surveying movies since 2002; like all our guides, this one is based on input from avid consumers - 20,773 moviegoers all told. Unlike other guidebooks whose choices (and opinions) come from one or two professional critics, this book tells it from the unique perspective of avid filmgoers like you. Our editors have synopsized your feedback and highlighted representative comments (in quotation marks within each review). We sincerely thank each of these participants - this book is really "theirs."

OUR PHILOSOPHY: Three simple premises underlie our ratings and reviews. First, we've long believed that the collective opinions of large numbers of consumers are more accurate than the opinions of a single critic. Second, we know that people often disagree about the films they see - a survey can reflect this, a single person can't. Third, because there is no single factor that determines a film's quality, we ask surveyors to separately rate acting, story and production values; we also provide an overall score. Finally, since people need reliable information in a fast, easy-to-digest format, we strive to be concise. Our Top Ratings lists (pages 6–28) and indexes (starting on page 212) are also designed to help you quickly choose the best movie for any occasion.

ABOUT ZAGAT: In 1979, we started asking friends to rate and review restaurants purely for fun. The term "user-generated content" had not yet been coined. That hobby grew into Zagat Survey; 31 years later, we have over 375,000 surveyors and cover airlines, bars, dining, fast food, entertaining, golf, hotels, movies, music, resorts, shopping, spas, theater and tourist attractions in over 100 countries. Along the way, we evolved from being a print publisher to a digital content provider, e.g. **ZAGAT.com, ZAGAT.mobi** (for web-enabled mobile devices), **ZAGAT TO GO** (for smartphones) and **nru** (for Android phones). We also produce customized gifts and marketing tools for a wide range of corporate clients. And you can find us on Twitter (twitter.com/zagatbuzz), Facebook and other social media networks.

JOIN IN: To improve our guides, we solicit your comments; it's vital that we hear your opinions. Just contact us at **nina-tim@zagat.com.** We also invite you to join our surveys at **ZAGAT.com.** Do so and you'll receive a choice of rewards in exchange.

New York, NY
September 13, 2010

Nina and Tim Zagat

Top Overall Quality

For Top Foreign Language Films, see page 28.

29 Godfather, The
Godfather Part II
Casablanca
Schindler's List
Lawrence of Arabia
To Kill a Mockingbird

28 Star Wars
Wizard of Oz
Lady Eve
Singin' in the Rain
Rear Window
It Happened One Night
Citizen Kane
Shawshank Redemption
All About Eve
Pianist, The
African Queen
Third Man
Finding Nemo
Dr. Strangelove
Lord of the Rings/Return
Best Years of Our Lives
Man for All Seasons
Grapes of Wrath
On the Waterfront
Paths of Glory
Lion in Winter
Fantasia
Hotel Rwanda
Bridge on the River Kwai
Some Like It Hot
Sunset Boulevard
All Quiet/Western Front
Sound of Music
Gone with the Wind
North by Northwest
High Noon
12 Angry Men
Double Indemnity
Maltese Falcon
Psycho
Raiders of the Lost Ark

27 One Flew Over Cuckoo's . . .
My Fair Lady
Sweet Smell of Success
I Never Sang for My Father
Snow White
Philadelphia Story
Woman of the Year
Up
Treasure of Sierra Madre
Usual Suspects
West Side Story
Heiress, The
Taxi Driver
Young Frankenstein
Notorious
Searchers, The*
Silence of the Lambs
Manchurian Candidate
Chinatown
Apocalypse Now
Ox-Bow Incident
Brief Encounter
Duck Soup
Holiday
Lord of the Rings/Fellowship
Patton
It's a Wonderful Life
Christmas Carol
Annie Hall
Great Expectations
Witness for the Prosecution
Sting, The
Big Sleep
Chicago
Night of the Hunter
Hamlet (1948)
Sullivan's Travels
Streetcar Named Desire
Lord of the Rings/Two Towers
Gandhi
Great Escape
Million Dollar Baby
Advise & Consent
Wild Bunch
Stalag 17
Princess Bride
How Green Was My Valley
Quiet Man
Graduate, The
Top Hat
Vertigo
Dinner at Eight
Rebecca
Roman Holiday
Spirited Away
Goodfellas
Gun Crazy*
Place in the Sun*
Wuthering Heights*

* Indicates a tie with film above

BY GENRE

ACTION/ADVENTURE

29 Lawrence of Arabia
28 Raiders of the Lost Ark
27 Treasure of Sierra Madre
Great Escape
26 Iron Man
Papillon
Dark Knight
Magnificent Seven
Spartacus
25 Man Who Would Be King
Deliverance
Adventures of Robin Hood
Professional, The
Mutiny on the Bounty (1935)
Bourne Ultimatum
King Kong
Inglourious Basterds
Blood Diamond
Kill Bill Vol. 2
Flight of the Phoenix

AMERICANA

29 To Kill a Mockingbird
28 Best Years of Our Lives
Grapes of Wrath
27 It's a Wonderful Life
26 Shadow of a Doubt
Christmas Story
Meet Me in St. Louis
Mr. Smith Goes to Washington
25 Yankee Doodle Dandy
Music Man
Member of the Wedding
Mr. Deeds Goes to Town
Badlands
All the King's Men
Seabiscuit
24 Stand by Me
American Graffiti
Far From Heaven
Forrest Gump
Oklahoma!

ANIMATED

28 Finding Nemo
Fantasia
27 Snow White
Up
Spirited Away
Toy Story
26 Shrek
Beauty/Beast (1991)
Pinocchio
Shrek 2
Incredibles, The
Cinderella
Bambi
Lady and the Tramp
WALL-E
Monsters, Inc.
Ratatouille
Toy Story 2
25 Lion King
Peter Pan

BIOGRAPHY

29 Lawrence of Arabia
28 Man for All Seasons
27 Patton
Gandhi
26 Raging Bull
Amadeus
Becket
Ray
Anne of the Thousand Days
Last Emperor
Queen, The
Capote
Funny Girl
25 Yankee Doodle Dandy
Milk
Sergeant York
Walk the Line
Finding Neverland
Cinderella Man
Last King of Scotland

CHILDREN/FAMILY

28 Wizard of Oz
Sound of Music
27 It's a Wonderful Life
Christmas Carol
Princess Bride
Mary Poppins
26 E.T. The Extra-Terrestrial
Christmas Story
Sounder
Willy Wonka
25 Babe
Whale Rider
Harry Potter/
Half-Blood Prince
24 Lili
Harry Potter/Goblet of Fire
Bells of St. Mary's
Oliver!
Black Stallion

Harry Potter/Order of Phoenix
Dark Crystal

COMEDY

28 Some Like It Hot
27 Woman of the Year
Young Frankenstein
Annie Hall
Graduate, The
Mister Roberts
26 Adam's Rib
Great Dictator
Man Who Came to Dinner*
Monkey Business
This Is Spinal Tap
When Harry Met Sally . . .
Harvey
Manhattan
Local Hero
25 Waiting for Guffman
Auntie Mame
Lavender Hill Mob
Blazing Saddles
Mr. Deeds Goes to Town

CRIME

29 Godfather, The
Godfather Part II
28 Rear Window
On the Waterfront
27 Usual Suspects
Sting, The
Chicago
Goodfellas
26 Departed, The
Pulp Fiction
Arsenic and Old Lace
Anatomy of a Murder
Capote
Mystic River
25 Fargo
Public Enemy
Experiment in Terror
Lavender Hill Mob
High Sierra
In Cold Blood

CULT

28 Star Wars
Wizard of Oz
Shawshank Redemption
All About Eve
Dr. Strangelove
Fantasia
Sound of Music
27 Manchurian Candidate
It's a Wonderful Life
Princess Bride
Gun Crazy
26 Monty Python/Holy Grail
Breakfast at Tiffany's
Red Shoes
Blade Runner
Willy Wonka
25 Harold and Maude
Waiting for Guffman
Forbidden Planet
Kill Bill Vol. 2

DRAMA

29 Godfather, The
Godfather Part II
Schindler's List
To Kill a Mockingbird
28 Citizen Kane
Shawshank Redemption
Pianist, The
Best Years of Our Lives
Grapes of Wrath
On the Waterfront
Paths of Glory
Lion in Winter
Hotel Rwanda
High Noon
12 Angry Men
27 I Never Sang for My Father
Heiress, The
Taxi Driver
Ox-Bow Incident
Great Expectations

DRAMEDY

28 All About Eve
African Queen
27 One Flew Over Cuckoo's . . .
It's a Wonderful Life
Sting, The
Sullivan's Travels
Stalag 17
Dinner at Eight
26 Breakfast at Tiffany's
Women, The
Crimes and Misdemeanors
Sense and Sensibility
Charade
Bend It Like Beckham
Mr. Smith Goes to Washington
Cool Hand Luke
25 Apartment, The
Sabrina
Fargo
Lady Vanishes

Visit ZAGAT.com

EPIC

29 Lawrence of Arabia
28 Bridge on the River Kwai
Gone with the Wind
27 Gandhi
Doctor Zhivago
26 Ben-Hur
Last Emperor
2001: A Space Odyssey
Braveheart
Spartacus
25 Empire of the Sun
Once Upon a Time/West
Mutiny on the Bounty (1935)
Gunga Din
Passage to India
24 Longest Day
Ten Commandments
Zulu
Giant
Once Upon a Time/America

FANTASY

28 Wizard of Oz
Lord of the Rings/Return
Raiders of the Lost Ark
27 Lord of the Rings/Fellowship
Christmas Carol
Lord of the Rings/Two Towers
Princess Bride
Mary Poppins
26 Harvey
Willy Wonka
25 King Kong
Lost Horizon
Harry Potter/Half-Blood Prince
24 Harry Potter/Goblet of Fire
Brazil
Ghost and Mrs. Muir
Harry Potter/Order of Phoenix
Alice in Wonderland (1951)
Dark Crystal
Harry Potter/Prisoner

FILM NOIR

28 Third Man
Sunset Boulevard
Double Indemnity
Maltese Falcon
27 Sweet Smell of Success
Chinatown
Big Sleep
Night of the Hunter
Gun Crazy
Laura
26 Out of the Past
Touch of Evil
Ace in the Hole
Blade Runner
Strangers on a Train
L.A. Confidential
Mildred Pierce
Memento
Key Largo
25 Fargo

HORROR

25 Exorcist, The
Frankenstein
Shining, The
Bride of Frankenstein
24 Dracula
Invasion/Body Snatchers
Rosemary's Baby
Hush . . . Hush, Sweet Charlotte
Mummy, The
23 Army of Darkness
Freaks
Thing, The (1982)
Cat People
Thing, The (1951)
22 Invisible Man
Poltergeist
Halloween

MUSICAL

28 Wizard of Oz
Singin' in the Rain
Sound of Music
27 My Fair Lady
West Side Story
Chicago
Top Hat
King and I
Mary Poppins
26 Fiddler on the Roof
American in Paris
Band Wagon
Cabaret
Meet Me in St. Louis
Swing Time
Funny Girl
25 Yankee Doodle Dandy
Music Man
Shall We Dance
Gay Divorcee

ROMANCE

29 Casablanca
28 Lady Eve
It Happened One Night
African Queen

Gone with the Wind
27 My Fair Lady
Philadelphia Story
West Side Story
Notorious
Brief Encounter
Holiday
Annie Hall
How Green Was My Valley
Quiet Man
Graduate, The
Top Hat
Vertigo
Rebecca
Roman Holiday
Place in the Sun
Wuthering Heights*

SCI-FI

28 Star Wars
26 E.T. The Extra-Terrestrial
Star Wars V/Empire Strikes
Avatar
Blade Runner
On the Beach
2001: A Space Odyssey
Star Trek
25 Matrix, The
Alien
Forbidden Planet
Day the Earth Stood Still
24 Star Wars VI/Return of Jedi
Close Encounters
Invasion/Body Snatchers
Terminator, The
X2
23 Star Wars III/Revenge of Sith
Aliens
Back to the Future

THRILLER

28 Rear Window
Third Man
North by Northwest
Psycho
27 Taxi Driver
Notorious
Silence of the Lambs
Manchurian Candidate
Night of the Hunter
Vertigo
39 Steps
26 Shadow of a Doubt
Gaslight
Jaws
Pulp Fiction
Strangers on a Train
Memento
Seven Days in May
Sixth Sense
25 Lifeboat

WAR

29 Schindler's List
Lawrence of Arabia
28 Pianist, The
Best Years of Our Lives
Paths of Glory
Bridge on the River Kwai
All Quiet/Western Front
Gone with the Wind
27 Apocalypse Now
Patton
Great Escape
Stalag 17
Caine Mutiny
Mister Roberts
26 MASH
Saving Private Ryan
Henry V
Hurt Locker
To Have and Have Not
Deer Hunter

WESTERN

28 High Noon
27 Searchers, The
Ox-Bow Incident
Wild Bunch
Stagecoach
26 Red River
Butch Cassidy/Sundance Kid
Shane
Hud
Unforgiven
Magnificent Seven
25 My Darling Clementine
Outlaw Josey Wales
Once Upon a Time/West
Man Who Shot Liberty Valance
Destry Rides Again
24 Oklahoma!
No Country for Old Men
Good, the Bad and the Ugly
She Wore a Yellow Ribbon

Visit ZAGAT.com

BY DECADE

1910s/1920s

28 General, The
Gold Rush
Napoléon
27 Potemkin
Metropolis
26 Cabinet of Dr. Caligari
Nosferatu
25 Birth of a Nation
24 Cocoanuts, The
Thief of Bagdad

1930s

28 Wizard of Oz
It Happened One Night
All Quiet on Western Front
Gone with the Wind
27 Snow White
Duck Soup
Holiday
Top Hat
Dinner at Eight
Wuthering Heights

1940s

29 Casablanca
28 Lady Eve
Citizen Kane
Third Man
Best Years of Our Lives
Grapes of Wrath
Fantasia
Double Indemnity
Maltese Falcon
27 Philadelphia Story

1950s

28 Singin' in the Rain
Rear Window
All About Eve
African Queen
On the Waterfront
Paths of Glory
Bridge on the River Kwai
Some Like It Hot
Sunset Boulevard
North by Northwest

1960s

29 Lawrence of Arabia
To Kill a Mockingbird
28 Dr. Strangelove
Man for All Seasons
Lion in Winter
Sound of Music
Psycho
27 My Fair Lady
West Side Story
Manchurian Candidate

1970s

29 Godfather, The
Godfather Part II
28 Star Wars
27 One Flew Over Cuckoo's . . .
I Never Sang for My Father
Taxi Driver
Young Frankenstein
Chinatown
Apocalypse Now
Patton

1980s

28 Raiders of the Lost Ark
27 Gandhi
Princess Bride
Breaker Morant
Fitzcarraldo
26 E.T. The Extra-Terrestrial
Raging Bull
Amadeus
Star Wars V/Empire Strikes
Soldier's Story

1990s

29 Schindler's List
28 Shawshank Redemption
27 Usual Suspects
Silence of the Lambs
Goodfellas
Toy Story
26 Saving Private Ryan
Beauty/Beast
Pulp Fiction
L.A. Confidential

2000s

28 Pianist, The
Finding Nemo
Lord of the Rings/Return
Hotel Rwanda
27 Up
Lord of the Rings/Fellowship
Chicago
Lord of the Rings/Two Towers
Million Dollar Baby
Spirited Away
26 Shrek
Shrek 2

Iron Man
Beautiful Mind
Slumdog Millionaire
Avatar
Incredibles, The
Crash
Departed, The
Ray

BY DIRECTOR

Woody Allen
27 Annie Hall
26 Crimes and Misdemeanors
Manhattan
24 Hannah and Her Sisters
23 Interiors
Bananas
Sleeper
Radio Days

Pedro Almodóvar
26 Talk to Her
25 All About My Mother
24 Women on the Verge
Volver
23 Bad Education

Robert Altman
26 MASH
25 3 Women
23 McCabe & Mrs. Miller
Player, The
Gosford Park
Nashville

Paul Thomas Anderson
23 There Will Be Blood

Wes Anderson
23 Rushmore

Hal Ashby
26 Being There
25 Harold and Maude
23 Coming Home

Ingmar Bergman
27 Seventh Seal
Persona
26 Wild Strawberries
Fanny and Alexander
Cries and Whispers
Smiles of a Summer Night
25 Scenes from a Marriage

Bernardo Bertolucci
26 Conformist, The
Last Emperor

Peter Bogdanovich
23 Last Picture Show

James L. Brooks
25 Terms of Endearment
23 Broadcast News

Mel Brooks
27 Young Frankenstein
26 Producers, The
25 Blazing Saddles

Richard Brooks
25 Elmer Gantry
In Cold Blood
Cat on a Hot Tin Roof
24 Sweet Bird of Youth
23 Blackboard Jungle

Tim Burton
23 Sweeney Todd
Alice in Wonderland

James Cameron
26 Avatar
24 Terminator, The
23 Aliens
Terminator 2: Judgment Day

Frank Capra
28 It Happened One Night
27 It's a Wonderful Life
26 Arsenic and Old Lace
Mr. Smith Goes to Washington
25 Mr. Deeds Goes to Town
Lost Horizon
24 Meet John Doe

John Cassavetes
24 Woman Under the Influence

Charlie Chaplin
28 City Lights
Gold Rush
Modern Times
26 Great Dictator
24 Limelight

Joel Coen
25 Fargo
24 Blood Simple
No Country for Old Men
23 Raising Arizona

Francis Ford Coppola

29 Godfather, The
Godfather Part II
27 Apocalypse Now
25 Conversation, The

George Cukor

27 My Fair Lady
Philadelphia Story
Holiday
Dinner at Eight
26 Adam's Rib
Gaslight
Women, The
Camille
Born Yesterday
25 Star Is Born

Michael Curtiz

29 Casablanca
26 Mildred Pierce
25 Yankee Doodle Dandy
Adventures of Robin Hood
White Christmas
24 Angels with Dirty Faces
23 Captain Blood

Jonathan Demme

27 Silence of the Lambs
24 Philadelphia

Vittorio De Sica

27 Bicycle Thief
25 Two Women
Garden of the Finzi-Continis

Stanley Donen

28 Singin' in the Rain
26 Charade
24 Funny Face
Two for the Road
24 Seven Brides/Seven Brothers
23 On the Town

Clint Eastwood

27 Letters from Iwo Jima
Million Dollar Baby
26 Gran Torino
Unforgiven
Mystic River
25 Outlaw Josey Wales
24 Invictus
23 Flags of Our Fathers
Changeling

Blake Edwards

27 Days of Wine and Roses
26 Breakfast at Tiffany's
25 Experiment in Terror
24 Pink Panther
23 Victor/Victoria
Shot in the Dark

Federico Fellini

27 La Strada
Nights of Cabiria
26 8½
Amarcord
25 La Dolce Vita
Juliet of the Spirits

Victor Fleming

28 Wizard of Oz
Gone with the Wind
25 Captains Courageous

John Ford

28 Grapes of Wrath
27 Searchers, The
How Green Was My Valley
Quiet Man
Stagecoach
Mister Roberts
25 My Darling Clementine
Man Who Shot Liberty Valance
24 She Wore a Yellow Ribbon
23 Fort Apache
How the West Was Won

Milos Forman

27 One Flew Over Cuckoo's . . .
26 Amadeus

Bob Fosse

26 Cabaret
24 Lenny
All That Jazz

Stephen Frears

26 Queen, The
24 Dangerous Liaisons
23 Dirty Pretty Things
My Beautiful Laundrette
Mrs. Henderson Presents

Christopher Guest

25 Waiting for Guffman
24 Best in Show
23 Mighty Wind

Howard Hawks

27 Big Sleep
Bringing Up Baby
26 Red River
His Girl Friday
To Have and Have Not

Ball of Fire
25 Sergeant York
24 Rio Bravo
23 Gentlemen Prefer Blondes

Werner Herzog
27 Fitzcarraldo
25 Aguirre: The Wrath of God

Alfred Hitchcock
28 Rear Window
North by Northwest
Psycho
27 Notorious
Vertigo
Rebecca
39 Steps
26 Shadow of a Doubt
Strangers on a Train
25 Lifeboat
Lady Vanishes
Suspicion
Dial M for Murder
To Catch a Thief
24 Man Who Knew Too Much
Birds, The
Foreign Correspondent
Spellbound
23 Torn Curtain
Saboteur

Ron Howard
26 Beautiful Mind
25 Cinderella Man
Frost/Nixon
24 Apollo 13

John Huston
28 African Queen
Maltese Falcon
27 Treasure of Sierra Madre
26 Key Largo
25 Man Who Would Be King
24 Asphalt Jungle
Dead, The
23 Night of the Iguana, The

Peter Jackson
28 Lord of the Rings/Return
27 Lord of the Rings/Fellowship
Lord of the Rings/Two Towers
24 Heavenly Creatures

Elia Kazan
28 On the Waterfront
27 Streetcar Named Desire
26 Gentleman's Agreement
Face in the Crowd
25 Splendor in the Grass
24 East of Eden
23 Viva Zapata!

Stanley Kramer
26 Inherit the Wind
On the Beach
Judgment at Nuremberg
25 Guess Who's Coming . . .
24 It's a Mad Mad Mad World
23 Ship of Fools

Stanley Kubrick
28 Dr. Strangelove
Paths of Glory
26 2001: A Space Odyssey
Spartacus
25 Killing, The
Shining, The
Clockwork Orange
24 Full Metal Jacket
Lolita

Akira Kurosawa
29 Seven Samurai
Rashomon
28 Yojimbo
27 Ran

David Lean
29 Lawrence of Arabia
28 Bridge on the River Kwai
27 Brief Encounter
Great Expectations
Doctor Zhivago
25 Oliver Twist
Passage to India
23 Summertime

Ang Lee
26 Sense and Sensibility
25 Eat Drink Man Woman
24 Crouching Tiger
Brokeback Mountain
22 Wedding Banquet

Spike Lee
23 Malcolm X
Do the Right Thing
Inside Man

Barry Levinson
25 Rain Man
Diner
24 Avalon
23 Natural, The

George Lucas

28 Star Wars
24 American Graffiti
23 Star Wars III/Revenge of Sith

Baz Luhrmann

23 Moulin Rouge!
Strictly Ballroom

Sidney Lumet

28 12 Angry Men
26 Pawnbroker, The
24 Fail-Safe
Network
Dog Day Afternoon
23 Serpico
Verdict, The*
Murder on the Orient Express
Before the Devil Knows . . .

David Lynch

24 Elephant Man
Straight Story

Terrence Malick

25 Badlands
23 Days of Heaven

Louis Malle

27 Au Revoir Les Enfants
24 Atlantic City

Joseph L. Mankiewicz

28 All About Eve
25 Sleuth
24 Ghost and Mrs. Muir
Barefoot Contessa
Guys and Dolls
Letter to Three Wives
Suddenly, Last Summer

Anthony Minghella

23 Truly Madly Deeply
22 Cold Mountain

Vincente Minnelli

26 American in Paris
Band Wagon
Meet Me in St. Louis
24 Gigi
Bells Are Ringing
Bad and the Beautiful
Cabin in the Sky
Brigadoon
23 Lust for Life
Father of the Bride

Mike Nichols

27 Graduate, The
25 Who's Afraid of V. Woolf?
Catch-22
22 Silkwood

Arthur Penn

25 Miracle Worker
Bonnie and Clyde
24 Little Big Man

Roman Polanski

28 Pianist, The
27 Chinatown
24 Rosemary's Baby
Knife in the Water

Sydney Pollack

25 Tootsie
Out of Africa
24 Way We Were
Three Days of the Condor
23 Jeremiah Johnson

Otto Preminger

27 Advise & Consent
Laura
26 Anatomy of a Murder
24 Man with the Golden Arm
23 Carmen Jones
Exodus

Robert Redford

25 Ordinary People
22 River Runs Through It

Martin Scorsese

27 Taxi Driver
Goodfellas
26 Raging Bull
Departed, The
24 Mean Streets
Alice Doesn't Live Here
23 King of Comedy
Aviator, The

Ridley Scott

26 Blade Runner
25 Alien
23 Gladiator
American Gangster
Thelma & Louise
Black Hawk Down

Steven Soderbergh

23 Traffic

Steven Spielberg

29 Schindler's List
28 Raiders of the Lost Ark
26 E.T. The Extra-Terrestrial
Saving Private Ryan
Jaws
Color Purple
25 Empire of the Sun
24 Indiana Jones/Last Crusade
Close Encounters
23 Munich
Catch Me If You Can

George Stevens

27 Woman of the Year
Place in the Sun
26 Shane
Swing Time
25 Gunga Din
24 Giant
23 Diary of Anne Frank

Preston Sturges

28 Lady Eve
27 Sullivan's Travels
25 Palm Beach Story
23 Miracle of Morgan's Creek

Quentin Tarantino

26 Pulp Fiction
25 Inglourious Basterds
Kill Bill Vol. 2
24 Reservoir Dogs
23 Kill Bill Vol. 1

François Truffaut

27 400 Blows
Day for Night
25 Shoot the Piano Player
24 Jules and Jim
Story of Adele H.
Last Metro

Gus Van Sant

25 Milk
24 Good Will Hunting

Orson Welles

28 Citizen Kane
26 Touch of Evil
25 Lady from Shanghai
Magnificent Ambersons

Billy Wilder

28 Some Like It Hot
Sunset Boulevard
Double Indemnity
27 Witness for the Prosecution
Stalag 17
26 Ace in the Hole
25 Apartment, The
Sabrina
Lost Weekend
24 Love in the Afternoon
23 Fortune Cookie
One, Two, Three
Seven Year Itch

Robert Wise

28 Sound of Music
27 West Side Story
25 Day the Earth Stood Still
24 I Want to Live!
Sand Pebbles

William Wyler

28 Best Years of Our Lives
27 Heiress, The
Roman Holiday
Wuthering Heights
26 Little Foxes
Ben-Hur
Funny Girl
25 Mrs. Miniver
Jezebel
24 Friendly Persuasion
Children's Hour
23 Collector, The

Fred Zinnemann

28 Man for All Seasons
High Noon
26 From Here to Eternity
25 Member of the Wedding
Day of the Jackal
Julia
24 Oklahoma!

Top Acting

29 Godfather Part II
Godfather, The
All About Eve
One Flew Over Cuckoo's . . .
Monster
Capote
Ray
Hamlet (1948)
Lion in Winter
Taxi Driver
On the Waterfront
Queen, The
Becket
To Kill a Mockingbird
Schindler's List
Last King of Scotland
Pianist, The
Brief Encounter
African Queen

28 Hotel Rwanda
Casablanca
Beautiful Mind
Million Dollar Baby
Streetcar Named Desire
Silence of the Lambs
Days of Wine and Roses
12 Angry Men
Gandhi
Man for All Seasons
Lady Eve
Patton
Shawshank Redemption
Lawrence of Arabia
Now, Voyager
Raging Bull
Adam's Rib
Notes on a Scandal
Philadelphia Story
Sweet Smell of Success
Inherit the Wind
Little Foxes
Milk
Crazy Heart
White Heat
Mystic River
Sophie's Choice
Doubt
Prime of Miss Jean Brodie
My Left Foot
Night of the Hunter
Midnight Cowboy
TransAmerica
Born Yesterday
Kind Hearts and Coronets
Grapes of Wrath
Chinatown
Heiress, The
Vera Drake
Departed, The
Woman of the Year
Apartment, The
Hud
Caine Mutiny
Walk the Line
Sunset Boulevard
Savages, The
Sleuth*
Frances
Witness for the Prosecution
Bridge on the River Kwai
American History X
Raisin in the Sun
My Brilliant Career
It Happened One Night
Hours, The
Face in the Crowd
Sweet Bird of Youth
Third Man
There Will Be Blood
Reader, The
Dr. Strangelove
Usual Suspects
Ball of Fire
Snake Pit
Accused, The
Requiem for a Heavyweight*
Pawnbroker, The
Miracle Worker
Henry V
His Girl Friday
Deer Hunter
Bad Day at Black Rock
Insider, The*

27 Being There
Treasure of Sierra Madre
Jezebel
Odd Couple
Sling Blade*
Citizen Kane
Some Like It Hot

Woody Allen

26 Annie Hall
Crimes and Misdemeanors
24 Manhattan
23 Front, The
21 Play It Again, Sam
20 Bananas
19 Sleeper

Julie Andrews

25 Sound of Music
24 Mary Poppins
Victor/Victoria
Americanization of Emily
Torn Curtain

Fred Astaire

26 On the Beach
24 Funny Face
23 Top Hat
Swing Time
Gay Divorcee
22 Shall We Dance
21 Band Wagon
Ziegfeld Follies
Easter Parade
20 Holiday Inn
19 Flying Down to Rio

Lauren Bacall

27 To Have and Have Not
Big Sleep
26 Key Largo
23 Murder on the Orient Express

Warren Beatty

25 Bonnie and Clyde
Splendor in the Grass
23 Parallax View
McCabe & Mrs. Miller

Ingrid Bergman

28 Casablanca
27 Notorious
Gaslight
Anastasia
26 For Whom the Bell Tolls
25 Bells of St. Mary's
Spellbound
23 Murder on the Orient Express

Cate Blanchett

28 Notes on a Scandal
27 Elizabeth
25 Aviator, The
Curious Case/Benjamin Button

Humphrey Bogart

29 African Queen
28 Casablanca
Caine Mutiny
27 Treasure of Sierra Madre
To Have and Have Not
Dark Victory
Maltese Falcon
Big Sleep
26 Key Largo
High Sierra
25 Sabrina
Barefoot Contessa
24 Angels with Dirty Faces

Marlon Brando

29 Godfather, The
On the Waterfront
28 Streetcar Named Desire
27 Apocalypse Now
24 Viva Zapata!
Mutiny on the Bounty
21 Guys and Dolls

Richard Burton

29 Becket
27 Who's Afraid of V. Woolf?
Anne of the Thousand Days
26 Spy Who Came in from Cold
Night of the Iguana

Nicolas Cage

25 Birdy
Moonstruck
23 Raising Arizona

James Cagney

28 White Heat
27 Mister Roberts
25 Public Enemy
Yankee Doodle Dandy
24 Angels with Dirty Faces
23 One, Two, Three
21 Footlight Parade

Michael Caine

28 Sleuth
26 Man Who Would Be King
Quiet American
24 Zulu
Ipcress File
21 Batman Begins

Charlie Chaplin

28 Gold Rush
City Lights

27 Great Dictator
26 Modern Times
25 Limelight

Julie Christie

27 Finding Neverland
26 Hamlet
Doctor Zhivago
Don't Look Now
25 Darling
Far from the Madding Crowd
23 McCabe & Mrs. Miller

Montgomery Clift

28 Heiress, The
27 From Here to Eternity
Place in the Sun
26 Suddenly, Last Summer
25 Red River

George Clooney

27 Good Night, and Good Luck
26 Michael Clayton
25 Up in the Air

Glenn Close

26 Reversal of Fortune
Dangerous Liaisons
24 Big Chill
21 Natural, The

Sean Connery

26 Man Who Would Be King
25 Wind and the Lion
24 Hunt for Red October
23 Goldfinger
Indiana Jones/Last Crusade
21 From Russia With Love
Thunderball
20 Dr. No

Gary Cooper

28 Ball of Fire
26 High Noon
For Whom the Bell Tolls
Mr. Deeds Goes to Town
Meet John Doe
25 Love in the Afternoon
Sergeant York
Friendly Persuasion
23 Beau Geste
22 Fountainhead, The

Kevin Costner

24 Silverado
20 Dances with Wolves

Joan Crawford

26 Grand Hotel
Women, The
25 Mildred Pierce

Russell Crowe

28 Beautiful Mind
Insider, The
27 Cinderella Man
L.A. Confidential
26 American Gangster
25 3:10 to Yuma
24 Master and Commander
23 Gladiator

Tom Cruise

27 Rain Man
26 Few Good Men
23 Last Samurai

Matt Damon

28 Departed, The
25 Invictus
Good Will Hunting
23 Bourne Ultimatum

Bette Davis

29 All About Eve
28 Now, Voyager
Little Foxes
27 Jezebel
Man Who Came to Dinner
All This, and Heaven Too
Dark Victory
26 Hush, Hush, Sweet Charlotte

Daniel Day-Lewis

28 My Left Foot
There Will Be Blood
25 In the Name of the Father
24 My Beautiful Laundrette
22 Last of the Mohicans

James Dean

27 East of Eden
24 Rebel Without a Cause
23 Giant

Olivia de Havilland

28 Heiress, The
Snake Pit
27 Gone with the Wind
26 Hush, Hush, Sweet Charlotte
22 Adventures of Robin Hood
21 Captain Blood

Catherine Deneuve

25 Last Metro
Belle de Jour
Indochine
22 Umbrellas of Cherbourg

Robert De Niro

29 Taxi Driver
28 Raging Bull
Deer Hunter
27 Goodfellas
Mean Streets
26 Once Upon a Time/America
King of Comedy
25 Bang the Drum Slowly
Midnight Run
24 Mission, The
23 Brazil

Johnny Depp

27 Finding Neverland
26 Sweeney Todd
25 Pirates Caribbean/The Curse
24 Chocolat
23 Alice in Wonderland

Leonardo DiCaprio

28 Departed, The
26 Blood Diamond
25 Aviator, The
24 Catch Me If You Can

Marlene Dietrich

28 Witness for the Prosecution
27 Judgment at Nuremberg
Blue Angel
25 Destry Rides Again

Kirk Douglas

27 Paths of Glory
26 Out of the Past
Ace in the Hole
25 Lust for Life
Bad and the Beautiful
24 Seven Days in May
Spartacus

Robert Downey Jr.

27 Good Night, and Good Luck
26 Iron Man

Faye Dunaway

28 Chinatown
25 Network
Bonnie and Clyde
Little Big Man
24 Three Days of the Condor
23 Thomas Crown Affair

Clint Eastwood

28 Million Dollar Baby
27 Gran Torino
26 Unforgiven
23 Outlaw Josey Wales
22 Escape from Alcatraz
21 For a Few Dollars More
Good, the Bad and the Ugly

Mia Farrow

26 Crimes and Misdemeanors
25 Hannah and Her Sisters
Rosemary's Baby
23 Radio Days

Henry Fonda

28 12 Angry Men
Lady Eve
Grapes of Wrath
27 Jezebel
Advise & Consent
Mister Roberts
On Golden Pond
Ox-Bow Incident
My Darling Clementine
25 Fail-Safe
24 Once Upon a Time/West
22 Fort Apache
21 How the West Was Won

Jane Fonda

27 Julia
On Golden Pond
26 Coming Home
24 Barefoot in the Park

Harrison Ford

24 Fugitive, The
Raiders of the Lost Ark
Witness
23 Indiana Jones/Last Crusade
22 Blade Runner
Star Wars
21 Star Wars V/Empire Strikes
20 Star Wars VI/Return of Jedi

Jodie Foster

29 Taxi Driver
28 Silence of the Lambs
Accused, The
26 Alice Doesn't Live Here
25 Inside Man

Jamie Foxx

29 Ray
24 Dreamgirls

Morgan Freeman

28 Million Dollar Baby
Shawshank Redemption
27 Driving Miss Daisy
26 Unforgiven
Gone Baby Gone
Glory
25 Invictus
23 Seven

Clark Gable

28 It Happened One Night
27 Gone with the Wind
25 Mutiny on the Bounty

Greta Garbo

27 Ninotchka
26 Camille
Grand Hotel
Anna Karenina

Ava Gardner

26 Night of the Iguana
On the Beach
25 Killers, The
Barefoot Contessa
20 Show Boat

Judy Garland

26 Wizard of Oz
Star Is Born
24 Meet Me in St. Louis
21 Ziegfeld Follies
Easter Parade

Richard Gere

26 Chicago
22 Pretty Woman
21 Days of Heaven

Mel Gibson

25 Year of Living Dangerously
Gallipoli
24 Braveheart
18 Road Warrior

Cary Grant

28 Philadelphia Story
His Girl Friday
27 Bringing Up Baby
Notorious
Holiday
26 North by Northwest
Suspicion
Arsenic and Old Lace
Awful Truth
25 Affair to Remember
Charade
To Catch a Thief
24 Gunga Din
Bishop's Wife
Mr. Blandings . . .
22 I'm No Angel

Tom Hanks

27 Philadelphia
26 Road to Perdition
Forrest Gump
Saving Private Ryan
25 Green Mile
24 Catch Me If You Can
Big
Apollo 13

Audrey Hepburn

27 My Fair Lady
Two for the Road
26 Children's Hour
Roman Holiday
Wait Until Dark
Breakfast at Tiffany's
25 Sabrina
Charade
Love in the Afternoon
24 Funny Face

Katharine Hepburn

29 Lion in Winter
African Queen
28 Adam's Rib
Philadelphia Story
Woman of the Year
27 Bringing Up Baby
Desk Set
On Golden Pond
Holiday
Guess Who's Coming . . .
26 Stage Door
Summertime
Suddenly, Last Summer

Charlton Heston

24 Touch of Evil
23 Ben-Hur
Agony and the Ecstasy
21 Ten Commandments
20 Planet of the Apes

Dustin Hoffman

28 Midnight Cowboy
27 Graduate, The
Rain Man
Tootsie
Lenny

Papillon
Marathon Man
26 All the President's Men
Kramer vs. Kramer
25 Little Big Man

Philip Seymour Hoffman

29 Capote
28 Doubt
Savages, The
27 Before the Devil Knows . . .
25 Happiness

William Holden

28 Born Yesterday
Sunset Boulevard
Bridge on the River Kwai
26 Country Girl
Stalag 17
Wild Bunch
25 Sabrina
Network
Counterfeit Traitor
24 Picnic
23 Love Is a Many-Splendored

Anthony Hopkins

28 Silence of the Lambs
27 Elephant Man
Remains of the Day

Tommy Lee Jones

27 No Country for Old Men
In the Valley of Elah
Coal Miner's Daughter
24 Fugitive, The

Diane Keaton

29 Godfather Part II
Godfather, The
26 Annie Hall
Something's Gotta Give
25 Interiors
24 Manhattan
21 Play It Again, Sam
19 Sleeper

Gene Kelly

28 Inherit the Wind
26 Singin' in the Rain
23 American in Paris
On the Town
21 Brigadoon
Ziegfeld Follies

Grace Kelly

27 Rear Window
26 High Noon
Country Girl
25 To Catch a Thief
24 Dial M for Murder
22 High Society

Nicole Kidman

28 Hours, The
24 Cold Mountain
23 Moulin Rouge!

Burt Lancaster

28 Sweet Smell of Success
27 Elmer Gantry
Atlantic City
From Here to Eternity
Judgment at Nuremberg
Leopard, The
25 Sorry, Wrong Number
Killers, The
24 Seven Days in May
Local Hero

Jessica Lange

28 Frances
27 Tootsie
23 All That Jazz

Vivien Leigh

28 Streetcar Named Desire
27 Gone with the Wind
25 Ship of Fools

Jack Lemmon

28 Days of Wine and Roses
Apartment, The
27 Odd Couple
Some Like It Hot
Glengarry Glen Ross
Mister Roberts
26 Missing
25 Fortune Cookie

Shirley MacLaine

28 Apartment, The
27 Being There
26 Children's Hour
Terms of Endearment
25 Turning Point

Tobey Maguire

25 Seabiscuit
20 Spider-Man 2

Marx Brothers

25 Duck Soup
Night at the Opera
24 Monkey Business
Animal Crackers

22 Cocoanuts, The
Horse Feathers
21 Day at the Races

Ewan McGregor

23 Moulin Rouge!
21 Black Hawk Down
16 Star Wars III/Revenge of Sith

Steve McQueen

27 Papillon
26 Sand Pebbles
Great Escape
25 Cincinnati Kid
23 Thomas Crown Affair
22 Magnificent Seven
Getaway, The

Marilyn Monroe

27 Some Like It Hot
23 Seven Year Itch
21 Gentlemen Prefer Blondes

Julianne Moore

28 Hours, The
27 Far From Heaven
24 Fugitive, The

Eddie Murphy

24 Dreamgirls
22 Trading Places

Bill Murray

27 Tootsie
25 Rushmore
20 Caddyshack

Paul Newman

28 Hud
Sweet Bird of Youth
27 Cat on a Hot Tin Roof
Cool Hand Luke
26 Sting, The
Hustler, The
Road to Perdition
Butch Cassidy/Sundance Kid
25 Verdict, The
24 Torn Curtain
23 Exodus

Jack Nicholson

29 One Flew Over Cuckoo's . . .
28 Chinatown
27 Five Easy Pieces
26 Shining, The
Terms of Endearment
Something's Gotta Give
Few Good Men

Laurence Olivier

29 Hamlet
28 Sleuth
27 Wuthering Heights
Rebecca
Marathon Man
26 Boys from Brazil
25 Pride and Prejudice
24 Spartacus

Al Pacino

29 Godfather Part II
Godfather, The
28 Insider, The
27 Glengarry Glen Ross
Dog Day Afternoon
26 Serpico
And Justice for All
25 Carlito's Way

Gregory Peck

29 To Kill a Mockingbird
27 Gentleman's Agreement
26 Cape Fear
Roman Holiday
On the Beach
Boys from Brazil
25 Twelve O'Clock High
Spellbound
22 Duel in the Sun
Guns of Navarone
21 How the West Was Won

Sean Penn

28 Milk
Mystic River
27 21 Grams
26 Dead Man Walking
25 Carlito's Way

Brad Pitt

25 Inglourious Basterds
Fight Club
24 Curious Case/Benjamin Button
23 Seven
Twelve Monkeys
River Runs Through It

Sidney Poitier

28 Raisin in the Sun
27 In the Heat of the Night
Guess Who's Coming . . .
26 Lilies of the Field
24 Blackboard Jungle

Robert Redford

26 Sting, The
Butch Cassidy/Sundance Kid

All the President's Men
25 Out of Africa
Way We Were
24 Barefoot in the Park
Three Days of the Condor
21 Jeremiah Johnson
Natural, The

Julia Roberts

22 Pretty Woman

Ginger Rogers

26 Stage Door
23 Top Hat
Swing Time
Gay Divorcee
22 Shall We Dance
19 Flying Down to Rio
Gold Diggers of 1933
18 42nd Street

Susan Sarandon

27 Atlantic City
26 Dead Man Walking
25 Thelma & Louise

Peter Sellers

28 Dr. Strangelove
27 Being There
24 Lolita
Pink Panther
23 Mouse That Roared
22 Shot in the Dark

Omar Sharif

28 Lawrence of Arabia
26 Doctor Zhivago
25 Funny Girl

Frank Sinatra

27 From Here to Eternity
26 Manchurian Candidate
Man with the Golden Arm
23 On the Town
22 High Society
21 Guys and Dolls

Will Smith

25 Pursuit of Happyness

Sissy Spacek

27 Badlands
Coal Miner's Daughter
Straight Story*
26 Missing
3 Women

James Stewart

28 Philadelphia Story
27 Rear Window
Anatomy of a Murder
Mr. Smith Goes to Washington
Harvey
It's a Wonderful Life
26 Vertigo
Flight of the Phoenix
25 Call Northside 777
Shop Around the Corner
Destry Rides Again
24 Man Who Shot Liberty Valance
Man Who Knew Too Much
21 How the West Was Won

Meryl Streep

28 Sophie's Choice
Doubt
Hours, The
Deer Hunter
26 Julie & Julia
Silkwood
Kramer vs. Kramer
25 Out of Africa
24 It's Complicated

Barbra Streisand

25 Funny Girl
Way We Were

Hilary Swank

28 Million Dollar Baby
27 Boys Don't Cry

Elizabeth Taylor

27 Who's Afraid of V. Woolf?
Cat on a Hot Tin Roof
Place in the Sun
26 Suddenly, Last Summer
Butterfield 8
25 Father of the Bride
24 National Velvet
23 Giant

Spencer Tracy

28 Adam's Rib
Inherit the Wind
Woman of the Year
Bad Day at Black Rock
27 Desk Set
Judgment at Nuremberg
Guess Who's Coming . . .
26 Captains Courageous
25 Father of the Bride
21 It's a Mad Mad Mad World

John Travolta

26 Pulp Fiction
19 Grease

Jon Voight

28 Midnight Cowboy
26 Coming Home
Deliverance
25 Catch-22

Denzel Washington

27 Philadelphia
26 American Gangster
Soldier's Story
Great Debaters
Malcolm X
Glory
Antwone Fisher
25 Inside Man

John Wayne

25 Red River
Searchers, The
Quiet Man
24 Man Who Shot Liberty Valance
Stagecoach
23 True Grit
22 She Wore a Yellow Ribbon
Rio Bravo
Fort Apache
20 Longest Day

Orson Welles

28 Third Man
27 Citizen Kane
Jane Eyre
24 Touch of Evil
23 Lady from Shanghai

Robin Williams

25 Dead Poets Society
Good Will Hunting

Bruce Willis

26 Pulp Fiction
25 Sixth Sense
23 Twelve Monkeys
19 Die Hard

Kate Winslet

28 Reader, The
27 Finding Neverland
Sense and Sensibility
Little Children
25 Heavenly Creatures
24 Eternal Sunshine

Natalie Wood

25 Splendor in the Grass
24 West Side Story
Rebel Without a Cause
23 Miracle on 34th Street

Renée Zellweger

27 Cinderella Man
26 Chicago
24 Cold Mountain

Top Story

29 Godfather, The
To Kill a Mockingbird

28 Schindler's List
Hamlet (1948)
Godfather Part II
Casablanca
Shawshank Redemption
Usual Suspects
All Quiet/Western Front
Star Wars
Paths of Glory
Witness for the Prosecution
Grapes of Wrath
Wizard of Oz
Manchurian Candidate
Great Expectations
Best Years of Our Lives
Double Indemnity
Rear Window
Christmas Carol
Hotel Rwanda
Seven Days in May

27 Man for All Seasons
All About Eve
Henry V
Wuthering Heights
On the Beach
Citizen Kane
Great Escape
Dr. Strangelove
Heiress, The
Raiders of the Lost Ark
12 Angry Men
Breaker Morant
Bridge on the River Kwai
Romeo and Juliet
39 Steps
Lord of the Rings/Return
Place in the Sun
Strangers on a Train
Psycho
Dial M for Murder
Gone with the Wind
Christmas Story
Pianist, The
House of Games
It's a Wonderful Life
Rebecca
Searchers, The
Sting, The
One Flew Over Cuckoo's . . .
Gun Crazy
Day of the Jackal
Killing Fields
Sunset Boulevard
Third Man
Lord of the Rings/Fellowship
Princess Bride
Brief Encounter
Maltese Falcon
Lawrence of Arabia
Anatomy of a Murder
Of Mice and Men
North by Northwest
Stalag 17
Inherit the Wind
Sixth Sense
I Never Sang for My Father
Laura
Gentleman's Agreement
Lion in Winter
West Side Story*
Gandhi
My Fair Lady
Memento
Sound of Music
Wait Until Dark
Lady Eve
Fiddler on the Roof
Advise & Consent
Face in the Crowd
Vertigo
Silence of the Lambs

26 Ox-Bow Incident
Blind Side
Doctor Zhivago
Lord of the Rings/Two Towers
Sweet Smell of Success
Chinatown
All the President's Men
Hope and Glory
Hunchback/Notre Dame
Some Like It Hot
Diary of Anne Frank
Member of the Wedding
Boy in the Striped Pajamas
Lady Vanishes
Twelve O'Clock High
Producers, The
Up

Top Production Values

29
Lord of the Rings/Return
Finding Nemo
Lord of the Rings/Two Towers
Fantasia
Lawrence of Arabia
Lord of the Rings/Fellowship
Godfather, The
Star Wars
Chicago
Godfather Part II
Wizard of Oz
Schindler's List
Gone with the Wind
Avatar

28
Star Wars V/Empire Strikes
Matrix, The
Last Emperor
Saving Private Ryan
Singin' in the Rain
Toy Story
Raiders of the Lost Ark
Pianist, The
Shrek 2
Doctor Zhivago
Spirited Away
Citizen Kane
Sound of Music
Shrek
Monsters, Inc.
Ben-Hur
Incredibles, The
Iron Man
Apocalypse Now
Up
Star Wars VI/Return of Jedi
Toy Story 2
Bridge on the River Kwai
Star Wars III/Revenge of Sith
Third Man
Nightmare Before Christmas

27
2001: A Space Odyssey
North by Northwest
Searchers, The
Beauty/Beast (1991)
West Side Story
Star Trek
Ratatouille
My Fair Lady
Patton
Braveheart
King and I
Brazil
Cars
Gandhi
American in Paris
Dark Knight
Last Samurai
Blade Runner
Harry Potter/Sorcerer's Stone
Wild Bunch
Casablanca
Harry Potter/Goblet of Fire
E.T. The Extra-Terrestrial
Quiet Man
Who Framed Roger Rabbit
Fantasia 2000
Sunset Boulevard
Psycho
Gettysburg
Lion King
Frida
Harry Potter/Order of Phoenix
Snow White
300
Harry Potter/Prisoner
Red River
Master and Commander
Moulin Rouge!
Amadeus
Aviator, The
Fitzcarraldo
Shawshank Redemption*
Pirates Caribbean/The Curse
Cabaret
Room with a View
Gladiator
Man for All Seasons
Out of Africa
X2
WALL-E
Ten Commandments
Wallace & Gromit
Harry Potter/Chamber
Rear Window
Mary Poppins
Chicken Run
Chronicles of Narnia/Prince
Close Encounters

26
Million Dollar Baby
Gold Diggers of 1933

Top Foreign Language Films

29
Seven Samurai
Rashomon

28
Lives of Others
Children of Paradise
Beauty/Beast (1947)
Grand Illusion
Battle of Algiers
Yojimbo
Das Boot

27
Ran
Bicycle Thief
Seventh Seal
Life Is Beautiful
La Strada
Persona*
Au Revoir Les Enfants
Letters from Iwo Jima
Jean de Florette
Pan's Labyrinth
Nights of Cabiria
400 Blows
Shop on Main Street
Wages of Fear
Day for Night

26
Cinema Paradiso
Conformist, The
Diving Bell and the Butterfly
King of Hearts
Babette's Feast
8½
Wild Strawberries
Amarcord
Black Orpheus
Fanny and Alexander*
Z
Cries and Whispers
Talk to Her
Delicatessen
Rififi
Smiles of a Summer Night
Alexander Nevsky
Amélie
M
Diabolique
Seven Beauties
Mon Oncle
Central Station

25
Mr. Hulot's Holiday
Two Women
Blue Angel
Antonia's Line
Garden of the Finzi-Continis
Leopard, The
Hiroshima, Mon Amour
Aguirre: The Wrath of God
Maria Full of Grace
Scenes from a Marriage
Farewell My Concubine
La Dolce Vita
Marriage of Maria Braun
All About My Mother
Contempt
Hero
My Life As a Dog
Like Water for Chocolate
Shoot the Piano Player
Juliet of the Spirits
Breathless
Eat Drink Man Woman
La Vie en Rose

24
Jules and Jim
Crouching Tiger
La Cage aux Folles
Swept Away
Il Postino
Story of Adele H.
Triplets of Belleville
Last Metro
House of Flying Daggers
Man and a Woman
Divorce Italian Style
Kite Runner
Belle de Jour
Discreet Charm
Wings of Desire
Women on the Verge
Volver
Diva
Dona Flor/Her Two Husbands
Red Violin
Monsoon Wedding
Umbrellas of Cherbourg
Knife in the Water
Y Tu Mamá También
L'Avventura

23
Motorcycle Diaries
Kung Fu Hustle
Bad Education
Indochine
La Femme Nikita

MOVIE DIRECTORY

	OVERALL	ACTING	STORY	PROD.

Accused, The ✉

23	28	23	21

1988 | Directed by Jonathan Kaplan | With Kelly McGillis, Jodie Foster, Bernie Coulson | 108 minutes | Rated R

Not for the "faint of heart", this "white-knuckle" thriller about a gang rape and its courtroom consequences is "based on true events" and dominated by a "phenomenal" Foster, who won an Oscar for her "captivating performance"; the "excruciating", "very graphic" reenactment of the crime is "definitely for mature audiences" - but far from gratuitous given the picture's "socially responsible" message.

Ace in the Hole ◑

26	26	26	24

1951 | Directed by Billy Wilder | With Kirk Douglas, Jan Sterling, Porter Hall, Bob Arthur | 111 minutes | Not Rated

One of the "most cynical films ever", this "long overlooked" but far-sighted "portrayal of the media circus" via Billy Wilder features "Kirk at his best - and least likable" - playing a "ruthless reporter" looking to "milk a story" about a cave-in victim awaiting rescue; it "bombed on release", but fans say this ace satire "lets no one off the hook" and note that "nothing has changed since '51."

Adam's Rib ◑

26	28	25	23

1949 | Directed by George Cukor | With Spencer Tracy, Katharine Hepburn, Judy Holliday | 101 minutes | Not Rated

"Chemistry abounds" in this "sparkling" matchup of Tracy and Hepburn, "probably the best pairing" of these "two pros", who are so "delightful" that many "wish they'd made even more movies together"; plot-wise, this "battle-of-the-sexes" comedy concerns "married attorneys on opposing sides of a case", but fans say it's worth watching for the "effortless comedic timing" alone.

Adventures of Priscilla, Queen of the Desert, The

23	24	22	22

1994 | Directed by Stephan Elliott | With Terence Stamp, Guy Pearce, Hugo Weaving | 104 minutes | Rated R

"Outlandish drag queens" and the "Australian outback" collide in this "razor-sharp" road comedy, a "flaming romp" about "boas, false eyelashes" and a bus "ride through the desert"; highlights include Stamp's "campy" performance as a "post-op transsexual looking for love" and a "fabulous" soundtrack that will thrill "ABBA fans."

Adventures of Robin Hood, The

25	22	24	24

1938 | Directed by Michael Curtiz, William Keighley | With Errol Flynn, Olivia de Havilland | 102 minutes | Not Rated

This "swashbuckliest swashbuckler of them all" is the "definitive telling" of the tale, filmed in "gorgeous Technicolor" and "acted with verve" by a "charismatic" Flynn and a "perfect" de Havilland; ok, it might be "a bit dated", but its "lightning-quick dialogue", "exciting" swordplay and those famous "green tights" are "still engaging" enough to inspire a "whole genre of films" - plus a "whole lot of parodies."

Advise & Consent ◑

27	27	27	24

1962 | Directed by Otto Preminger | With Henry Fonda, Charles Laughton, Walter Pidgeon, Don Murray | 139 minutes | Not Rated

A "grown-up study of Washington" (which should be "required viewing for all of Congress"), this "interesting", "behind-the-scenes" drama stars Fonda as a Cabinet candidate whose confirmation hearings inaugurate a "gutsy" exposé of hardball politics; voters consent it's a "talky chestnut", but it's still a front-runner for "one of Preminger's best."

Affair to Remember, An 26 | 25 | 25 | 23

1957 | Directed by Leo McCarey | With Cary Grant, Deborah Kerr, Richard Denning | 119 minutes | Not Rated

The "ultimate chick flick", this "three-hanky tearjerker" begins with a "glamorous" "shipboard romance" that turns "tragic" after an "unexpected twist" at the "Empire State Building"; though the "inspiration for many other weepies" (notably *Sleepless in Seattle*), this one's the "standard", thanks to the "captivating banter", ultra-"suave Grant" and some "classic NY" scenery; just don't bother to see it with your boyfriend – men "don't get it."

African Queen, The ✉ 28 | 29 | 26 | 26

1951 | Directed by John Huston | With Humphrey Bogart, Katharine Hepburn, Robert Morley | 105 minutes | Not Rated

"Curmudgeonly riverboat captain" Bogie and "feisty missionary" Hepburn "sizzle" as they take a "trip up a hellish river" and "discover love, courage" and the "best use of leeches since the Middle Ages" in this "beautifully crafted" drama; its "legendary reputation" owes a lot to Huston's "no-nonsense direction", James Agee's "witty" screenplay, the fine "location shots" of "deepest Africa" and, of course, that "undeniable chemistry" between the two shining stars; in sum, "they don't make 'em like this anymore."

Agony and the Ecstasy, The 23 | 23 | 22 | 24

1965 | Directed by Carol Reed | With Charlton Heston, Rex Harrison, Diane Cilento | 138 minutes | Not Rated

"All who love art" can get a "romanticized history lesson" via this "well-made epic" featuring Heston as Renaissance man Michelangelo, commissioned to limn the ceiling of the Sistine Chapel while "sparring" with "foil" Pope Julius (the "excellent" Harrison); "good storytelling" makes for an "unparalleled study of the artistic process", even if a few philistines agonize "could this movie be any longer?"

Aguirre: The Wrath of God F 25 | 25 | 23 | 25

1977 | Directed by Werner Herzog | With Klaus Kinski, Helena Rojo | 100 minutes | Not Rated

"Shot on a small budget under unbelievable conditions", this "staggering" saga of 16th-century Spaniards seeking El Dorado by crossing the Andes and then descending the Amazon stars Kinski as a "hopelessly mad" "megalomaniac conquistador" opposite "more monkeys than you can shake a stick at"; the film's "hauntingly beautiful" but "static" pacewise, and it's "hard to tell who's more obsessed – the characters in the movie or the director and actors who made it."

Airplane! 24 | 19 | 20 | 19

1980 | Directed by Jim Abrahams, David Zucker, Jerry Zucker | With Robert Hays, Julie Hagerty, Lloyd Bridges, Leslie Nielsen, Peter Graves, Robert Stack | 88 minutes | Rated PG

"Funny as heck", this "laugh-a-second spoof" mocks "'70s-era disaster films" with a "scatter-gag" barrage of "relentless slapstick", "constant plays on words" and the "best appearance by Ethel Merman in decades"; granted, it's "infantile" and some of the humor might be perceived as "politically incorrect" today, but there are so many "one-liners you'll remember years later" – 'don't call me Shirley!' – that it's no surprise this flick "launched a thousand imitators."

Akira 23 | - | 21 | 26

1990 | Directed by Katsuhiro Otomo | Animated | 124 minutes | Rated R

"Defining the anime genre", this "groundbreaking" "classic" "based on the Japanese comic book" is "blazingly kinetic", though "more violent than it needs to be" and thus "not for younger viewers"; the "confusing" sci-fi plot (something to do with "how power corrupts") might "make you wonder if something was lost in translation", but it's so "visually stunning" you won't care.

Aladdin 24 | - | 22 | 25

1992 | Directed by Ron Clements, John Musker | Animated | 90 minutes | Rated G

Disney's "fast-moving" animated version of the Aladdin story is "stolen" by Robin Williams' "infectiously manic", "whirlwind" vocal performance as a "genius" genie; overall, its "likable characters" and "humorous storyline" appeal to both "adults and kids alike", while the "enchanting" Oscar-winning soundtrack will leave you "singing for days."

Alexander Nevsky ◑ F 26 | 22 | 25 | 26

1939 | Directed by Sergei Eisenstein | With Nikolai Cherkassov | 107 minutes | Not Rated

"Propaganda" was never better than this "exceptional" war epic, made to rally Soviet support for Stalin; shot in "haunting" black-and-white and set to a "superb Prokofiev score", it recounts the trials and tribulations of a 13th-century Russian prince, and even if the "clanky" script "ultimately collapses under the weight of all the ideological baggage", it's still a "triumph of expressionism" from "genius" director Eisenstein.

Alice Doesn't Live Here Anymore ✉ 24 | 26 | 23 | 21

1974 | Directed by Martin Scorsese | With Ellen Burstyn, Kris Kristofferson, Jodie Foster | 112 minutes | Rated PG

In this "early Scorsese" drama, Burstyn won an Oscar for her role as a "blue-collar" gal "trying to find herself" after a marriage breakup, and the "poignant", very "real" outcome marked a "watershed" for "feminists" in a "time when men and women were changing their roles."

Alice in Wonderland 24 | - | 25 | 25

1951 | Directed by Clyde Geronimi, Wilfred Jackson, Hamilton Luske | Animated | 75 minutes | Rated G

Disney's wonderfully "wacky" animation transforms Lewis Carroll's children's book into an "intelligent cartoon" rife with "hidden messages" and a slightly "schizophrenic" edge to boot; indeed, "family entertainment" mavens say this "imaginative" production is such a "terrific adaptation" that it "almost makes you forget the classic Tenniel illustrations."

Alice in Wonderland 23 | 23 | 20 | 25

2010 | Directed by Tim Burton | With Johnny Depp, Mia Wasikowska, Helena Bonham Carter, Anne Hathaway | 108 minutes | Rated PG

Lewis Carroll's "classic" gets a "surreal reconfiguration" via Tim Burton in this "lavish" fantasy following Alice's "mind trip" down the rabbit hole and into a "vivid" CGI spectacle; props go to Depp's "plain weird" Mad Hatter and Carter's "deliciously evil" Red Queen, though the "jabberwocky" side plot "needs work"; ultimately, for "sheer pizzazz" "there's plenty to love" here.

Alien 25 | 22 | 25 | 26

1979 | Directed by Ridley Scott | With Sigourney Weaver, Tom Skerritt, Veronica Cartwright | 117 minutes | Rated R

"Often imitated but never equaled", this "fierce" sci-fi "horror classic" could pass as a "Hitchcock-in-space" thriller thanks to its "jaw-dropping visuals" and "heart-pounding" plot about an outer space "survey team" that inadvertently brings a "new guest" home to dinner; "Weaver rocks" in "macho-man" mode and is only upstaged by the "slimy", "really gross" title character, the "best movie monster this side of Frankenstein."

Aliens 23 | 21 | 22 | 26

1986 | Directed by James Cameron | With Sigourney Weaver, Michael Biehn, Bill Paxton | 137 minutes | Rated R

This "second installment" in the *Alien* franchise is just as "scream-out-loud scary" as its predecessor, with a "*Rambo*-esque" emphasis; expect the "same high-quality production values" and "edge-of-your-seat tension", and if there's debate as to whether it "trumps" or "just lives up to" the original, one thing's certain: Weaver is still one "bad-ass" chick.

All About Eve ✉◑ 28 | 29 | 27 | 26

1950 | Directed by Joseph L. Mankiewicz | With Bette Davis, Anne Baxter, Gary Merrill, George Sanders, Celeste Holm | 138 minutes | Not Rated

"Fasten your seatbelts" – the "ladies lunch on each other" in this "scalding", "wickedly funny" look at the "vicious world of showbiz"; a "boffo" Davis is "electrifying" as the "fading star" (opposite a "strong" Baxter as the rising one), but both are indebted to Mankiewicz's "perfect script", a "catty" catalog of "sharp-tongued dialogue" that "puts today's scenarios to shame"; in sum, this is one of the "best backstage bitchfests of all time."

All About My Mother ✉F 25 | 26 | 25 | 23

1999 | Directed by Pedro Almodóvar | With Cecilia Roth, Penélope Cruz, Marisa Paredes | 101 minutes | Rated R

Though "all the major characters are women", this "captivating story" via Spanish director Almodóvar is definitely "not a chick flick": rather, this "unusual", Oscar-winning drama about a mother searching for her dead son's transsexual dad provides a very "modern definition of what makes a family"; fans single out Roth's "stunning" work and Cruz's "breakout performance" – that is, when they're not "crying their hearts out" or "laughing their heads off."

All Quiet on the Western Front ✉◑ 28 | 26 | 28 | 25

1930 | Directed by Lewis Milestone | With Lew Ayres, Louis Wolheim, Raymond Griffith | 131 minutes | Not Rated

"One of the first anti-war films" (and the "last word" on the subject for many), this "devastating" WWI saga is a "harrowing" glimpse at the "unglorious nature" of battle; over 75 years later, it "still packs a wallop", and though a bit "slow" by modern standards, this "faithful adaptation of the novel" will "stay with you."

All That Jazz

OVERALL	ACTING	STORY	PROD.
24	23	22	26

1979 | Directed by Bob Fosse | With Roy Scheider, Jessica Lange, Ann Reinking, John Lithgow | 123 minutes | Rated R

A "brilliantly original" "autobiopic" from Bob Fosse about Bob Fosse, this "prescient" drama might be "self-indulgent" and plainly "inspired by *8½*", but it's also a "warts-and-all" "character sketch" with, no surprise, "imaginative choreography"; look for a "great star turn" by Scheider and lots of "sardonic" dialogue.

All the King's Men ✉◑

OVERALL	ACTING	STORY	PROD.
25	26	25	22

1949 | Directed by Robert Rossen | With Broderick Crawford, John Ireland, Mercedes McCambridge | 109 minutes | Not Rated

The "American dream goes sour" in this "classic political drama" adapted from the Pulitzer Prize–winning novel about the rise and fall of a Huey Long–esque politician "corrupted by power"; this Best Picture winner is memorable for its "strong story" - and "even stronger acting by Crawford" (who also won a statuette).

All the President's Men

OVERALL	ACTING	STORY	PROD.
25	26	26	23

1976 | Directed by Alan J. Pakula | With Robert Redford, Dustin Hoffman, Jason Robards | 138 minutes | Rated PG

"History comes alive" in this "truth-is-stranger-than-fiction" account of the "Watergate" scandal, a "riveting", torn-"from-the-headlines thriller" that "captures you every time" "even though you know the outcome"; as reporters Woodward and Bernstein, Redford and Hoffman are truly "memorable" (ditto those "ties and sideburns"), and in the end this "gripping" effort brings "clarity to the events of that confusing time."

All This, and Heaven Too ◑

OVERALL	ACTING	STORY	PROD.
26	27	25	25

1940 | Directed by Anatole Litvak | With Bette Davis, Charles Boyer, Barbara O'Neil, Jeffrey Lynn | 141 minutes | Not Rated

"Davis and Boyer shine" in this "classy classic", a "poignant", mid-19th century tale of "love and loss" wherein a "self-sacrificing" governess yearns for an aristocratic charmer, only to be suspected of murder after his spouse is killed; granted, it's an "eight-hanky blubberfest", but old-school romance junkies are sure to be on cloud nine.

Almost Famous ✉

OVERALL	ACTING	STORY	PROD.
23	24	24	22

2000 | Directed by Cameron Crowe | With Billy Crudup, Frances McDormand, Kate Hudson | 122 minutes | Rated R

"Almost perfect" filmmaking, director Crowe's "feel-good" "semi-autobiographical story" about his work as a "teenage *Rolling Stone* reporter" "on the road with a rock band" is half "coming-of-age" romance, half unadulterated "love song" to the '70s; while Crudup's "underrated" portrayal of a rocker and McDormand's "outstanding" mom earn kudos, "Hudson steals the show" as the "vulnerable groupie."

Amadeus ✉

OVERALL	ACTING	STORY	PROD.
26	27	25	27

1984 | Directed by Milos Forman | With F. Murray Abraham, Tom Hulce, Elizabeth Berridge | 158 minutes | Rated PG

"Genius thwarted by mediocrity" is the theme of this "lively" Mozart biopic that's admittedly "not historically accurate", given its depiction of the "tortured" composer as something of a cross between a "twerp" and a "rock god"; awash in "lush period details", "timeless music" and

	OVERALL	ACTING	STORY	PROD.

"surprisingly nuanced performances" by Abraham and Hulce, it even manages to "make classical music seem racy" – and was quite the Oscar magnet, taking home eight of them.

Amarcord ✉ **F** 26 | 25 | 25 | 26

1975 | Directed by Federico Fellini | With Magali Noël, Bruno Zanin, Pupella Maggio | 127 minutes | Rated R

"Fellini's warmhearted look back to his childhood", this Foreign Language Oscar winner is a "wonderful depiction" of "small-town life" in 1930s "fascist Italy", an "evocative" film that's simultaneously "lyric, tragic, vulgar and comic"; fans say this "beautiful reminiscence" reveals the famed director "at his most accessible" – and most "surreal."

Amélie **F** 26 | 26 | 24 | 25

2001 | Directed by Jean-Pierre Jeunet | With Audrey Tautou, Mathieu Kassovitz | 122 minutes | Rated R

"Sweet as *sucre*", this "candy-coated" "picture postcard" of a romance concerns a "modern-day Pollyanna from Montmartre" "who wants to fix everyone's life" to make up for "what's missing in hers"; in the title role, a "new star has arrived" in "gamine" Tautou, a "21st-century Audrey Hepburn" whose "doe-eyed", "cute-as-a-button" looks alone will "put a huge grin on your face"; indeed, this "brimming-with-goodwill" picture is so "magical", you'll "hardly notice the subtitles."

American Beauty ✉ 24 | 27 | 23 | 24

1999 | Directed by Sam Mendes | With Kevin Spacey, Annette Bening, Wes Bentley, Thora Birch | 121 minutes | Rated R

The "desperation of modern suburban life" is the theme of this "engrossing" Best Picture winner that polarizes viewers: fans hail this tale of a man's "midlife awakening" and "resurrection" as a "truthful commentary on American society", but thornier types fuss it's a "pretentious", "angry" tract "disguised as existentialist philosophy"; nonetheless, there are plenty of bouquets for Spacey's "dead-on" performance and Alan Ball's "seriously meaty", "rapierlike screenplay."

American Gangster 23 | 26 | 23 | 24

2007 | Directed by Ridley Scott | With Denzel Washington, Russell Crowe, Ruby Dee | 157 minutes | Rated R

Denzel is one "amazing bad guy" in this "powerful" crime epic that traces (and maybe "glamorizes") the rise and fall of a real-life "Harlem drug kingpin" who amassed riches selling heroin in the '70s; on the law-and-order side, Crowe is equally "outstanding" as an "honest cop" pitted against a "worthy opponent" in this "deliciously violent", if "overlong", picture.

American Graffiti 24 | 23 | 23 | 23

1973 | Directed by George Lucas | With Richard Dreyfuss, Ron Howard, Cindy Williams | 110 minutes | Rated PG

"Spot future stars" (including an early Harrison Ford) in this "end-of-an-era" dramedy that "launched a dozen careers" and proves that "Lucas once directed actors, not just pixels"; "covering one night" in 1962 – "but what a night" – it "captures a time and place" in teenage, West Coast America by mixing "cool cars", "period jukebox hits" and "Wolfman Jack" into a "classic growing-up story" that really "makes nostalgia compelling."

OVERALL ACTING STORY PROD.

American History X 25 | 28 | 24 | 23

1998 | Directed by Tony Kaye | With Edward Norton, Edward Furlong, Beverly D'Angelo | 119 minutes | Rated R

"Neo-Nazi violence" and "racism" lie at the heart of this "scalding" drama about "white supremacists" that's "like a punch in the gut" thanks to the "gifted" Norton's "all-too-convincing" portrait of a "scary" "skinhead"; though surely "horrifying", this "powerful" film will also "make you think."

American in Paris, An ✉ 26 | 23 | 22 | 27

1951 | Directed by Vincente Minnelli | With Gene Kelly, Leslie Caron, Oscar Levant, Nina Foch | 113 minutes | Not Rated

A "debonair" Kelly and "beautiful Caron" "dance up a storm" in this "unforgettable" Gershwin musical that might tempt you to "visit Paris"; sure, the "silly story" is a bit "hackneyed", but "who cares?" when the production's so "visually compelling" (especially that climactic ballet "integrating Impressionist art" in its settings); no surprise, it took home six Oscars, including Best Picture.

Americanization of Emily, The ◑ 24 | 24 | 22 | 21

1964 | Directed by Arthur Hiller | With James Garner, Julie Andrews, James Coburn, Melvyn Douglas | 115 minutes | Not Rated

"Considered controversial in its day", this "powerful anti-war" film tells the story of a "cynical" American naval officer scheming to avoid duty in the D-day invasion while romancing a priggish English lass; Andrews is "quite good" in her "first role to depart from her sweet image", though Paddy Chayefsky's screenplay gets mixed notices: "literate" vs. "preachy."

American Splendor 23 | 25 | 22 | 22

2003 | Directed by Shari Springer Berman, Robert Pulcini | With Paul Giamatti, Hope Davis, Harvey Pekar | 101 minutes | Rated R

An "average slob" gets the big-screen treatment in this "subversive" biopic of underground comics scribe Harvey Pekar, a "schlubby" "anti-hero" complete with a "file-clerk" day job; deftly employing "three parallel realities" – "actors, cartoons" and Harvey himself – to tell its story, this "offbeat" picture is nothing if not "original", though some feel it "falls short of its potential" and wonder "what does it amount to in the end?"

Anastasia ✉ 23 | 27 | 24 | 23

1956 | Directed by Anatole Litvak | With Ingrid Bergman, Yul Brynner, Helen Hayes | 105 minutes | Not Rated

The Oscar-winning, ever "appealing" Bergman and a "great" Brynner make quite a "combo" in this dramatic biography of Anastasia, the legendary daughter of the last Russian czar and pretender to the throne – or is she?; told with "sympathy and empathy", it's a "cuddle-up-with-your-honey" picture with acting "so good you find yourself rooting for those inept royals"; "is it true?" – c'mon, "does it matter?"

Anatomy of a Murder ◑ 26 | 27 | 27 | 24

1959 | Directed by Otto Preminger | With James Stewart, Lee Remick, Ben Gazzara, Arthur O'Connell | 160 minutes | Not Rated

Stewart "pulls out all the stops" as a "down-to-earth" lawyer in this courtroom drama that's a "spellbinding" look at a "sensational" "backwoods" revenge killing; "considered risqué" in the '50s given Remick's "sultry" turn and its use of the then-verboten word "'panties'", it remains as "riveting" as ever; P.S. "Duke Ellington and his band" lay down the cool progressive jazz soundtrack.

And Justice for All 23 | 26 | 22 | 22

1979 | Directed by Norman Jewison | With Al Pacino, Jack Warden, Christine Lahti | 119 minutes | Rated R

The "innocent get tossed by the wayside" in this "compelling" courtroom drama indicting an "out-of-control legal system" in its story of an "honest young lawyer" defending a "risk-taking" judge accused of rape; Pacino is in "vintage" form, delivering an "incandescent" performance highlighted by an "explosive rant": "you're out of order, the whole trial is out of order!"

Angels with Dirty Faces ◑ 24 | 24 | 22 | 20

1938 | Directed by Michael Curtiz | With James Cagney, Pat O'Brien, Humphrey Bogart | 97 minutes | Not Rated

Two toughs from the slums take different career paths - one becoming a "lowlife", the other a priest - in this "cautionary melodrama" from the days when "good was good and bad was bad"; "cliché-ridden" though it may be, it was designed to "scare the bejesus out of would-be delinquents" - or at least have them "doing Cagney impersonations for weeks" afterward.

Animal Crackers ◑ 26 | 24 | 18 | 20

1930 | Directed by Victor Heerman | With the Marx Brothers, Lillian Roth, Margaret Dumont | 97 minutes | Rated G

"Hooray for Captain Spaulding!"; this "timeless" Marx Brothers "romp" is best remembered for Groucho's "priceless entrance" and "fabulously stupid" quips ("I shot an elephant in my pajamas, but how he got in my pajamas, I'll never know"); needless to say, the "storyline isn't the point" here, but the "zany" pace doesn't leave time for logic anyway.

Animal House 24 | 20 | 21 | 20

1978 | Directed by John Landis | With John Belushi, Tim Matheson, Tom Hulce, John Vernon | 109 minutes | Rated R

"Raunchy and vulgar", this much-admired "granddaddy of the frat boy gross-out comedies" features the much-"missed" Belushi "at his side-splitting best" as Bluto Blutarsky, a "seven-year college" vet; "no, it ain't Shakespeare", but rather a "textbook" study of "toga parties", "road trips", "food fights" and "anarchic libidos on parade" that's so much of a "guy's movie" that some fellas say they "thought it was a documentary."

Anna Karenina ◑ 26 | 26 | 26 | 25

1935 | Directed by Clarence Brown | With Greta Garbo, Fredric March, Freddie Bartholomew | 95 minutes | Not Rated

"Let's hear it for Tolstoy", whose "huge novel" gets a "brilliant" celluloid spin in this romance of "choices and consequences", starring "Garbo at her best" as the restless Russian who trades mundane wedlock with husband Rathbone for notoriety with the "marvelous" March; classicists insist it's a "moving" ride "from the second it starts" to the climactic encounter between Anna and "the train."

OVERALL | ACTING | STORY | PROD.

Anne of the Thousand Days

26 | 27 | 26 | 26

1969 | Directed by Charles Jarrott | With Richard Burton, Geneviève Bujold, Irene Papas | 145 minutes | Rated PG-13

"History buffs" and "Anglophiles" like this "top-notch" period drama, a "powerful" recounting of "Henry VIII's inability to commit", featuring "brilliant" work by Burton as the "boorish" king and Bujold as the "sensuous Anne Boleyn"; the "beautiful production" is alternately "transporting" and "heart-wrenching", while the Oscar-winning "costumes alone are worth the watch."

Annie Hall ✉

27 | 26 | 25 | 24

1977 | Directed by Woody Allen | With Woody Allen, Diane Keaton, Tony Roberts | 93 minutes | Rated PG

"Every neurotic's favorite comedy", this Oscar-winning Allen film about an "insecure" "Jewish nebbish" smitten with a nutty, "la-di-da"-spouting "shiksa" is "among his deftest creations"; its "pitch-perfect NY" setting, "pure-genius script" and "very funny" set pieces (the "lobster-cooking episode", the "split-screen family dinner scene") make for "essential Woody."

Antonia's Line ✉ F

25 | 26 | 25 | 24

1996 | Directed by Marleen Gorris | With Willeke van Ammelrooy, Els Dottermans | 102 minutes | Rated R

"About women and for women", this "liberating" drama recounts 50 years in one lady's life, told in "flashback" from her "death bed"; "shockingly feminist" to chauvinists, its "charming performances" and "empowering message" are so "unforgettable" that it more than "deserves the Best Foreign Film Oscar" it received.

Antwone Fisher

23 | 26 | 24 | 22

2002 | Directed by Denzel Washington | With Derek Luke, Denzel Washington, Joy Bryant | 120 minutes | Rated PG-13

"Buy a box of tissues before you rent" this "inspiring true-life story about a boy from the 'hood who makes something of himself despite many obstacles"; this "emotional roller coaster" is "wonderfully acted" and represents a "terrific directorial debut by Denzel", who "manages to bring realism to what could have been a manipulative storyline."

Apartment, The ✉ ◑

25 | 28 | 25 | 23

1960 | Directed by Billy Wilder | With Jack Lemmon, Shirley MacLaine, Fred MacMurray | 125 minutes | Not Rated

"Sex in the big, bad city" has never been as "realistic" or "touching" as in this "sad-edged romance", recounting the exploits of a "hapless" "junior exec in love with his boss' mistress"; it pits a "baby-faced" Lemmon opposite a "tender" MacLaine, and besides being "very amusing", it's also a "powerful social comment masquerading as comedy."

Apocalypse Now

27 | 27 | 25 | 28

1979 | Directed by Francis Ford Coppola | With Martin Sheen, Marlon Brando, Robert Duvall | 153 minutes | Rated R

The "Vietnam nightmare" meets Joseph "Conrad's *Heart of Darkness*" in this "landmark" Coppola opus that's one part "gut churner", one part "acid trip" as it examines the "insanity of war"; true, it's "long", the "last half hour is disappointing" and many wonder "what the heck Brando's saying", but ultimately this "sprawling" "meditation on the human mind" just plain "grabs you"; P.S. the expanded version (*Apocalypse Now Redux*) divides voters.

Apollo 13 24 | 24 | 25 | 26

1995 | Directed by Ron Howard | With Tom Hanks, Bill Paxton, Kevin Bacon, Gary Sinise | 140 minutes | Rated PG

"Even though you [presumably] know the outcome", this "space race" drama based on the "remarkable true story" of the "perilous voyage of Apollo 13" stays "suspenseful"; with a roster of "big-name actors" exuding the "right stuff", it delivers "get-up-and-cheer escapism" that might be "a tad corny" but will "make you proud to be an American" – "isn't history wonderful?"

Army of Darkness 23 | 17 | 20 | 19

1993 | Directed by Sam Raimi | With Bruce Campbell, Embeth Davidtz | 81 minutes | Rated R

"Leading with his chin", "B-movie god" Campbell plays a "chainsaw"-wielding, "time-traveling" slacker pitted against Dark Ages hordes in this "witty" horror comedy (known in geekdom as the "third episode of the *Evil Dead* series"); "deliberately cheesy" production values and an "abundance of quotable lines" – i.e. "gimme some sugar, baby" – have earned it "cult-classic" status.

Arsenic and Old Lace ◑ 26 | 26 | 25 | 22

1944 | Directed by Frank Capra | With Cary Grant, Priscilla Lane, Raymond Massey | 118 minutes | Not Rated

"Elderberry wine" makes for "murderous fun" in this "macabre" black comedy about two "vengeful old ladies" killing off bachelors while "chewing the scenery"; as their nephew, a "frantic" Grant "hams it up unashamedly" and delivers the "world's best double takes" in this "funny" adaptation of the Broadway hit.

Asphalt Jungle, The ◑ 24 | 24 | 24 | 23

1950 | Directed by John Huston | With Sterling Hayden, Louis Calhern, Sam Jaffe, Marilyn Monroe | 112 minutes | Not Rated

Sure, this "prime example of juicy film noir" is one of the "original caper" pictures, about a "carefully planned" "jewel heist gone terribly wrong", but it's also appealing for an "early" turn by Marilyn Monroe in a "blow-you-away" bit part; otherwise, this "dark tale" of "greed" and "emotion" supplies enough "twists and compelling characters" to make it "one of Huston's most underrated films."

Atlantic City 24 | 27 | 22 | 22

1980 | Directed by Louis Malle | With Burt Lancaster, Susan Sarandon, Kate Reid | 104 minutes | Rated R

This "valentine to a lost city" pairs a "stunning" Lancaster and Sarandon as unlikely lovers "trying to redeem their lives" in a "dying" town; "sad, bittersweet" and "overlooked", it boasts a "superb" John Guare script full of "characters worth caring about" but is most remembered for the scene of "our heroine bathing herself with sliced lemons."

Auntie Mame 25 | 25 | 24 | 25

1958 | Directed by Morton DaCosta | With Rosalind Russell, Forrest Tucker, Coral Browne | 143 minutes | Not Rated

"Defining diva-dom for generations", this "stylish" comedy about a wide-eyed kid's "wacky rich" auntie stars a "larger-than-life Russell" as a "great old broad"-cum-"force of nature"; it might be "overlong and underplotted", but "great one-liners" barbed with "sharp wit" ("life is a banquet and most poor suckers are starving to death") assure its rep as the "campiest of camp classics."

Au Revoir Les Enfants F 27 | 26 | 27 | 24

1987 | Directed by Louis Malle | With Gaspard Manesse, Francine Racette | 104 minutes | Rated PG

"Powerful and haunting", this "must-see" drama explores "anti-Semitism" in WWII "occupied France" via its depiction of a "Jewish boy hidden" in a French school; though there's certainly "no happy ending" here, it "brings the events of the Holocaust to a personal level" so devastatingly that you'll "never forget" it.

Avalon 24 | 25 | 24 | 23

1990 | Directed by Barry Levinson | With Aidan Quinn, Elizabeth Perkins, Armin Mueller-Stahl | 126 minutes | Rated PG

"Touching" and "oh-so-true", this third installment of director Levinson's "semi-autobiographical" "homage to the immigrant experience" (and "growing up in Baltimore") follows a "bravura cast" across several generations; the "wistful humor" and "nostalgic" sense of time and place make for a "rare" dose of "heartfelt" entertainment, best summed up by its most renowned line: "why did you cut the turkey?"

Avatar 26 | 20 | 20 | 29

2009 | Directed by James Cameron | With Sam Worthington, Zoe Saldana, Sigourney Weaver, Stephen Lang | 162 minutes | Rated PG-13

With a "gargantuan budget" and ambition to match, James Cameron "sets the new standard" for CGI cinema with this "groundbreaking" sci-fi epic, a visual "wonder" that immerses viewers in an alien "rain-forest" world as it chronicles an Earthling's engagement with an "indigenous" civilization threatened by a "greedy corporation"; sure, the story's a bit "preachy" and rather "derivative" (hello, "*Dances with Wolves* in space"), but "gazillion"-dollar grosses don't lie - the "production values alone are a must-see."

Aviator, The 23 | 25 | 22 | 27

2004 | Directed by Martin Scorsese | With Leonardo DiCaprio, Cate Blanchett, Kate Beckinsale, John C. Reilly | 170 minutes | Rated PG-13

Martin Scorsese takes off with a "bottomless budget" in this "sweeping" biopic of "eccentric" gazillionaire Howard Hughes, where the lift-off is supplied by "sumptuous" production design (including one of the "most realistic plane crashes" ever filmed) and Cate Blanchett's "dead-on", Oscar-grabbing take on Kate Hepburn; more debatable is Leo's title turn ("formidable" or "hollow"), though most agree on the "too-long" running time and "soulless", "conventional" windup.

Awful Truth, The ✉◑ 25 | 26 | 24 | 23

1937 | Directed by Leo McCarey | With Irene Dunne, Cary Grant, Ralph Bellamy, Alexander D'Arcy | 91 minutes | Not Rated

"Two spoiled rich people" on the verge of divorce try to "win each other back" in this "laugh-out-loud" romantic comedy top-billing the "classic combo" of Grant and Dunne; it's "one of the better screwball" pictures "from Hollywood's golden age" with enough "crackling dialogue" and sheer "fun" to leave fans saying "they don't make 'em like this anymore."

	OVERALL	ACTING	STORY	PROD.

Babe

25	22	25	26

1995 | Directed by Chris Noonan | With James Cromwell, Magda Szubanski, Danny Mann | 89 minutes | Rated G

"Believe the hype": fans are in "hog heaven" over this "porcine" comedy about a "talking pig" who "wants to be a sheepherder so he won't get eaten"; "cute without being cutesy", it features Oscar-winning "computer effects" that allow "animals to interact" with humans so realistically that it may "turn you into a vegetarian."

Babette's Feast ✉ F

26	26	26	25

1988 | Directed by Gabriel Axel | With Stéphane Audran, Bibi Andersson, Jarl Kulle | 102 minutes | Rated G

"Sumptuous enough to make vegetarians drool" (though "slow as molasses"), this "classic foodie" dramedy is an "unusual" tale based on the Isak Dinesen story about the "power of redemption" cooked up in one "magnificent meal"; "still mouthwatering after all these years", this "intriguing" Danish treat is so "delectable" and "savory" that it could be the "Zagat signature movie."

Back to the Future

23	20	25	24

1985 | Directed by Robert Zemeckis | With Michael J. Fox, Christopher Lloyd, Lea Thompson | 111 minutes | Rated PG

A "time-traveling DeLorean" propels the "delectably dimpled Fox" into a "fun ride to the past" (and an opportunity to observe his parents as "goofy teenagers") in this "perfect blend of sci-fi, fantasy and pop culture"; "irrepressibly entertaining" and very popular, it spawned an "incredible ride" at the Universal theme park as well as two "terrible sequels."

Bad and the Beautiful, The ✉ ◑

24	25	24	24

1952 | Directed by Vincente Minnelli | With Lana Turner, Kirk Douglas, Walter Pidgeon, Dick Powell | 118 minutes | Not Rated

Douglas is at his "jaw-clenching best" playing a "manipulative producer" in this knowing, "behind-the-scenes" look at Tinseltown that could be "Hollywood's best movie about itself"; told in a series of flashbacks by a director, an actress and a screenwriter, it's "lush, hammy" stuff that's "over the top in just the right way"; P.S. "never loan Lana Turner your car."

Bad Day at Black Rock

24	28	24	22

1955 | Directed by John Sturges | With Spencer Tracy, Robert Ryan, Anne Francis | 81 minutes | Not Rated

This "taut little thriller" is "mean, lean" moviemaking about "bigotry and intolerance" in a "small town with a secret", starring an "excellent" Tracy in "one of his more unusual roles"; although somewhat "forgotten" today, it's "just as relevant as it was in the post-McCarthy '50s", "giving you plenty to think about" as it "profiles American prejudices."

Bad Education F

23	26	23	24

2004 | Directed by Pedro Almodóvar | With Gael García Bernal, Fele Martínez, Daniel Giménez Cacho | 106 minutes | Rated R

"Bad boy" director Almodóvar proves he's at the "head of the class" with this "visually hypnotic", "gender-bending" mystery that pays homage to both "film noir" and "Hitchcock"; boasting a "bravura" performance by rising star Bernal (who's just as "sexy in drag"), this "out-there" flick is rife with "racy", "taboo"-smashing material (e.g. "drugs", "transvestites", "priest abuse") and "not for the easily offended."

Badlands 25 | 27 | 24 | 24

1973 | Directed by Terrence Malick | With Martin Sheen, Sissy Spacek, Warren Oates | 95 minutes | Rated PG

The "banality of evil" is dissected in this "dark, disturbing" depiction of a true-life teen crime spree; playing "shallow", "disaffected" lovers on the run, a "very young" Spacek and Sheen are "first rate", while Malick's "trademark sweeping cinematography" acts as "visually stunning" counterpoint to the "bitingly tragic" story; in short, it's "gutsy", "twisted" and "not nearly as well known as it should be."

Bad Seed, The ◑ 22 | 23 | 25 | 20

1956 | Directed by Mervyn LeRoy | With Nancy Kelly, Patty McCormack, Eileen Heckart | 129 minutes | Not Rated

"Not for the faint of heart", this "very creepy" thriller is the story of a "perky little deranged girl" who's the "world's most evil child" (think "Ted Bundy in a pinafore"); "unsettling and unforgettable" in its time, it's still "way, way over the top", and even if the Broadway play "had a better ending", this one will positively "send chills down your spine."

Ball of Fire ◑ 26 | 28 | 24 | 23

1941 | Directed by Howard Hawks | With Gary Cooper, Barbara Stanwyck, Oskar Homolka, Dana Andrews | 111 minutes | Not Rated

Fired-up admirers praise the "classic" hilarity in this "delightful" screwball comedy, wherein "sassy" burlesque queen Stanwyck holes up with "eight straight-laced" linguists to school them in "early '40s slang"; add Cooper in a "droll", "deadpan" turn as a "timid bookworm", and sparks fly as the "splendid cast" lets fly with the "witty" repartee.

Bambi 26 | - | 25 | 26

1942 | Directed by David Hand | Animated | 70 minutes | Rated G

"Don't forget those tissues" before settling into this dear coming-of-age story that's best remembered for the "absolutely heart-wrenching" "death of Bambi's mother", a "cruel lesson in life" that will "make you think twice about showing it" to young children; otherwise, it's arguably the "most beautiful" example of vintage Disney animation, "warm and fuzzy" but "not mawkish."

Bananas 23 | 20 | 22 | 19

1971 | Directed by Woody Allen | With Woody Allen, Louise Lasser, Carlos Montalban | 82 minutes | Rated PG-13

"For Allen purists mostly", this "early" comic romance "relies heavily on sight gags and slapstick humor" in its "anarchic" story of a nebbish turned "Latin American dictator" that's a "zany" satire to some, but "intermittently funny shtick" to others; P.S. hang on for a "young" Sylvester Stallone's cameo as a "thug on the subway."

Band Wagon, The 26 | 21 | 20 | 26

1953 | Directed by Vincente Minnelli | With Fred Astaire, Cyd Charisse, Nanette Fabray, Oscar Levant | 111 minutes | Not Rated

A "worthy companion to *Singin' in the Rain*", this "solid musical" comedy boasts the "most romantic moment in movie history" – the "lovely 'Dancing in the Dark' number in Central Park" – performed by Astaire and Charisse in "top form"; thanks to its "fantastic music" and "delightful cast", nostalgists sigh "they don't make 'em like this anymore."

Bang the Drum Slowly 23 | 25 | 24 | 18

1973 | Directed by John Hancock | With Michael Moriarty, Robert De Niro, Vincent Gardenia | 96 minutes | Rated PG

Moriarty and De Niro deliver "two moving performances" in this memorably "sad" drama about a hayseed baseball catcher with a terminal illness and the star pitcher who befriends him; both a "real tearjerker" and a "powerful story of friendship", it's a "well done", "humbling" experience that still has "staying power."

Barefoot Contessa, The 24 | 25 | 23 | 23

1954 | Directed by Joseph L. Mankiewicz | With Humphrey Bogart, Ava Gardner, Edmond O'Brien | 128 minutes | Not Rated

"Romantic to the nth degree", this "enjoyable" drama centers on a "ravishing" performance by the "amazing Ava" as a "gorgeous" ingenue who rises to "old Hollywood" stardom and ultimately marries into minor royalty; if some say the "thin plot" reveals feet of clay, it's still loaded with "elegance" and "real quality" – "those were movies!"

Barefoot in the Park 23 | 24 | 22 | 21

1967 | Directed by Gene Saks | With Robert Redford, Jane Fonda, Charles Boyer, Mildred Natwick | 106 minutes | Rated G

Channeling "how delightful the first rush of true love is", this "light" romantic comedy pairs "ingénue" Fonda with "heartthrob" Redford in a "cute tale" of newlyweds who "try on marriage in a small NY flat"; there's "great chemistry" between the "beautiful" leads and Neil Simon's script is "witty", even if some say its "strong period quality" makes the film feel "a bit dated" today.

Batman Begins 23 | 21 | 23 | 26

2005 | Directed by Christopher Nolan | With Christian Bale, Michael Caine, Katie Holmes | 141 minutes | Rated PG-13

After a "worrisome decline" into "cartoonish goofery", the Batman franchise is "back on track" with this "quality" revival, a "rollicking ride" that revels in the "dark" tone of the "original comic book" as it recounts the Caped Crusader's "early years"; as for acting, the "brooding" Bale "soars" in the lead role, shedding new "insight" into his character's "inner turmoil", though romantic interest Holmes is deemed the "weak link."

Battle of Algiers, The ◐ F 28 | 24 | 27 | 26

1967 | Directed by Gillo Pontecorvo | With Jean Martin, Yacef Saadi | 117 minutes | Not Rated

"Terrorism and military response" are the up-to-the-minute subjects of this "decades-ahead-of-its-time" feature delineating the Algerian struggle for independence from French rule; the "riveting" footage is "so lifelike" that it "looks like a documentary", but even as a "docudrama" it remains "timely, essential" viewing.

Beaches 22 | 23 | 22 | 21

1988 | Directed by Garry Marshall | With Bette Midler, Barbara Hershey, John Heard | 123 minutes | Rated PG-13

Alternately "heartwarming and heartbreaking", this "major chick flick" (a bona fide "10-hanky" special) captures the "intensity of friendship" as it recounts the "lifelong" alliance of "two opposites": the "always passionate" Midler and the more "detached" Hershey; hard-hearted sorts yawn it's a "sappy soap opera", but others say when you need a "good cathartic cry", this "guilty pleasure" is the "one to watch."

Beau Geste ◑ 25 | 23 | 25 | 22

1939 | Directed by William A. Wellman | With Gary Cooper, Ray Milland, Robert Preston | 120 minutes | Not Rated

"Heroic heroes and villainous villains" populate this "ultimate" war picture about "friendship and honor" that's "perhaps the best Foreign Legion movie" ever made; ok, there are "no special effects" and it might seem "corny" today, but it still supplies plenty of "first-class adventure" right up to that "majestic ending."

Beautiful Mind, A ✉ 26 | 28 | 25 | 25

2001 | Directed by Ron Howard | With Russell Crowe, Ed Harris, Jennifer Connelly | 134 minutes | Rated PG-13

"What *Rain Man* did for autism", this "absorbing" Oscar winner about a "brilliant mathematician's" battle with mental illness "does for schizophrenia", revealing the "thin line between genius and insanity"; "phenomenally acted" by Crowe and Connelly, it "celebrates the triumph of the human spirit" – though foes say its "Hollywoodized" script "strays too far from historical accuracy."

Beauty and the Beast ◑F 28 | 25 | 27 | 28

1947 | Directed by Jean Cocteau | With Jean Marais, Josette Day, Marcel André | 93 minutes | Not Rated

Enter a "highly stylized universe" in this "hallucinatory" take on the classic "fairy tale" that's both "dreamlike" and "complex" owing to "Cocteau's wit and imagination"; "still unsurpassed by more lavish productions", this "amazing visual feast" demonstrates the artistry possible with "ancient technology" – and enough "sexuality beneath the surface" to keep things throbbing.

Beauty and the Beast 26 | - | 25 | 27

1991 | Directed by Gary Trousdale, Kirk Wise | Animated | 84 minutes | Rated G

A "sensational score" complements the cast of "lovable characters" in this "magical milepost" that "set the bar for a new wave of animated classics"; told with a "fresh approach", it has an "intelligent" "heroine with chutzpah" trilling "catchy", "singable songs" that will "keep tots of all ages entranced"; in short, this "modern masterpiece" – the first animated film ever nominated for Best Picture – is nothing less than "Disney at its high-flying best."

Becket ✉ 26 | 29 | 26 | 26

1964 | Directed by Peter Glenville | With Richard Burton, Peter O'Toole, John Gielgud | 148 minutes | Not Rated

"Big drama writ large", this biopic about England's King Henry II and his "deep bond with Thomas Becket" features the "brilliant teaming" of "two high-powered actors" – the "winning" O'Toole and "wonderful" Burton – in "histrionic, bellowing performances"; sure, it's "a bit talky", but otherwise this "beautifully filmed period piece" is living proof of the way "history should be experienced."

	OVERALL	ACTING	STORY	PROD.

Before Sunrise
23	23	22	21

1995 | Directed by Richard Linklater | With Ethan Hawke, Julie Delpy | 105 minutes | Rated R

A "thinking person's" romance, this "bittersweet gem" examines a "passionate meeting of the minds" between Hawke and the "enchanting" Delpy as "star-crossed" Eurorailing students who hook up for a single night; the duo's "winning chemistry" is framed by "beautiful" Viennese backdrops, and "what might have been" will dawn on those who catch the "10-years-later follow-up", *Before Sunset*.

Before the Devil Knows You're Dead
23	27	23	22

2007 | Directed by Sidney Lumet | With Philip Seymour Hoffman, Ethan Hawke, Albert Finney, Marisa Tomei | 117 minutes | Rated R

"Crime doesn't pay" in this "dark" "American tragedy" about two brothers' botched robbery of a mom-and-pop store owned by their own mom and pop; Hoffman and Hawke are "killer" as the "morally bankrupt" siblings, and their "downward spiral" is rife with "unpredictable plot twists", although you might want to avert your eyes from "Phil's nude scene."

Being John Malkovich
22	24	24	22

1999 | Directed by Spike Jonze | With John Cusack, Cameron Diaz, John Malkovich, Catherine Keener | 112 minutes | Rated R

"'Original' does not even begin to describe" this "surreal romp" that mixes "dark fantasy" with "smart comedy" in its "off-the-wall" account of a regular guy who finds a portal that takes him "inside the head" of actor John Malkovich; though it "rewards rather than insults the audience's intelligence", it's definitely "not for everybody", variously described as "engrossing", "audacious fun" or just plain "confusing as hell."

Being Julia
23	27	21	24

2004 | Directed by István Szabó | With Annette Bening, Jeremy Irons | 104 minutes | Rated R

Bening "steals the show" with her "luminous" portrayal of a "fading English actress undertaking one last fling" with a young Yank in this "enjoyable" Brit "comedy of manners" based on the Somerset Maugham novella; overall, it's a "fluffy period piece" perhaps best suited for devotees of the "theatuh", but it's still "worth watching" all the way through for that "deliciously wicked climax."

Being There
26	27	25	23

1979 | Directed by Hal Ashby | With Peter Sellers, Shirley MacLaine, Melvyn Douglas | 130 minutes | Rated PG

"Politics and hypocrisy" get a skewering in this "classic allegory" about a "slow-thinking" gardener who proves that "80 percent of life is just showing up"; "Sellers glows" in this "faithful" adaptation of Jerzy Kosinski's story, which "requires patience with its slow pace" but does "allow you to form your own conclusions."

Belle de Jour F
24	25	23	23

1968 | Directed by Luis Buñuel | With Catherine Deneuve, Jean Sorel | 101 minutes | Rated R

Deneuve was "never sexier" than in this "marvelously perverse" French drama, a peek at the "dark side" of a "chichi housewife" pent up in "bourgeois" wedlock whose "S&M fantasies" compel her to take a "side job" at the local bordello; more "Dali painting" than *Playboy* centerfold, it's a "stylish", "complex" window into director Buñuel's "surreal world", and the leading lady's "intense", "alluring" performance spices up the "slow" spots.

Bells Are Ringing 24 | 24 | 22 | 22

1960 | Directed by Vincente Minnelli | With Judy Holliday, Dean Martin, Fred Clark | 127 minutes | Not Rated

A "funny" Broadway musical becomes a "fine vehicle" for the "wonderful" Holliday in this story of a singing switchboard girl hung up on a playwright (the slightly "out-of-his-league" Martin); yet despite a "classic" score and a "famous song" ('The Party's Over'), some say this "stage-bound" production's "outdated."

Bells of St. Mary's, The ◑ 24 | 25 | 23 | 23

1945 | Directed by Leo McCarey | With Bing Crosby, Ingrid Bergman | 126 minutes | Not Rated

Bergman and "ring-a-ding Bing" take turns "tugging your heart" in this "*Going My Way* sequel", a "heartwarming" drama (and "Christmas fave") about a crooning clergyman sent to a parochial school's rescue with a message of "selfless giving"; the "old-fashioned sweetness" strikes a "treacly" note for cynics, but "sentimental" sorts still delight in its "touching", "keep-a-hanky-handy" style of filmmaking that's "now extinct."

Bend It Like Beckham 26 | 24 | 25 | 23

2003 | Directed by Gurinder Chadha | With Parminder K. Nagra, Keira Knightley, Jonathan Rhys Meyers | 112 minutes | Rated PG-13

"Bend it like anything you want" – this "thoroughly entertaining", "cross-cultural feel-good movie" about an "Indian girl in England who wants to play soccer" scores with its "empowering" storyline and "fantastic ensemble acting"; a "true delight" "for young and old alike", it's the "best ethnic-themed movie since *My Big Fat Greek Wedding*" – "but no TV series, please."

Ben-Hur ✉ 26 | 23 | 25 | 28

1959 | Directed by William Wyler | With Charlton Heston, Jack Hawkins, Stephen Boyd | 212 minutes | Rated G

Unleashed four decades "before *Gladiator*", this "bigger than big" sword-and-sandals "masterpiece" features Heston exuding "hammy", bare-chested "bravura" as a Judean prince betrayed into Roman slavery only to seek payback via "breathtaking" bouts of action (including that "stunner" of a "chariot race"); a colossal hit and major Oscar magnet, it epitomizes the "grand Hollywood historical epic", built on "biblical" bedrock.

Best in Show 24 | 25 | 23 | 22

2000 | Directed by Christopher Guest | With Christopher Guest, Eugene Levy, Catherine O'Hara | 90 minutes | Rated PG-13

"Three woofs" and "four paws up" for this "quirky riot" of a mockumentary about a "gaggle of fanatical dog show participants" and their "pedigreed pooches"; the wacky repartee makes for a "beautifully inappropriate", "laugh-a-minute satire" that "can be viewed 100 times without becoming dog-eared."

	OVERALL	ACTING	STORY	PROD.

Best Years of Our Lives, The ✉◑ | 28 | 27 | 28 | 25

1946 | Directed by William Wyler | With Myrna Loy, Fredric March, Dana Andrews, Teresa Wright | 172 minutes | Not Rated

"Have the Kleenex handy" – there's no denying the "pure heart" of this "compelling" drama exploring the "uneasy readjustment" of WWII "vets coming home" to Main Street USA; its all-around "riveting" acting and "no-miss script" perfectly capture the "next-door" post-war mood, taking Best Picture (plus six more Oscars) and resonating as a "quintessentially American period piece."

Bicycle Thief, The ✉◑F | 27 | 26 | 27 | 24

1949 | Directed by Vittorio De Sica | With Lamberto Maggiorani, Enzo Staiola | 93 minutes | Not Rated

"Poetry put on film", this early slice of "Italian neorealism" is "so sad" but so "beautifully executed" that it's ultimately "not a downer"; using "nonprofessional actors" in a drama of a father and son searching impoverished post-war Rome for the stolen bike that's key to their livelihood, De Sica tugs hearts with a "timeless pathos" that's most "affecting" for its "charm and simplicity."

Big | 23 | 24 | 24 | 22

1988 | Directed by Penny Marshall | With Tom Hanks, Elizabeth Perkins, Robert Loggia | 104 minutes | Rated PG

Getting literal with its "inner child", this "cute" "kid-in-a-man's-body" comedy stars a "winning", "never-so-lovable" Hanks, who "makes the movie" (and moves into the big time) as a 13-year-old who "becomes an adult overnight" and gains entrée to NYC's corporate playground; though some of the "fantasy" is "on the sappy side", a large contingent calls it "most rewatchable."

Big Chill, The | 23 | 24 | 22 | 21

1983 | Directed by Lawrence Kasdan | With Glenn Close, William Hurt, Kevin Kline, Jeff Goldblum, Mary Kay Place, JoBeth Williams, Tom Berenger | 105 minutes | Rated R

Trace the tracks of their tears as this '60s-era "nostalgia" trip tries to "define a generation" via a "superb ensemble", an "iconic soundtrack" and the "soul-searching" premise of "boomers regathering" at a friend's funeral (fun fact: Kevin Costner "plays the stiff"); anyone bummed by the "contrived" setup and "smug" "yuppie angst" can still groove to the "perfect" tune selection.

Big Clock, The ◑ | 25 | 25 | 25 | 23

1948 | Directed by John Farrow | With Ray Milland, Charles Laughton, Maureen O'Sullivan, Elsa Lanchester | 95 minutes | Not Rated

"Nice and twisty", this "classic noir" stars Ray Milland as a crime magazine editor in a "real predicament" after witnessing "his publisher killing his lover"; the "suspenseful" story was filmed again in 1987 as *No Way Out*, but pundits say the original "dances rings around" the remake.

Big Heat, The ◑ | 25 | 25 | 24 | 22

1953 | Directed by Fritz Lang | With Glenn Ford, Gloria Grahame, Lee Marvin, Carolyn Jones | 90 minutes | Not Rated

"Considered daring in its time", this "ultimate noir picture" features a rogues' gallery of hard-boiled "tough guys" and gals in a story about an honest cop "obsessed with getting revenge" following his wife's murder; though tepid types say the heat's "cooled off over the years", there's "one horrifying scene" involving a pot of "scalding hot coffee" that's still quite a "shocker."

Big Night 24 | 26 | 23 | 23

1996 | Directed by Campbell Scott, Stanley Tucci | With Stanley Tucci, Tony Shalhoub, Minnie Driver | 107 minutes | Rated R

"Yum": this "quirky", "thoroughly enjoyable" dramatic "feast" tracks two "Italian immigrant brothers" in their "endearing" effort to keep their restaurant and culinary "vision" alive on the '50s-era Jersey coast; hailed as an "overlooked gem", its slow-simmering pace allows admirers to "savor" "brilliant performances" that are rivaled only by "stunning food shots" – "don't catch it on an empty stomach."

Big Sleep, The ◑ 27 | 27 | 24 | 24

1946 | Directed by Howard Hawks | With Humphrey Bogart, Lauren Bacall, Martha Vickers | 114 minutes | Not Rated

"Whodunit? who cares?" as long as the legendary Bogie and Bacall keep up the "snappy" patter and "heavy-lidded" "chemistry" in this "dizzying" film noir "classic" featuring Bogart as "fast-talking" gumshoe Philip Marlowe prowling Raymond Chandler territory (1940s Los Angeles at its most "atmospheric"); if the notoriously "incomprehensible plot" is seriously in need of a clue, at least the "crackling" pace and "salty" repartee always "entertain and enthrall."

Billy Elliot 25 | 26 | 25 | 23

2000 | Directed by Stephen Daldry | With Julie Walters, Jamie Bell | 110 minutes | Rated PG-13

It takes *Swan Lake* to break the "working-class shackles" of a Northern England mining town in this "coming-of-age" drama about a "boy who loves ballet" and his hardscrabble dad; behind the "thick British accents", fans discover a "captivating" if "unlikely tale" propelled by "talent, desire" and lots of "fancy footwork", with an "uplifting" finale that's apt to inspire "a good cry."

Birds, The 24 | 20 | 24 | 25

1963 | Directed by Alfred Hitchcock | With Tippi Hedren, Rod Taylor, Jessica Tandy, Suzanne Pleshette | 119 minutes | Rated PG-13

"Nature strikes back, Hitchcock style", in this "improbably terrifying" "nail-biter" about "birds gone mad" that "still packs enough of a punch" to leave the timid "traumatized"; though critics aren't chirping about the "hokey", "no-rhyme-or-reason" plot that takes "too long to get going", ultimately you'll "never think of pigeons in the same way" after a gander at this one.

Birdy 23 | 25 | 22 | 21

1984 | Directed by Alan Parker | With Matthew Modine, Nicolas Cage | 120 minutes | Rated R

Much "emotional" flutter marks this "haunting" drama that "gets into the psyches" of a "pair of outcasts": Modine as a "traumatized" Vietnam-era vet with a "disturbing" fixation on "birdlike" behavior and a "brilliant" Cage as the childhood friend out to revive him; thanks to the leads' "breadth and heart", it's a "neglected minor classic" nested within a "surreal" story – "this film can fly."

	OVERALL	ACTING	STORY	PROD.
Birth of a Nation, The ◑	25	20	19	27

1915 | Directed by D.W. Griffith | With Lillian Gish, Mae Marsh, Henry B. Walthall | 190 minutes | Not Rated

A "masterful" technical feat that could be the "most influential movie ever made", Griffith's "landmark" silent epic "wrote the book" on "camera movement" and "cinema as storytelling" while offering a "morally irresponsible" version of Reconstruction replete with "blatantly racist" "stereotyping" and the "Ku Klux Klan presented as heroes"; so even though this work marks the "birth of the feature" film, be prepared for a storyline that's a "mess" - "even by 1915" standards.

Bishop's Wife, The ◑	24	24	24	23

1947 | Directed by Henry Koster | With Cary Grant, Loretta Young, David Niven | 105 minutes | Not Rated

Although "less well known" than some of its "holiday movie" peers, this "Christmasy" romance stars Grant as a "guardian angel" blessed with "elegance and style" ("duh!") who's sent to "restore faith" to a clergyman and his spouse but "falls in love" along the way; overall, it's an "amusing, touching" display of "old-fashioned" "star power" that sentimental souls will "never forget."

Blackboard Jungle ◑	23	24	22	19

1955 | Directed by Richard Brooks | With Glenn Ford, Anne Francis, Vic Morrow, Sidney Poitier | 101 minutes | Not Rated

See "the '50s in a new way" via this "gritty" drama, a standout of the "juvenile delinquent genre" set in an "inner-city school" where "danger is only a heartbeat away" as idealistic teacher Ford is forced to "tame" a horde of punks; notable for Hollywood's "first use of a rock 'n' roll" soundtrack, it may "feel a bit dated", though cynics shrug "schools haven't changed" that much.

Black Hawk Down	23	21	23	26

2001 | Directed by Ridley Scott | With Josh Hartnett, Ewan McGregor, Tom Sizemore | 144 minutes | Rated R

It's "hard to watch, but it's even harder to turn away" from this "astoundingly gripping" (and "surprisingly accurate") account of a 1993 Mogadishu "military misadventure", which pitted a handful of U.S. Army Rangers against a huge enemy force; "Scott puts you on the ground with the soldiers", "brilliantly showing the total chaos of the Somalian battle" in all its "gory", "graphic" and "grueling" detail; indeed, even peaceniks agree this "salute to our servicemen" "doesn't simplify or sensationalize" combat.

Black Orpheus ✉ F	26	23	25	25

1959 | Directed by Marcel Camus | With Marpessa Dawn, Breno Mello | 100 minutes | Rated PG

"Brazilian backdrops" and "bossa nova" rhythms cast their "spell" over Greek legend in this "enchanting", "lyrical" foreign flick, an "exotic retelling" of the Orpheus and Eurydice myth transposed to "modern-day Rio" during Carnival; "sexy", "lush" and full of "beautiful shots" of "cinema verité" revelry, it takes its Dionysian devotees to Hades and back in "unmatched" style - and oh, that "moving-in-your-seat" soundtrack!

	OVERALL	ACTING	STORY	PROD.
Black Stallion, The	24	20	23	25

1979 | Directed by Carroll Ballard | With Mickey Rooney, Kelly Reno, Teri Garr | 118 minutes | Rated G

Equestrians of "all ages" ponder the "bond between boy and horse" in this "captivating" family film about an Arabian steed who's shipwrecked with a youngster on a desert island only to be entered in a turf race after they're rescued and resettled to a Western ranch; though saddled with a "somber" side, it "wins the roses" with a "skillful blend" of "breathtaking" scenery and "luminous cinematography."

Blade Runner 26 | 22 | 25 | 27

1982 | Directed by Ridley Scott | With Harrison Ford, Rutger Hauer, Sean Young, Daryl Hannah | 117 minutes | Rated R

This "awesome" "blueprint" for "modern sci-fi" is a "visually stunning" picture best watched with "your brain switched on"; an ultra-"stylish" "noir take" on LA as a 21st-century "dystopia" where "commercialism and biotech run amok", it's also a "hard-boiled" "morality play" with one of "Ford's best acting jobs" as a PI "hunting cyborg replicants while falling in love with one"; connoisseurs tout the "superior director's cut."

Blazing Saddles 25 | 22 | 23 | 23

1974 | Directed by Mel Brooks | With Cleavon Little, Gene Wilder, Harvey Korman, Madeline Kahn | 93 minutes | Rated R

"You'll never look at a horse the same way" after a peek at this "hilarious", "decidedly un-PC" comedy via Mel Brooks, an "off-the-wall" Wild West "spoof" that "insults everyone" with a mix of "slapstick", "quotable one-liners" and really "tasteless" routines (like the sound effects-ridden "campfire scene"); most call it "enjoyable" if "overdone."

Blind Side, The ✉ 26 | 27 | 26 | 25

2009 | Directed by John Lee Hancock | With Sandra Bullock, Tim McGraw, Quinton Aaron | 129 minutes | Rated PG-13

Whether you're a "sports fan or not", this "uplifting" "true-life" drama "hits home" "without any sugarcoating" as "sassy, brassy" Bullock (who "definitely earned her Oscar") takes in a "disadvantaged" young "underdog" who grows up to be NFL player Michael Oher; with the "predictable tug at the heart" held in check by the "wonderful performances", the "stirring" story scores a "real touchdown."

Blood Diamond 25 | 26 | 25 | 26

2006 | Directed by Edward Zwick | With Leonardo DiCaprio, Djimon Hounsou, Jennifer Connelly | 143 minutes | Rated R

"You'll rethink your jewelry purchases" after a look at this "engaging" production mining the "horror of the African diamond trade" for "socially relevant" drama and featuring an "intense" DiCaprio as an "unlikable" smuggler whose "hint of a golden heart" helps a father – the "spectacular" Hounsou – find his kidnapped son; "violent" action scenes drive home the "savagery" of the conflict while indicting the "wealth-obsessed" culture that nurtures it.

Blood Simple 24 | 25 | 25 | 22

1985 | Directed by Joel Coen | With Frances McDormand, John Getz, Dan Hedaya | 97 minutes | Rated R

"Complex" is more like it as the Coen brothers' first feature "pumps new blood" into the "low-budget crime thriller" in this "brilliant" "film noir homage" filled with "wicked" "thrills delivered with a drawl"; it's a "twisty", "nerve-jangling" tale of betrayal and revenge in a dusty Texas town, told with a "quirky" slant that "foreshadows" the filmmakers' "masterpiece, *Fargo*."

Blowup 26 | 23 | 25 | 25

1966 | Directed by Michelangelo Antonioni | With David Hemmings, Vanessa Redgrave, Sarah Miles | 111 minutes | Not Rated

"Forget *Austin Powers*", baby, "this is the *real* Swinging London": a "riveting existential thriller" that tracks a happening fashion photographer obsessed with both Redgrave and a "mysterious death in a park"; hipsters hail it as an "enigmatic" (or "infuriating") milestone of the "alienation genre" possessed by the "spirit of the '60s" – and that tasty "period flavor" is still "too cool for words."

Blue Angel, The ◑ 🅵 25 | 27 | 24 | 22

1930 | Directed by Josef von Sternberg | With Marlene Dietrich, Emil Jannings | 99 minutes | Not Rated

Behold the "magnificent Dietrich" "at her best" in this "Weimar-era" German drama, the story of "naughty Lola", a garter-flashing chanteuse who "seduces an old fool" of a schoolmaster and expedites his "descent into the gutter"; though it's a "dated" dose of "ennui and moral rot" in a "world now lost", fräulein Marlene's "tour-de-force", career-launching turn is "music to the eyes."

Body and Soul ◑ 25 | 26 | 23 | 23

1947 | Directed by Robert Rossen | With John Garfield, Lilli Palmer, Anne Revere, Hazel Brooks | 104 minutes | Not Rated

If "you think *Rocky* was good", lace up for this noirish boxing drama and go the distance with Garfield's "raw", "moving" portrayal of a ham-and-egger who makes the big time only to get "tangled up" in mobster connections and "his own flaws"; thanks to "perfect" casting and Oscar-winning editing, it's "one of the great fight movies" and a "provocative" warm-up for *Raging Bull*.

Body Heat 24 | 25 | 25 | 23

1981 | Directed by Lawrence Kasdan | With William Hurt, Kathleen Turner, Richard Crenna, Mickey Rourke | 113 minutes | Rated R

"Whew!" this "palpably steamy" "noir thriller" stars "what-a-babe" Turner as a trophy wife who "burns up the screen" as she seduces "small-town lawyer" Hurt into a "spiraling" web of "deceit" that "keeps you guessing" to the last frame; in short, it's a sexed-up "version of the old help-me-kill-my-husband story", a kind of "*Double Indemnity* for a new generation."

Bonnie and Clyde 25 | 25 | 24 | 25

1967 | Directed by Arthur Penn | With Warren Beatty, Faye Dunaway, Gene Hackman, Estelle Parsons | 111 minutes | Rated R

More a piece of "film history than real history", this "stunning" 1930s "crime-spree" biopic "broke a lot of old rules" in its "revisionist" take on the title characters, real-life "losers" reconceived by Beatty and Dunaway as the "screen's best-ever antiheroes"; the "letter-perfect" cast, "impeccable" direction and "gorgeously gory" photography all add up to way-"ahead-of-its-time" moviemaking, even if the "indelible images" of the "bloody ballet at the end" unsettle the squeamish.

	OVERALL	ACTING	STORY	PROD.

Born Free

24	19	24	23

1966 | Directed by James Hill | With Virginia McKenna, Bill Travers, Geoffrey Keen | 95 minutes | Rated PG

The "theme song alone" is enough to set off "shameless weeping" as this "well-told" family flick unfolds, focusing on a husband and wife in "wild Africa" and their effort to "protect the lioness Elsa"; a "major tearjerker" in its day, it remains "vivid" for boomers who tell of "loving it as a child" even though it's "so sad."

Born Yesterday ✉◑

26	28	25	23

1950 | Directed by George Cukor | With Judy Holliday, Broderick Crawford, William Holden | 103 minutes | Not Rated

"Still magical today", this "zany" screwball comedy revolves around a "not-so-dumb blonde", the mistress of a shady tycoon, who undergoes a *My Fair Lady*-like transformation and "breaks out of her bimbo chains"; thanks to her unique voice and "great timing", the "perfectly cast" Holliday took home an Oscar for her "pure gold" performance, a "pièce de résistance" that the 1993 remake "can't match."

Bourne Ultimatum, The

25	23	23	26

2007 | Directed by Paul Greengrass | With Matt Damon, Julia Stiles, David Strathairn | 115 minutes | Rated PG-13

"From the opening scene" through the "amazing" windup, the "action doesn't stop" in this "outstanding" Bourne threequel, an "adrenaline"-soaked "cherry on top of the franchise" packed with "cloak-and-dagger intrigue", "dizzying" car chases and "exotic international locales"; reprising his role as the titular amnesiac spy, Damon proves again he was "born to play the part", and fans hope the "door's open for more" installments.

Boy in the Striped Pajamas, The

26	26	26	24

2008 | Directed by Mark Herman | With Asa Butterfield, Amber Beattie, David Thewlis, Vera Farmiga | 94 minutes | Rated PG-13

The "son of a Nazi officer" and a "Jewish boy" on opposite sides of a concentration camp fence "become friends" in this "grim" Holocaust "fable" that "brings a horrific chapter of history down to size" through a "child's eyes"; provided you can "overlook several implausibilities" and stomach some "difficult" depictions, an "emotional, eye-opening" experience awaits.

Boys Don't Cry ✉

23	27	23	21

1999 | Directed by Kimberly Peirce | With Hilary Swank, Chloë Sevigny, Peter Sarsgaard | 118 minutes | Rated R

Turning a "dark situation" into a "tough" study of "intolerance", this "disturbing" drama is a "faithful telling of the story of Teena Brandon", a small-town girl who "dresses and acts the part" of a boy, leading to "powerful" complications; though the Oscar-winning Swank is "beyond convincing", the "brutal" ending is "not easy to watch", but "will stay with you" – "unfortunately, it's true."

Boys from Brazil, The

24	26	25	22

1978 | Directed by Franklin J. Schaffner | With Gregory Peck, Laurence Olivier, Steve Guttenberg, James Mason | 123 minutes | Rated R

"Old Nazis" plan new terror via a brood of "Hitler clones" in this "taut thriller" starring the "powerful" Olivier as a war-criminal tracker who

	OVERALL	ACTING	STORY	PROD.

goes "mano a mano" with Peck's "evil Dr. Mengele"; it's a trove of "delightfully creepy" scenes ("loved the Dobermans"), and the "over-the-top" scenario still holds up given that a "genetic-engineering nightmare" is "even scarier now."

Boyz N the Hood

23 | 22 | 24 | 21

1991 | Directed by John Singleton | With Ice Cube, Cuba Gooding Jr., Laurence Fishburne | 107 minutes | Rated R

The "gangsta flick" that "sets the bar" for the competition "keeps it real" as it takes a "hard-core" look at ghetto "gang wars in South Central" LA; an "important" breakthrough with some "surprising acting turns", it's a "fantastic first film" from Singleton, whose later work doesn't "get anywhere near this one."

Braveheart ✉

26 | 24 | 25 | 27

1995 | Directed by Mel Gibson | With Mel Gibson, Sophie Marceau, Catherine McCormack | 177 minutes | Rated R

"It's got everything" say fans of this "awe-inspiring" medieval "history lesson" about an "underdog" Scottish hero ("Mel in a kilt" and "war paint") "knocking heads" in an anti-Brit "rebellion"; the "gory", "hackin'-and-hewin'" battles, "heartfelt" acting and "huge scope" help justify Gibson's Best Director win, even if some warn of three "long", "melodramatic" hours.

Brazil

24 | 23 | 23 | 27

1985 | Directed by Terry Gilliam | With Jonathan Pryce, Robert De Niro, Bob Hoskins | 131 minutes | Rated R

Even as "fantasy", Monty Python alumnus Gilliam's "twisted", "utterly original" vision of a "part-Orwell, part-Python" future is definitely "a little out there"; it demands "perseverance" - what with its "baffling" "whirlwind" of "bizarre" effects and chin-scratching "black comedy" plot about one man's struggle with a "Kafka-esque" "bureaucracy" - but rewards those who hang in there with a "totally crazy ride."

Breach

23 | 26 | 24 | 23

2007 | Directed by Billy Ray | With Chris Cooper, Ryan Phillippe, Laura Linney | 110 minutes | Rated PG-13

Based on the "actual events" surrounding the case of Robert Hanssen, the notorious FBI agent caught "spilling the beans to the Soviets", this "taut" espionage thriller pits the "brilliant" Cooper against an "amazing" Phillippe in a "chess game of the minds" that has you "engaged from the get-go"; don't expect any "over-the-top pyrotechnics" or "easy answers" here, just good old "edge-of-your-seat tension" that doesn't quit "even if you know the ending."

Breaker Morant

27 | 27 | 27 | 24

1980 | Directed by Bruce Beresford | With Jack Thompson, Edward Woodward, Bryan Brown | 107 minutes | Rated PG

"Guy's-flick" fans salute this "solid Aussie" drama of "kangaroo" justice, a "small masterpiece" in its "gripping" depiction of "betrayal" at a military trial during the Boer War; told with "moving realism", it tackles the "question of morals in warfare" using a "top-notch" cast to "demonstrate bravery" and "bravura", turning the fate of "appointed scapegoats" into an "inspiration."

OVERALL	ACTING	STORY	PROD.

Breakfast at Tiffany's 26 | 26 | 24 | 24

1961 | Directed by Blake Edwards | With Audrey Hepburn, George Peppard, Patricia Neal | 115 minutes | Rated PG

In the "role she was born to play", a "mesmerizing" Hepburn brings Truman Capote's "messed-up" "free spirit" Holly Golightly to life in "peerless style"; fans find everything about it "irresistible" – "Henry Mancini's divine score", Audrey's "timeless clothes", the "love-letter-to-NY" cinematography – and call this "dream-making, heartbreaking" tribute to the "power of romance" their "all-time favorite."

Breaking Away ✉ 24 | 21 | 24 | 20

1979 | Directed by Peter Yates | With Dennis Christopher, Dennis Quaid, Daniel Stern | 100 minutes | Rated PG

A "rousing ride", this "*Rocky*-esque" "Hoosier tale" is a "coming-of-age" drama on two wheels, with Christopher leading a cast of "cutie-pie" "underdogs" as a cyclist who pedals straight into a "town-and-gown" "class conflict"; it's cheered on as a "big-hearted" "buddy film" that delivers a "socko" bike race finale.

Breaking the Waves 23 | 27 | 20 | 20

1996 | Directed by Lars von Trier | With Emily Watson, Stellan Skarsgård | 153 minutes | Rated R

"Be prepared" for "emotionally devastating" doings in this "raw" drama of "delusion" and "doomed romance" about a "dimwitted girl" who "sacrifices everything for her paralyzed husband"; most pronounce it "strange" yet "so well done it's painful" (the "musical interludes give one time to weep"), though foes call it a "silly" parable that's a most "depressing" picture of "female martyrdom."

Breathless ◑ F 25 | 24 | 21 | 23

1961 | Directed by Jean-Luc Godard | With Jean-Paul Belmondo, Jean Seberg | 87 minutes | Not Rated

"So hip" and as "refreshing" now as at its debut, this French "New Wave masterpiece" breathes "pure pleasure" into a "silly gangster story" with "luscious" leads Belmondo and Seberg as lovers on the lam (even the late-'50s Paris setting is a "terrific character"); while scholars speak of genre-"defining" technical feats – the "jump cut is born!" – most simply find it "charming" and way "ahead of its time."

Bride of Frankenstein, The ◑ 25 | 21 | 23 | 23

1935 | Directed by James Whale | With Boris Karloff, Colin Clive, Elsa Lanchester | 75 minutes | Not Rated

Bolt-necked Frankie gets "his one shot at love" in this "excellent sequel" to the hoary "'30s horror classic", wherein Karloff reprises his signature role with "panache" and Lanchester's shocked fiancée simply has "great hair"; fright fiends cherish the "creepy" results as "campy", "funny" and not a little "whacked."

Bridge on the River Kwai, The ✉ 28 | 28 | 27 | 28

1957 | Directed by David Lean | With William Holden, Alec Guinness, Jack Hawkins, Sessue Hayakawa | 161 minutes | Rated PG

Those "stiff upper lips" do some "memorable" whistling in director Lean's "grand", "engrossing" Japanese POW camp epic, an "old-fashioned" yarn about the "timeless themes" of "honor", "conviction" and the "madness" of war; a lock for the top Oscars of 1957, it "suc-

	OVERALL	ACTING	STORY	PROD.

ceeds" mightily with "great performances" – led "heart and soul" by a "hubris"-afflicted Guinness – enhanced by "splashy" scenery and an "explosive ending."

Brief Encounter ◑ 27 29 27 25

1946 | Directed by David Lean | With Celia Johnson, Trevor Howard, Stanley Holloway | 86 minutes | Not Rated

For a "truly romantic" fix, this "quiet" "masterpiece of yearning" from David Lean (via Noël Coward) is "right up there" in the running as the "definitive tearjerker"; the "never better" Johnson and Howard play "ordinary people" whose meeting on a commuter line develops into a "short but intense" "connection", with swells of Rachmaninoff to seal the deal; in brief, an "unforgettable" trip.

Brigadoon 24 21 22 24

1954 | Directed by Vincente Minnelli | With Gene Kelly, Van Johnson, Cyd Charisse | 108 minutes | Not Rated

A Lerner and Loewe "stage show turned into a movie", this "lesser-known" MGM musical is set in a mythical Scottish town that can be visited by outsiders only once every 100 years; though some criticize the "corny" concept, "phony accents" and "cardboard back-lot" sets, most "suspend disbelief" once the music starts and the "magical" Kelly and Charisse begin "dancing in the heather."

Bringing Up Baby ◑ 27 27 24 24

1938 | Directed by Howard Hawks | With Katharine Hepburn, Cary Grant | 102 minutes | Not Rated

"One continuous roar", director Hawks' "screwiest of screwball comedies" is propelled at a "frenetic pace" by the Hepburn-Grant "chemistry" and a "tons-of-fun" scenario touching on "dinosaur bones, crazy rich folk" and a lost leopard; it's an old-school "madcap" "champ", and fans of "farce" still bring it up as the "funniest movie ever."

Broadcast News 23 25 22 20

1987 | Directed by James L. Brooks | With William Hurt, Albert Brooks, Holly Hunter | 127 minutes | Rated R

"Appearance over substance" is the subject of this "smart" "send-up of the media" about a "love triangle" in a "career-driven", *Network*-esque TV newsroom that hums with "behind-the-scenes" one-upmanship; nominated for a slew of Oscars (but winner of none), this "ahead-of-its-time" comedy remains "totally engaging", due to the efforts of its "sharp-as-a-tack" cast.

Brokeback Mountain ✉ 24 26 23 26

2005 | Directed by Ang Lee | With Heath Ledger, Jake Gyllenhaal, Michelle Williams, Anne Hathaway | 134 minutes | Rated R

Widely pegged as the "gay cowboy movie", this "star-crossed" "Romeo-and-Romeo" romance is as "controversial" as they come, yet its "gimmick-free" rendition of "forbidden love" "avoids sensationalism" thanks to an "understated" performance by Ledger (and an "underrated" one by Gyllenhaal), backed up by "stunning scenery", a "ravishing score" and "Angst" Lee's "heartfelt", Oscar-winning direction; ultimately, this "timeless" film has had a "real cultural influence", even if it's best remembered for the "most spoofed line of the year": "I wish I knew how to quit you."

	OVERALL	ACTING	STORY	PROD.
Brother from Another Planet, The	23	22	23	19

1984 | Directed by John Sayles | With Joe Morton, Steve James, Bill Cobbs | 108 minutes | Rated R

"Truly original for its time", this "low-budget" "cult favorite" via John Sayles examines "race relations and urban life" in its "offbeat" story of a black extraterrestrial who lands in Harlem; despite the sci-fi underpinnings, it's more of a "funny social commentary" about "what it means to be human", with a mute title character (the very "likable" Morton) and one of the "greatest on-screen card tricks ever."

Bug's Life, A 24 | - | 22 | 26

1998 | Directed by John Lasseter, Andrew Stanton | Animated | 96 minutes | Rated G

"Even parents" bug out on the "mind-blowing creativity" of the Disney/ Pixar team's "step-ahead animation" in this "cute" parable of "insect politics" rendered in "sharp, colorful" computer graphics that "look incredible", even if the "social satire" is "geared for kids"; most maintain it's "superior to *Antz*" and advise sticking around for the fake outtakes as the credits roll (the "best part").

Butch Cassidy & the Sundance Kid ✉ 26 | 26 | 25 | 25

1969 | Directed by George Roy Hill | With Paul Newman, Robert Redford, Katharine Ross | 110 minutes | Rated PG

"Compulsive charmers" Newman and Redford play a pair of wise-cracking, "magnetic" antiheroes trying to stay ahead of the law in this "outstanding" Western "buddy movie", loaded with "adventure and humor"; it fuses a "snappy" script, Burt Bacharach soundtrack and "too many classic scenes to count" into a "sentimental favorite" that's "never boring" from start to "unforgettable" finish.

Butterfield 8 ✉ 23 | 26 | 24 | 23

1960 | Directed by Daniel Mann | With Elizabeth Taylor, Laurence Harvey, Eddie Fisher, Dina Merrill | 109 minutes | Not Rated

A "bombshell" call girl with a "taste for the good life" falls for a "rich, married heartbreaker" in this "expertly done" drama that landed Taylor her first Oscar; no question, Liz "sizzles", but some say this sanitized version of the 1935 John O'Hara novel is "hardly one for the ages."

Cabaret ✉ 26 | 25 | 25 | 27

1972 | Directed by Bob Fosse | With Liza Minnelli, Michael York, Joel Grey | 124 minutes | Rated PG

Comprised of equal parts "love, angst", "singing, dancing and Nazis", this "seminal modern musical" set in pre-WWII Berlin is a "touchstone" of the genre that "hasn't lost its luster"; old chums cheer Fosse's "superb direction" and the "starmaking performances" from Minnelli and Grey (who all took home Oscars), and even though the mood of the piece can careen from "dark" to "raunchy", it's always "fun to watch."

Cabinet of Dr. Caligari, The ◑ 26 | 21 | 24 | 26

1921 | Directed by Robert Wiene | With Conrad Veidt, Werner Kraus | 67 minutes | Not Rated

"They don't get any freakier" than this "fascinating antique", a "menacingly atmospheric" silent horror flick that uses "German expressionism" and "twisted sets" to kindle a "nightmare" tale of murder told by a "tortured mind"; "stark, powerful" and "spooky" right down to the

	OVERALL	ACTING	STORY	PROD.

pioneering "surprise ending", it's "still being imitated" and still makes many modern chillers "look lame."

Cabin in the Sky ◑ 24 | 23 | 23 | 22

1943 | Directed by Vincente Minnelli | With Ethel Waters, Eddie "Rochester" Anderson, Lena Horne | 98 minutes | Not Rated

A "rare major studio release with an all African-American cast", this "classic musical" is worth seeing since nearly "every black actor or singer of the era was in it"; the rather "dated" plot - something to do with a husband's temptation and its consequences - pales in comparison to the "wonderful music", including "gems" like 'Taking a Chance on Love' and 'Happiness is a Thing Called Joe.'

Caddyshack 24 | 20 | 19 | 19

1980 | Directed by Harold Ramis | With Chevy Chase, Rodney Dangerfield, Bill Murray | 99 minutes | Rated R

"Dumb as it is", this "goofy" comedy of "golfers gone amok" is a "classic" of "un-ironic" (some say "sophomoric") humor featuring a "priceless" ensemble cast and a fake gopher; "ok, it's a guy thing", but it "stands the test of time" as "oft-quoted" "mindless fun."

Caine Mutiny, The 27 | 28 | 26 | 23

1954 | Directed by Edward Dmytryk | With Humphrey Bogart, Jose Ferrer, Van Johnson | 124 minutes | Not Rated

This "briny" blend of "powerful wartime story" and "engrossing" courtroom drama gets its ballast from Bogart's "brilliant", "pull-out-all-the-stops" turn as Queeg, the "demented sea captain" compulsively "click, click, clicking" a set of "steel balls"; the "classic script" follows a "totally believable" high-seas rebellion to a court-martial and is "must-see" material for maritime mavens.

Calendar Girls 23 | 25 | 23 | 22

2003 | Directed by Nigel Cole | With Helen Mirren, Julie Walters, John Alderton | 108 minutes | Rated PG-13

"Older can be beautiful" is the "serious message behind the tea and scones" of this comic tale of "plucky", middle-aged English gals who pose for a nude calendar to raise funds for a cancer center; the "talent-laden cast" does a "charming" job with this "female version of *The Full Monty*", and let's face it, "who doesn't love Helen Mirren naked?"; wags note certain parts "sag" a bit.

Call Northside 777 ◑ 25 | 25 | 25 | 23

1948 | Directed by Henry Hathaway | With James Stewart, Richard Conte, Lee J. Cobb, Helen Walker | 111 minutes | Not Rated

Depicting the "quest for truth before *CSI*", this "gritty" crime drama stars "Stewart as many people haven't seen him", playing a worldly-wise reporter who reinvestigates a decade-old murder and gets "caught up in a crusade to free a convict"; shot in a "semi-documentary" style that alludes to its "true-story" source, this "period piece" still "holds up well."

Camille ◑ 26 | 26 | 25 | 26

1937 | Directed by George Cukor | With Greta Garbo, Robert Taylor, Lionel Barrymore | 109 minutes | Not Rated

The "epitome of classic romance", this ultra-"tragic love story" stars "Garbo at her peak" playing a 19th-century Parisian courtesan with a cough who falls for a rather naïve young man; although Taylor is "marginal in an admittedly thankless role", his leading lady's "charm" and "breathtaking beauty" is "fascinating" enough to keep admirers enthralled; P.S. "have plenty of Kleenex on hand."

Cape Fear ◑

25 | 26 | 26 | 23

1962 | Directed by J. Lee Thompson | With Gregory Peck, Robert Mitchum, Polly Bergen | 105 minutes | Not Rated

It's high tide for "rage and revenge" in this "doozy" of a noir thriller, a real "nail-biter" starring Peck as an upright dad who "gets down in the gutter" to protect his family from a "deeply frightening" ex-con at large in the marsh and "as evil as they come"; most rate it "scarier than the remake", "without the histrionics."

Capote 🖂

26 | 29 | 24 | 25

2005 | Directed by Bennett Miller | With Philip Seymour Hoffman, Catherine Keener, Chris Cooper | 114 minutes | Rated R

Not content to do a mere "uncanny impression", "genius" Hoffman delves "inside the mind" of "flamboyant" writer Truman Capote to render the "iconoclast" "in all his complexity" – while nabbing a "well-deserved" Oscar along the way – in this "fascinating" biopic, a behind the scenes look at the writing of Tru's "watershed" book *In Cold Blood*; abetted by Keener's "sturdy" supporting turn, this "world-class study" also works well as a "meditation on journalistic ethics."

Captain Blood ◑

23 | 21 | 20 | 21

1935 | Directed by Michael Curtiz | With Errol Flynn, Olivia de Havilland, Basil Rathbone | 119 minutes | Not Rated

Avast, there's "salty" "popcorn fun" aplenty in this "smashing" swashbuckler, featuring "Flynn's first starring role" as an enslaved wretch who becomes a "devil-may-care" pirate of the Caribbean; armchair buccaneers jump on board for the "roguish" baddies, "high-seas action" and "men in tights", not minding that the old vessel is "on the creaky side."

Captains Courageous 🖂◑

25 | 26 | 24 | 21

1937 | Directed by Victor Fleming | With Spencer Tracy, Freddie Bartholomew, Lionel Barrymore | 115 minutes | Not Rated

Fashioned from a Kipling tale that's "every boy's dream of excitement", this "tearjerker" adventure stars Bartholomew as a bratty rich kid who's rescued at sea and matures under the helm of a salty sailor, the Oscar-winning Tracy; the lad's "highly touching" transformation is conveyed through "phenomenal" acting that's "too often forgotten."

Carlito's Way

22 | 25 | 22 | 22

1993 | Directed by Brian De Palma | With Al Pacino, Sean Penn, Penelope Ann Miller | 145 minutes | Rated R

Scarface cohorts De Palma and Pacino go "gangster" again in this "tight, tense" crime thriller about a Latino drug lord just out of prison who's "trying to go straight but not getting there"; with the principals "in peak form" (Penn "steals the show" as a "slimy, coke-addicted" lawyer), it's a "cool", if "underrated" look at the underworld with a "subtle" slant.

Carmen Jones

23 | 23 | 23 | 23

1954 | Directed by Otto Preminger | With Dorothy Dandridge, Harry Belafonte, Pearl Bailey | 105 minutes | Not Rated

A "modern", "Americanized" version of Bizet's "classic" *Carmen*, this "beautiful reimagining" was a "breakthrough for its time" given its all-black cast, led by the "sassy" Dorothy and "hot" Harry; while the concept's "superb" and the music "beautiful", it's docked a few points since the stars' songs were dubbed by "real opera singers."

Carousel

24 | 22 | 22 | 25

1956 | Directed by Henry King | With Gordon MacRae, Shirley Jones, Cameron Mitchell | 128 minutes | Not Rated

"Girl meets wrong boy" at the traveling show in this silver screen go-round of Rodgers and Hammerstein's "sentimental" musical, which draws on a "lovely" score and "fine cast" of "first-rate" singers to spin a tale that's "romantic, sad" and "not always pretty"; while it's regarded as a "neglected great" to devotees, it's also seen as a squandering of "talent" on a "corny", "tarnished-with-age" storyline.

Cars

24 | - | 23 | 27

2006 | Directed by John Lasseter, Joe Ranft | Animated | 116 minutes | Rated G

Disney/Pixar's "well-oiled" animation outfit rigs a "familiar fish-out-of-water story" ("*Doc Hollywood*", anyone?) to "talking cars" and rolls out this "delightful" joyride featuring "exceptional" renderings and "adorable" vocal characterizations by Owen Wilson, Paul Newman and comic Larry The Cable Guy; parents appreciate the "great" soundtrack and "offbeat" cultural references – real lifesavers when the young 'uns "watch it for the 30th time."

Casablanca ✉◑

29 | 28 | 28 | 27

1942 | Directed by Michael Curtiz | With Humphrey Bogart, Ingrid Bergman, Paul Henreid, Claude Rains | 102 minutes | Rated PG

We'll always have the "magic" of this "most compelling" of romances, a showcase for "legendary" turns from an "enigmatic" Bogart, "radiant" Bergman and "top-shelf" supporting cast set against the "unforgettable" backdrop of WWII occupied North Africa; the "fast-paced" plot of passion and "intrigue" is an "unsurpassed" model of good, "old-fashioned storytelling" and a bona fide "runner-up to Shakespeare" for "classic lines" – there's no choice but to "play it again and again."

Casino Royale

23 | 22 | 21 | 26

2006 | Directed by Martin Campbell | With Daniel Craig, Eva Green, Mads Mikkelsen, Judi Dench | 144 minutes | Rated PG-13

A "strong reboot for the franchise", this "excellent prequel" based on Ian Fleming's first 007 novel goes "back to basics" with "fewer gadgets" and "more brains" to give the long-running series a "needed jolt"; "blond Bond" Daniel Craig's "blue-collar" take on the character makes him a "worthy successor to Connery, Sean Connery", and though the picture "bogs down in the card scenes", it's worth seeing for that "amazing opening foot chase" alone.

Catch Me If You Can

23 | 24 | 25 | 24

2002 | Directed by Steven Spielberg | With Leonardo DiCaprio, Tom Hanks, Christopher Walken | 141 minutes | Rated PG-13

Spielberg's "fast-paced" "cat-and-mouse game" ("based on a true story" about a charming con man) is "mischievous, delicious fun from the delightful opening credits until the final frame", with "lots of '60s color" and "awesome acting" by the "engaging DiCaprio" and "rock-solid" Hanks; it's a "wild ride" that shows us "sometimes crime *does* pay."

	OVERALL	ACTING	STORY	PROD.

Catch-22 — 25 | 25 | 25 | 23

1970 | Directed by Mike Nichols | With Alan Arkin, Jon Voight, Anthony Perkins, Bob Newhart, Art Garfunkel, Orson Welles, Richard Benjamin, Paula Prentiss | 122 minutes | Rated R

A "faithful" adaptation of Joseph Heller's "classic novel", this "wicked black comedy" about the "absurdity of war" skewers the "brutality and bureaucracy" of combat in its "devastating" look at a squadron of WWII flyboys (played by a "sterling" ensemble cast led by Arkin); simultaneously "hilarious" and "appalling", it's a "cultural artifact" of the "cynical '60s" to some, "never more relevant" to others.

Cat on a Hot Tin Roof — 25 | 27 | 24 | 23

1958 | Directed by Richard Brooks | With Elizabeth Taylor, Paul Newman, Burl Ives | 108 minutes | Not Rated

"Man, these people have problems": "steamy Liz" in that "white slip" and a "dynamite" Newman "burn up the screen" in this "sex-soaked" Tennessee Williams drama of "love, rejection" and "Southern family politics"; the "towering" Ives presides as the ragin' Big Daddy, adding an "incredibly interesting" *Lear*-like thread to all that "eye candy."

Cat People ◑ — 23 | 20 | 21 | 22

1942 | Directed by Jacques Tourneur | With Simone Simon, Kent Smith, Tom Conway, Jane Randolph | 73 minutes | Not Rated

"More scary than many modern films", this "wonderfully weird" "low-budget" horror flick tells the story of a "tortured soul" who believes "she's cursed to become a killer panther"; it may be "relatively tame by today's standards" (and "not for *Friday the 13th* fans"), but does achieve an "eerie tension" via its "mysterious characters", "dark sets" and "incredible use of light and shadow."

Central Station F — 26 | 27 | 25 | 22

1998 | Directed by Walter Salles | With Fernanda Montenegro, Marília Pêra, Vinícius de Oliveira | 113 minutes | Rated R

The unexpected bonding between a "world-weary woman" and a "sweet young boy" lies at the heart of this "flawless" Brazilian drama hailed for its "absorbing performances" ("Montenegro is a revelation") played out against "stark inner city" and "colorful countryside" locales; a "tug-at-your-heart" "tearjerker" if there ever was one, its "haunting" "story of redemption" makes for one "very special movie."

Changeling — 23 | 24 | 23 | 23

2008 | Directed by Clint Eastwood | With Angelina Jolie, John Malkovich, Jeffrey Donovan, Michael Kelly | 141 minutes | Rated R

"Corruption, mystery and maternal love" collide in '20s LA in this "dark period thriller", a "gripping" story of a "distraught" single mom (the "gorgeous" Jolie) whose "son vanishes" and her subsequent "harrowing" treatment by "out-of-control" authorities; Eastwood "captures the era superbly" in a "cautionary" opus that's "emotionally charged" but "oh-so-gloomy."

Charade — 26 | 25 | 26 | 25

1963 | Directed by Stanley Donen | With Cary Grant, Audrey Hepburn, Walter Matthau | 113 minutes | Not Rated

Expect "plenty of plot twists" in this "quintessential romantic comedy/thriller" (the "best Hitchcock flick that Hitchcock didn't make") about the scramble for a missing fortune; its very "easy-on-the-eyes" stars, "luscious Paris" scenery, magical "Mancini melodies" and "Audrey's fab wardrobe" make for "perfect" moviemaking – "murder was never so much fun."

Chariots of Fire ✉ 26 | 25 | 25 | 25

1981 | Directed by Hugh Hudson | With Ben Cross, Ian Charleson, Ian Holm | 123 minutes | Rated PG

Remembered for "running off with" a Best Picture Oscar, this "inspiring" drama paces itself in "superb" style as it follows the "trials and triumph" of a British track team bound for the 1924 Olympics; thanks to "uplifting" legwork and a very "hummable" soundtrack, it breaks the tape as a "never boring" movie.

Charlotte's Web 23 | 22 | 25 | 24

2006 | Directed by Gary Winick | With Dakota Fanning | 97 minutes | Rated G

There are "no surprises" in this "delightful rendering" of E. B. White's "classic" farm fable, just "sweet" storytelling made "magical" by the "amazing" Fanning and a barnyard bunch brought to life by "believable" effects and "wonderful" celeb voice work ("Julia Roberts is fabulous as Charlotte"); though an itsy-bitsy minority maintains the 1973 animated version "can't be beat", most exalt this "much-needed break" from today's family-unfriendly fare.

Chicago ✉ 27 | 26 | 25 | 29

2002 | Directed by Rob Marshall | With Renée Zellweger, Catherine Zeta-Jones, Richard Gere, Queen Latifah | 113 minutes | Rated PG-13

"Bob Fosse would have been proud" of this "absolutely brilliant" adaptation of his boffo Broadway "tale of murder, greed and corruption" in 1920s Chicago; "astounded" surveyors swear this "razzle-dazzle" "visual masterpiece" "deserved every Oscar it won" thanks to its "phenomenal acting", "sexy cinematography", "spine-tingling music" ("who knew the big three could sing?") and "major dance moves that'll leave you gasping for air"; even critics who complain of "miscasting" and "MTV camerawork" hope it sparks a "return to old-fashioned movie musicals."

Chicken Run 23 | - | 23 | 27

2000 | Directed by Peter Lord, Nick Park | Animated | 84 minutes | Rated G

Pure "poultry in motion", this "ingenious", "touching" barnyard saga uses "fantastic" claymation to portray a "darn appealing" bunch of British fowl and their "valiant struggle" to get off the farm; "subtle references" make it a "hilarious take" on all the *Stalag 17*-style POW pics, so while kids can enjoy the "innocent" animated escapade, it "doesn't chicken out" on "tongue-in-cheek", grown-up undertones; in an eggshell, a "good run for the money."

Children of a Lesser God ✉ 23 | 25 | 22 | 21

1986 | Directed by Randa Haines | With Marlee Matlin, William Hurt, Piper Laurie | 119 minutes | Rated R

This "touching" drama "does justice to the original play" on the strength of "sexy, compelling" turns from Hurt as a speech teacher at a school for the deaf and Best Actress winner Matlin, "signing throughout" as a hearing-impaired woman with a complex past; expect "moving scenes" as their intimacy develops, and though an "enjoyable" intro to the "deaf community", it might be a "little overdramatized."

Children of Paradise ◑ F 28 | 27 | 27 | 26

1946 | Directed by Marcel Carné | With Arletty, Jean-Louis Barrault, Pierre Renoir | 190 minutes | Not Rated

Filmed in France "under the noses of the Nazis", this "legendary" romance "lovingly re-creates 1840s Paris" in a "multilayered" story of a "lovesick" mime's passion for a vampish stage siren; built on "profound" themes and "stylized" performances (that come off as "melodramatic" but are rich with "beauty and feeling"), it "continues to fascinate" as a "masterpiece of world cinema" and the big screen's "greatest tribute to live theater."

Children's Hour, The ◑ 24 | 26 | 24 | 22

1961 | Directed by William Wyler | With Audrey Hepburn, Shirley MacLaine, James Garner, Miriam Hopkins | 107 minutes | Not Rated

"Way ahead of its time", this "groundbreaking" adaptation of the Lillian Hellman play examines "scandal and reputation", specifically what happens after a "malicious child" fingers two schoolteachers as lesbians; despite a "predictable" ending and subject matter that's "tragic" verging on "depressing", the "performances still pack a wallop."

Chinatown ✉ 27 | 28 | 26 | 26

1974 | Directed by Roman Polanski | With Jack Nicholson, Faye Dunaway, John Huston | 131 minutes | Rated R

This "taut drama" about "stolen water" and "bottled-up emotion" in 1930s LA is a "nearly perfect" exercise in "Technicolor film noir" that's simultaneously "funny, bleak and knowing"; credit the "dynamite" cast, "ravishingly beautiful" cinematography and "superb script" (that ends with a "shocking", "untypical-Hollywood ending") for its success; most memorable scene: Dunaway's "slap"-happy "she's-my-sister-she's-my-daughter" tour de force.

Chocolat 22 | 24 | 22 | 23

2000 | Directed by Lasse Hallström | With Juliette Binoche, Alfred Molina, Johnny Depp | 121 minutes | Rated PG-13

A "yummy escape" "bordering on a fairy tale", this "funny" romance finds "lovely" "rebel spirit" Binoche pitted against "petty-minded villagers" when she opens a chocolate shop in a French hamlet and takes up with Depp; the blend of a "beautiful setting" mixed with some "uplifting whimsy" makes for one "tasty bonbon."

Christmas Carol, A ◑ 27 | 26 | 28 | 23

1951 | Directed by Brian Desmond Hurst | With Alastair Sim, Kathleen Harrison, Mervyn Johns | 86 minutes | Not Rated

"Sim is the best Scrooge ever" in this Dickens of a "holiday delight", a "magical adaptation" of the "timeless" fable concerning a rich old paragon of "grouchiness" transformed by a Yuletide visit from a posse of ghosts; cherished as "superb" family fare that "inspires" without drowning in the "happily-ever-after tone" of other versions, it has fans replaying it "religiously" because there's "no way" to do "Christmas without it."

	OVERALL	ACTING	STORY	PROD.
Christmas Story, A	26	23	27	22

1983 | Directed by Bob Clark | With Peter Billingsley, Melinda Dillon, Darren McGavin | 94 minutes | Rated PG

A "sweet but not sugary" look at the "debacle that's Christmas in America", this "irresistible" family fave takes a "fond glimpse back" with a "funny-till-it-hurts" "exposition of a '40s childhood" centered on a kid bent on a "BB gun" under the tree; "most rewatchable" and "quotable" thanks to its "excellent cast and script", it's "good clean fun" for all ages and now widely deemed a seasonal "must."

	OVERALL	ACTING	STORY	PROD.
Chronicles of Narnia: Prince Caspian	23	21	22	27

2008 | Directed by Andrew Adamson | With Ben Barnes, Georgie Henley, Skandar Keynes, William Moseley | 144 minutes | Rated PG

The Pevensie children return to the magical realm of Narnia to find it threatened by an "evil king" in this "darker" but "fun" follow-up, a "sweeping" saga that's "as grand as the first" and equally "respectful" of novelist C.S. Lewis' "timeless" vision; the young cast "continues to delight", the production's "breathtaking" and the big battle scenes are both "exhilarating" and "goreless", for the ultimate in "kid enjoyment."

	OVERALL	ACTING	STORY	PROD.
Chronicles of Narnia: The Lion, the Witch & the Wardrobe	23	21	24	26

2005 | Directed by Andrew Adamson | With Georgie Henley, Skandar Keynes, Tilda Swinton | 140 minutes | Rated PG

C.S. Lewis' "classic" children's fantasy is "faithfully" rendered on celluloid via this "masterful production", a veritable "feast for the eyes" whose mane highlights include "lovely" performances, "beautiful" costumes and "spectacular" effects ("you can almost touch Aslan"); its "religious overtones" court controversy, however, with defenders declaring the "Christian themes are dealt with appropriately" and skeptics suggesting "it feels like a sermon."

	OVERALL	ACTING	STORY	PROD.
Cincinnati Kid, The	24	25	22	22

1965 | Directed by Norman Jewison | With Steve McQueen, Edward G. Robinson, Ann-Margret, Karl Malden | 102 minutes | Rated PG

This "gritty" drama that "predates today's poker craze" still "antes up" some "real entertainment" thanks to a "royal flush of a cast" led by the "never-cooler" McQueen, whose portrayal of a "professional card sharp" pays off in a "riveting, big-game sequence"; though basically "*The Hustler* with cards", bettors wager it's one of the all-time "best gambling flicks."

	OVERALL	ACTING	STORY	PROD.
Cinderella	26	-	25	26

1950 | Directed by Clyde Geronimi, Wilfred Jackson, Hamilton Luske | Animated | 74 minutes | Rated G

"You know the drill": "breathtaking" animation from "Disney's golden age" merges with the stuff "countless girlish dreams" are made of in this "beautiful fantasy" about an "overworked, abused orphan" who bags her Prince Charming, with a little help from her fairy godmother and some "industrious", very finely feathered friends; if "short on characterization", it remains an "old-fashioned favorite" that's a shoe-in to be a "classic for generations to come."

	OVERALL	ACTING	STORY	PROD.
Cinderella Man	25	27	25	25

2005 | Directed by Ron Howard | With Russell Crowe, Renée Zellweger, Paul Giamatti | 144 minutes | Rated PG-13

The "dreary" "look of the Great Depression" permeates this "superbly crafted" sports biopic 'bout James Braddock, the "down-on-his-luck pug" who "battled back" from poverty and injury for a "shot at the heavyweight title"; given its "superb" combo of the "incredibly believable" Crowe and "wonderful" Giamatti, fans feel this "worthy" contender "should have been a bigger hit."

Cinema Paradiso ✉ F	26	26	26	25

1990 | Directed by Giuseppe Tornatore | With Philippe Noiret, Jacques Perrin | 123 minutes | Rated R

This Italian "heart-warmer" is an "endearing" look at "love and loss" as well as a "nostalgic valentine" to the "magic of cinema"; based on the "charming" story of a "projectionist in the local movie house" who "mentors a fatherless child", it rolls a "colorful" cast, "*bellissimo*" camerawork and a "lovely" score into an "engrossing", frankly "sentimental" film.

Citizen Kane ✉ ◑	28	27	27	28

1941 | Directed by Orson Welles | With Orson Welles, Joseph Cotten, Agnes Moorehead, Everett Sloane | 119 minutes | Rated PG

"Loosely based on the life of William Randolph Hearst", this "magnum opus" about a "ruthless megalomaniac" who "mourns the loss of his innocent childhood" is an "undisputed masterpiece" that's "often imitated, never duplicated" and "as fresh as ever"; starring and directed by wunderkind Welles, it "revolutionized the cinema" and forever changed the meaning of the word "rosebud" – "by comparison, all other films are home movies."

City Lights ◑	28	28	26	25

1931 | Directed by Charlie Chaplin | With Charlie Chaplin, Virginia Cherrill | 87 minutes | Not Rated

"Humor, pathos and poignancy" make this silent "Chaplin masterpiece" glow with "old-fashioned sentimentality" as the Little Tramp's "devotion for a blind flower girl" leads to a series of "classic" sequences; from famed bits like the "balletic boxing match" to the "heartbreaking" closing, this early flicker is a testament to a master "on top of his game."

Claire's Knee F	23	24	22	23

1971 | Directed by Eric Rohmer | With Jean-Claude Brialy, Aurora Cornu, Laurence de Monaghan | 105 minutes | Rated PG

The "antithesis of an action movie", this "insightful" look at "erotic desire done without conventional sex scenes" tells the story of a "midlife crisis"-bound Frenchman "obsessed with, well, the title says it all"; knockers rap all the "cerebral ooh-la-la" as too "talky", though admirers insist this "sweet paean to romantic longing" is "probably the high point of Rohmer's career."

Clerks ◑	23	17	22	16

1994 | Directed by Kevin Smith | With Brian O'Halloran, Jeff Anderson, Marilyn Ghigliotti | 92 minutes | Rated R

"Crude" acting and "bottom-of-the-barrel production" values are redeemed by "wicked black humor" and "inspired", "raunchy" dia-

	OVERALL	ACTING	STORY	PROD.

logue in this "microbudget indie" effort, a "fast-paced" comedy that pumps life into the "dead-end job" scene with a "realistic" look at "minimart" wage slavery; the "first foray" in Smith's "New Jersey series", it's a "slacker" "cult classic" that's "painfully funny" but unsafe for the "squeamish."

Clockwork Orange, A

25 | 24 | 24 | 25

1971 | Directed by Stanley Kubrick | With Malcolm McDowell, Patrick Magee | 137 minutes | Rated R

"Not for the weak of heart", this "ingenious Kubrick" cult parable is a "bold", "nightmarish" "mix of sex, ultraviolence" and "mind control" set in a "freaky", "futuristic" Britain; following the travails of "unhinged" "bad boy" McDowell (the "sinister yet strangely likable" head of a "vicious gang of droogies") through his "chilling" crimes to his "brainwashing" rehab, it threads "brilliant visuals" and "twisted" "social satire" into "riveting", "artful stuff" – helped by a bit of the old "Ludwig van."

Close Encounters of the Third Kind

24 | 22 | 25 | 27

1977 | Directed by Steven Spielberg | With Richard Dreyfuss, François Truffaut, Teri Garr | 135 minutes | Rated PG

"It's ok to believe in UFOs" thanks to this "landmark" sci-fi "spectacle", a "mesmerizing", "believable contact film" wherein Spielberg's "sense of wonder" first embraces the "aliens-come-to-earth" formula; the "hopeful" plotline involves a race to "figure it all out" when strange signals arrive from the sky, and the result is a "mind-blowing" "visual treat" with plenty of "heart" (and "mountains of mashed potatoes") that delivers a "jaw-dropping" climax with a "sentimental streak" a light-year wide.

Coal Miner's Daughter ✉

24 | 27 | 23 | 22

1980 | Directed by Michael Apted | With Sissy Spacek, Tommy Lee Jones, Levon Helm | 125 minutes | Rated PG

Kentucky moonshine and "bravura performances" brighten this "charming biopic" of country crooner Loretta Lynn, led by the Oscar-winning Spacek as the daughter of Appalachia who "makes it huge" in Nashville; a down-home, "down-to-earth fairy tale", its "realistic portrayal" of a star's "rise to fame" and bout with burnout plays like an "interesting" C&W take on *Behind the Music.*

Cocoanuts, The ◑

24 | 22 | 19 | 19

1929 | Directed by Robert Florey, Joseph Santley | With the Marx Brothers, Kay Francis | 96 minutes | Not Rated

Never mind the "technical primitiveness", this first Marx Brothers comedy is as "zany" as their later work; though this "crude" rendering of the sibs' Broadway show is burdened with "trite musical numbers" and a "weak" story involving Florida real estate, die-hard Marxists say ya "gotta love" it as an "intriguing mess" that's at worst a guarantee of "better things to come."

Cold Mountain

22 | 24 | 22 | 26

2003 | Directed by Anthony Minghella | With Jude Law, Nicole Kidman, Renée Zellweger | 152 minutes | Rated R

The "cinematic equivalent of a coffee table book", this "beautifully shot" Civil War saga of separated lovers "adapted from Homer's

	OVERALL	ACTING	STORY	PROD.

Odyssey" stars a "smokin'" Law opposite a "too-beautiful" Kidman, ever the "fashion plate" when she's "supposed to be starving"; never mind the too-"long" running time, "watching-the-grass-grow" pacing and controversy over Renée's Oscar win ("much deserved" vs. "Granny Clampett"), at the very least, this one is certainly "worth falling asleep on the sofa for."

Collector, The 23 | 26 | 25 | 22

1965 | Directed by William Wyler | With Terence Stamp, Samantha Eggar | 119 minutes | Not Rated

A "deeply disturbed recluse" kidnaps a "lovely young woman" in this "chilling story of obsession" adapted from John Fowles' "devastating" first novel; "terrific acting by Stamp and Eggar" keeps folks "fascinated", and if this "creepy stalker film" can be "hard to watch" at times, it's still "wonderfully done."

Color Purple, The 26 | 27 | 26 | 25

1985 | Directed by Steven Spielberg | With Whoopi Goldberg, Danny Glover, Oprah Winfrey | 154 minutes | Rated PG-13

A "heartfelt" rendering of Alice Walker's "breakthrough" best-seller, this "moving" drama of "empowerment" "really hits home" with its depiction of a "post-slavery black family" in the Deep South and a wronged woman's "redemption and liberation"; the "breathtaking" lenswork, "Goldberg's best-ever showing" and a "brilliant" supporting cast ("Oprah can act!") make for a "teary triumph" that some cite as "Oscar's biggest snub."

Coming Home ✉ 23 | 26 | 23 | 21

1978 | Directed by Hal Ashby | With Jane Fonda, Jon Voight, Bruce Dern, Penelope Milford | 126 minutes | Rated R

"Jon and Jane are magic together" in this "ultimate anti-war message" drama-cum-love triangle involving a paraplegic Vietnam vet, an "inconveniently married" hospital volunteer and a gung-ho marine; expect "moving performances" (Voight and Fonda took home Oscars) and "loads of emotion" that manage to convey a "coming of age for both the characters - and the times."

Commitments, The 24 | 23 | 23 | 21

1991 | Directed by Alan Parker | With Robert Arkins, Andrew Strong, Colm Meaney | 118 minutes | Rated R

Roddy Doyle's "classic" tale of "lower-class" Dublin youths trying to bring soul music to Ireland is a "poignant", "feel-good" take on the "passions and perils of putting your dreams into flight"; but it's the "infectious", "toe-tapping" soundtrack that really "steals the show", making this "charming" film "eminently watchable" - and "rewatchable."

Conformist, The F 26 | 26 | 27 | 26

1971 | Directed by Bernardo Bertolucci | With Jean-Louis Trintignant, Stefania Sandrelli, Dominique Sanda | 115 minutes | Rated R

Director "Bertolucci is at his absolute best" in this "supercool, superstylized" Italian psychological drama set in the '30s about an "emotionally troubled civil servant" turned "fascist agent"; nonconformists warn "beware the dubbed version" but concur that Vittorio Storaro's "haunting" cinematography transcends dialogue; hottest moment: that "erotic tango" between Sanda and Sandrelli.

	OVERALL	ACTING	STORY	PROD.

Constant Gardener, The 23 | 26 | 23 | 24

2005 | Directed by Fernando Meirelles | With Ralph Fiennes, Rachel Weisz | 129 minutes | Rated R

The "politically pertinent" topic of pharmaceutical companies' alleged "exploitation of third-world citizens" forms the "fascinating" backdrop of this "tautly woven" thriller-cum-"haunting" love story featuring the "ever dependable" Fiennes as an "uptight English diplomat" who unravels a "mystery" involving his activist wife (the "fabulous" Weisz); based on John Le Carré's "complex" novel, it's undoubtedly "more exciting than its title might suggest", and provides plenty of "food for thought."

Contempt F 25 | 24 | 22 | 24

1964 | Directed by Jean-Luc Godard | With Brigitte Bardot, Michel Piccoli, Jack Palance, Fritz Lang | 104 minutes | Not Rated

The "struggle between commerce and artistic integrity" gets the Godard treatment in this "scathing" "movie about movies" that details a screenwriter's struggle to adapt James Joyce's *Ulysses* and simultaneously keep his marriage from unraveling; with a "coquettish" Bardot and a "full-throttle" Palance on board, "stunning" Mediterranean vistas and a "cameo from director Fritz Lang", it's a fine example of "classic French New Wave" that's "showy, smart" and "enjoyably pretentious."

Conversation, The 25 | 26 | 25 | 23

1974 | Directed by Francis Ford Coppola | With Gene Hackman, John Cazale, Frederic Forrest | 113 minutes | Rated PG

A "brilliant" thriller about a "paranoid" surveillance specialist who comes undone, this "little-known" Coppola feature features a "virtuoso performance by Hackman", whose gradual "deterioration is amazing" (there's also an appearance by a very young Harrison Ford); though a bit "slow-moving", the script is so "superbly constructed" that "if this flick doesn't put you on edge, nothing will."

Cool Hand Luke 26 | 27 | 24 | 22

1967 | Directed by Stuart Rosenberg | With Paul Newman, George Kennedy, Strother Martin | 126 minutes | Not Rated

"One of the best movie lines ever" ('what we have here is a failure to communicate') and that "famous hard-boiled egg scene" make this "damn great" Deep South prison drama memorable - not to mention the efforts of "consummate pro" Newman playing one cool con, abetted by a "strong" Kennedy, who grabbed an Oscar for his supporting work.

Coraline 23 | - | 22 | 25

2009 | Directed by Henry Selick | Animated | 100 minutes | Rated PG

A "weird" "feast for the eyes", this "very Tim Burton-esque" take on Neil Gaiman's "dark" novel uses "eye-popping" stop-motion animation to tell the "out-there" tale of a girl escaping her "real-life childhood" via a mysterious door leading into a "creepy" parallel universe; even those who knock the "odd" story concede it's a "visually stunning ride", albeit "a bit intense for young kids."

Counterfeit Traitor, The 25 | 25 | 26 | 23

1962 | Directed by George Seaton | With William Holden, Lili Palmer, Hugh Griffith | 140 minutes | Not Rated

"Based on a true story", this "classy" (albeit "forgotten") WWII spy thriller revolves around a Swedish "quisling" blacklisted by the Allies after trading with the Nazis; in the title role, the "dashing" Holden is in his "gracefully aging prime", though some say the "deeply moving" Palmer steals the show as his "noble" confederate.

Country Girl, The ✉◑ 24 | 26 | 23 | 23

1954 | Directed by George Seaton | With Bing Crosby, Grace Kelly, William Holden | 104 minutes | Not Rated

Kelly ventures "out of her normal range" into Oscar-winning territory as a "frumpy" gal married to an alcoholic "actor on the skids" in this "top-notch" drama adapted from the Clifford Odets play; Crosby also "plays against type" to "memorable" effect, while the "brilliant" Holden completes the trifecta by supplying the romantic "tension."

Court Jester, The 24 | 25 | 23 | 24

1955 | Directed by Melvin Frank, Norman Panama | With Danny Kaye, Glynis Johns, Basil Rathbone, Angela Lansbury | 101 minutes | Not Rated

It's "a laugh a minute" with Kaye at his "funniest" in this musical-comedy lensed in "fabulous Technicolor", which has him posing as the fool in a medieval court run by a scheming knight and "mugging away" with "wordplay", "song-and-dance" routines and "one-liners to spare" – notably the 'pellet-with-the-poison' shtick, a routine that "you'll never forget."

Crash ✉ 26 | 27 | 26 | 25

2005 | Directed by Paul Haggis | With Sandra Bullock, Don Cheadle, Matt Dillon, Brendan Fraser, Terrence Howard, Ludacris, Thandie Newton, Ryan Phillippe | 113 minutes | Rated R

"Everyone's a little bit racist" according to this "provocative" treatment of "prejudice in America", a Best Picture Oscar grabber about "intertwined lives" in LA that "damn near hits the mark" in its attempts to "break down stereotypes" and "make you rethink your values"; with a "dream-team cast" enlivening the "incredible writing", expect to collide with some "tough", "wonderfully unpredictable" scenes that deliver a "powerful message."

Crazy Heart ✉ 25 | 28 | 22 | 24

2009 | Directed by Scott Cooper | With Jeff Bridges, Maggie Gyllenhaal, Robert Duvall, Colin Farrell | 112 minutes | Rated R

Ok, it's a story you've "seen before" – a "washed-up country musician" gets a "second chance at life and love" – but this "variation on *Tender Mercies*" and its ilk commands "sleeper" status on the strength of Bridges' crazy "believable", "booze"-soaked rendition of the archetypal "self-destructive" troubadour; fans also tout Gyllenhaal's "terrific" supporting turn, the "great" soundtrack and that "surprising" Colin Farrell cameo.

Cries and Whispers F 26 | 28 | 24 | 26

1972 | Directed by Ingmar Bergman | With Harriet Andersson, Liv Ullmann, Ingrid Thulin | 106 minutes | Rated R

"Compelling is an understatement" when it comes to this "tortured masterpiece", a "raw", "close-in study of three sisters and their prickly relationship" that's "quintessential Bergman"; although it's "well acted" and "handsomely mounted", its depiction of "pain" is so "hard to watch" that some ask "are you sure 'angst' isn't a Swedish word?"

	OVERALL	ACTING	STORY	PROD.

Crimes and Misdemeanors

26	26	25	24

1989 | Directed by Woody Allen | With Woody Allen, Mia Farrow, Anjelica Huston, Martin Landau | 107 minutes | Rated PG-13

"Crime does pay" in this "deeply serious" Allen dramedy with dual plotlines, one about a murderous philanderer, the other a "socially inept" filmmaker; "ruthlessly truthful", it manages to be alternately "scathing", "thought-provoking" and "hilarious", with "dead-on casting" and an "expert" scenario to boot.

Crossing Delancey

23	23	23	21

1988 | Directed by Joan Micklin Silver | With Amy Irving, Peter Riegert, Sylvia Miles | 97 minutes | Rated PG

This "romantic comedy with a Jewish twist" earns "*mazel tovs*" for its "endearing" story of "intellectual" striver Irving, set up with "pickle vendor" Riegert thanks to "old-school matchmaking" from her "meddling" Lower East Side bubbe; despite crossing into "schmaltzy" territory, it's "well acted" and "relevant for all those single gals" who hope "all's well that ends well."

Crouching Tiger, Hidden Dragon ✉ F

24	23	21	28

2000 | Directed by Ang Lee | With Chow Yun-Fat, Michelle Yeoh, Zhang Ziyi | 120 minutes | Rated PG-13

Whether it's a "kung fu chick flick", a "thinking person's" martial arts film or "'chop-socky' translated into art", this "surreal" fantasy is full of "eye-popping fight sequences" that are half "ballet", half "Bruce Lee"; most memorable for its "strong female characters" and that "encounter in the bamboo forest", it's nothing less than a "breath of fresh air on the stale movie landscape."

Curious Case of Benjamin Button, The

23	24	22	24

2008 | Directed by David Fincher | With Brad Pitt, Cate Blanchett, Taraji P. Henson, Tilda Swinton | 166 minutes | Rated PG-13

In this "thought-provoking" drama based on a Scott Fitzgerald story, Pitt is "born old" and "ages in reverse" (thanks to "incredible" makeup and effects), resulting in a "curious" look at the "transitory nature of life"; an "unlikely love story" with Blanchett and the "drawn-out" plot has hotheads hitting the "snooze button", but most maintain the "original premise" and "star power" make it work.

Damned, The

23	24	21	23

1969 | Directed by Luchino Visconti | With Dirk Bogarde, Helmut Berger, Ingrid Thulin, Charlotte Rampling | 157 minutes | Rated R

Steel yourself for "decadence on parade" in this "sick, slick" look at a family of "jaded" German industrialists who ally themselves with the Nazis on the eve of WWII; both "absorbing and repellent in equal measure", it's "kinky" alright, though "outstanding production values" and the "beautiful Rampling" make it slightly more palatable for general audiences.

Damn Yankees

24	23	23	24

1958 | Directed by George Abbott, Stanley Donen | With Gwen Verdon, Tab Hunter, Ray Walston | 111 minutes | Not Rated

This screen adaptation of the Faust-influenced Broadway musical recounts how a "man makes a pact with the devil" to guarantee that the "Washington Senators win the pennant"; reprising their stage roles,

Walston is at his "evil best" as Lucifer, while the "too-rarely-seen" Verdon gets what she wants as his sidekick, Lola; it's a "perfect evocation of the national optimism of the '50s" with a "great score" and a bonus: "Bob Fosse's mambo."

Dances with Wolves ✉ 23 | 20 | 22 | 25

1990 | Directed by Kevin Costner | With Kevin Costner, Mary McDonnell, Graham Greene | 183 minutes | Rated PG-13

For once, American Indians are portrayed in a "human light" in this "picturesque, sweeping epic" about a Civil War soldier who goes West, joins the Sioux and finds love along the way; although "beautifully shot" and quite the Oscar magnet (seven statuettes, including Best Picture), this "guy flick that women love" has critics citing a "monotonous", way-"too-long" running time.

Dangerous Liaisons ✉ 24 | 26 | 24 | 26

1988 | Directed by Stephen Frears | With Glenn Close, John Malkovich, Michelle Pfeiffer | 119 minutes | Rated R

"Malkovich quietly chews up the scenery" opposite "perfectly evil" "ice queen" Close in this "flawless" drama set in "decadent", 17th-century France rife with "treachery, betrayal and sexual games" among the "upper classes" ("no wonder the peasants revolted"); still, its "sumptuous production" and Oscar-winning screenplay make the "manipulating" characters more palatable.

Dark Crystal, The 24 | - | 24 | 26

1982 | Directed by Jim Henson, Frank Oz | With puppet characters | 93 minutes | Rated PG

"Sinister muppets" take the stage in this "classic" "all-puppet feature", a "magical fairy tale" with an "otherworldly good and evil" storyline that represents the "culmination of Jim Henson's imagination"; while the "stunning visuals" please crowds, some warn that the "dark" plot "may be too scary" for smaller fry.

Dark Knight, The 26 | 26 | 23 | 27

2008 | Directed by Christopher Nolan | With Christian Bale, Heath Ledger, Aaron Eckhart, Maggie Gyllenhaal | 152 minutes | Rated PG-13

"Visionary director" Nolan's follow-up to his franchise-rebooting *Batman Begins*, this "very dark", "very good" sequel is an "action-packed", star-studded extravaganza with "top-of-the-genre" cred due largely to Heath Ledger's "iconic", "thoroughly creepy" portrayal of the Joker, which won him a posthumous Oscar; indeed, its "show-stealing" arch-villain aside, it's "hard to remember much else", although "bat-maniacs" who "watch it again and again" avow it "delivers in all areas."

Dark Victory ◑ 25 | 27 | 23 | 23

1939 | Directed by Edmund Goulding | With Bette Davis, George Brent, Humphrey Bogart | 104 minutes | Not Rated

"Sensational" Bette at her "Warner Brothers peak" "turns camp into classic" in this melodramatic "tearjerker" about an heiress who's got everything – including a brain tumor; sob sisters say it's "worth every hanky" for Davis' "valiant" turn (one of the "best performances of 1939") and keep their eye out for a very "young Ronald Reagan" in a supporting role.

	OVERALL	ACTING	STORY	PROD.

Darling ✉◑

22	25	20	21

1965 | Directed by John Schlesinger | With Julie Christie, Dirk Bogarde, Laurence Harvey | 128 minutes | Not Rated

Get a "glimpse of the Swinging '60s" via this "quintessential" story of a "self-absorbed" "model/party girl" who "makes it to the top" only to find "there's nothing there"; if the film feels "a bit dated", at least it's "cast to perfection" – the "smashing", Oscar-winning Christie is "at the height of her beauty and acting powers" here.

Das Boot F

28	26	26	27

1982 | Directed by Wolfgang Petersen | With Jürgen Prochnow, Herbert Grönemeyer | 149 minutes | Rated R

When it comes to "underwater über alles" action, it's hard to top this "sweaty, claustrophobic" saga of "doomed German sailors" engaged in a "battle of egos" in a U-boat at the "bottom of the ocean"; though it's almost an "anti-recruiting film" given its "harrowing" realism, it exhibits enough "depth" to prove that "fear has no nationality" – you'll almost "root for" the Nazis.

Day at the Races, A ◑

24	21	20	19

1937 | Directed by Sam Wood | With the Marx Brothers, Maureen O'Sullivan, Margaret Dumont | 111 minutes | Not Rated

The "Marx Brothers at their zenith of zaniness" horse around in this "very funny" comedy about a veterinarian turned human doctor; though some say it's a "slightly second-tier" also-ran (only "sporadically funny" and even a tad "racist"), it was nevertheless one of the boys' "biggest box office hits."

Day for Night ✉F

27	25	25	25

1973 | Directed by François Truffaut | With Jacqueline Bisset, Valentina Cortese, Jean-Pierre Léaud | 115 minutes | Rated PG

"Truffaut's homage to American filmmaking", this "quintessential movie about making movies" "perfectly captures" all the "behind-the-scenes" "neuroses" and "joy" from an insider's point of view; though it shows the director "at his lightest", the "magical" result was both "charming" and "wacky" enough for it to take home a Best Foreign Language picture Oscar.

Day of the Jackal, The

25	24	27	22

1973 | Directed by Fred Zinnemann | With Edward Fox, Michael Lonsdale, Delphine Seyrig | 145 minutes | Rated PG

"Grip the edge of your seat and hang on" for a "fast-paced" game of "cat and mouse" as this "riveting" thriller follows the race to foil a "legendary" hit man's "plot to assassinate Charles de Gaulle"; a "top-notch cast" and "true-to-the-book intelligence" keep things "tense until the very end", so fans of "crackling suspense" call it the "real deal" – and wonder "why they bothered to remake it."

Days of Heaven

23	21	20	25

1978 | Directed by Terrence Malick | With Richard Gere, Brooke Adams, Sam Shepard | 95 minutes | Rated PG

"Underseen but not underappreciated", this "gorgeous" if "bleak" drama detailing a love triangle between two dirt-poor migrant workers and a loaded landowner "broke new ground" in its use of "beautiful cinematography" to take the place of conventional exposition; though it "speaks volumes without much dialogue", low-attention-span types yawn "not terribly compelling."

Days of Wine and Roses ◑ 27 | 28 | 25 | 24

1962 | Directed by Blake Edwards | With Jack Lemmon, Lee Remick, Charles Bickford | 117 minutes | Not Rated

For a "tough look" at a "serious issue", this "harrowing" drama about the "ravages of alcoholism" was a "huge breakthrough in its day" and remains "relevant" thanks to "tear-your-heart-out" performances from Lemmon and Remick as "desperate" young marrieds "lost in the bottom of the bottle"; "Henry Mancini's haunting title song" won the Oscar and "says it all."

Day the Earth Stood Still, The ◑ 25 | 20 | 26 | 21

1951 | Directed by Robert Wise | With Michael Rennie, Patricia Neal, Sam Jaffe | 92 minutes | Rated G

"Fifties-era real-life fears about the fate of humanity" are the backbone of this "Cold War sci-fi" flick about a "benevolent alien" invasion of Washington, DC; sure, the "less-is-more special effects" seem "dated" and "primitive by today's standards", but the "underlying message" – "world peace or else!" – makes this one "very enlightened for its time."

Dead, The 24 | 26 | 24 | 25

1987 | Directed by John Huston | With Anjelica Huston, Donal McCann, Dan O'Herlihy, Donal Donnelly | 83 minutes | Rated PG

Director Huston's "worthy last hurrah", this "sterling" adaptation of James Joyce's "classic" short story features Angelica leading a "wonderful cast" in an "atmospheric" period drama about a married couple's "quiet" reckoning at a Christmas gathering; awash in the "luminous" "Irish flavor" of 1890s Dublin, its "deft" "small touches" make for a "subtle yet heartbreaking" "gem" that's a "perfect final film."

Dead Again 22 | 24 | 24 | 22

1991 | Directed by Kenneth Branagh | With Kenneth Branagh, Andy Garcia, Emma Thompson | 107 minutes | Rated R

There are "good twists and mind tricks" aplenty in this "stylish, pseudo-noir thriller" about a detective drawn into a decades-old murder mystery; fans dig its "riveting performances", "Dali-esque imagery" and that "wonderful twist at the end", swearing you'll never look at a "pair of scissors" the same way after seeing this "over-the-top" "nail-biter."

Dead Man Walking ✉ 23 | 26 | 23 | 21

1995 | Directed by Tim Robbins | With Susan Sarandon, Sean Penn, Robert Prosky | 122 minutes | Rated R

"Based on a true story", this "enlightening" study of capital punishment is also a "profound lesson in human compassion" thanks to "poignant" turns from a "riveting" Penn as a "condemned killer" and the Oscar-winning Sarandon as a nun bent on leading him to "redemption"; although "unsettling and disturbing", the picture "provides both sides of the death-penalty argument" in an "objective", "unflinching" manner.

Dead Poets Society ✉ 24 | 25 | 24 | 23

1989 | Directed by Peter Weir | With Robin Williams, Robert Sean Leonard, Ethan Hawke | 128 minutes | Rated PG

"Living with rules" vs. "living with passion" gets the big-screen treatment in this "uplifting" drama about an "inspirational teacher" who

OVERALL | ACTING | STORY | PROD.

admonishes his students with a ringing "'carpe diem!'"; thanks to the Oscar-winning screenplay and Williams' ultra-"convincing" turn as the "influential mentor", many say this "wake-up call" of a movie should be "mandatory classroom viewing."

Death in Venice 24 | 26 | 24 | 24

1971 | Directed by Luchino Visconti | With Dirk Bogarde, Marisa Berenson, Bjorn Andresen, Silvana Mangano | 130 minutes | Rated PG

"Delicious but depressing", this "exquisitely sad meditation on love and loss" adapted from the Thomas Mann novella stars a "memorable" Bogarde as a man who becomes obsessed by a boy while on holiday in circa-1910 Venice; though the scenery's certainly "beautiful to look at" (and the "take-your-breath-away" Mahler soundtrack equally "haunting"), the film's "slow" pace and long, "languid" shots make some shrug "gorgeous but tedious."

Deer Hunter, The ✉ 26 | 28 | 24 | 24

1978 | Directed by Michael Cimino | With Robert De Niro, Christopher Walken, Meryl Streep, John Cazale, John Savage | 183 minutes | Rated R

"Ordinary guys from an ordinary American town" undergo the "ravages" of Vietnam in this "unforgettable war film", a "deeply moving", "epic-in-every-way" work that netted five Oscars (including Best Picture); brace yourself for "tough-as-nails" performances from De Niro and Walken, some "profound" if "heavy-handed symbolism" plotwise and a wrenching "Russian roulette scene" that will "leave you drained"; P.S. it also features "someone new named Streep."

Delicatessen F 26 | 23 | 24 | 26

1992 | Directed by Jean-Pierre Jeunet, Marc Caro | With Dominique Pinon, Jean-Claude Dreyfus | 99 minutes | Rated R

Cannibalism is on the menu of this "wonderfully twisted" black comedy about a "*boulangerie* serving cuts of meat" fit for "Hannibal Lecter" or Sweeney Todd; definitely "not for everyone", it's certainly "original", with enough "quirky characters" and "macabre" twists to make for an "inventive", if offbeat, "late-night snack."

Deliverance 25 | 26 | 25 | 23

1972 | Directed by John Boorman | With Jon Voight, Burt Reynolds, Ned Beatty, Ronny Cox | 109 minutes | Rated R

This "allegorical nightmare" about four "city slickers" on a "weekend canoe trip" "did for camping in the woods what *Jaws* did for swimming in the ocean", mainly because of that infamous "squeal-like-a-pig" "rape scene" (to the tune of "those damn 'Dueling Banjos'"); more important, it also "proves that thought and testosterone can coexist" and "debunks the long-held myth that Reynolds can't act."

Departed, The ✉ 26 | 28 | 25 | 26

2006 | Directed by Martin Scorsese | With Leonardo DiCaprio, Matt Damon, Jack Nicholson, Mark Wahlberg | 151 minutes | Rated R

Scorsese brought home a "well-deserved, long-overdue" Oscar for directing this "dynamite" Boston "crime opera", a "complex" cops 'n' mobsters flick that's "overflowing with superstars" but so "violent" that "your ears will ring from the gunshots"; set to an "excellent" soundtrack and featuring a finale that will have you "picking your jaw up off the floor", this "instant classic" simply "delivers on all cylinders."

	OVERALL	ACTING	STORY	PROD.

Desk Set 25 27 23 23

1957 | Directed by Walter Lang | With Katharine Hepburn, Spencer Tracy, Gig Young, Joan Blondell | 103 minutes | Not Rated

Set in the "dawn of the computer age", this "brisk" romantic comedy brings the "battle of the sexes into the workplace" by pitting "efficiency expert" Tracy against "research librarian" Hepburn; while the "two pros" display "perfect chemistry" and "flawless timing", a few say it's "not their finest hour" – though "Kate's wardrobe" alone makes it "worth the rental" for fashionistas.

Destry Rides Again ◑ 25 25 23 23

1939 | Directed by George Marshall | With Marlene Dietrich, James Stewart, Mischa Auer | 94 minutes | Not Rated

A "surprisingly modern approach to the code of the Old West", this "funny" oater tells the tale of a "reluctant", "soft-spoken" lawman aiming to tame a corrupt town; there's "strong chemistry" between Stewart's "aw-shucks" deputy and Dietrich's "heart-of-gold" floozy, not to mention a "classic saloon fight" and an "irresistible" song – 'The Boys in the Backroom' – later "parodied in *Blazing Saddles*."

Diabolique ◑F 26 25 28 23

1955 | Directed by Henri-Georges Clouzot | With Simone Signoret, Véra Clouzot | 116 minutes | Not Rated

"Leave it to the French" to serve up this "nasty little thriller" about a murderous love triangle set in a boarding school that "scares the socks" off surveyors; granted, it "looks pretty primitive today", but ultimately "Signoret still smolders", the "clever plot twists" keep coming and "whoa, what an ending!"

Dial M for Murder 25 24 27 24

1954 | Directed by Alfred Hitchcock | With Ray Milland, Grace Kelly, Robert Cummings | 105 minutes | Rated PG

A "jilted husband seeks revenge on his philandering wife" in this "taut" Hitchcock thriller, a "stagey story" transformed into a "suspenseful" movie (fun fact: it was "originally shot in 3-D"); actingwise, "Kelly shines", Milland is "subtly sinister" and Cummings "drags down every scene he appears in."

Diary of Anne Frank, The ◑ 23 23 26 21

1959 | Directed by George Stevens | With Millie Perkins, Shelley Winters, Richard Beymer | 180 minutes | Not Rated

"Every young person should see" this true story of a Jewish family hiding from the Nazis in an Amsterdam attic that "brings to life a dark time in history"; "man's inhumanity to man" is depicted "from a child's point of view" and "though we know the outcome", the "suspense" is truly "heartbreaking."

Die Hard 23 19 22 24

1988 | Directed by John McTiernan | With Bruce Willis, Bonnie Bedelia, Alan Rickman | 131 minutes | Rated R

This "flawless" "granddaddy of the '80s action" flick spawned "countless imitations but no equals" thanks to its "thrill-a-minute" mix of suspense, explosions and "comic one-liners"; die-hard diehards tout Willis' "ass-kicking" turn as a "loser whom fate requires to be a hero" as well as "chic bad guy" Rickman, who supplies the "cool quips and fashion tips."

	OVERALL	ACTING	STORY	PROD.
Diner	25	25	23	22

Diner

1982 | Directed by Barry Levinson | With Steve Guttenberg, Mickey Rourke, Kevin Bacon, Ellen Barkin | 110 minutes | Rated R

Levinson's first Baltimore drama "centers on the lives of a group of '50s high school grads" "who spent their youth in diners"; a "finely observed" "guy flick" that's both "smart and funny", it features a "wonderful ensemble cast" that delivers the snappy patter so "brilliantly" it served as a "springboard" for the careers of "many future stars."

	OVERALL	ACTING	STORY	PROD.
Dinner at Eight	27	27	24	25

Dinner at Eight ◑

1933 | Directed by George Cukor | With Marie Dressler, John Barrymore, Jean Harlow | 113 minutes | Not Rated

It seems as if "every star at MGM appears" in this frothy dramedy about a social-climbing hostess' "high society" dinner party where nothing goes as planned; look for plenty of "art deco sparkle" productionwise, a "joy" of a script and "suave, understated" performances from Dressler and John Barrymore; biggest surprise: Harlow's "snappy" turn as a gum-popping, gold-digging hussy.

	OVERALL	ACTING	STORY	PROD.
Dirty Pretty Things	23	24	24	21

Dirty Pretty Things

2003 | Directed by Stephen Frears | With Chiwetel Ejiofor, Audrey Tautou, Sergi López | 97 minutes | Rated R

London's illegal "immigrant underworld" goes under the microscope in this "atmospheric", "suspenseful" crime thriller detailing "shady goings-on" (think prostitution, drug dealing and "macabre" trafficking in human organs) at a "swanky UK hotel"; the "low-budget look" works well with the "gritty performances", "thought-provoking" scenario and "unexpected ending."

	OVERALL	ACTING	STORY	PROD.
Discreet Charm of the Bourgeoisie, The	24	23	23	22

Discreet Charm of the Bourgeoisie, The ✉ F

1972 | Directed by Luis Buñuel | With Fernando Rey, Delphine Seyrig, Stéphane Audran | 102 minutes | Rated PG

"Controversial" in its day, this Oscar-winning "satirical portrait of the French bourgeoisie" tells the "elliptical" tale of "six people in search of a hot meal" who are "confounded at every turn" by bizarre goings-on; Buñuel serves up enough "dream-within-a-dream sequences" to turn this dark comedy into a "thoughtful, surreal delight" that further enhances his reputation as the "Dali of cinema."

	OVERALL	ACTING	STORY	PROD.
District 9	22	21	23	23

District 9

2009 | Directed by Neill Blomkamp | With Sharlto Copley, Jason Cope, Nathalie Boltt | 112 minutes | Rated R

"Unexpectedly smart" and "subversive", this sci-fi allegory gives a "fresh" spin to the "alien-invader" genre when a spacecraft stalls in South Africa and its passengers are "resettled in shantytowns", suggesting "undertones of apartheid"; shot "documentary-style" with a "no-name cast" and the obligatory "gory action", it's both "destined for cult status" and "perfectly set up for a sequel."

	OVERALL	ACTING	STORY	PROD.
Diva	24	20	24	24

Diva F

1982 | Directed by Jean-Jacques Beineix | With Wilhelmenia Fernandez, Frederic Andrei | 123 minutes | Rated R

Perhaps the "greatest opera/action flick ever", this "oh-so-stylish" French thriller creates a "complicated world" about a "scooter-riding

kid" obsessed by a "reclusive soprano"; "glorious to look at", with "wonderful images of Paris", it's most memorable for that "fast-paced motorcycle chase" in the Métro.

Diving Bell and the Butterfly, The F — 26 | 28 | 26 | 26

2007 | Directed by Julian Schnabel | With Mathieu Amalric, Emmanuelle Seigner, Marie-Josée Croze, Max von Sydow | 112 minutes | Rated PG-13

Overcoming its "depressing subject" matter with "intelligence, humanity" and even "humor", this "heartfelt" true story of a "playboy incapacitated by a stroke" who can communicate "only by blinking a single eyelid" certainly "puts life in perspective"; though much of the film is "shot through the victim's eye", you "can tell the director is a painter" given the "artistic sensibility" and "remarkable visuals"; indeed, it's "full of feeling", but there's "not a sentimental moment in it."

Divorce Italian Style ✉ ◐ F — 24 | 25 | 23 | 22

1962 | Directed by Pietro Germi | With Marcello Mastroianni, Daniela Rocca, Stefania Sandrelli | 104 minutes | Not Rated

"Mastroianni's a hoot" playing an "unfortunately married" man "lusting for greener pastures" in this "*molto bene*" comedy set way back when divorce was illegal in Italy; its "silly but sweet" Oscar-winning screenplay is both a "condemnation of the law" as well as a "nice satire", and if it "loses a little in translation", it compensates with black-and-white cinematography that's "lusher than most color films."

Doctor Zhivago ✉ — 27 | 26 | 26 | 28

1965 | Directed by David Lean | With Omar Sharif, Julie Christie, Geraldine Chaplin, Rod Steiger | 197 minutes | Rated PG-13

Lean's "timeless" – others say "long" – Oscar-winning evocation of Boris Pasternak's "sweeping" novel of "love and war" is the "epic to end all epics", merging "brilliant historical storytelling" with "romantic extravaganza"; set during the Russian Revolution, it "humanized the USSR during the Cold War" due to the "tear-jerking" relationship between Christie and Sharif – though its "balalaika"-heavy theme song and the scenes in that "winter wonderland" of an "ice palace" resonate most.

Dog Day Afternoon ✉ — 24 | 27 | 22 | 20

1975 | Directed by Sidney Lumet | With Al Pacino, John Cazale, Chris Sarandon, Charles Durning | 124 minutes | Rated R

This "funny/sad" true tale of a botched "bank heist" committed by "hapless" amateurs is transformed into a "deep, character-driven" example of director Lumet "at his best"; expect "great performances from the entire cast" (from the nervous bank tellers "right down to the pizza delivery guy"), with particular kudos to an "ass-kicking" Pacino and a "brilliant" Sarandon as his gay lover.

Dona Flor and Her Two Husbands F — 24 | 24 | 24 | 21

1978 | Directed by Bruno Barreto | With Sonia Braga, José Wilker, Mauro Mendonça | 110 minutes | Rated R

The "superb" Braga floors fans in this "charming" but "sexy Brazilian fantasy" (from Jorge Amado's novel) about a woman whose "exciting" first marriage to a "cheat" seemingly ends with his death until his "ghost returns" to haunt her new life with a "dull" second husband; aficionados applaud the "memorable characters", "inventive screenplay" and "very hot" love scenes.

Donnie Darko

22 | 23 | 23 | 21

2001 | Directed by Richard Kelly | With Jake Gyllenhaal, Drew Barrymore, Mary McDonnell | 113 minutes | Rated R

"*Harvey*" meets "*Psycho*" in this indie "cult favorite" that combines "trippy sci-fi" FX with "John Hughes high-school angst" in its story of a "delusional" teen who sees visions of "demonic bunny rabbits"; sure, you might "need a few viewings to understand it" (after which it may still "make no sense"), but its "huge fan base" goes bonkers over the "original" script, "top-notch soundtrack" and the "solid" Jake, in the breakout role that made him a star.

Don't Look Now

24 | 26 | 24 | 24

1973 | Directed by Nicolas Roeg | With Julie Christie, Donald Sutherland | 110 minutes | Rated R

"Venice at its most eerie" is the backdrop for this "disturbing" psychological thriller with an "atmosphere of dread" so pervasive that you'll be "on the edge of your gondola" throughout; based on a Daphne du Maurier story about "grieving parents" mourning the death of their child, it weaves a "blind clairvoyant" and a "murderous dwarf" into its "thoroughly adult" web – and tops things off with "one of the best sex scenes in the history of cinema."

Do the Right Thing

23 | 23 | 22 | 21

1989 | Directed by Spike Lee | With Spike Lee, Danny Aiello, Ossie Davis, Ruby Dee | 120 minutes | Rated R

"Italian-American pizza parlor owners in Brooklyn" and the "African-American community who patronize the shop" clash "on the hottest day of the year" in this "anatomy of a race riot" from Spike Lee, who "deftly balances tragedy with comedy" to telegraph a "message as clear as black and white" that still "resonates years later."

Double Indemnity ◑

28 | 27 | 28 | 25

1944 | Directed by Billy Wilder | With Fred MacMurray, Barbara Stanwyck, Edward G. Robinson | 107 minutes | Not Rated

"From the chiaroscuro settings to the world-weary voice-over", Wilder's "refreshingly sour" slice of "hard-boiled" noir "sets the standard for the genre"; the story of "another dumb cluck done in by a woman", it features a "fast-talking" MacMurray, a "knockout" Stanwyck ("love the anklet") and a "fantastic" Robinson, with enough plot "twists" and sly "killer banter" to make it the cinematic equivalent of "bonded bourbon"; best scene: shopping at the "supermarket."

Doubt

25 | 28 | 25 | 24

2008 | Directed by John Patrick Shanley | With Meryl Streep, Philip Seymour Hoffman, Amy Adams, Viola Davis | 104 minutes | Rated PG-13

"No doubt" you'll have "lots to think about" after a look at this "tense" church drama depicting a "battle of wills" between an "old-school nun" and a "reformist priest" suspected of child abuse; "acting heavyweights" Streep and Hoffman "go *mano a mano*" to "mesmerizing" effect, though the "ambiguous", "did-he-or-didn't-he?" denouement has surveyors reaching "differing conclusions."

	OVERALL	ACTING	STORY	PROD.

Down by Law ◑ — 24 | 23 | 23 | 22

1986 | Directed by Jim Jarmusch | With Tom Waits, John Lurie, Roberto Benigni | 107 minutes | Rated R

A "trio of unlikely fugitives" – a DJ, a pimp and an Italian tourist – takes it on the lam from a Louisiana slammer in this "odd", "brooding" comedy from indie king Jarmusch that's best remembered for "introducing Benigni" to American audiences; but even though this B&W "original" has attained "compulsory" "cult classic" status over time, a few say its "slow pace is not for everyone."

Dracula ◑ — 24 | 21 | 23 | 20

1931 | Directed by Tod Browning | With Bela Lugosi, Helen Chandler, Dwight Frye | 75 minutes | Not Rated

Granted, the "special effects are nonexistent", but this "definitive Dracula" is still "scarier than anything made today", leaving "plenty of room for imagination" thanks to Lugosi's "riveting" take on the "immortal vampire"; though it uses music sparingly to evoke an "eerie atmosphere", a new, souped-up DVD with a "Philip Glass score" is highly touted; best line: "I never drink . . . wine."

Dreamgirls — 23 | 24 | 22 | 26

2006 | Directed by Bill Condon | With Jamie Foxx, Beyoncé Knowles, Eddie Murphy, Jennifer Hudson | 131 minutes | Rated PG-13

This "glitzy" Motown musical chronicles the "roller-coaster" fortunes of a "Supremes"-like trio and marks the "breathtaking" big-screen debut of "*American Idol*" manqué Hudson, who "pours on the pathos" with an "exquisite" Beyoncé and "dy-no-mite" Murphy at her side; busting out "gorgeous" costumes to accompany the "top-notch" tunes, it "feels like being at a Broadway show – minus the ticket prices."

Driving Miss Daisy ✉ — 24 | 27 | 23 | 22

1989 | Directed by Bruce Beresford | With Morgan Freeman, Jessica Tandy, Dan Aykroyd | 99 minutes | Rated PG

"Race relations" in the South and the "loss of dignity" that can come with aging are "wonderfully depicted" in this "heartwarming" story of an "unconventional friendship" between a matriarch and her chauffeur; the "sterling" Tandy and Freeman exhibit "incredible onscreen chemistry" (she drove home with an Oscar) in this "uplifting yet down-to-earth" drama.

Dr. No — 23 | 20 | 22 | 23

1963 | Directed by Terence Young | With Sean Connery, Ursula Andress, Jack Lord | 110 minutes | Rated PG

The "first Bond outing" is a "lean and mean" thriller "unhindered by political correctness", with "fewer gadgets" and gals than usual (though the image of Andress in that "white bikini" is "seared forever onto many a man's brain"); while the "dashing" Connery "makes it all look effortless", "purists" note this "unadulterated" "template" is the "closest they ever came to Ian Fleming's vision."

Dr. Strangelove ◑ — 28 | 28 | 27 | 26

1964 | Directed by Stanley Kubrick | With Peter Sellers, George C. Scott, Sterling Hayden | 93 minutes | Rated PG

"Nuclear annihilation was never funnier" than in Stanley Kubrick's "stinging Cold War satire", a "chillingly comic" examination of "distressingly familiar government officials" and their "precious bodily fluids"; as members of "our military at work", Scott is "magnificent" and Sellers "phenomenal" (in "three, count 'em, three roles"), while "Slim Pickens riding the bomb" remains one of the cinema's most indelible images; doomsday devotees dub it "apocalypse now and forever."

Duck Soup ◑

27 | 25 | 23 | 22

1933 | Directed by Leo McCarey | With the Marx Brothers, Margaret Dumont | 70 minutes | Not Rated

"Hail, hail Freedonia" cry fans of the "anarchic" Marx foursome, whose trademark "lunacy" is at its "peak" in this "political satire" about a "mythical dictatorship"; "absurdly funny" – it includes the "legendary mirror scene with Groucho and Harpo" – it's the brothers' "finest hour" and voted top of the Marxes in this Survey.

Duel in the Sun

23 | 22 | 22 | 24

1946 | Directed by King Vidor | With Jennifer Jones, Gregory Peck, Joseph Cotten, Lillian Gish | 146 minutes | Not Rated

Producer David O. Selznick "goes for baroque" in this "overripe", "overacted", "overly long" horse opera about a "hot" half-breed and the two brothers who desire her; its "shockingly sexual" undercurrent led to its "nickname, *Lust in the Dust*", though what's "campy" and "over the top" for some is "epic" and "operatic" to others; no question, "they don't make 'em like this anymore."

Dumbo

24 | - | 23 | 24

1941 | Directed by Ben Sharpsteen | Animated | 64 minutes | Rated G

"Elephants fly" in this "short but sweet" animated Disney classic message movie "about the importance of being yourself"; though the politically correct disparage its "racist undertones" and find it "too sad" for smaller fry, fans laud its "fabulous", Oscar-winning score and "unforgettable sequences" – particularly the "tripped-out" "hallucination" of those pink pachyderms on parade.

Eastern Promises

24 | 27 | 23 | 23

2007 | Directed by David Cronenberg | With Viggo Mortensen, Naomi Watts, Vincent Cassel | 100 minutes | Rated R

Fasten your seatbelts for a "brutal" slice of gangster life depicted in this "stomach-clenching" thriller starring a "stunning" Mortensen as a Russian mobster with "nice tattoos" caught in a vicious "spiral of murder"; the "strong" supporting cast and "killer ending" supply bonus thrills, but the "take-your-breath-away" moment is Viggo's Full Monty "steam room fight scene."

Easter Parade

22 | 21 | 17 | 24

1948 | Directed by Charles Walters | With Judy Garland, Fred Astaire, Ann Miller | 107 minutes | Not Rated

"It isn't really Easter" till you've watched this "grand Irving Berlin musical" boasting 17 songs and "lots of frills upon it" – including Fred and Judy at their "singing and dancing best" in their "only screen appearance together"; the slender story has Astaire trying to make a star out of chorus girl Garland, but this "wonderful" MGM "showcase" transcends its plot with sheer star power.

OVERALL | ACTING | STORY | PROD.

East of Eden 24 | 27 | 24 | 23

1955 | Directed by Elia Kazan | With James Dean, Julie Harris, Raymond Massey, Jo Van Fleet | 115 minutes | Not Rated

An "unforgettable" Dean eats "every actor on the set for breakfast" in his "searing" big-screen debut as the "proverbial bad seed" in this adaptation of John Steinbeck's tale of "sibling rivalry"; sure, there are also "beautiful" CinemaScope panoramas and an Oscar-winning turn from Van Fleet, but Jimmy makes it "memorable."

Easy Rider 23 | 23 | 20 | 20

1969 | Directed by Dennis Hopper | With Peter Fonda, Dennis Hopper, Jack Nicholson | 94 minutes | Rated R

"Sex, drugs and rock 'n' roll" explode on the silver screen in this "seminal" "road movie" that "defined a generation" by capturing the essence of the "tumultuous" '60s; famed for "Nicholson's starmaking performance" and Hopper's "manic", "revolutionary" direction, this "trippy" "time capsule" might have also "invented the music video" thanks to that "amazing soundtrack"; still, Gen-Y types protest it "doesn't hold up" today, unless you "get high" first.

Eat Drink Man Woman F 25 | 24 | 24 | 24

1994 | Directed by Ang Lee | With Sihung Lung, Wu Chien-Lien, Yang Kuei-Mei, Wang Yu-Wen | 123 minutes | Not Rated

Gourmands eat up this "tasty" Taiwanese look at a "different culture" that tells the story of a traditional "Asian father who shows his love by cooking for his daughters"; director Lee's "visual feast" contrasts "ticklish relationships" with "stupendous food scenes" so adroitly that many "get hungry just thinking about it."

Education, An 25 | 27 | 24 | 24

2009 | Directed by Lone Scherfig | With Carey Mulligan, Peter Sarsgaard, Alfred Molina, Olivia Williams | 100 minutes | Rated PG-13

A "starry-eyed" school girl's seduction by a "charming older man" is given "earnest" treatment in this "well-done" coming-of-ager set in "Swinging '60s London"; newcomer Mulligan's "breakout performance" as the ingénue earns the highest marks, with Sarsgaard's "quintessential cad", Molina's "socially awkward dad" and Emma Thompson's "tough-as-nails headmistress" also making the honor roll.

8½ ✉◐F 26 | 26 | 24 | 26

1963 | Directed by Federico Fellini | With Marcello Mastroianni, Claudia Cardinale, Anouk Aimée | 145 minutes | Not Rated

"Navel-gazing has never been more profound" than in this "semi-autobiographical" "Italian masterpiece" about a blocked "director trying to make a film" by using his "life as material for his work"; told in "stream of consciousness", it also features "luscious" art direction and a "career-defining turn by Mastroianni" – no wonder many call this "heartfelt" flick the "definitive movie about movies."

Eight Men Out 24 | 24 | 25 | 23

1988 | Directed by John Sayles | With John Cusack, David Strathairn, D.B. Sweeney, Charlie Sheen | 119 minutes | Rated PG

A "black eye for baseball" gets a "dark" retelling in Sayles' "insightful" sports story, recounting the "legendary 1919 Black Sox scandal" that left eight players "forever banned" for "throwing the World Series";

with a "superb" ensemble cast and an "uncanny re-creation" of "post-WWI" times, it's pitched as a "contender" for best diamond drama.

Elephant Man, The ◑ 24 | 27 | 25 | 23

1980 | Directed by David Lynch | With Anthony Hopkins, John Hurt, Anne Bancroft | 125 minutes | Rated PG

The "dignity in deformity" is defined in this "unflinching" true story about a "Victorian-era" freak who "tests the compassion of a horrified society"; "brilliant acting and makeup" make it a "gloriously Gothic" "voyage into the human heart" – a "perfect match of director and material", it will "touch you deep inside."

Elizabeth 24 | 27 | 23 | 26

1998 | Directed by Shekhar Kapur | With Cate Blanchett, Geoffrey Rush, Joseph Fiennes | 124 minutes | Rated R

"Captivating" Cate displays "unbelievable range" in this bio of England's "Virgin Queen" that follows her progress from "lusty young woman" to "ice-cold, calculating icon"; though it "feels like a fantasy version of Elizabeth I's life" to skeptics, scholars swear it's "historically on the mark", with "excellent costume design" and a "gripping" plot.

Elmer Gantry ✉ 25 | 27 | 24 | 23

1960 | Directed by Richard Brooks | With Burt Lancaster, Jean Simmons, Shirley Jones | 146 minutes | Not Rated

Disciples of this "rip-roaring" adaptation of the Sinclair Lewis novel testify that Lancaster's Oscar-winning, "fire-and-brimstone" performance as a "street preacher"-cum-"con man" in a "hypocritical" traveling ministry is the "best of his career" (while some "get religion" watching Jones' take on a jilted prostitute); its "excellent script" detailing a "flesh vs. the spirit" conflict also took home a statuette.

Empire of the Sun 25 | 23 | 24 | 26

1987 | Directed by Steven Spielberg | With Christian Bale, John Malkovich | 154 minutes | Rated PG

Perhaps Spielberg's most "underappreciated" picture, this "touching story of a British child's internment in a World War II Japanese prison camp" is an "ambitious" epic replete with "dazzling" acting, "David Lean-worthy" imagery and an "especially moving John Williams score"; maybe the "storyline drags" a bit midway, but overall its "sheer power" supplies the "magic moments."

Enchanted 23 | 22 | 22 | 25

2007 | Directed by Kevin Lima | With Amy Adams, Patrick Dempsey, James Marsden | 107 minutes | Rated PG

Disney simultaneously "parodies and pays homage" to itself in this "clever" musical fairy tale about a maiden from a generic "cartoon world" (complete with talking "woodland creatures") who's unwittingly transposed to "rough-and-tumble" NYC; look for amusingly "kitschy" song-and-dance routines and "lovely chemistry" between the "exuberant" Adams and "McDreamy" Dempsey.

Enchanted April 24 | 26 | 22 | 25

1992 | Directed by Mike Newell | With Joan Plowright, Miranda Richardson, Josie Lawrence | 95 minutes | Rated PG

For a "wonderfully rich pick-me-up", take a look at this "genteel" "getaway" of a movie about four "risk-taking" women who decide to "leave their dreary English lives behind" and are "transformed" during an April vacation in "lush, sunny" Tuscany; the perfect "antidote to winter", it's "more complex than it first appears", and Plowright's "terrific performance" will brighten any "rainy day."

Enter the Dragon 23 | 16 | 17 | 20

1973 | Directed by Robert Clouse | With Bruce Lee, John Saxon, Jim Kelly | 98 minutes | Rated R

"Martial arts" mavens maintain that this "all-time best kung fu" flicker is "butt-kicker" Lee's "magnum opus", the "standard by which all karate films are judged"; sure, the "production's cheesy" and its "James Bond" "rip-off" plot is "unoriginal", but the "balletic, ballistic" fight scenes are so "spectacular" that this one "spawned many forgettable imitators" – not to mention many "video games."

Escape from Alcatraz 23 | 22 | 23 | 21

1979 | Directed by Don Siegel | With Clint Eastwood, Fred Ward, Patrick McGoohan | 112 minutes | Rated PG

"Actually filmed on The Rock", this "edge-of-your-seat thriller" based on a real-life "amazing escape" from the "infamous" prison stars Eastwood as a "likable bad guy" in one of his "best non-Western performances"; the "good pace" and "solid action" are "thoroughly entertaining", with some "socially conscious" commentary on the justice system thrown in to boot.

Eternal Sunshine of the Spotless Mind 23 | 24 | 24 | 23

2004 | Directed by Michel Gondry | With Jim Carrey, Kate Winslet, Tom Wilkinson, Mark Ruffalo, Kirsten Dunst | 108 minutes | Rated R

A "one-of-a-kind experience", this "quirky, deeply romantic" fantasy follows a "balanced" Carrey and "winning" Winslet as broken-up lovers who biologically erase their memories of each other, then struggle to erase the erasure; though "not likely to be everyone's cup of tea", the "zany", "head-trip" script is "cerebral", "comical" and "complex" (given a "juggled time sequence" à la "*Memento*"), yet skillfully steered by director Gondry's "deft hand."

E.T. The Extra-Terrestrial 26 | 22 | 26 | 27

1982 | Directed by Steven Spielberg | With Dee Wallace, Henry Thomas, Drew Barrymore | 115 minutes | Rated PG

Arguably the "*Wizard of Oz* for a brand-new generation", this "irresistible" sci-fi "fairy tale" is the "endearing story of a boy", the "cutest alien of all time" and their attempts to "phone home"; there's agreement that Spielberg's "incredibly imaginative" "genius strikes again", managing to express "every human emotion in less than two hours", so gather the "entire family" along with a "big bowl of Reese's Pieces" and get ready for some "true magic."

Exodus 23 | 23 | 26 | 25

1960 | Directed by Otto Preminger | With Paul Newman, Eva Marie Saint, Sal Mineo | 210 minutes | Not Rated

An "all-star cast" drives this story of the "founding of modern Israel", a "stunning", "satisfying" Preminger epic "faithfully adapted" from Leon Uris' best-seller; fans single out the star turn from a "too-gorgeous-for-words" Newman "in his prime", and if the plot has some "bathos" mixed into its "high drama", it's ultimately a "moving" moving picture.

	OVERALL	ACTING	STORY	PROD.
Exorcist, The ✉	25	24	26	25
Experiment in Terror ◑	25	24	25	23
Eye of the Needle	23	25	26	22
Eyewitness	23	24	23	21
Face in the Crowd, A ◑	26	28	27	24
Fail-Safe ◑	24	25	26	21

Exorcist, The ✉

1973 | Directed by William Friedkin | With Ellen Burstyn, Max von Sydow, Linda Blair | 122 minutes | Rated R

"Horror and religion" collide in this "head-spinning", "nightmare-inducing" "shocker" about a child possessed by the devil that "grossed out America" with its "revolting" language and that infamous "pea-soup vomit scene"; though some say it's "slid into camp" over the years, most maintain it's still "one of the scariest movies ever" – but stick to the "original" cut that's much more "terrifying" than the recent 'restored' reissue.

Experiment in Terror ◑

1962 | Directed by Blake Edwards | With Glenn Ford, Lee Remick, Stefanie Powers, Ross Martin | 123 minutes | Not Rated

A rare thriller from Blake Edwards, this "little-known gem" is "one of the better woman-in-danger pictures" thanks to "chilling" performances by Remick as a "sexy" bank teller and Martin as an "asthmatic" extortionist; a jazzy Henry Mancini soundtrack and "mesmerizing" San Francisco settings (particularly that knockout windup at Candlestick Park) supply the atmosphere.

Eye of the Needle

1981 | Directed by Richard Marquand | With Donald Sutherland, Kate Nelligan, Christopher Cazenove | 112 minutes | Rated R

"Overlooked but worthwhile", this "engrossing" WWII thriller about a Nazi spy out to alert Hitler about D-day is suspenseful enough to "keep your heart in your throat" throughout; Sutherland is "fantastic" as the "creepy" lead, somehow "convincing you to cheer for him", especially when conducting a "waves-crashing-against-the-rocks" romance with the "excellent" Nelligan.

Eyewitness

1981 | Directed by Peter Yates | With William Hurt, Sigourney Weaver, Christopher Plummer | 103 minutes | Rated R

"Early starring roles" bear witness to the promise of "sexy" Bill and "stunning" Sigourney, who "both do excellent work" in this "absorbing" thriller about a janitor fixated on a TV newswoman, who meet after he discovers a murder victim; it's a "solid enough plot", and the "noir" atmosphere is enhanced by the "lovely" NYC settings.

Face in the Crowd, A ◑

1957 | Directed by Elia Kazan | With Andy Griffith, Patricia Neal, Walter Matthau, Anthony Franciosa | 125 minutes | Not Rated

Griffith's "stunning" film debut (decidedly "pre-Mayberry") has the actor playing a country bumpkin who parlays his "likable" cornpone persona into a "national political force" – only to morph into a radio and TV "demagogue"; a "hard-hitting" combination of "media satire" and "morality play", this "prescient" flick "still packs a punch" and remains a "fascinating study of fame and how it can corrupt."

Fail-Safe ◑

1964 | Directed by Sidney Lumet | With Henry Fonda, Walter Matthau, Larry Hagman | 112 minutes | Not Rated

The "Cold War gets hot" in this "chilling", "hypnotic" nuclear-war melodrama about an American President forced to make some "horrifying choices" as an atom bomb hurtles its way toward Moscow; devotees note that the storyline is strikingly similar to that of *Dr. Strangelove* (though decidedly laugh-free) but insist its "what if?" plot is especially "gripping – and hopefully not prophetic."

Fanny and Alexander ✉ F 26 | 25 | 25 | 26

1983 | Directed by Ingmar Bergman | With Pernilla Allwin, Bertil Guve, Gunn Wallgren | 188 minutes | Rated R

"Proof that Bergman wasn't miserable all the time", this "semi-autobiographical look back at his childhood" in Sweden "told from two siblings' point of view" features the "master" "at his most accessible"; sure, the "pacing's slow" and the film "long" (in fact, it's a pared-down version of a six-hour TV miniseries), yet the overall "visual magnificence" makes for something "rich and interesting."

Fantasia 28 | - | - | 29

1940 | Directed by Ben Sharpsteen et al | Animated | 120 minutes | Rated G

Disney's "magnificent merger" of "mind-blowing" animation with a symphonic orchestra conducted by "maestro Leopold Stokowski" is a piece of "unbeatably creative" "eye candy" that's "never been equaled"; though a "flop when it first came out", it was later revived as a "'60s head movie" (thanks to trippy sequences like those "dancing hippos in tutus" and "Mickey Mouse as the sorcerer's apprentice"); modernists maintain this "original music video" remains a "perfect way to introduce a child to classical" sounds.

Fantasia 2000 24 | - | - | 27

1999 | Directed by James Algar et al | Animated | 75 minutes | Rated G

The "perfect companion" to the 1940 "classic", this "worthy" sequel marrying animation to music of great composers is "terrific Disney" that might be "more for adults than kids"; it "keeps the spirit of the original beautifully" (right down to the "cloying celebrity" intros to each vignette), and although the "flamingo-with-the-yo-yo" scene enthralls many, the "best segment" is "'Rhapsody in Blue' via Al Hirschfeld."

Farewell My Concubine F 25 | 26 | 24 | 26

1993 | Directed by Chen Kaige | With Leslie Cheung, Gong Li, Zhang Feng-Yi | 171 minutes | Rated R

"Worthy of David Lean on every level", this "sumptuous", "epic achievement" traces a complex friendship between two Peking Opera singers over a "fascinating sweep of history" from the '30s to the '70s; "stunning both visually and emotionally", it boasts "superb acting" and "outstanding scenery", but make sure to sit up straight: its "overlong" running time can be "draining."

Far From Heaven 24 | 27 | 23 | 26

2002 | Directed by Todd Haynes | With Julianne Moore, Dennis Quaid, Dennis Haysbert | 107 minutes | Rated PG-13

Haynes' "gorgeous homage to director Douglas Sirk's '50s melodramas" takes a "grippingly bittersweet" look at the "reality of the suburban picket-fence dream" and "genteel Northern racism"; though the pace is "slow" and the story "a little weak", it remains a "must-see" thanks to "flawless performances" from Moore and Quaid as well as "colorful", "stunning cinematography" that "captures the time period with brilliance" – the "costumes alone are close to heaven."

Far from the Madding Crowd

OVERALL	ACTING	STORY	PROD.
23	25	23	24

1967 | Directed by John Schlesinger | With Julie Christie, Terence Stamp, Peter Finch, Alan Bates | 168 minutes | Rated PG

A "precursor of *Masterpiece Theater*", this "wonderfully visual" romantic drama based on the Thomas Hardy novel brings on a "terrific cast" led by the "luscious" Christie as a British country lass drawn into "poignant" entanglement with a trio of suitors, led by "unforgettable" cavalryman Stamp; though it was far from box-office gold, those with a taste for Victorian eye candy simply "love it."

Fargo ✉

OVERALL	ACTING	STORY	PROD.
25	27	25	25

1996 | Directed by Joel Coen | With Frances McDormand, William H. Macy, Steve Buscemi | 98 minutes | Rated R

This "comic noir" treatment of "crime in the heartland" shows "how funny Minnesota can be" in the hands of the Coen brothers, who spin a "folksy", violent yarn that makes the "outrageous seem everyday" and the "mundane interesting"; but the pièce de résistance is McDormand's "deadpan", Oscar-winning turn as a "pregnant crime-stopper" whose "goofy dialogue" alone is – "you betcha" – worth the price of admission.

Father of the Bride ◑

OVERALL	ACTING	STORY	PROD.
23	25	21	20

1950 | Directed by Vincente Minnelli | With Spencer Tracy, Joan Bennett, Elizabeth Taylor | 92 minutes | Not Rated

Hollywood legends Tracy (in the "harried" title role) and Taylor (as the bride) walk down the aisle together in this "heartwarming" chestnut about the "havoc surrounding the planning of a wedding"; while most vow it's something that "all fathers and daughters should watch" together, a few pronounce it "dated and slow."

Ferris Bueller's Day Off

OVERALL	ACTING	STORY	PROD.
23	22	23	21

1986 | Directed by John Hughes | With Matthew Broderick, Alan Ruck, Mia Sara | 98 minutes | Rated PG-13

"Every teenager's fantasy" of "ditching high school" for the day is realized in this "brilliant comedy" about a "sly slacker" on the loose in Chicago who "gets away with everything" and "does it with style"; the "smug-mugged" Broderick exudes "bravado" in the role that "launched his career", while "underappreciated" director Hughes offhandedly produces a picture so "influential" that it "belongs in a time capsule of the '80s."

Few Good Men, A

OVERALL	ACTING	STORY	PROD.
23	26	23	22

1992 | Directed by Rob Reiner | With Tom Cruise, Jack Nicholson, Demi Moore, Kevin Bacon | 138 minutes | Rated R

"Star-driven", "crackerjack courtroom drama" about a military murder investigation that's both "intelligent and entertaining"; no question, there are more than a few good performances, especially the "adorable-as-ever" Cruise in a "gritty", change-of-pace role playing against Nicholson's "riveting" if "pompous" marine colonel, who delivers the picture's most "infamous line: 'you can't handle the truth.'"

Fiddler on the Roof

OVERALL	ACTING	STORY	PROD.
26	25	27	26

1971 | Directed by Norman Jewison | With Topol, Leonard Frey, Norma Crane | 181 minutes | Rated G

One of the "last of the epic musicals", this "uplifting" adaptation of the "Broadway classic" finds "wide-screen resonance" in its "memorable" score and "elaborate production" values; despite the unmusical subject matter (19th-century "Jews fleeing the pogroms"), it's still a "joyous" film that's as "moving as a moving picture can be."

Fight Club 23 | 25 | 24 | 24

1999 | Directed by David Fincher | With Brad Pitt, Edward Norton, Helena Bonham Carter | 139 minutes | Rated R

"Love-it-or-hate-it" moviemaking is alive and well in this "testosterone-ridden" "cult classic" that uses "top-notch effects", "twisted humor" and a "killer" soundtrack in its depiction of "ultraviolent, disenfranchised males"; an "amazing Norton" and "underrated Pitt" provide the fireworks in this "gore"-drenched drama, with a "surprise finish" that's either "mind-blowing" or "nonsensical", depending on who's talking.

Finding Nemo 28 | - | 25 | 29

2003 | Directed by Andrew Stanton, Lee Unkrich | Animated | 100 minutes | Rated G

"No matter what your age", you'll be "riveted to your seat" by this "Pixar masterpiece" about a "neurotic father fish searching for his son" in a "beautifully rendered undersea world"; voters insist it's "one of the best animated films of all time", blending "superb visual effects" with a "touching" yet "hilarious script" (laced with "adult references that the tots will certainly miss") and "fully developed, brilliantly voiced characters."

Finding Neverland 25 | 27 | 24 | 26

2004 | Directed by Marc Forster | With Johnny Depp, Kate Winslet, Julie Christie | 106 minutes | Rated PG

"Even if you're a rock-hearted cynic", get out your handkerchiefs for this "pixie dust-coated", "semi-biographical" reflection on *Peter Pan* playwright J.M. Barrie's "fantastic imagination" and the people who inspired it; "do-no-wrong" Depp and Winslet "fly high" with "stellar performances", though most agree it's the "adorable child" actors who "steal the show" demonstrating the "simple power of play."

Fish Called Wanda, A 23 | 24 | 22 | 21

1988 | Directed by Charles Crichton | With John Cleese, Jamie Lee Curtis, Kevin Kline | 108 minutes | Rated R

It's easy getting hooked on this "nonstop", "kitchen-sink comedy" about a heist perpetrated by a "bumbling gang" portrayed by a "few chaps of Python fame" as well as the "show-stealing", Oscar-winning Kline; be prepared for "lots of giggles", but "forget political correctness", as "stutterers" and some unfortunate "goldfish" are gleefully abused.

Fitzcarraldo 27 | 26 | 26 | 27

1982 | Directed by Werner Herzog | With Klaus Kinski, Claudia Cardinale | 158 minutes | Rated PG

"Absolute perseverance" verging on "outlandish obsession" is the theme of this "very bizarre" story of a "quixotic" fellow determined to "build an opera house in the middle of the South American jungle"; "awe-inspired" types say "you've never seen anything like it", starting with that "scene of a ship being carried over a mountain", done with "no special effects"; P.S. try it as a "double feature with *Burden of Dreams*", the "spectacular making-of documentary."

	OVERALL	ACTING	STORY	PROD.

Five Easy Pieces

24	27	22	21

1970 | Directed by Bob Rafelson | With Jack Nicholson, Karen Black, Lois Smith | 96 minutes | Rated R

"Nicholson's at the height of his powers" in this "deliberately paced character study" about "disaffection", "wasted ambition and dreams" that's a "must-see" for die-hard Jack fans; it "captures the restlessness of its era" with an expert "mix of comedy and serious drama" – and offers explicit instructions on "how not to be a waitress" in that "unforgettable chicken-salad sandwich" scene.

(500) Days of Summer

22	23	22	21

2009 | Directed by Marc Webb | With Joseph Gordon-Levitt, Zooey Deschanel | 95 minutes | Rated PG-13

"Not your ordinary rom-com", this "bittersweet" take on "young romance" follows a "lovesick puppy" "hopelessly smitten" with a gal who "keeps him at length and off balance"; the "well-paced" narrative with a "shifting timeline" of "flashbacks and flash-forwards" is told with "quirky charm" (not to mention a "bouncy soundtrack"), and "refreshingly avoids a cliché ending."

Flags of Our Fathers

23	23	23	26

2006 | Directed by Clint Eastwood | With Ryan Phillippe, Jesse Bradford, Adam Beach | 132 minutes | Rated R

As an "elegiac" tribute to "our military heroes", Clint's snapshot of the "real history" behind the "Iwo Jima flag-raisers" – subjects of the "famous photo" that "won WWII" – focuses on the "flipside of heroism" to document the "brutal realities" encountered "both on and off the battlefield"; the ensemble cast is "outstanding", the action scenes "gritty" (if a bit "hard to follow") and the "insights" into "government propaganda" specially resonant "in today's climate."

Flight of the Phoenix, The

25	26	24	21

1965 | Directed by Robert Aldrich | With James Stewart, Richard Attenborough, Peter Finch | 147 minutes | Not Rated

"Jimmy Stewart can fly anything" and does in this post-*Spirit of St. Louis* adventure flicker about a desert plane crash that leaves its survivors facing a "seemingly hopeless future"; "realistically shot" and "brilliantly acted", it's a "feel-good", "can-do" kind of picture "without violence" that "really stays with you."

Flying Down to Rio ◑

23	19	16	25

1933 | Directed by Thornton Freeland | With Dolores del Rio, Gene Raymond, Fred Astaire, Ginger Rogers | 89 minutes | Not Rated

It was made as a Dolores del Rio vehicle, but this "often overlooked" musical is best remembered as the "first pairing" of "scene stealers" Fred and Ginger who are "pure heaven" performing the "infectious" 'Carioca'; most choose to "forget the plot" and "fast-forward to the dance routines", particularly the "amazing" "girls-dancing-on-airplane-wings" number.

Footlight Parade ◑

23	21	18	25

1933 | Directed by Lloyd Bacon | With James Cagney, Joan Blondell, Ruby Keeler, Dick Powell | 104 minutes | Not Rated

A "low-budget troupe" of show folk struggles to stay afloat during the Depression in this "zany" musical that's worth seeing for "Busby

Berkeley's grand production numbers", as well as the chance to "watch James Cagney" cut a rug; maybe the "dated" story's just "so-so", but the "amazing" dance routines (including 'By a Waterfall', 'Honeymoon Hotel' and 'Shanghai Lil') are nothing short of "electric."

For a Few Dollars More 23 | 21 | 21 | 20

1967 | Directed by Sergio Leone | With Clint Eastwood, Lee Van Cleef, Gian Maria Volentè | 130 minutes | Rated R

"No one's tougher than Clint" (who "doesn't smile once" but sure "looks good in a poncho") in this "tasty spaghetti western", the second installment in the Man With No Name trilogy; even though the dialogue's "dubbed", the characters "cardboard" and the bounty-hunter plot "weird", this "guilty pleasure" is still "fun to watch" – and "oh, that music!"

Forbidden Planet 25 | 18 | 25 | 24

1956 | Directed by Fred M. Wilcox | With Walter Pidgeon, Anne Francis, Leslie Nielsen | 98 minutes | Rated G

Its long-before-digital FX "may seem quaint" today, but this "top-notch psychological thriller" represents the "true start of the sci-fi genre" to many; despite a compelling storyline "based on Shakespeare's *Tempest*" and some halfway decent acting from the humans, "Robby the Robot is the real star" here.

Foreign Correspondent ◑ 24 | 22 | 24 | 22

1940 | Directed by Alfred Hitchcock | With Joel McCrea, Laraine Day, Herbert Marshall, George Sanders | 120 minutes | Not Rated

One of Hitchcock's "forgotten movies", this "crackling" espionage drama set on the eve of WWII follows a political reporter across Europe, and is worth seeing for its "terrific set pieces" (the "famous windmill scene", those "umbrellas in the rain"); still, a minority finds the "pro-American" sentiment a tad "too preachy", saying the director is "more the master of propaganda than the master of suspense" here.

Forrest Gump ✉ 24 | 26 | 24 | 25

1994 | Directed by Robert Zemeckis | With Tom Hanks, Robin Wright, Gary Sinise | 142 minutes | Rated PG-13

"Even macho guys" get misty over this "sentimental" story of "hope and perseverance" that explores recent American history through the "unlikely eyes" of a "simple-minded", Zelig-like hero (the "triumphant", Oscar-winning Hanks); though picky viewers find "not much assortment in this box of chocolates", they're overruled by "enchanted" believers who say its "basic good-heartedness" makes it "remarkably touching."

Fort Apache ◑ 23 | 22 | 23 | 22

1948 | Directed by John Ford | With John Wayne, Henry Fonda, Shirley Temple, Ward Bond | 125 minutes | Not Rated

This "great" Golden-Age-of-Hollywood Western is the first of the Ford trilogy that both mythologized and humanized the cavalry; Fonda's effectively "cast against type" as a by-the-numbers commander who takes over a frontier fort and can't connect with his men or the local Indians, while Wayne is "perfect" as the more understanding captain with whom he clashes; tame for the TV generation, its fight scenes are "remarkable for its era."

	OVERALL	ACTING	STORY	PROD.

Fortune Cookie, The ◑ 23 | 25 | 22 | 21

1966 | Directed by Billy Wilder | With Walter Matthau, Jack Lemmon | 125 minutes | Not Rated

The first (and many say the "best) pairing of the Lemmon-Matthau combo", this biting black comedy via Billy Wilder takes aim at our litigious society in its story of a sports cameraman faking an injury in exchange for insurance money; a "top-notch script" intertwining "big laughs" and "nonstop snickers" keeps things moving at a fast clip, even if the ending "veers uncomfortably between drama and humor."

42nd Street ◑ 24 | 18 | 20 | 26

1933 | Directed by Lloyd Bacon | With Ruby Keeler, Ginger Rogers, Bebe Daniels | 89 minutes | Not Rated

Alright, it's a "bit corny by modern standards", but this "brassy" "mother of all backstage musicals" showcases choreographer "Busby Berkeley at his glossy best" applying his "inventive" genius to all those "dancing feet"; "every actress' dream" come true, it's a real "classic", so just ignore the "hackneyed" plot and Keeler's "clunky" footwork.

For Whom the Bell Tolls 25 | 26 | 26 | 22

1943 | Directed by Sam Wood | With Gary Cooper, Ingrid Bergman, Katina Paxinou | 170 minutes | Not Rated

Fans swear this adaptation of Hemingway's Pulitzer Prize-winner about an American fighting fascism in '30s Spain "gets every single nuance right", starting with its "poignant", "old-fashioned love story" right down to the very convincing battle sequences; though a minority dubs it "schmaltz in macho drag", it strikes a chord as a "true classic by any measure" for most bell-ringers.

Fountainhead, The ◑ 22 | 22 | 23 | 22

1949 | Directed by King Vidor | With Gary Cooper, Patricia Neal, Raymond Massey | 114 minutes | Not Rated

Ayn Rand's mammoth novel "brought to life", this Hollywood version fortunately "doesn't take six months to watch" as it profiles the life of an independent, "Frank Lloyd Wright"-esque architect intent on being a "genuine individual"; foes find it too talky and "hokey" (except for the "delicious Neal") and advise you "read the book before seeing the movie."

400 Blows, The ◑ F 27 | 26 | 25 | 24

1959 | Directed by François Truffaut | With Jean-Pierre Léaud, Robert Beauvais | 94 minutes | Not Rated

"Anyone who survived adolescence" can relate to this French "coming-of-age" film, a "semi-autobiographical" effort that marked Truffaut's directorial debut; as his "great alter ego", Léaud "depicts the pain and joy of growing up" in a winsomely "giddy" turn, though the picture earned its "place in film history" by "breaking a lot of rules" while demonstrating a "true love of movies."

Frances 23 | 28 | 23 | 22

1982 | Directed by Graeme Clifford | With Jessica Lange, Kim Stanley, Sam Shepard | 140 minutes | Rated R

"Disturbing" but still "quite fine", this "harrowing" biography of "Hollywood nonconformist" Frances Farmer pulls no punches in its exploration of the actress' "demons" and "society's response to her mental illness"; in the title role, Lange is "magical" (and "matched by Stanley as her mother"), but this one's "not for the timid" given its ultimately "desperate, depressing" tone.

Frankenstein ◑ 25 | 21 | 25 | 23

1931 | Directed by James Whale | With Boris Karloff, Colin Clive, Mae Clarke | 71 minutes | Not Rated

The "granddaddy of all horror films" adds a touch of "pathos" and "camp" to its story of a mad scientist who "goes against nature" and builds a creature "prone to violence"; beyond monster-mashing, it also explores the "theme of loneliness" via Karloff's "heartbreaking" ghoul, and though "a bit overacted", it's still "goose-bumps time when Colin Clive shouts '*it's alive!*'"

Freaks ◑ 23 | 18 | 22 | 19

1932 | Directed by Tod Browning | With Wallace Ford, Leila Hyams, Olga Baclanova | 64 minutes | Not Rated

"Dated" perhaps, but "as creepy as ever", this "subversive" look at "circus sideshow" performers still shocks 75 years later since it casts "actual human oddities" – real midgets, pinheads and Siamese twins – in leading roles; "banned for years" after its initial release and "hardly politically correct", it's either "exploitative", "sympathetic" or a "nightmare-inducing" "train wreck" that "you can't take your eyes off of."

French Connection, The ✉ 25 | 26 | 25 | 24

1971 | Directed by William Friedkin | With Gene Hackman, Roy Scheider, Fernando Rey | 104 minutes | Rated R

Famed for the "most harrowing car chase ever", this "seminal hard-boiled cop drama" is a "fast-paced" "exposé of the drug underworld" that's also "superbly cast and acted", starting with Hackman's "explosive", Oscar-winning turn as the tough-talking 'Popeye' Doyle; sure, it might seem "dated" to modernists, but that's "only because it's aped so frequently."

Frida 25 | 27 | 25 | 27

2002 | Directed by Julie Taymor | With Salma Hayek, Alfred Molina | 123 minutes | Rated R

"Fiery" Hayek "put her heart and soul" into this "underrated little" bio of "eccentric" Mexican artist Frida Kahlo, "and it shows"; she delivers her "finest performance", capturing the "pain, grief and personal tragedy that the painter expressed in her art" against a "visually stunning tapestry" of "color and texture" in which her "actual paintings come to life"; "wonderful" acting by Molina and an "amazing soundtrack" are more reasons "not to miss it."

Fried Green Tomatoes 23 | 25 | 23 | 22

1991 | Directed by Jon Avnet | With Kathy Bates, Jessica Tandy, Mary Stuart Masterson | 130 minutes | Rated PG-13

"Southern-fried memories" are the basis of this "heartwarming" dramedy detailing how a "pathetic excuse for a woman" transforms herself into a "take-charge wonder"; its "sweet story" might feature a dash of "male bashing", but it's "genuinely touching and involving" – no wonder many fried-food fans find this "feel-good" "tear-jerking" "chick flick" so gosh darn "yummy."

	OVERALL	ACTING	STORY	PROD.

Friendly Persuasion

24	25	25	23

1956 | Directed by William Wyler | With Gary Cooper, Dorothy McGuire, Anthony Perkins | 140 minutes | Not Rated

"One for thy heart", this story of "Quakers during the Civil War" "trying to be pacifists" is an "all-around solid" picture thanks to a "strong storyline"; its "endearing characters" include the ultra-"believable" Cooper (the "Harrison Ford of his time") as well as a "moving" McGuire and Oscar-nominated Perkins.

From Here to Eternity ✉◑

26	27	24	24

1953 | Directed by Fred Zinnemann | With Burt Lancaster, Montgomery Clift, Deborah Kerr, Frank Sinatra, Donna Reed | 118 minutes | Not Rated

Based on James Jones' "powerful" novel, this "gold standard" of war dramas depicts military life in Honolulu's Pearl Harbor just before the Japanese attack; the "all-star cast" (including an Oscar-winning "Ol' Blue Eyes") and a "technically brilliant" production make this a "compelling classic" – though it's best remembered for Burt and Deborah's iconic "kissing-on-the-beach" scene.

From Russia With Love

23	21	23	23

1964 | Directed by Terence Young | With Sean Connery, Robert Shaw, Lotte Lenya, Daniela Bianchi | 115 minutes | Rated PG

Ride the "Orient Express from Istanbul to Venice" – with plenty of stops for "exotic locales", "scantily clad" gals and "great fight scenes" – in this early James Bonder; the "formula never works better" thanks to an "incomparable" Connery pitted against "non-cartoon" villains, especially Lenya at her most "sadomasochistic."

Front, The

23	23	25	21

1976 | Directed by Martin Ritt | With Woody Allen, Zero Mostel, Andrea Marcovicci | 95 minutes | Rated PG

The "one great Woody movie" that he "didn't direct", this "dark comedy" is a "flashback" to "McCarthyism in the '50s" starring Allen as a "reluctant hero" shilling scripts penned by "blacklisted writers" (though "Mostel steals the show" as a comedian pressured into the "witch hunt"); suitably "sharp and cynical", it delivers a "powerful message" that "may still have resonance today."

Front Page, The ◑

24	24	25	20

1931 | Directed by Lewis Milestone | With Adolphe Menjou, Pat O'Brien, Edward Everett Horton | 101 minutes | Not Rated

Based on the timeless stage comedy from Ben Hecht and Charles MacArthur, this zany satire of tabloid journalism is propelled by a fast-moving plot delivered with rapid-fire, overlapping dialogue; since it's an early talkie, it hasn't aged well, but the story was well-regarded enough to inspire three remakes, including *His Girl Friday,* arguably the best of the bunch.

Frost/Nixon

25	27	24	23

2008 | Directed by Ron Howard | With Frank Langella, Michael Sheen, Sam Rockwell, Kevin Bacon | 122 minutes | Rated R

A "clinic in great acting", this "Watergate-aftermath" docudrama reprises the "taut stage play" with Sheen as British journalist David Frost and the "bravura" Langella as Richard Nixon, going head to head in the "interview of a lifetime" (along with an "eye-opening back story");

"full accuracy" is dubious, but the "riveting verbal jousting" and "nuanced" characterizations will "even generate empathy" for Tricky Dick.

Fugitive, The 23 | 24 | 24 | 23

1993 | Directed by Andrew Davis | With Harrison Ford, Tommy Lee Jones, Sela Ward, Julianne Moore | 127 minutes | Rated PG-13

From the "ultimate adrenaline rush" of the opening "train wreck" to the "smashing grand finale", you'll be "on the edge of your seat" throughout this "thinking person's action flick", based on the "long-ago" TV series about a doctor unjustly accused of murder; the "cat-and-mouse" plot lends a "Hitchcockian" feel to the proceedings, while Ford and Jones deliver "pitch-perfect performances."

Full Metal Jacket 24 | 25 | 22 | 25

1987 | Directed by Stanley Kubrick | With Matthew Modine, Adam Baldwin, Vincent D'Onofrio | 116 minutes | Rated R

"Kubrick does Vietnam" in this "intense" war picture that's really "two amazing films in one": first up is the "disturbingly funny" depiction of "boot-camp" basic training, followed by an abrupt about-face to the "total hell" of the front-line war; "first-rate production and acting" keep things "compelling" throughout, even if peaceniks feel the "uneven" second half is a tad too "violent."

Funny Face 24 | 24 | 21 | 25

1957 | Directed by Stanley Donen | With Audrey Hepburn, Fred Astaire, Kay Thompson | 103 minutes | Not Rated

"Cinderella" goes to Paris in this "fashion industry musical" wherein a "gracefully aging", "debonair" Astaire turns a "bookish" Hepburn into an "ethereal", "luminous" supermodel; despite "no story to speak of", it's "thoroughly enchanting" thanks to "magic" dancing and Gershwin's "s'wonderfully" "dreamy" score; best number: Thompson's "steal-the-movie" rendition of 'Think Pink.'

Funny Girl ✉ 26 | 25 | 24 | 26

1968 | Directed by William Wyler | With Barbra Streisand, Omar Sharif, Walter Pidgeon | 151 minutes | Rated G

"Hello, gorgeous!"; Babs' "big movie debut" in one of the "last great traditional Hollywood musicals" made her the "greatest star" thanks to some "chutzpah", some "charm" and a voice "like buttah"; indeed, her Oscar-winning turn as comedienne Fanny Brice is so "socko" that it's easy to ignore the "schmaltzy" plot about the "man who got away."

Gallipoli 25 | 25 | 25 | 24

1981 | Directed by Peter Weir | With Mel Gibson, Mark Lee, Bill Kerr, David Argue | 110 minutes | Rated PG

A "fresh-faced" Gibson "comes of age" as an actor in this "oh-so-sad war movie" about a "disastrous WWI" battle in Turkey that points out the "pointlessness" of combat; "one of the best of the Australian New Wave" films, it winds up with a "10-hanky tragic ending" that "tugs at the heartstrings without being corny."

Gandhi ✉ 27 | 28 | 27 | 27

1982 | Directed by Richard Attenborough | With Ben Kingsley, Candice Bergen, Edward Fox | 188 minutes | Rated PG

"Big Hollywood at its best", this "meticulously detailed" bio of the Indian leader is "*The Ten Commandments* of the '80s", "long but riveting" and "emotionally wrenching"; Kingsley's "searing", Oscar-winning portrayal of the figure "who brought the British Empire to its knees" is the movie's "glorious centerpiece", and if a few find it "ponderous" and "overblown", there's no debate that it "captures the spiritual essence of the man perfectly."

Garden of the Finzi-Continis, The ✉ F — 25 | 24 | 27 | 25

1971 | Directed by Vittorio De Sica | With Dominique Sanda, Lino Capolicchio, Helmut Berger | 94 minutes | Rated R

"Complacency leads to disaster" in this "haunting" WWII drama about "upper-class Italian Jews" who "close their eyes to the looming evil" of fascism by believing that "money and position will insulate them"; it's most notable for making the "beautiful" young Sanda a star.

Gaslight ✉ ◑ — 26 | 27 | 26 | 24

1944 | Directed by George Cukor | With Ingrid Bergman, Charles Boyer, Joseph Cotten | 114 minutes | Not Rated

Anything but light, this "high-tension" thriller stars a "glowing", Oscar-winning Bergman as a newlywed who thinks she's "going insane - or is she?"; "mesmerized" fans say the "original" storyline "maintains the suspense to the end", helped by an atmospheric "Victorian setting" and a particularly "villainous villain" in Boyer.

Gay Divorcee, The ◑ — 25 | 23 | 20 | 25

1934 | Directed by Mark Sandrich | With Fred Astaire, Ginger Rogers, Edward Everett Horton | 107 minutes | Not Rated

"No one could dance like Fred and Ginger", and this footloose '30s musical "whirls" with production numbers "par excellence" as Rogers plays a spouse untying the knot in high style as Astaire duly falls into step; the "silly story" is trumped by the "dreamy" tunes and, of course, that terpsichorean team-up "can't be beat."

General, The ◑ — 28 | 27 | 26 | 27

1927 | Directed by Clyde Bruckman, Buster Keaton | With Buster Keaton, Marion Mack | 75 minutes | Not Rated

One of the "most remarkable" silent films, this pioneering effort "establishes gags still used today" in its story of a Civil War–era Southern engineer in hapless pursuit of a stolen locomotive; the "Great Stoneface's" most "ambitious" work, it also incorporates some "amazing physical comedy" - Keaton "does all his own stunts."

Gentleman's Agreement ✉ ◑ — 26 | 27 | 27 | 24

1947 | Directed by Elia Kazan | With Gregory Peck, Dorothy McGuire, Celeste Holm | 118 minutes | Not Rated

A once-"controversial exposé" of "American anti-Semitism", this "earnest" "message drama" offers Peck in a "wonderfully emotional" turn as an investigative reporter who passes himself off as Jewish and becomes a first-hand witness to "subtle prejudice"; if the final result seems a bit "dated" and "simplistic" today, it's still "interesting" as an early attempt at social criticism.

Gentlemen Prefer Blondes — 23 | 21 | 20 | 24

1953 | Directed by Howard Hawks | With Jane Russell, Marilyn Monroe, Charles Coburn | 91 minutes | Rated PG

You'll probably prefer Monroe's "ingenious, ingenuous" "dumb blonde" to the "nonexistent storyline" in this "guilty-pleasure" musical comedy, a "deliciously over-the-top" story of "gold diggers" on the make made all the more vivid in "spectacular Technicolor"; it's "one for the time capsule", if only for Marilyn's "dazzling", iconic rendition of 'Diamonds Are a Girl's Best Friend.'

Georgy Girl ◑ 23 | 25 | 21 | 20

1966 | Directed by Silvio Narizzano | With Lynn Redgrave, James Mason, Alan Bates, Charlotte Rampling | 99 minutes | Not Rated

An "ever optimistic ugly duckling" takes on "London in the Swinging '60s" in this "poignant, bittersweet comedy" that makes you "laugh and cry" as you "root for the protagonist"; starring a "moving", "before-Weight-Watchers" Redgrave as the "odd person out", it "still holds up" over 40 years later, but beware: that "theme song will stick in your head for days."

Getaway, The 22 | 22 | 21 | 21

1972 | Directed by Sam Peckinpah | With Steve McQueen, Ali MacGraw, Ben Johnson | 122 minutes | Rated PG

"Steve and Ali sizzle" with their "on-screen (and off-screen) love affair" in this "essential" "crime spree road trip" flick about an ex-con and his missus "on the run from basically everyone they know"; McQueen is his "usual stoic yet likable self", MacGraw's deliciously "icy" and director Peckinpah provides enough "slo-mo" action to make for "exciting B-movie" thrills.

Gettysburg 25 | 24 | 25 | 27

1993 | Directed by Ronald F. Maxwell | With Tom Berenger, Jeff Daniels, Martin Sheen, Stephen Lang | 261 minutes | Rated PG

Perhaps the "definitive" depiction of the "ferocious" 1863 Civil War battle that "determined the course of American history", this "powerful" epic achieves full "factual accuracy" with authentic locations buttressed by an "excellent" cast enacting the "conflict's backstory" and commemorating the "bravery on both sides"; still, the four-hours-plus running time leaves even "history buffs" huffing "too long and drawn out."

Ghost and Mrs. Muir, The ◑ 24 | 25 | 25 | 22

1947 | Directed by Joseph L. Mankiewicz | With Rex Harrison, Gene Tierney, George Sanders | 104 minutes | Not Rated

This "timeless" fantasy details the unlikely "love story" between a widow and a "crusty old" sea captain who's "full of life" - even though he's a ghost; the "otherworldly" romance that ensues avoids being "sentimental goop" thanks to "superb performances" from Tierney, Harrison and little "eight-year-old Natalie Wood."

Giant ✉ 24 | 23 | 24 | 24

1956 | Directed by George Stevens | With Elizabeth Taylor, Rock Hudson, James Dean, Dennis Hopper | 201 minutes | Rated G

As "sprawling" as the Lone Star state itself, this "all-out wonderful", big-time Texas "epic" about money, love and oil "burns with star power", featuring some mighty "big names" - Liz, Rock and Jimmy (in his last role) - "in their prime"; but cynics say this "way too long" picture is an example of "Hollywood bloat" and just "cornball hooey", but aficionados insist this super-"colossal '50s production" still "holds your interest."

	OVERALL	ACTING	STORY	PROD.
Gigi ✉	24	23	23	26

1958 | Directed by Vincente Minnelli | With Leslie Caron, Maurice Chevalier, Louis Jourdan | 119 minutes | Rated G

"Thank heaven" for this "fine rendering" of the Lerner and Loewe musical, an "unorthodox love story" about a "turn-of-the-century" Parisian courtesan and the client who wants to marry her; winner of nine Oscars, this "stunner" boasts a "radiant" Caron, suave Jourdan, "*amusant*" Chevalier and "top-notch" production values, so even if the end result might look like a "lavish" wad of "cotton candy", "just give in" and enjoy it.

Gilda ◑	24	23	21	23

1946 | Directed by Charles Vidor | With Rita Hayworth, Glenn Ford, George Macready | 110 minutes | Not Rated

Noir was never more "delectable" than in this "solid" love triangle starring a "delicious" "Hayworth in her signature role" as the "glamorous", hair-tossing Gilda; though her "modified striptease" in the 'Put the Blame on Mame' number is the "only reason to see it" for some, others find enough "mystery and suspense" to make it "memorable."

Gladiator ✉	23	23	22	27

2000 | Directed by Ridley Scott | With Russell Crowe, Joaquin Phoenix, Oliver Reed, Richard Harris | 155 minutes | Rated R

"Everything a big Hollywood blockbuster should be", this "old-fashioned" "sword-and-sandal" extravaganza features lots of "action, adventure and backstabbing" in its story of a Roman general turned wretched slave; the "intense", Oscar-winning Crowe oozes "testosterone" and the "lavish re-creation of Ancient Rome" brings the "Coliseum to life", but thumbs-downers dismiss it as "bombastic beefcake."

Glengarry Glen Ross	23	27	22	20

1992 | Directed by James Foley | With Al Pacino, Jack Lemmon, Ed Harris, Alec Baldwin | 100 minutes | Rated R

"High-pressure" real-estate salesmen "with an axe about to fall on their jobs" get the David Mamet treatment in this "dark", "lacerating drama" about the "predatory world of business"; its "talky", expletive-laden scenario can be "intensely disturbing", but ultimately it "shows what can be done with a small cast, limited sets and Godzilla talent."

Glory	25	26	26	26

1989 | Directed by Edward Zwick | With Matthew Broderick, Denzel Washington, Morgan Freeman | 122 minutes | Rated R

Based on the "true tale" about the "first black Civil War regiment and the white Union officer who led them", this "period piece" is a fine "evocation of a story few people know"; expect "great battle scenes", even if it "doesn't end the way you want it to."

Godfather, The ✉	29	29	29	29

1972 | Directed by Francis Ford Coppola | With Marlon Brando, Al Pacino, Diane Keaton, Robert Duvall, James Caan, John Cazale | 175 minutes | Rated R

Perhaps the "best three hours you can spend sitting still", this "ultimate gangster film" and "cultural phenomenon" is ranked the Most Popular film in this Survey; an "absolutely flawless" American epic, it recounts the "operatic" lives of the Corleone family via an "intricate"

plot, "bravura photography" and "iconic performances" from Brando and Pacino; in fact, the end result is so "killer" that "nothing else comes close – except maybe the sequel"; favorite line: "leave the gun, take the cannoli."

Godfather Part II, The ✉ 29 | 29 | 28 | 29

1974 | Directed by Francis Ford Coppola | With Al Pacino, Robert Duvall, Diane Keaton, Robert De Niro, John Cazale | 200 minutes | Rated R

A "real rarity – a sequel as good as the original" – this "true masterpiece" "stands on its own laurels" as it "delves deeper into the Corleone family" saga; a "moody meditation on the emptiness of power", its "complex" plot "masterfully intercuts" two stories separated by a half-century into a "taut", "heartbreaking tale of innocence lost", and though "never overshadowing its big brother", it just might be "even more subtle and sublime"; most chilling moment: the "kiss between Michael and Fredo."

Gods and Monsters ✉ 23 | 27 | 23 | 22

1998 | Directed by Bill Condon | With Ian McKellen, Brendan Fraser, Lynn Redgrave | 105 minutes | Rated R

McKellen's "brilliant" performance is the backbone of this "innovative biopic" detailing an "encounter between a hedge clipper and a has-been" moviemaker that's based on the life of 1930s "gay director" James Whale; partisans point to the Oscar-winning script as proof of why "indie films are such a delight."

Going My Way ✉◑ 24 | 23 | 22 | 21

1944 | Directed by Leo McCarey | With Bing Crosby, Barry Fitzgerald, Risë Stevens | 126 minutes | Not Rated

"Sing along with Bing" in this "hokey but pleasant" musical drama showcasing Crosby "at his best" as a "popular priest" with heavenly pipes who converts a parish house choir to his feel-good philosophy; though multiple Oscars came its way, it looks "very dated" now since they "stopped making" this brand of "engaging schmaltz" "long ago."

Gold Diggers of 1933 ◑ 25 | 19 | 16 | 26

1933 | Directed by Mervyn LeRoy | With Joan Blondell, Ruby Keeler, Dick Powell, Ginger Rogers | 96 minutes | Not Rated

An attempt to "cheer up" Depression-wracked America, this "wonderfully dated" "art deco musical" about down-and-out show people putting on a revue is best remembered for choreographer Busby Berkeley's "endlessly inventive" dance routines that evoke "joy and naughtiness" – along with a "bittersweet undercurrent of desperation"; don't-miss moment: "Ginger Rogers' pig latin version of 'We're in the Money.'"

Goldfinger 26 | 23 | 25 | 25

1964 | Directed by Guy Hamilton | With Sean Connery, Honor Blackman, Gert Frobe | 112 minutes | Rated PG

Rated the Top 007 picture in this Survey, this "classic" has it all: "formidable villains", the "coolest gadgets", an "out-of-this-world", "robbing-Fort-Knox" plot, a "fabulous theme song" "belted out by Shirley Bassey" and perhaps the "best-named" babe of them all, the one-and-only "Pussy Galore"; most memorable exchange: "do you expect me to talk? – no, Mr. Bond, I expect you to *die!*"

	OVERALL	ACTING	STORY	PROD.

Gold Rush, The ◑ 28 | 28 | 25 | 26

1925 | Directed by Charlie Chaplin | With Charlie Chaplin, Mack Swain | 82 minutes | Not Rated

Chaplin's "amazing talent" (as a writer, director and actor) is evident in this "brilliant" silent flicker, featuring the Little Tramp as a prospector "fighting the elements in the Klondike" and "overcoming all hurdles to get the girl" – and the gold; rife with "classic sequences" (the "bread-roll dance", the boiled "shoe for dinner", the cabin teetering on the edge of a cliff), it doesn't need dialogue "to evoke both laughter and pathos" – indeed, over 80 years later, many report a "lasting emotional impact."

Gone Baby Gone 24 | 26 | 23 | 23

2007 | Directed by Ben Affleck | With Casey Affleck, Michelle Monaghan, Morgan Freeman, Amy Ryan | 114 minutes | Rated R

The "Affleck brothers impress on both sides of the camera" in this "hard-driving" crime drama, with first-time director Ben flexing his "potential as a filmmaker" and sibling Casey delivering a "star-making performance" as a P.I. from "gritty" South Boston hired to "search for a missing girl"; rife with "moral quandaries", "surprising twists" and "spot-on" supporting turns ("authentic accents" included), it will "leave you thinking" "long after the lights go up."

Gone with the Wind ✉ 28 | 27 | 27 | 29

1939 | Directed by Victor Fleming | With Clark Gable, Vivien Leigh, Leslie Howard, Olivia de Havilland, Hattie McDaniel, Butterfly McQueen | 238 minutes | Rated G

A bona fide piece of "American pop culture", this Civil War melodrama based on Margaret Mitchell's "beloved book" is a "timeless", "sweeping" saga of love and loss in dwindling Dixieland; frankly, legions of admirers "do give a damn", rating it an "epic with a capital E" for its incredibly "beautiful production", "amazing" costumes and "perfect cast", especially Gable's "dashing" Rhett and Leigh's "performance of a lifetime" as the "feisty", "fiddle-dee-deeing" Scarlett; sure, it's a "long sit", yet in the end this "gorgeous triumph" "still thrills."

Goodbye, Mr. Chips ✉◑ 25 | 27 | 25 | 23

1939 | Directed by Sam Wood | With Robert Donat, Greer Garson, Paul Henreid | 114 minutes | Not Rated

More proof for the theory that "1939 was the best film year ever", this "touching" tale depicting 40 years in the life of everyone's "favorite" British schoolmaster is an unabashedly "sentimental story that will leave nary an eye dry"; credit "wonderful turns" from both Garson (in her screen debut) and Donat (who copped an Oscar) for making this "classic" "withstand the test of time."

Goodfellas 27 | 27 | 26 | 25

1990 | Directed by Martin Scorsese | With Robert De Niro, Ray Liotta, Joe Pesci | 146 minutes | Rated R

"Not for the faint of heart", "mob-master" Scorsese's "harrowing modern gangster" classic careens from "hysterically funny to terrifyingly violent" owing to an "electrifying" screenplay based on the true story of "'made' guys and greed" that reveals "mobsters as human beings" – albeit "vicious and heartless" ones; "beautiful lensing" and "stellar performances" make this one boil with "brutal power."

Good Night, and Good Luck ◑ 25 | 27 | 24 | 26

2005 | Directed by George Clooney | With David Strathairn, George Clooney, Robert Downey Jr. | 93 minutes | Rated PG

"History doesn't get much better" than George Clooney's recreation of the "tense", "smoke-filled" ambiance of CBS's 1950s-era newsroom, scene of an "intriguing showdown" between Senator Joseph McCarthy and broadcaster Edward R. Murrow ("they don't make journalists like that anymore"); crackling with "sharp dialogue" and blessed with a "sterling cast" headlined by the "phenomenal" Strathairn, it raises enough "thoughtful criticism" to incite "discussion about government censorship."

Good, the Bad and the Ugly, The 24 | 21 | 23 | 23

1967 | Directed by Sergio Leone | With Clint Eastwood, Lee Van Cleef, Eli Wallach | 161 minutes | Rated R

A "delicious spaghetti Western" drenched in "tasty dramatic marinara sauce", this Clint-essential "Man-With-No-Name" oater about a trio of Civil War–era gunmen battling over Confederate treasure is a "true classic"; sure, Eastwood's "penetrating glare" is "hypnotic", but some say Wallach "steals the show" by injecting some "subtle comedy" into the mix, while composer Ennio Morricone's "memorable score" will "stick in your head for days."

Good Will Hunting ✉ 24 | 25 | 24 | 22

1997 | Directed by Gus Van Sant | With Robin Williams, Matt Damon, Ben Affleck | 126 minutes | Rated R

Written by the "then-unknown" team of Damon and Affleck, this "intelligent" drama is built on an "uplifting", "powerful" screenplay about a "troubled petty criminal" who's coincidentally a "brilliant math genius"; its "searing yet subtle" performances include an Oscar-winning turn from Williams at his "most moving", and though the ill-willed badmouth it as "predictable", overall most folks "like them apples."

Goonies, The 23 | 19 | 23 | 21

1985 | Directed by Richard Donner | With Sean Astin, Josh Brolin, Corey Feldman | 114 minutes | Rated PG

One of the "best kids' adventures ever", this "smart, finely crafted" "family movie" about a gang of "pre-teen treasure hunters" who wield "go-go gadgets" and thwart bad guys is a fun "roller-coaster ride" "for all ages" (and a bona fide "nostalgia" trip for "Gen-Xers"); ok, it may have "some flaws", but at least it "doesn't take itself too seriously."

Gosford Park ✉ 23 | 27 | 21 | 25

2001 | Directed by Robert Altman | With Clive Owen, Alan Bates, Maggie Smith, Helen Mirren, Kristin Scott Thomas | 137 minutes | Rated R

"Agatha Christie meets *Upstairs, Downstairs*" in this "jolly good show" of a "whodunit" that's an "insightful", "behind-the-scenes skewering of the British class system" set in a "'30s country estate"; "one of Altman's best", it boasts "rich atmosphere", "scintillating dialogue" and a "bloody great" ensemble cast all "acting up a storm", and if contrarians complain about its "convoluted", "hard-to-follow" plot, fans claim it "gets better every time you see it."

	OVERALL	ACTING	STORY	PROD.

Graduate, The ✉ | 27 | 27 | 26 | 24

1967 | Directed by Mike Nichols | With Dustin Hoffman, Anne Bancroft, Katharine Ross | 105 minutes | Rated PG

The "benchmark coming-of-age comedy", this "knowing" look at a "confused young man" and his "older seductress" is the "definitive '60s alienation" flick and "somehow never ages"; credit its "witty script", Mike Nichols' "ahead-of-its-time direction", a "groovy" Simon-and-Garfunkel soundtrack and "superb" turns from the "fab" Hoffman and the "unforgettable" Bancroft as – "koo-koo-ka-choo" – Mrs. Robinson; best word: "plastics."

Grand Hotel ✉◑ | 25 | 26 | 24 | 25

1932 | Directed by Edmund Goulding | With Greta Garbo, John Barrymore, Joan Crawford, Lionel Barrymore | 112 minutes | Not Rated

"Intertwined lives" are the basis of this star-studded "early MGM talkie", one of the first multicharacter dramas set in a hotel; in addition to its "sumptuous" production and "literate" screenplay, it's endured thanks to a "brilliant" cast, particularly an "amazing Crawford", the "show-stealing" Barrymores and the "breathtaking Garbo", who utters her most famous line here: "I vant to be alone."

Grand Illusion ◑F | 28 | 28 | 27 | 26

1938 | Directed by Jean Renoir | With Jean Gabin, Erich von Stroheim, Pierre Fresnay | 114 minutes | Not Rated

"It's no illusion": this "compelling" WWI "masterpiece" has "inspired generations" with its "crushing portrayal of the futility of war" and is "still as powerful as ever"; director Renoir "shows how it should be done" in this "ahead-of-its-time" picture that's on "everyone's greatest list" simply because it "touches on every human emotion."

Gran Torino | 26 | 27 | 25 | 25

2008 | Directed by Clint Eastwood | With Clint Eastwood, Christopher Carley, Bee Vang | 116 minutes | Rated R

Eastwood takes his trademark "cantankerous vigilante" out for a valedictory spin in this "fine morality play" about a "racist" war vet who "confronts his prejudices" after a Chinese "immigrant family moves in next door"; an "honest" exercise from start to "showstopper" finish, it's "violent", "intense" and "to the point" – i.e. "classic Clint" – and will certainly "make your day."

Grapes of Wrath, The ✉◑ | 28 | 28 | 28 | 25

1940 | Directed by John Ford | With Henry Fonda, Jane Darwell, John Carradine | 128 minutes | Not Rated

"Every frame is a work of art" in this "faithful rendition" of Steinbeck's "eloquent" novel about dispossessed Depression-era farmers living through "desperate" times; quite possibly "Ford's best", it's a "classic for a reason" and "ranks high on the list of great American films" as an "important statement about life", the "depth of man's sorrow and the zenith of man's spirit."

Grease | 23 | 19 | 21 | 23

1978 | Directed by Randal Kleiser | With John Travolta, Olivia Newton-John, Stockard Channing | 110 minutes | Rated PG

"Fun" is the word for this "campy" comedy "classic", a "high-energy" "adaptation of the Broadway musical" that's a "'70s" take on a "hokey

'50s" story enacted by some of the "oldest high-school students ever"; still, the "hunky Travolta" and "stunning Newton-John" "light up the screen", and the "slick production" numbers are so "irresistible" that "cult followers" watch this "guilty pleasure" "over and over."

Great Debaters, The 25 26 25 24

2007 | Directed by Denzel Washington | With Denzel Washington, Nate Parker, Jurnee Smollett, Forest Whitaker | 126 minutes | Rated PG-13

"It doesn't get any better than Washington and Whitaker" in this "earnest", "fact-based" tale of a "black college debate team" that "overcomes stacked odds" in the "racially tense", Depression-era South; though chances are "you can guess how it ends", the "extraordinary perspectives on African-American history" it offers are both "uplifting" and "inspirational."

Great Dictator, The ◑ 26 27 25 23

1940 | Directed by Charlie Chaplin | With Charlie Chaplin, Jack Oakie, Paulette Goddard | 124 minutes | Not Rated

The normally "silent Chaplin" "fearlessly" takes "aim at Hitler" in this rare talkie, a "scathing satire of fascist tyranny" in which he "plays two roles": a Jewish barber and "rabid" dictator Adenoid Hynkel, a "brilliant parody" of Der Führer; although "overly sentimental" and "preachy" to some, most find this "masterpiece of physical comedy" "thought-provoking and perpetually relevant."

Great Escape, The 27 26 27 26

1963 | Directed by John Sturges | With Steve McQueen, James Garner, Richard Attenborough | 169 minutes | Not Rated

"Guy movies don't get any better" than this "absorbing" "prison break" flick "based on a true escape" from a WWII "German war camp"; featuring McQueen backed up by an "all-star" ensemble, it also boasts "excellent writing", a "hummable score" and "flawless action" scenes, including the "best motorcycle scene ever filmed"; though on the "long" side, it's "worth every minute."

Great Expectations ◑ 27 27 28 26

1947 | Directed by David Lean | With John Mills, Valerie Hobson, Alec Guinness, Jean Simmons | 118 minutes | Not Rated

A "pip of a movie", David Lean's "superb realization" of Dickens' novel about an orphan and his mysterious benefactor is a "masterpiece in every sense of the word"; it's "hauntingly shot" in "living black and white", and memorable moments include the "stunning graveyard sequence", Miss Havisham's "cobwebby wedding table" and "wonderful early performances by Simmons and Guinness"; in sum, "when they talk about a classic, this is what they mean."

Great White Hope, The 25 27 25 23

1970 | Directed by Martin Ritt | With James Earl Jones, Jane Alexander | 103 minutes | Rated PG-13

"Way before Darth Vader", Jones is rematched with his "Broadway hit" role and delivers a "phenomenal" performance as a "Jack Johnson-esque heavyweight champion" whose devotion to Alexander is "doomed by racism and resentment"; in a unanimous decision, judges say this "riveting" drama "captures an era" with "tremendous emotion" and packs a "powerful punch."

	OVERALL	ACTING	STORY	PROD.

Green Mile, The 23 | 25 | 23 | 24

1999 | Directed by Frank Darabont | With Tom Hanks, David Morse, Michael Clarke Duncan | 188 minutes | Rated R

Stephen King's "harrowing" serial novel is now "wonderfully translated to the screen" in this "disturbing drama" that "tugs at your emotions" with its "touching depiction" of "humanity at its best and worst"; despite "fine acting", this "very long" Mile makes some "wish it was an hour shorter."

Guess Who's Coming to Dinner ✉ 25 | 27 | 25 | 22

1967 | Directed by Stanley Kramer | With Spencer Tracy, Sidney Poitier, Katharine Hepburn | 108 minutes | Not Rated

"Daring for its day", this '60s "commentary on race relations" is the "final film of Hollywood's finest couple", "class acts Hepburn and Tracy", at their most "powerful"; sure, its "controversial subject" of "interracial marriage" might seem a bit "stagy" and "dated" now, but its "poignant and charming" treatment assures that the "issues remain" relevant.

Gun Crazy ◑ 27 | 24 | 27 | 22

(aka Deadly Is the Female)

1949 | Directed by Joseph H. Lewis | With Peggy Cummins, John Dall | 86 minutes | Not Rated

"Eat your heart out, *Bonnie and Clyde*" – this "tight little thriller" about "gun-toting lovers on the run" is film noir at its most "brilliant" and "economical", despite its "B-list stars" and "zero-budget" budget; there's plenty of "subtly kinky" innuendo too, but it's best remembered for an "influential" robbery sequence, shot in one take from the backseat of a car.

Gunga Din ◑ 25 | 24 | 25 | 24

1939 | Directed by George Stevens | With Cary Grant, Victor McLaglen, Douglas Fairbanks Jr. | 117 minutes | Not Rated

This "rousing adventure flick" from "Hollywood's golden age" recounts the "golden age of the British Empire" via the "story of three soldiers in imperial India" and the titular native lad who befriends them; some snappy "byplay between Grant, McLaglen and Fairbanks" makes it a "buddy film" prototype, though a few are troubled by the "superior", "racist attitude" of the colonialists.

Guns of Navarone, The 23 | 22 | 24 | 23

1961 | Directed by J. Lee Thompson | With Gregory Peck, David Niven, Anthony Quinn | 158 minutes | Rated PG

"Even people who hate war movies love" this "star-studded" production about WWII Allied commandos plotting to destroy Nazi artillery; "pounding" suspense and a "splendid cast" put this action-adventurer "head-and-shoulders above" the rest – and that "climactic sequence" will have you "holding your breath."

Guys and Dolls 24 | 21 | 24 | 24

1955 | Directed by Joseph L. Mankiewicz | With Marlon Brando, Jean Simmons, Frank Sinatra | 150 minutes | Not Rated

"Brando sings!" in this "colorful" musical rendition of the "Damon Runyon stories" about "gamblers, evangelists" and racehorses, all dolled up into one "heavyweight" extravaganza set around Times Square, rife with "catchy tunes" and "showstopping" numbers; foes think Marlon's "miscast", pointing to his "bored", "sexually smug" rendition of 'Luck Be a Lady.'

Halloween

22 | 16 | 20 | 19

1978 | Directed by John Carpenter | With Donald Pleasence, Jamie Lee Curtis | 91 minutes | Rated R

"Changing the face of horror movies forever", this "almost bloodless chiller shows that gore doesn't equal terror" as it depicts a "masked psycho stalker" who preys on "rowdy teens"; despite "zero-budget" production values and so-so acting (but mighty "great screaming by Jamie Lee"), this "influential" "slasher" flick spawned a slew of sequels and "still holds up."

Hamlet ✉◑

27 | 29 | 28 | 24

1948 | Directed by Laurence Olivier | With Laurence Olivier, Eileen Herlie, Basil Sydney, Jean Simmons | 153 minutes | Not Rated

"Probably the best Shakespeare film ever made with the greatest Shakespearean actor", this Oscar-winning epic is a "brilliantly visual" take on the Bard's "greatest drama"; director/producer/star Olivier does Hamlet as a blond "as only he can do it", and if the action scenes are less vivid than in other versions, overall it's still "unfailingly great."

Hamlet

24 | 26 | 26 | 25

1996 | Directed by Kenneth Branagh | With Kenneth Branagh, Julie Christie, Derek Jacobi | 242 minutes | Rated PG-13

This oft-done (maybe "overdone") Shakespearean tragedy gets "expansive" treatment from "modern master" Branagh, who uses the Bard's full text, resulting in a "four-hour adaptation"; though "engrossing, suspenseful" and "beautifully reimagined" to fans, those who say "enough already" call it "*too much* of a good thing."

Hangover, The

22 | 22 | 22 | 21

2009 | Directed by Todd Phillips | With Bradley Cooper, Ed Helms, Zach Galifianakis, Justin Bartha, Heather Graham | 100 minutes | Rated R

A "totally hilarious" inventory of "things that definitely should stay in Vegas", this "shameless" "guys-gone-wild" comedy about a Sin City "bachelor party gone wrong" delivers nonstop "crass humor", "sight gags" and "great cameos" (e.g. "Mike Tyson and a tiger"); it's "not high art", but "resistance is futile" – you'll be having "too much fun" to care; P.S. "don't miss the final credits."

Hannah and Her Sisters ✉

24 | 25 | 23 | 23

1986 | Directed by Woody Allen | With Mia Farrow, Barbara Hershey, Dianne Wiest | 103 minutes | Rated PG-13

A "nice balance of jokes and philosophy", this "pertinent" romantic comedy about three sisters and their "struggle with the meaning of life" "brims with so much intelligence and heart" that many call it "Allen's most life-affirming" picture; featuring "all-around wonderful" acting, it's a "valentine" to "NYers in all their neurotic glory" that manages to "convey a message without tempering the laugh-out-loud humor."

Happiness

23 | 25 | 22 | 20

1998 | Directed by Todd Solondz | With Jane Adams, Jon Lovitz, Philip Seymour Hoffman | 134 minutes | Not Rated

Forget the "truly ironic title": this extremely "dark" "feel-bad" comedy is "*American Beauty* with a lot more acid" and so "unrelentingly bleak"

	OVERALL	ACTING	STORY	PROD.

that it's "not for the faint of heart"; given some "taboo subject matter", the unhappy call it a "sicko train wreck" that's "probably the worst first-date movie ever", but fans tout its "brave" if "perverted" take on the "middle classes."

Hard Day's Night, A ◑ 24 | 19 | 19 | 24

1964 | Directed by Richard Lester | With The Beatles, Wilfrid Brambell | 87 minutes | Rated G

"Before there was MTV", there was this "best rock movie ever", an "ahead-of-its-time" "groundbreaker" shot with documentary-style "quick edits" that brilliantly convey the "lunacy" and the "pure joy of Beatlemania" in the "days of innocence"; it's "still a film of wonder", and, of course, there's that "incredible soundtrack" of "Fab Four" classics.

Harold and Maude 25 | 25 | 25 | 21

1972 | Directed by Hal Ashby | With Ruth Gordon, Bud Cort, Vivian Pickles | 91 minutes | Rated PG

Ok, it "starts with a hanging", but this "counterculture cult classic gets funnier", managing to be both "morbid" and "absurdly wonderful" in its "May-December story" of a "death-obsessed" kid who finds love with a "free-spirited old lady"; while certainly "not for everyone", this "original" features a "phenomenal" Gordon and a "gem" of a "Cat Stevens soundtrack."

Harry Potter and the Chamber of Secrets 24 | 22 | 24 | 27

2002 | Directed by Chris Columbus | With Daniel Radcliffe, Rupert Grint, Emma Watson, Kenneth Branagh | 161 minutes | Rated PG

This "rare spectacular sequel" is "much darker and scarier than the first", but "fantastic fantasy fare for the family" nevertheless and an "excellent adaptation of the book" "within the limits of time"; the special effects are "amazing", of course, and "the young stars have grown into their roles and do an even better job" this time around, but fans who "can't wait for the next one" admit that "Dumbledore is going to be tough to replace."

Harry Potter and the Goblet of Fire 24 | 22 | 25 | 27

2005 | Directed by Mike Newell | With Daniel Radcliffe, Rupert Grint, Emma Watson, Gary Oldman | 157 minutes | Rated PG-13

"Dragons", a giant "maze" and "puberty" spell trouble for Harry and the Hogwarts gang in this "fine addition" to a series that's "progressed beyond the kids movie" milieu and ventured into "darker" territory thanks to the maturing Potter's "increasing angst"; a "faithful compression" of Rowling's tome, it summons more "impressive" effects wizardry and "strong acting", keeping the franchise "on fire" as the wand passes to future episodes.

Harry Potter and the Half-Blood Prince 25 | 23 | 24 | 26

2009 | Directed by David Yates | With Daniel Radcliffe, Rupert Grint, Emma Watson, Jim Broadbent | 153 minutes | Rated PG

Potter loyalists still "hopelessly hooked" on Harry herald this sixth "compression" of J.K. Rowling's wizard saga as a "worthy" entry, praising its "darker" mood and "lavish" production values; those who "haven't followed the series" might be more than half-"confused" by the goings-on, but can still scrape by on the charms of its numerous cameos by "British acting nobility."

	OVERALL	ACTING	STORY	PROD.

Harry Potter and the Order of the Phoenix 24 | 23 | 25 | 27

2007 | Directed by David Yates | With Daniel Radcliffe, Rupert Grint, Emma Watson, Ralph Fiennes | 138 minutes | Rated PG-13

The *Potter* franchise "continues to soar" with this "fine" fifth entry, an "exciting" adventure that finds the "maturing" but ever "vulnerable" Harry spinning "out of control" just as the villainous Voldemort makes another bid for supremacy; acolytes applaud the scenarist for "keeping the story moving", the young cast for "getting better with age" and the "first-rate" production for its reliably "stellar" visuals.

Harry Potter and the Prisoner of Azkaban 24 | 22 | 25 | 27

2004 | Directed by Alfonso Cuarón | With Daniel Radcliffe, Rupert Grint, Emma Watson | 141 minutes | Rated PG

Rowling's third installment in the "beloved" series of children's books about a triumvirate of young wizards is "as wonderful and fanciful as the others", with particularly "fabulous production values"; featuring just the "right touch of menace and darkness" to win over "older moviegoers", it has appeal for all ages, but since the "kids are growing up", some wonder "will Harry have a beard in the next one?"

Harry Potter and the Sorcerer's Stone 24 | 23 | 25 | 27

2001 | Directed by Chris Columbus | With Daniel Radcliffe, Rupert Grint, Emma Watson | 152 minutes | Rated PG

It's "Hogwarts brought to magic life": this "reverent" screen adaptation of the ultra-"popular children's book" about a school for young witches and wizards is simply "spellbinding" – nothing less than a "21st-century *Wizard of Oz*"; fans zero in on the "eye-popping special effects", "outstanding" ensemble cast and "perfect" scenario that "gets every character right", "just like you imagined them"; still, the "length and scariness factors" might mean it's "wasted on little kids."

Harvey ◑ 26 | 27 | 25 | 22

1950 | Directed by Henry Koster | With James Stewart, Josephine Hull, Peggy Dow | 104 minutes | Not Rated

"So sweet and genuine that it's never become dated", this ever "classic comedy" concerning an "adorable sot" and his "imaginary six-foot rabbit" is such an "enchanting, grown-up fairy tale" that the "word 'heartwarming' was coined for it"; "delightful performances" elevate this "feel-good" flick into the "can't-miss" category.

Heart Is a Lonely Hunter, The 25 | 27 | 24 | 22

1968 | Directed by Robert Ellis Miller | With Alan Arkin, Sondra Locke, Stacy Keach, Chuck McCann | 123 minutes | Not Rated

If you're in the mood for a "tearjerker", among the "best of its kind" is this "beautifully told" drama featuring Arkin "hitting all the right notes" as a "deaf-mute saint" who comes to a Southern town and alters "lonely" local lives; the cast is "incredible" at conveying "unspoken dialogue", and the poignant "parable" provides a "tug at the heartstrings" "you'll never forget."

Heaven Can Wait 24 | 24 | 24 | 22

1943 | Directed by Ernst Lubitsch | With Gene Tierney, Don Ameche, Charles Coburn | 112 minutes | Not Rated

The famed "Lubitsch touch" is rendered in Technicolor in this "witty, unsentimental" comedy about a deceased playboy at the gate of Hell hoping to be admitted by listing his many transgressions; it's a "clever" yet "charming" trifle about how "life doesn't meet up to one's expectations", with a "devilishly nice ending."

Heavenly Creatures 24 | 25 | 26 | 24

1994 | Directed by Peter Jackson | With Kate Winslet, Melanie Lynskey, Clive Merrison | 99 minutes | Rated R

One part "fantasy", one part "true crime", this "absolutely riveting" drama about two teens plotting "matricide" is a "surreal", "haunting descent into the imagination" as it details an "attachment that turns deadly"; Winslet's "career-launching" performance is so "astounding" that some say "*this* is the movie" that the *Titanic* star "should have gotten an Oscar nomination for."

Heiress, The ✉◑ 27 | 28 | 27 | 26

1949 | Directed by William Wyler | With Olivia de Havilland, Montgomery Clift, Miriam Hopkins | 115 minutes | Not Rated

There's "not a weak link" in this "haunting" "old-world" version of Henry James' *Washington Square,* with Oscar winner de Havilland leading an "aces" cast in a "multilayered" turn as a "plain-Jane heiress yearning to be loved" by "gold digger" Clift over the veto of her "stern" father; indeed, her "riveting" makeover "from wallflower to woman" generates "expertly crafted" drama.

Henry V 26 | 28 | 27 | 26

1989 | Directed by Kenneth Branagh | With Kenneth Branagh, Derek Jacobi | 137 minutes | Rated PG-13

"Brush up on your Shakespeare" via this "revisionist" adaptation of the Bard's "difficult" history play about an English monarch at war with France; "both spectacular and approachable", it makes the 17th-century dialogue "completely understandable to modern ears", and first-time director Branagh's "lavish, lusty" brio is so "brilliant" that many acolytes ask "Sir Laurence who?"

Hero F 25 | 22 | 23 | 27

2004 | Directed by Zhang Yimou | With Jet Li, Zhang Ziyi | 99 minutes | Rated PG-13

"Not your typical martial-arts movie", this Chinese "homage to *Rashomon*" told from multiple perspectives in "non-linear" format explodes with "luscious visuals", "chop-'em-up kung fu" fight scenes and even some "noble" performances ("Jet Li can act!"); still, while fans see a "thought-provoking" epic about "politics, loyalty and truth", a few Sinophobes can't help but read a "propaganda" message in the "nationalist storyline."

High Noon ✉◑ 28 | 26 | 26 | 25

1952 | Directed by Fred Zinnemann | With Gary Cooper, Grace Kelly, Lloyd Bridges | 85 minutes | Not Rated

Voted the "best classic Western" in this Survey, this "tense drama" filmed in "real time" "breaks the mold" by combining all the "grit of the West" with a "strong comment on the McCarthyist '50s" and a touch of "Greek drama" to boot; as a "single-minded sheriff" with "principles", Cooper took home an Oscar, though many admit they're drawn to this timeless "allegory" for its "theme song" alone; in short, it's "absolutely tops" – nothing else "comes close."

	OVERALL	ACTING	STORY	PROD.

High Sierra ◑ | 25 | 26 | 24 | 23

1941 | Directed by Raoul Walsh | With Humphrey Bogart, Ida Lupino, Alan Curtis | 100 minutes | Not Rated

Hard-boiled with a heart, this "gritty gangster pic" features a sneering Bogie in a "part made for him" as a "bad crook gone worse" who puts on a "tough" front to cover up the sentimental sap underneath; noir connoisseurs call it "dated but great", heaping high praise on Lupino's incredibly "hot" performance.

High Society | 23 | 22 | 22 | 23

1956 | Directed by Charles Walters | With Bing Crosby, Grace Kelly, Frank Sinatra, Celeste Holm | 107 minutes | Not Rated

"What a swell party" is this Cole Porter "musical rendition of *The Philadelphia Story*", a "sophisticated comedy of manners" set in a "Newport mansion" inhabited by some "fantastic talent": a "gorgeous Grace", "swingin' Bing" and "delightful Sinatra"; sure, the original might be "far superior" plotwise, but fans dub this "softer" take the "Tiffany" of the singing-and-dancing genre.

Hiroshima, Mon Amour ◑F | 25 | 24 | 24 | 23

1960 | Directed by Alain Resnais | With Emmanuelle Riva, Eiji Okada | 90 minutes | Not Rated

Simultaneously "harrowing and beautiful", this "inventive", "intellectual" drama "explores the tragedies of war and the meaning of memory" by intercutting an "interracial love story" with "documentary footage" of the ruins of Hiroshima; though too "enigmatic" and "arty" for some ("I really want to like it, but . . ."), others tout the "cinematic importance" of this French New Wave "masterpiece."

His Girl Friday ◑ | 26 | 28 | 24 | 22

1940 | Directed by Howard Hawks | With Cary Grant, Rosalind Russell, Ralph Bellamy | 92 minutes | Not Rated

"Pay attention" now: the "superfast-moving plot" "comes at you at 100 mph" in this "biting" screwball comedy that's a "wonderful adaptation" of "*The Front Page*"; Grant and Russell "snap and crackle" as a "newspaper editor and star reporter chasing the story of a lifetime – and each other" – and if the "breakneck speed" of this zippy "roller-coaster ride" can be "exhausting", the payoff is "absolute hilarity."

Holiday ◑ | 27 | 27 | 25 | 23

1938 | Directed by George Cukor | With Katharine Hepburn, Cary Grant, Doris Nolan, Lew Ayres | 95 minutes | Not Rated

"Nonconformity" and "high society" collide in this "glorious" romantic comedy about a "charming" average Joe on the verge of marrying into a wealthy family; "crisp" dialogue, "wonderful character actors" and "radiant" stars make this somewhat "overlooked" Kate-and-Cary vehicle the perfect choice when you "can't watch *Bringing Up Baby* or *The Philadelphia Story* one more time"; P.S. "who knew Grant could do such a good backflip?"

Holiday Inn ◑ | 23 | 20 | 20 | 23

1942 | Directed by Mark Sandrich | With Bing Crosby, Fred Astaire, Marjorie Reynolds | 100 minutes | Not Rated

"Crooner Bing" and "hoofer Astaire" are "rivals" in this "lively" "musical romance" that's chock-full of "Irving Berlin favorites" but most remembered for introducing 'White Christmas'; sure, the plot's pretty "lightweight", but at least the songs of this "holiday bonbon" will "stick in your brain well into the new year."

Hoosiers

23 | 22 | 24 | 19

1986 | Directed by David Anspaugh | With Gene Hackman, Barbara Hershey, Dennis Hopper | 114 minutes | Rated PG

A modern-day "David and Goliath on the basketball court", this "inspirational" "classic of the small-town-team-rises-up genre" is a "corporate team builder" flick; as the "motivational" but "down-and-out coach trying to make a comeback", Hackman captures the spirit of "rural" hoops culture and supplies this "underdog story" with some "real heart."

Hope and Glory

26 | 26 | 26 | 25

1987 | Directed by John Boorman | With Sarah Miles, Ian Bannen, Sebastian Rice-Edwards, Sammi Davis | 113 minutes | Rated PG-13

It's "chins way up" in Boorman's "nostalgic" drama set in WWII England, a "touching" tale told "through a boy's eyes" about a family escaping the London blitz to decamp in "small-town" Britannia; with "endearing honesty" that balances humor with the "heavy subject" of war, this "priceless gem" also boasts a "stellar" cast "mostly made up of unknowns."

Horse Feathers ◑

24 | 22 | 20 | 18

1932 | Directed by Norman Z. McLeod | With the Marx Brothers, Thelma Todd | 68 minutes | Not Rated

"One of the Marxes' zaniest comedies" showcases the boys in "peak form" in a college setting, in which Groucho is the incoming university president; expect the usual "breezy lunacy" "based on years of vaudeville antics" – especially the "hilarious" "French-farcical wooing of Todd" – and ignore that "abrupt ending."

Hotel Rwanda

28 | 28 | 28 | 26

2004 | Directed by Terry George | With Don Cheadle, Sophie Okonedo, Joaquin Phoenix, Nick Nolte | 121 minutes | Rated PG-13

A "heartwrenching" reminder of the "horrors" committed during the 1994 Rwandan genocide ("a modern-day Holocaust"), this "true story" of a hotel manager who "helped save 1,200 lives" eschews "preachy" moralizing and overt carnage in order to emphasize the "redemptive" notion that "courage can turn the tide"; the "magnificent" Cheadle and "brilliant" supporting cast "do a great service" to this "important piece of history", inspiring "much hope" that such an "appalling" tragedy "doesn't happen again."

Hound of the Baskervilles, The ◑

22 | 22 | 25 | 20

1939 | Directed by Sidney Lanfield | With Basil Rathbone, Nigel Bruce, Richard Greene | 80 minutes | Not Rated

Critics call this the "most successful" take on Arthur Conan Doyle's "classic" thriller, featuring Rathbone's "quintessential" Sherlock Holmes sleuthing around an English castle; it's "must" viewing for detective devotees, complete with "campy" ambiance and "over-the-top" emoting.

Hours, The ✉

25 | 28 | 24 | 25

2002 | Directed by Stephen Daldry | With Nicole Kidman, Julianne Moore, Meryl Streep, Ed Harris | 114 minutes | Rated PG-13

There's "no action, only acting" in this "intelligent, challenging" adaptation of the "brilliant" book about three women of different generations whose "not perfect" lives are linked by a Virginia Woolf novel – and the "acting by all three leading ladies" "deserved an Oscar" (Kidman "won by a nose"); "don't watch it if you're in a good mood", however, because it's "hopelessly depressing" and "so slow moving it should have been called *The Days.*"

House of Flying Daggers F 24 | 22 | 21 | 27

2004 | Directed by Zhang Yimou | With Takeshi Kaneshiro, Zhang Ziyi, Andy Lau | 119 minutes | Rated PG-13

"Exhilarating fight sequences" and "feast-for-the-eyes" scenery team up with a "tearjerker" story of "star-crossed lovers" in this "outstanding" Chinese epic from "virtuoso" director Zhang that kicks the martial arts genre to "new heights"; still, visual beauty aside, not everyone's flying high over the kung-fusing plot (with "more twists and turns than the Yangtze River"), ditto the seemingly "interminable" ending.

House of Games 24 | 23 | 27 | 21

1987 | Directed by David Mamet | With Lindsay Crouse, Joe Mantegna, Lilia Skala | 102 minutes | Rated R

"Cold characters and clipped conversations" make this "mind-bending thriller" pure Mamet "at his most manipulative"; its "twisty" con-game plot (something like "*The Sting,* all grown-up") "keeps you guessing", and though the dialogue reminds some critics of "cartoons talking", it's "chilling on many levels", with a "head-spinning" ending that stays with you "long after the movie's over."

House of Sand and Fog 23 | 27 | 22 | 23

2003 | Directed by Vadim Perelman | With Jennifer Connelly, Ben Kingsley, Shoreh Aghdashloo | 126 minutes | Rated R

A "brilliant rendering" of the "moral stand-off" between a "slacker who loses her home" and a "desperate" Iranian who purchases it for his exiled family, this "taut", "heart-wrenching" drama explores "everything that the American dream is – and isn't"; "balanced directing" and "amazingly nuanced performances" by Kingsley, Connelly and Aghdashloo turn this inherently "dour material" into a "gripping", "haunting" tragedy.

How Green Was My Valley ✉◑ 27 | 26 | 26 | 26

1941 | Directed by John Ford | With Walter Pidgeon, Maureen O'Hara, Anna Lee, Donald Crisp | 118 minutes | Not Rated

Director Ford's "gentler side" is showcased in this "sentimental", "soulful" story of a Welsh mining family over the course of 50 years; renowned as the movie that "beat out *Citizen Kane*" for the year's Best Picture Oscar, it may seem a tad "corny" to modernists, but traditional types laud its "compassion, humanity" and "old-fashioned values."

How the West Was Won ✉ 23 | 21 | 22 | 25

1963 | Directed by John Ford, Henry Hathaway, George Marshall | With Gregory Peck, Henry Fonda, James Stewart, George Peppard, Carroll Baker, Eli Wallach | 162 minutes | Rated G

A "true epic" that feels like "five films in one", this "sprawling Western" boasts an "all-star cast" hitting the trail to follow "compelling storylines" ranging from the Civil War to a prairie-schooner drive, all in blazing "Cinerama"; the "long overview" of the "taming" of the territories makes for a grand, "sweeping tale" that's "plenty entertaining", but see it in "wide-screen" or else "don't bother."

	OVERALL	ACTING	STORY	PROD.
Hud ✉◑	26	28	24	24

1963 | Directed by Martin Ritt | With Paul Newman, Melvyn Douglas, Patricia Neal, Brandon De Wilde | 112 minutes | Not Rated

"Stud muffin" Newman is at his "bad boy best" playing an "alienated", "black-hearted" cowboy in this "truly adult" "modern Western" about a "struggle between a father and son"; sure, "Neal got the Oscar" (as did "heartbreaker Douglas" and that "gorgeous black-and-white cinematography"), but in the end, Paul's "heartbreakingly cool" anti-hero gets the most reaction.

Hunchback of Notre Dame, The ◑ 26 | 26 | 26 | 24

1939 | Directed by William Dieterle | With Charles Laughton, Cedric Hardwicke, Maureen O'Hara | 116 minutes | Not Rated

One of the more "remarkable" adaptations of the much-filmed Victor Hugo novel of 15th-century Paris, this "timeless" picture about a hunchback's love for a gypsy girl garners praise for its "terrific story and wonderful production"; in the flashy title role, the "spectacular" Laughton gives Lon Chaney's 1923 silent performance a run for its money; best word: "sanctuary!"

Hunt for Red October, The 24 | 24 | 25 | 24

1990 | Directed by John McTiernan | With Sean Connery, Alec Baldwin, Scott Glenn | 134 minutes | Rated PG

The "first and best Jack Ryan thriller", this "entertaining" "Cold War guy flick" about a "renegade Russian submarine captain" combines "heart-pounding" suspense with "characters you can root for" (i.e. the "powerhouse" Connery and "holding-his-own" Baldwin); the "twisting plot" supplies enough "white-knuckle" moments to make it every bit "as good as the book."

Hurt Locker, The ✉ 26 | 26 | 25 | 26

2009 | Directed by Kathryn Bigelow | With Jeremy Renner, Anthony Mackie, Brian Geraghty, Ralph Fiennes | 131 minutes | Rated R

"You'll be on the edge of your seat" throughout Kathryn Bigelow's "brilliant", Oscar-winning Iraq War flick, a "suspenseful psychological study" of an "adrenaline-addicted" Army bomb defuser whose "white-knuckle" battlefield travails are rivaled in intensity by his "battles within"; between the "understated" acting and "documentary"-like feel, it's as "realistic" as it gets, resulting in a "sensitive tribute to soldiers" that smartly spares any "maudlin gush."

Hush . . . Hush, Sweet Charlotte ◑ 24 | 26 | 23 | 23

1964 | Directed by Robert Aldrich | With Bette Davis, Olivia de Havilland, Joseph Cotten, Agnes Moorehead | 133 minutes | Not Rated

Playing a "faded Dixie belle" with a "Lizzie Borden" rep, Davis "demonstrates the fine art of overacting" in this "Gothic horror classic" made as a follow-up (but not a sequel) to *Whatever Happened to Baby Jane?*; it's a "campy, creepy" ride revolving around a long-ago murder and its consequences that "holds your attention throughout."

Hustle & Flow 23 | 26 | 21 | 21

2005 | Directed by Craig Brewer | With Terrence Howard, Anthony Anderson, Taryn Manning, Ludacris | 116 minutes | Rated R

This "gritty", "gutter-to-glory" story of a Southern "street hustler" chasing "rap star" dreams has a simple message: "it's tough out there for a pimp"; "emerging star" Howard turns in a "hard-to-the-bone" performance that morphs an "unlovable" character into "someone you root for", while his chief co-star – that "catchy soundtrack" – will "stick in your head for days."

Hustler, The ◑ 25 | 26 | 24 | 22

1961 | Directed by Robert Rossen | With Paul Newman, Jackie Gleason, Piper Laurie | 134 minutes | Not Rated

"Dark, tense and beautifully delivered", this "ultimate movie about winning" is simultaneously a "love poem to the game of pool", featuring "Newman on a roll" playing opposite Gleason in a rare dramatic performance that nearly "steals the picture"; it's "convincing", "gripping" stuff, and though Paul reprised the character of Eddie Felson in *The Color of Money,* connoisseurs claim this first take is so "much better."

Ice Age 23 | – | 21 | 25

2002 | Directed by Chris Wedge, Carlos Saldanha | Animated | 81 minutes | Rated G

The "oddest combination" of ice-age mammals sets out to save a little girl in this "cute", "cross-generational animated flick" featuring a "perfectly chosen" "all-star" vocal cast (e.g. Ray Romano as a "whiney" woolly mammoth); although it's "not up to the current high animated film standards", the "laugh-out-loud-funny" script and "well-done graphics" certainly "won't leave you cold."

Illusionist, The 23 | 24 | 24 | 25

2006 | Directed by Neil Burger | With Edward Norton, Paul Giamatti, Jessica Biel | 110 minutes | Rated PG-13

A "lush production" lit up by "gorgeous" cinematography reproduces the "old-world charm" of "fin de siècle" Vienna in this "clever", "lyrical musing on love and magic" starring the "brilliant" Norton as a "sly" soothsayer smitten by a nobleman's dame; the "intricate" plot "pleases and teases", with some appropriately "enchanting" contributions by Giamatti and Biel.

Il Postino F 24 | 25 | 24 | 24

1995 | Directed by Michael Radford | With Massimo Troisi, Philippe Noiret | 108 minutes | Rated PG

A "charming" mix of "poetry and postal services", this "small treasure" "could only have been made in Italy", given its "lyrical", "humble" airs; the "sweet tale" of a "simple" postman "with the heart of a poet", it manages to be both a "great love story" and a "haunting" tale of "inspiration", with "bravura" acting and "beautiful scenery" that come together for "winning" moviemaking.

I'm No Angel ◑ 23 | 22 | 21 | 21

1933 | Directed by Wesley Ruggles | With Mae West, Cary Grant | 87 minutes | Not Rated

Mae's a "hoot" in this "made-to-order vehicle" about a "brazen" sideshow performer and the many men in her life, including a hot millionaire whom she sues for breach of promise; the "risqué dialogue" showcases her sexy, "sassy sense of humor", though the picture's most famous line – "Beulah, peel me a grape" – isn't racy, just plain "hilarious."

	OVERALL	ACTING	STORY	PROD.
In America	26	27	25	24

2003 | Directed by Jim Sheridan | With Paddy Considine, Samantha Morton, Djimon Hounsou | 107 minutes | Rated PG-13

Sheridan's "beautiful" retelling of the "immigrants-come-to-NY" story is brought to life by an "exceptional ensemble" cast in this "small movie with a big heart"; while its "bittersweet" scenario of a poor Irish family trying to "rebuild after the tragic loss" of a child has many "crying like babies", it's executed so "brilliantly" that even the dry-eyed concur it's "without a single false moment."

In Cold Blood ◑	25	26	26	22

1967 | Directed by Richard Brooks | With Robert Blake, Scott Wilson, John Forsythe | 134 minutes | Rated R

Brooks' "brilliant" adaptation of Truman Capote's "true-crime" "spellbinder" is "one of the most chilling films" about random murders ever made ("remember when not showing blood was more scary than showing it?"); shot "in almost documentary style" and all the more frightening thanks to Quincy Jones' evocative score, it "still works today" as "powerful" albeit "disturbing" moviemaking.

Incredibles, The	26	-	25	28

2004 | Directed by Brad Bird | Animated | 115 minutes | Rated PG

"Not everyone can be Batman", and this animated Pixar satire "with brains" depicts the everyday "humdrum" lives of "has-been superheroes" drawn into an "edge-of-your-seat" rescue; it's "not just for kids" what with its "existential take on superherodom", though its "stunning animation" and "witty" set pieces (the "Jack Jack attack", that "show-stealing costumer") appeal to "all ages"; in fact, its "old-fashioned" message – the "family comes first" – makes many "love cartoons again."

Indiana Jones and the Last Crusade	24	23	23	26

1989 | Directed by Steven Spielberg | With Harrison Ford, Sean Connery, Denholm Elliott | 127 minutes | Rated PG-13

"Almost as good as the first" installment, this third foray in the "Indy adventure" series is a "search-for-the-Holy-Grail" tale that alternates "lighthearted humor" with plenty of "gee-whiz", "close-call action sequences"; Ford is the "perfect hero", but Connery (as his dad) "takes the cake" in this fond salute to "old-fashioned Saturday afternoon movie serials" "brought up to date."

Indochine ✉ F	23	25	23	25

1992 | Directed by Régis Wargnier | With Catherine Deneuve, Vincent Perez | 152 minutes | Rated PG-13

A "haunting", "epic" tale of French Indochina, this Foreign Language Oscar winner details an "enthralling romance" played out against the background of a country in turmoil; as a "beautiful" plantation owner, Deneuve "looks smashing in great clothes", though some say the end result is a "little too picture perfect."

I Never Sang for My Father ∅	27	27	27	23

1970 | Directed by Gilbert Cates | With Melvyn Douglas, Gene Hackman, Estelle Parsons | 92 minutes | Rated PG

Guys get their own "tearjerker" thanks to this stage drama adaptation that "hits home" with its "knowing depiction" of a "tortured son" forced to care for his widower father; the "excellent" Hackman's "controlled exasperation" in dealing with Douglas' "family patriarch" makes for a refrain that's manfully "maudlin" but rings "so true."

Inglourious Basterds 25 | 26 | 24 | 25

2009 | Directed by Quentin Tarantino | With Brad Pitt, Mélanie Laurent, Christoph Waltz, Diane Kruger, Eli Roth | 153 minutes | Rated R

"Tarantino rewrites WWII" with his "usual snappy dialogue", "dark humor" and "graphic violence" in this "twisted" war flick, a "revenge fantasy" with Pitt ("laughable" Southern accent and all) leading "*Dirty Dozen*"-style commandos in occupied France, though Oscar-winner "Waltz steals the show" as the "Nazi you love to hate"; sure, it's "squirmy at times" and "factually incorrect" – "to say the least" – but it stays "intriguing" right up to the "surprise ending."

Inherit the Wind ◑ 26 | 28 | 27 | 22

1960 | Directed by Stanley Kramer | With Spencer Tracy, Fredric March, Gene Kelly | 128 minutes | Rated PG

"You'll go ape" for this "fictionalized account of the Scopes monkey trial", based on the true story of a teacher trying to bring Darwin into his classroom; a "magnificent Tracy and March" are "at the top of their game" trying to "reconcile creationism with evolution" in this "thought-provoker" that many call the "ultimate in intelligent courtroom drama."

In-Laws, The 24 | 24 | 24 | 20

1979 | Directed by Arthur Hiller | With Peter Falk, Alan Arkin, Richard Libertini | 103 minutes | Rated PG-13

If you have any "weird" relatives-by-marriage, you'll "laugh out loud" at this "sidesplitting" comedy pitting a "chameleonic Falk" against a "befuddled Arkin" ("one of the great pairings of the cinema") as about-to-be in-laws; "totally unpredictable", it's "worth watching" if only to "find out where *Meet the Parents* came from."

Inside Man 23 | 25 | 23 | 23

2006 | Directed by Spike Lee | With Denzel Washington, Clive Owen, Jodie Foster | 129 minutes | Rated R

A "clever bank robber" undertakes an "elaborate" heist while trying to elude an "embattled cop" in this "intense" thriller driven by a "tight", "fast-paced" script that "keeps you guessing until the end"; featuring a "top-flight" cast led by the "sensational" Denzel and Clive, it marks a "graceful" foray into "mainstream commercial" fare for Spike Lee.

Insider, The 25 | 28 | 25 | 23

1999 | Directed by Michael Mann | With Al Pacino, Russell Crowe, Christopher Plummer | 157 minutes | Rated R

Crowe turns in a "quietly intense" performance (while Pacino is intense but definitely not quiet), in this dramatic thriller about a tobacco company "whistle-blower" trying to "do the right thing no matter what the consequences"; although a "disillusioning behind-the-scenes look" at "big business, the media and public opinion", it's "absolutely riveting" and an "inspirational" profile in "courage."

Interiors 23 | 25 | 22 | 23

1978 | Directed by Woody Allen | With Geraldine Page, Diane Keaton, Mary Beth Hurt, Maureen Stapleton | 93 minutes | Rated PG

"Nuanced performances" and "brilliant cinematography" are the highlights of this Woody Allen "homage to Ingmar Bergman", a "thoughtful" drama that examines "family dynamics" and "sibling rivalry" in the wake of a divorce; though some say the director should "stick to comedy", others counter this "wonderfully depressing" flick "didn't get its due when first released."

In the Heat of the Night ✉ 24 | 27 | 24 | 22

1967 | Directed by Norman Jewison | With Sidney Poitier, Rod Steiger, Warren Oates | 109 minutes | Rated PG

The "faint smell of honeysuckle hangs over" this "excellent" crime drama, a "statement on race relations" about a "black Yankee cop" suspected of murder in a small Southern town; it "generated of controversy in its day" and was quite the Oscar magnet, taking home five statuettes including Best Picture and Best Actor for the "perfect Steiger."

In the Name of the Father 23 | 25 | 24 | 21

1993 | Directed by Jim Sheridan | With Daniel Day-Lewis, Emma Thompson, Pete Postlethwaite | 133 minutes | Rated R

This "shattering" look at "desperate times" in Northern Ireland is a "riveting" true story about a "father and son jailed for a crime they did not commit"; "Day-Lewis is mesmerizing" and "totally believable" in this "troubling" account of "love and respect" amid a "terrible civil war."

In the Valley of Elah 22 | 27 | 23 | 21

2007 | Directed by Paul Haggis | With Tommy Lee Jones, Charlize Theron, Jason Patric | 121 minutes | Rated R

"Capturing the desperation of a parent" seeking answers about his son's disappearance after returning from Iraq, Jones "breaks your heart" with an "understated", "dead-on" performance in this "gripping, introspective" mystery; delineating the "emotional scars" incurred by modern soldiering, the film conveys a "powerful", "anti-any-war" message that's "thought-provoking" to some, "preachy" to others.

Into the Wild 23 | 25 | 24 | 24

2007 | Directed by Sean Penn | With Emile Hirsch, Marcia Gay Harden, Hal Holbrook, William Hurt | 148 minutes | Rated R

Penn's "fine" direction and Hirsch's "excellent" performance drive this "haunting", fact-based account of an idealistic youth whose quest to achieve "harmony with nature" led him to the "isolated wilds of Alaska" and an "inevitably sad" end; "breathtaking" shots of "wonderful scenery" make it "memorable", though cynics say it "romanticizes" the meanderings of a "spoiled kid."

Invasion of the Body Snatchers ◑ 24 | 19 | 25 | 19

1956 | Directed by Don Siegel | With Kevin McCarthy, Dana Wynter, Larry Gates | 80 minutes | Not Rated

"Don't fall asleep!"; this '50s slice of "paranoid science fiction" posits that there are "alien pod people among us" "plotting to take over our hearts and minds"; alright, it's a "classic Red Scare parable", but "still perfectly effective today" despite "wooden acting" and that studio-enforced optimistic ending.

Invictus 24 | 25 | 25 | 23

2009 | Directed by Clint Eastwood | With Morgan Freeman, Matt Damon | 134 minutes | Rated PG-13

Freeman was "born to play" Nelson Mandela in Eastwood's "rousing" drama, a "credible retelling" of the "savvy" leader's effort to "unite post-apartheid South Africa" behind the national rugby squad; a few cry foul at "drawn-out" scenes, but "dead-on" thesping makes for a "convincing" story of "forgiveness and inspiration" – "cue the triumphant tears."

Invisible Man, The ◑ 22 | 20 | 21 | 20

1933 | Directed by James Whale | With Claude Rains, Gloria Stuart, William Harrigan | 71 minutes | Not Rated

"Fabulous effects" ("especially for its time") and some slyly "campy" moments make this "classic" creature feature worthy of "every movie lover's repertoire"; the tale of an inventor whose invisibility serum transforms him into a crazed killer, it stars Rains in the "scary" title role, whose amazing acting has more to do with vocalizing than visibility.

Ipcress File, The 24 | 24 | 26 | 23

1965 | Directed by Sidney J. Furie | With Michael Caine, Nigel Green, Guy Doleman, Sue Lloyd | 109 minutes | Not Rated

"Caine rocks" in an "early" role as a distinctly non-Bond British agent in this "totally engaging" Cold War spy thriller, centering on a "heart-pounding" hunt for a top-secret file through a "bleak" underworld of brainwashing and betrayal; based on the Len Deighton novel, its "exciting" intelligence proves that "classic espionage never gets old."

Iron Giant, The 24 | - | 25 | 25

1999 | Directed by Brad Bird | Animated | 86 minutes | Rated PG

"Markedly different from other animated films", this story of a "quirky boy and an enormous robot from outer space" is both a "sly satire of the '50s" and a "message" flick about "tolerance and non-violence"; "criminally underrated" (it "slipped through the cracks due to poor marketing"), it's "entertaining and deserves to be seen."

Iron Man 26 | 26 | 24 | 28

2008 | Directed by Jon Favreau | With Robert Downey Jr., Terrence Howard, Jeff Bridges, Gwyneth Paltrow | 126 minutes | Rated PG-13

Lending his signature "edge" to the role of "playboy arms dealer" turned metal-suited "crusader", the "gifted" Downey "excels" in this "top-notch" "thinking person's comic book movie", a "turbo-charged" FX extravaganza that "sparkles" with "intelligence, humor" and "explosions galore"; enthusiasts are already "eagerly awaiting the sequel", flickers of which are screened in the "footage following the credits."

It Happened One Night ✉◑ 28 | 28 | 26 | 25

1934 | Directed by Frank Capra | With Clark Gable, Claudette Colbert | 105 minutes | Not Rated

"Gable and Colbert are swell together" in this "great Depression spirit-lifter", the "mother of all screwball comedies" about a "wisecracking tabloid reporter" and a "snooty heiress" "on the run"; the first picture to "sweep all the major Oscars", it was also considered rather "racy for its time": indeed, Gable's baring of his chest in the "walls of Jericho" sequence sent the "undershirt industry" into a tizzy.

It's a Mad Mad Mad Mad World 24 | 21 | 22 | 23

1963 | Directed by Stanley Kramer | With Spencer Tracy, Milton Berle, Sid Caesar, Buddy Hackett, Mickey Rooney, Ethel Merman, Edie Adams, Jonathan Winters | 192 minutes | Rated G

The ultimate "car comedy", this "sprawling gut-buster" features a "huge cast" of "crème de la crème" comedians in an "every-man-for-himself" "race to find a hidden fortune"; sure, it's a "long long long long movie", but it's "still terrifically entertaining" with plenty of "silly slapstick" and "great cameos" to keep things lively; best moment: "Jonathan Winters tearing up the gas station."

It's a Wonderful Life ◑ 27 | 27 | 27 | 25

1946 | Directed by Frank Capra | With James Stewart, Donna Reed, Henry Travers | 130 minutes | Not Rated

"Nobody tells a story like Capra", and this "inspirational" film "strikes a fundamental chord with lots of people" via its "small-town" tale about a "good guy" coping with "hard times" and proving "how one life can make a difference"; sure, it's a "little schmaltzy" and "surprisingly dark", but most say "it's a wonderful picture" and "Christmas wouldn't be Christmas without it" – even if you've seen it a "million times" on TV.

It's Complicated 22 | 24 | 21 | 22

2009 | Directed by Nancy Meyers | With Meryl Streep, Alec Baldwin, Steve Martin, John Krasinski | 120 minutes | Rated R

"Sex with your ex" is the setup of this "rare" rom-com for "grown-ups", with "spot-on" Streep as a divorcée who hooks up with her former hubby after the "nest empties", generating "likable chemistry" and "belly laughs" for the "boomer crowd"; the "routine" story is "nothing complicated", but thanks to a "strong cast", "easy to watch."

I Want to Live! ✉◑ 24 | 27 | 25 | 23

1958 | Directed by Robert Wise | With Susan Hayward, Simon Oakland, Theodore Bikel | 120 minutes | Not Rated

For "Susan Hayward at her most Susan Hayward", check out her "scenery-chewing", Oscar-grabbing turn in this "gut-wrenching" true story about a "tough cookie" "party girl" headed for the gas chamber; though cynics hiss this overheated "potboiler" as "extremely dated", more feel it's "not easily forgotten", particularly its still "effective" "anti-death penalty" theme.

Jane Eyre ◑ 25 | 27 | 26 | 22

1944 | Directed by Robert Stevenson | With Orson Welles, Joan Fontaine, Margaret O'Brien | 97 minutes | Not Rated

A "moody rendition of the Brontë novel", this "damn good" Gothic romance concerns a "frail" governess, a rich landowner and a houseful of dark secrets; expect plenty of "gloom and doom from the get-go" followed by atmospheric "shadows" and "Orson scowling" throughout – but as for that "disappointingly contrived ending", blame the author, not Hollywood.

Jaws 26 | 22 | 25 | 26

1975 | Directed by Steven Spielberg | With Roy Scheider, Robert Shaw, Richard Dreyfuss | 124 minutes | Rated PG-13

"Sink your teeth" into this "classic summer" scarefest that "gets the adrenaline pumping", since it's got "everything": "horrifying shark attacks", "missing limbs", "crackling" John Williams music and even "fully developed characters"; it "launched the Spielberg juggernaut" by cleverly "making you fear what you don't see", and if the title character looks a bit dated today, the "seasick" wonder "will it ever be safe to go back in the water?"

	OVERALL	ACTING	STORY	PROD.
Jean de Florette 🄵	27	27	26	26

1987 | Directed by Claude Berri | With Yves Montand, Gérard Depardieu | 120 minutes | Rated PG

"As Balzacian as French cinema can get", this "epic" drama about farmers feuding over a natural spring in the "pastoral paradise of Provence" is "stunningly beautiful" and "totally compelling"; since it's only the "first half of a genuinely tragic tale", "make sure to see *Manon of the Spring*" (its sequel) afterward to get the full scope of this truly "unforgettable story."

	OVERALL	ACTING	STORY	PROD.
Jeremiah Johnson	23	21	23	22

1972 | Directed by Sydney Pollack | With Robert Redford, Will Geer, Stefan Gierasch | 108 minutes | Rated PG

"One of the earliest Westerns to change the movie stereotypes of Indian ways", this saga relates the story of an American soldier turned "mountain man" and his pitched, emotional battle with Crow Nation warriors; a precursor of *Dances with Wolves,* it showcases Redford "at his best" and is a "classic" to true believers.

	OVERALL	ACTING	STORY	PROD.
Jezebel ✉◑	25	27	23	23

1938 | Directed by William Wyler | With Bette Davis, Henry Fonda, George Brent, Fay Bainter | 103 minutes | Not Rated

"Bette does *Gone with the Wind*" in this familiar-sounding "period piece" about an "obstinate Southern belle who defies a way of life about to be blown away"; granted, the "melodramatic" plot may be a bit "overbaked", but Davis' Oscar-winning performance as a "most delicious bitch" is sheer "perfection"; most "legendary" moment: the "red dress scene."

	OVERALL	ACTING	STORY	PROD.
Joy Luck Club, The	25	25	26	24

1993 | Directed by Wayne Wang | With Ming-Na Wen, Tamlyn Tomita, Lauren Tom, Rosalind Chao | 139 minutes | Rated R

Both an "intergenerational" drama and a "class-A weeper", this "evocative" rendering of Amy Tan's best-seller traces the "interwoven stories" of four Chinese women and their daughters with "complex insight" made more "vivid" by "superb acting"; admirers who identify with this "real look at family dynamics" that "transcends all cultures" declare it "a joy to watch."

	OVERALL	ACTING	STORY	PROD.
Judgment at Nuremberg ✉◑	26	27	25	22

1961 | Directed by Stanley Kramer | With Spencer Tracy, Burt Lancaster, Richard Widmark, Marlene Dietrich, Maximilian Schell, Judy Garland, Montgomery Clift | 178 minutes | Not Rated

Based on the "historic" 1948 Nazi war criminal trials, this "excellent courtroom drama" "asks some tough questions" and boasts "uniformly fine" players "often cast against type", as well as a "brilliant", Oscar-winning script; though the issues it raises are "unsettling", it remains a "relevant flick that everyone should see."

	OVERALL	ACTING	STORY	PROD.
Jules and Jim ◑🄵	24	26	24	23

1962 | Directed by François Truffaut | With Jeanne Moreau, Oskar Werner, Henri Serre | 100 minutes | Not Rated

One of the "milestones of the French New Wave", this charming "Truffaut masterpiece" is the "ultimate" "love triangle", wherein Moreau's "enigmatic beauty" makes her the "elusive muse" of two best friends; the "chemistry" between the players is "haunting and lyrical", and though that "bad-dream" ending is mighty "sad", the "fascinating story" proves "how complicated life can be."

Julia ✉ 25 | 27 | 25 | 24

1977 | Directed by Fred Zinnemann | With Jane Fonda, Vanessa Redgrave, Jason Robards | 118 minutes | Rated PG

"Fonda and Redgrave are radiant" in this "fascinating" drama, a "superb pairing of two actresses" cast as playwright Lillian Hellman and her "beloved childhood friend" Julia, a lefty resisting the Nazis in '30s Europe; fans applaud the "nervous" suspense and "moving" moments in this "frightening portrayal" of fraught times.

Julie & Julia 24 | 26 | 23 | 24

2009 | Directed by Nora Ephron | With Meryl Streep, Amy Adams, Stanley Tucci, Chris Messina | 123 minutes | Rated PG-13

"Stellar Streep" "lights up the screen" as Julia Child in this "better-than-the-book" comedy/biopic soufflé that chronicles the culinary queen's years in "postwar Paris"; the "parallel plot" about a "yuppie blogger" bent on preparing every recipe in her idol's cookbook is "less nourishing" ("wish it were just *Julia*"), but overall it's a "tasty romp" and the perfect "date movie for foodies."

Juliet of the Spirits F 25 | 26 | 22 | 26

1965 | Directed by Federico Fellini | With Giulietta Masina, Mario Pisu, Sandra Milo | 142 minutes | Not Rated

"Fellini's first color feature", this "dreamlike" tale is the story of an unhappy housewife who escapes her "dreary marriage" and slides into "fantasy" after a séance; it "still haunts" fans who dub it a "vivid" look at the power of "imagination", thanks to the performance of the director's "likable" real-life wife Masina, along with a "surrealistic platter" of "fascinating" character actors.

Jungle Book, The 24 | 21 | 25 | 24

1942 | Directed by Zoltan Korda | With Sabu, Joseph Calleia, Rosemary DeCamp | 109 minutes | Not Rated

Talk to the animals: this "great children's movie" is a picturesque take on the Kipling yarn of Mowgli, a lad reared by wolves who returns to village life only to face mercenary types hot on the scent of hidden riches; it's a wild eyeful of "classic" family fare that even outdoes "one of the best Disneys", the Mouse House's animated version made 25 years later.

Jungle Book, The 23 | - | 23 | 24

1967 | Directed by Wolfgang Reitherman | Animated | 78 minutes | Rated G

Kipling's "Tarzan-like character and all his friends" pop up in this "charming" Disney cartoon that "makes an impression" with a "crowd-pleasing" story full of "family fun"; it might not be the studio's "best animation", but its "enchanting" soundtrack has enough "delightful songs" to make for a thing of "pure joy."

Juno ✉ 25 | 26 | 24 | 23

2007 | Directed by Jason Reitman | With Ellen Page, Michael Cera, Jennifer Garner | 96 minutes | Rated PG-13

A "feel-good film about teen pregnancy" may sound like an oxymoron, but this "savvy" take on a "controversial" subject "rings with authenticity" thanks to a "humane", Oscar-winning script and Page's "spirited" portrayal of a "wisecracking", knocked-up kid set on "giving her baby up for adoption"; maybe the "snappy" repartee is "occasionally over-cute", but the overall result is "refreshing", especially synched against that "great soundtrack."

Key Largo ◑ 26 | 26 | 23 | 23

1948 | Directed by John Huston | With Humphrey Bogart, Edward G. Robinson, Lauren Bacall | 101 minutes | Not Rated

"Tough guys and dolls bring back the golden Warner Brothers days" in this "hard-hitting" noir showcase about a group held hostage by a "super-rat" of a gangster - until "anti-hero" Bogart shows up; near the "top of Huston's body of work", it features a "highly suspenseful" plot, "stellar performances" and some "vintage" Bogie and Bacall moments - "'nuff said."

Kill Bill Vol. 1 23 | 22 | 21 | 25

2003 | Directed by Quentin Tarantino | With Uma Thurman, Lucy Liu, Vivica A. Fox, Sonny Chiba | 111 minutes | Rated R

"Violence and gore abound" in this "over-the-top", "occasionally ridiculous" first installment of Quentin Tarantino's two-part salute to "comic strips", "spaghetti westerns" and "grindhouse kung fu flicks"; starring a "butt-kicking" Uma as a "revenge"-seeking "killing machine", it's "not for everyone" what with all the "spurting blood", "flying limbs" and "gross sound effects", but thrill freaks purr its "adrenaline" rush is simply "cool as heck" - provided you "check your brains at the door" before viewing.

Kill Bill Vol. 2 25 | 24 | 24 | 26

2004 | Directed by Quentin Tarantino | With Uma Thurman, David Carradine, Michael Madsen, Daryl Hannah | 136 minutes | Rated R

A continuation that "improves upon the original", this "gentler cousin" of the "obscenely graphic" *Vol. 1* features "less red food coloring" and more "character development", while remaining a "wickedly referential" homage to martial arts movies; as the ever-vengeful assassin, Thurman still "burns bright" and despite "trademark" Tarantino dialogue that gets a bit "long-winded", fans say there's a "true heart beating at the center of all the fighting" that lends "emotional heft" to both parts.

Killers, The ◑ 25 | 25 | 25 | 23

1946 | Directed by Robert Siodmak | With Burt Lancaster, Ava Gardner, Edmond O'Brien | 105 minutes | Not Rated

"Lancaster makes a powerful film debut" backed up by an "outstanding" Gardner in this "riveting" flick "expanded from the Hemingway short story" about a mysterious small-town murder and its aftermath; it gets to the "core of film noir" through a burbling mix of "moral ambiguity, sexual tension and crime."

Killing, The ◑ 25 | 24 | 25 | 24

1956 | Directed by Stanley Kubrick | With Sterling Hayden, Coleen Gray, Elisha Cook Jr. | 85 minutes | Not Rated

"Long before Quentin Tarantino", this "hardened noir" from the "early Kubrick" elevated a "B-list cast" and "run-of-the-mill" racetrack robbery story into a "nail-biting knockout" that typifies "taut" pacing and

	OVERALL	ACTING	STORY	PROD.

"tough-guy" attitude; an "overlooked" but "influential" effort with a diced-up structure that's "ahead of its time", it's a killer calling card from "one of the masters."

Killing Fields, The

26 | 26 | 27 | 25

1984 | Directed by Roland Joffé | With Sam Waterston, Haing S. Ngor, John Malkovich | 141 minutes | Rated R

"Friendship is tested by war" in this "harrowing" true story "told through the eyes of a journalist" relating the "atrocities in Cambodia" and the "horrors of the Khmer Rouge" following the U.S. pullout from Vietnam; "worthy Oscar-winner Ngor" (a real-life survivor of this "holocaust") turns in an "honest" performance that "will move you to tears" and "make you think" a lot.

Kind Hearts and Coronets ◑

26 | 28 | 26 | 24

1950 | Directed by Robert Hamer | With Alec Guinness, Dennis Price, Valerie Hobson | 106 minutes | Not Rated

For "quintessential" "English humor" that "gets better with each viewing", check out this "matchless black comedy" about the disinherited scion of a noble family who tries to achieve dukedom through serial murder; in an inspired twist, his victims – all eight of them – are played by the one-and-only Alec Guinness, whose spot-on performance squarely places this one on the "forever best list."

King and I, The ✉

27 | 26 | 25 | 27

1956 | Directed by Walter Lang | With Yul Brynner, Deborah Kerr, Rita Moreno | 133 minutes | Rated G

The "'Shall We Dance' scene" alone is "worth the price of admission" to this regally "sumptuous" version of Rodgers and Hammerstein's "terrific, old-fashioned" Broadway musical; though it may be "historically inaccurate", "who cares?" given the "stunning production", "gorgeous score" and "totally engaging" team of the "lovely Kerr" "getting to know" Oscar-winner Brynner.

King Kong ◑

25 | 15 | 24 | 24

1933 | Directed by Merian C. Cooper, Ernest B. Schoedsack | With Fay Wray, Robert Armstrong, Bruce Cabot | 100 minutes | Rated PG

This "granddaddy of all monster flicks" "still rules the roost" as an "essential piece of cinema history" and the inspiration for "countless" imitators; ok, the "stop-motion" special effects are "Stone Age stuff by today's standards", but this "warped beauty-and-the-beast saga" remains memorable for its "indelible" imagery, that iconic "climax atop the Empire State Building" and most of all for the "irreplaceable" Fay Wray, "filmdom's finest screamer."

King of Comedy, The

23 | 26 | 23 | 21

1983 | Directed by Martin Scorsese | With Robert De Niro, Jerry Lewis, Sandra Bernhard | 101 minutes | Rated PG

"Sharp, insightful and totally original", this pitch-black comedy about a wannabe comedian and the talk-show host he stalks is a different kind of "De Niro psycho flick" that's "complex and unsettling, but kind of fun"; as the stalkee, Lewis is both "funny and sad" ("maybe the French do know something"), and the picture itself is the "most underrated of Scorsese's career."

	OVERALL	ACTING	STORY	PROD.
King of Hearts F	26	26	26	24

1967 | Directed by Philippe de Broca | With Alan Bates, Geneviève Bujold, Pierre Brasseur, Adolfo Celi | 100 minutes | Not Rated

One of the "best anti-war flicks", this "satiric" allegory tells of a World War I soldier's attempt to dismantle a bomb set in a village solely inhabited by "insane asylum inmates"; while some snort its "pacifist" message is too "simplistic" and "heavy-handed", more say this "cult classic" is a "thought-provoking" indictment of the "madness of war."

	OVERALL	ACTING	STORY	PROD.
Kiss Me Deadly ◑	24	20	23	21

1955 | Directed by Robert Aldrich | With Ralph Meeker, Albert Dekker, Paul Stewart, Marian Carr | 104 minutes | Not Rated

"Cold War propaganda has never been more frightening" than in this "mesmerizing" example of "classic film noir" rife with girls, guns and "cynicism", topped off with some "nuclear paranoia"; based on Mickey Spillane's lurid best-seller, it "bears repeat viewing" thanks to Aldrich's "superb direction", a "memorable ending" and that famous "suitcase", later "paid homage to in *Pulp Fiction*."

	OVERALL	ACTING	STORY	PROD.
Kiss Me Kate	24	21	24	25

1953 | Directed by George Sidney | With Howard Keel, Kathryn Grayson, Ann Miller | 109 minutes | Not Rated

"Cole Porter's Broadway smash" gets the "Hollywood treatment" in this "sparkling film version" that's a reworking of "*The Taming of the Shrew*"; even though the "principals lack star power", you can still "brush up on your Shakespeare" nicely with "great musical numbers" and "exciting dancing", which come together famously in Miller's "knock-'em-dead" turn in 'Too Darn Hot.'

	OVERALL	ACTING	STORY	PROD.
Kiss of Death ◑	23	24	22	22

1947 | Directed by Henry Hathaway | With Victor Mature, Brian Donlevy, Richard Widmark, Coleen Gray | 98 minutes | Not Rated

A "decent ex-con" hoping to lead a straight life fends off a "very bad man" from his criminal past in this "classic" noir best remembered for Widmark's Oscar-nominated, big-screen debut as "chilling" hit man Tommy Udo ("you'll remember his cackle forever"); creepiest scene: when the "old lady in the wheelchair" meets her fate.

	OVERALL	ACTING	STORY	PROD.
Kite Runner, The F	24	24	25	24

2007 | Directed by Marc Forster | With Khalid Abdalla, Atossa Leoni, Shaun Toub | 128 minutes | Rated PG-13

Novelist Khaled Hosseini's "gripping" tale of two friends in conflict-torn Afghanistan is "tastefully" transferred to the big screen in this "simplified" adaptation, sparing many "background details" while still conveying the narrative's "moralistic" core – i.e. "how childhood events determine the course of an entire life"; enriched by a "vivid" production and some "wonderful kid actors", it packs a "powerful" punch.

	OVERALL	ACTING	STORY	PROD.
Knife in the Water ◑ F	24	23	24	22

1963 | Directed by Roman Polanski | With Leon Niemczyk, Jolanta Umecka, Zygmunt Malanowicz | 94 minutes | Not Rated

Polanski's "breakthrough" movie achieves "suspense in a boat" via its story of a married couple who invite a hitchhiker along on their sailing

	OVERALL	ACTING	STORY	PROD.

expedition; despite a "small cast" and "obvious low budget", the "mesmerizing" result achieves "Hitchcock-level tension", no mean feat considering that it was the director's first feature.

Kramer vs. Kramer ✉ 23 | 26 | 23 | 21

1979 | Directed by Robert Benton | With Dustin Hoffman, Meryl Streep, Justin Henry | 105 minutes | Rated PG

"All about the acting", this "riveting drama" won Oscars for Hoffman and Streep as a married couple undergoing the "trauma of divorce and child custody"; overturning the "gender-biased view of parenting", its depiction of a growing "father-son" bond is the core of the story, though its "heart-wrenching" theme "hits you hard" – "there are no winners" in this split-up.

Kung Fu Hustle F 23 | 20 | 21 | 24

2005 | Directed by Stephen Chow | With Stephen Chow, Yuen Wah, Qiu Yuen | 95 minutes | Rated R

"Move over Jackie Chan!": this "wildly imaginative" piece of "chop-socky" merges "mind-boggling fight choreography" with "genre-blending" aplomb in its tale of "unlikely heroes" facing off against mobsters; its "spaghetti-western-meets-*Crouching-Tiger*" approach is equal parts "Bruce Lee, Wile E. Coyote and Quentin Tarantino", with a dash of "Bob Fosse" thrown in for good measure.

La Cage aux Folles F 24 | 26 | 25 | 22

1979 | Directed by Edouard Molinaro | With Michel Serrault, Ugo Tognazzi, Remy Laurent | 100 minutes | Rated R

"Funnier than the American remake", the "Broadway musical" and the "two sequels", this "absurd" French farce is "light-years ahead of its time" telling the story of two gay blades forced to "play it straight" in order to impress prospective in-laws; "overacted to perfection" by an "unbeatable" cast, it defines flaming "frivolity", even if a few cluck it's become "a bit faded" with time.

L.A. Confidential ✉ 26 | 27 | 25 | 26

1997 | Directed by Curtis Hanson | With Kevin Spacey, Russell Crowe, Guy Pearce, Kim Basinger | 138 minutes | Rated R

"Every nuance is perfect" in this "steamy" period crime drama, an "explosive exposé" about "crooks, hookers" and "police corruption" in '50s LA that's "sharp", "detailed" and "violent as hell"; though it "made a star of Crowe", the overall "dead-on casting" advances the "case for an ensemble acting award", while the "smart", Oscar-winning script has "all the grit" of a "film noir" classic, boosted by "21st-century production values."

La Dolce Vita ◑ F 25 | 25 | 23 | 25

1961 | Directed by Federico Fellini | With Marcello Mastroianni, Anita Ekberg, Anouk Aimée | 167 minutes | Not Rated

"Celebrity-obsessed culture" goes under the microscope in this "scandalous" study of "decadence", "damnation and redemption" as seen in '60s Rome through the eyes of a jaded gossip columnist (Mastroianni "at his best") fed up with the "sweet life"; arguably "Fellini's most famous" film, it's a "decidedly unglamorous look at glamour" that "introduced the word 'paparazzi'" into the world lexicon; most iconic scene: "Ekberg in the Trevi Fountain."

	OVERALL	ACTING	STORY	PROD.
Lady and the Tramp	26	-	24	25

1955 | Directed by Wilfred Jackson, Hamilton Luske, Clyde Geronimi | Animated | 75 minutes | Rated G

Puppy love gets a "gorgeous vintage Disney" spin in this "cute" canine romance awash in "lush animation" and lensed in "beautiful" CinemaScope; doggy devotees adore its fetching characters, "endearing story" and "great songs" ("highlighted by Peggy Lee's" sultry rendition of 'He's a Tramp'), though the most unforgettable moment has to be its "famous spaghetti kiss."

	OVERALL	ACTING	STORY	PROD.
Lady Eve, The ◑	28	28	27	26

1941 | Directed by Preston Sturges | With Barbara Stanwyck, Henry Fonda, Charles Coburn | 97 minutes | Not Rated

"Steamy innuendo" and "wacky pratfalls" coexist in this "smart" Preston Sturges "romp" about a "scheming con artist" out to snare an "unsuspecting" "wealthy geek", aided by an "outstanding supporting cast" of "cardsharps"; a "sassy", "shameless" Stanwyck does "that sultry thing" so well that Fonda's "bumbling rube" "doesn't stand a chance" in this "slyly amusing" screwball comedy that many pronounce "perfect."

	OVERALL	ACTING	STORY	PROD.
Lady from Shanghai, The ◑	25	23	22	26

1948 | Directed by Orson Welles | With Orson Welles, Rita Hayworth, Everett Sloane | 87 minutes | Not Rated

"Another Orson Welles achievement", this "bravura" "B movie" is "completely enjoyable" for many, thanks to some memorable "standout scenes": the "shootout in the hall of mirrors", "Rita Hayworth speaking Chinese"; still, skeptics shrug the plot is a "confusing mess" that "looks like it's been cut to death."

	OVERALL	ACTING	STORY	PROD.
Lady Vanishes, The ◑	25	24	26	23

1938 | Directed by Alfred Hitchcock | With Margaret Lockwood, Michael Redgrave, Dame May Whitty | 97 minutes | Not Rated

A first-class ticket to "intrigue", this "crackerjack Hitchcock classic" finds the master at his "most fleet" and "fascinating", cooking up a "sublime combination" of the comic and the thrilling; its story of a strange disappearance on a train full of "memorable characters" is such "sheer entertainment" that even those who "know the ending" "never tire" of jumping back aboard.

	OVERALL	ACTING	STORY	PROD.
La Femme Nikita F	23	22	24	23

1991 | Directed by Luc Besson | With Anne Parillaud, Jean-Hugues Anglade, Jeanne Moreau | 115 minutes | Rated R

The "intelligent foreign film" gets a "violent jolt of adrenaline" in this "fast-paced" but "thought-provoking" "tough chick" flick about a punk junkie turned professional assassin; as the "kick-ass" lead, the "mesmerizing" Parillaud performs "spectacular stunts" that "hold your attention" so completely that it's more than "worth the effort to read the subtitles."

	OVERALL	ACTING	STORY	PROD.
Last Emperor, The ✉	26	24	25	28

1987 | Directed by Bernardo Bertolucci | With John Lone, Joan Chen, Peter O'Toole | 160 minutes | Rated PG-13

"Truly an epic, and a darned good one" at that, this "sweeping", "large-scale" bio tells the story of China's "final monarch" from his ascent to the throne at age three through war, occupation and "revolutionary

changes" in his kingdom; credit "lavish" sets, "spectacular scenery" and "outstanding" acting by Lone and O'Toole for its winning an impressive "nine Academy Awards"; P.S. several versions exist, but all are on the "long" side.

Last King of Scotland, The ✉ 25 | 29 | 24 | 25

2006 | Directed by Kevin Macdonald | With Forest Whitaker, James McAvoy, Kerry Washington, Gillian Anderson | 123 minutes | Rated R

"Perfectly capturing the charisma and paranoia" of Ugandan dictator Idi Amin, Whitaker's "transcendental", Oscar-winning performance is an "indelible achievement" that brings a "barbarous" chapter in African history to light; told from the perspective of a "fictionalized" doctor, it features several depictions of "gruesome" violence, including "one of the most horrific torture scenes ever."

Last Metro, The F 24 | 25 | 23 | 23

1981 | Directed by François Truffaut | With Catherine Deneuve, Gérard Depardieu, Jean Poiret | 131 minutes | Rated PG

"Love and loyalty" are the underlying themes of this "wistful" tale of a French theatrical troupe staging a play in Nazi-occupied Paris; it's "vintage Truffaut" with "beautiful" work from the "haunting" Deneuve, and might work best as a "double bill with *Day For Night*", the same director's "tribute to movies and movie folk."

Last of the Mohicans, The 22 | 22 | 22 | 25

1992 | Directed by Michael Mann | With Daniel Day-Lewis, Madeleine Stowe, Russell Means | 122 minutes | Rated R

For a "realistic portrayal of the French and Indian War", this "historical adventure set in the battle-torn American colonies" doesn't stint on the "barbarism", though it's tempered by "beautiful scenery" and an "incredible score"; "truly evil villains and larger-than-life heroes" make this "wonderful realization of James Fenimore Cooper's book" "top-notch filmmaking."

Last Picture Show, The ◑ 23 | 23 | 23 | 22

1971 | Directed by Peter Bogdanovich | With Timothy Bottoms, Jeff Bridges, Cybill Shepherd, Ben Johnson | 118 minutes | Rated R

This "gritty portrait of a small Texas town on the brink of extinction" is "stunningly realized" in Bogdanovich's "masterpiece" that captures the loss so well "you can practically hear the death rattle"; the "birthplace of many new stars", it features some mighty "raw performances" from its "marvelous ensemble", a "strong script" and ultra-"realistic production values"; in short, it's a "lovely" if "sad" tribute to "something intrinsically American."

La Strada ✉◑F 27 | 28 | 26 | 25

1956 | Directed by Federico Fellini | With Giulietta Masina, Anthony Quinn, Richard Basehart | 108 minutes | Not Rated

Set in a "traveling circus", Fellini's "parable of goodness thwarted by cruelty" pairs a "strongman who's all muscle and no heart" with a "peasant girl who's nothing but heart"; the "waiflike" Masina is "luminous" opposite a "surprisingly good" Quinn, and combined with "beautiful imagery" and "sad" "music that will stay with you", it's plain to see why this "masterwork" won the very first Best Foreign Film Oscar.

	OVERALL	ACTING	STORY	PROD.
Last Samurai, The	23	23	22	27

2003 | Directed by Edward Zwick | With Tom Cruise, Ken Watanabe, Tony Goldwyn | 154 minutes | Rated R

"*Shogun*" meets "*Dances with Wolves*" in this "rousing" epic, wherein a haunted, "drunken Civil War vet" goes to feudal Japan to fight the samurai and is instead taken hostage by their "honor and spirit"; while Cruise garners an equivocal appraisal ("bang-up job" vs. "doesn't cut it"), "Watanabe wildly outshines him" as the "noble, betrayed" samurai leader; despite "slow pacing" and way "too much blood", this "clash of cultures" still swells with "sweeping vistas", "beautiful cinematography" and "amazing fight scenes."

	OVERALL	ACTING	STORY	PROD.
Last Seduction, The	22	24	22	20

1994 | Directed by John Dahl | With Linda Fiorentino, Peter Berg, Bill Pullman | 110 minutes | Rated R

"Fiorentino sizzles" as a "bad"-to-the-bone "femme fatale" in this "deliciously wicked" neo-noir crime thriller about a "very sexy" gal who rips off her husband and takes cover with a love-struck doofus; sure, it's "low budget" and there may be more than a few "holes in the plot", but "man, what a ride!"

	OVERALL	ACTING	STORY	PROD.
Laura ◑	27	25	27	26

1944 | Directed by Otto Preminger | With Gene Tierney, Dana Andrews, Clifton Webb | 88 minutes | Not Rated

A "suspenseful, elegant whodunit with a twist" – the "detective falls in love with the murder victim" – this "chic" take on film noir provides plenty of "romantic goose bumps" owing to the simmering "chemistry" between the "brooding" Andrews and "exquisite" Tierney; throw in some "haunting music" and a "nicely paced" if somewhat "silly plot", and the result is "Preminger's best flick."

	OVERALL	ACTING	STORY	PROD.
Lavender Hill Mob, The ✉◑	25	26	23	22

1951 | Directed by Charles Crichton | With Alec Guinness, Stanley Holloway | 78 minutes | Not Rated

"Wittily whimsical", this British comic "gem" helped introduce Alec Guinness – an "actor's actor with the most expressive raised eyebrow in film" – to America; the caper-gone-awry story involving a milquetoast bank clerk who dreams up the "perfect crime" is "delightfully funny" thanks to its "wonderful" script.

	OVERALL	ACTING	STORY	PROD.
La Vie en Rose ✉F	25	28	23	25

2007 | Directed by Olivier Dahan | With Marion Cotillard, Sylvie Testud, Emmanuelle Seigner, Gérard Depardieu | 140 minutes | Rated PG-13

The "tumultuous life" of "tragic" French chanteuse Édith Piaf is revealed in this "engrossing" biopic that's rather "ironically titled" given "a rose whose life was all thorns"; while the "hard-to-follow" story unfolds via "constant flashbacks" and "confusing time shifts", Cotillard's "*magnifique*", Oscar-winning performance has "not a false note" and manages to "redefine the phrase 'soul music'" along the way.

	OVERALL	ACTING	STORY	PROD.
L'Avventura ◑F	24	23	22	25

1961 | Directed by Michelangelo Antonioni | With Gabriele Ferzetti, Monica Vitti, Lea Massari | 145 minutes | Not Rated

A real art-house "landmark" and one of "Antonioni's most accessible" films, this "minimalist masterwork" follows a jaded playboy as he

OVERALL	ACTING	STORY	PROD.

hunts for his missing mistress on a Mediterranean isle; its "stark visual and intellectual" values are hailed as "revolutionary", though literalists wading through the "ennui" come up "baffled and confused."

Lawrence of Arabia ✉ 29 | 28 | 27 | 29

1962 | Directed by David Lean | With Peter O'Toole, Omar Sharif, Alec Guinness | 222 minutes | Rated PG

The "biggest epic of them all", this bio of WWI British soldier T.E. Lawrence "sets the standard for large-scale filmmaking" with its "stunning" desert cinematography, "suspense by the duneful" and "stupendous cast", led by the "perfect" O'Toole; thanks to Lean's "painterly techniques", the "background is as consistently amazing as the foreground" in this "gold standard" of an Oscar magnet that "demands to be seen on the big screen."

Lenny ◑ 24 | 27 | 23 | 21

1974 | Directed by Bob Fosse | With Dustin Hoffman, Valerie Perrine | 111 minutes | Rated R

"Blue comic" Lenny Bruce gets the Bob Fosse scrutiny in this "ahead-of-its-time" biopic that's alternately "depressing and funny"; the amused applaud the "virtuoso" Hoffman, "excellent" Perrine ("who knew?") and "gritty" black-and-white cinematography that perfectly "captures the kind of seedy clubs" where the "self-destructive" comedian got his start.

Leopard, The F 25 | 27 | 24 | 27

1963 | Directed by Luchino Visconti | With Burt Lancaster, Claudia Cardinale, Alain Delon | 187 minutes | Rated PG

"Historical sweep", "stunning visuals" and "personal reverie" combine in this "magnificent period piece" from Luchino Visconti, a "sumptuous" epic set in 19th-century Italy detailing the rise of Garibaldi and subsequent "decline of the aristocracy"; despite a "sluggish pace" and mixed marks for Lancaster's title turn as an Italian prince, "awesome" production values and the finale's "lauded" ballroom sequence make this one a "must-see" for cineasts.

Letters from Iwo Jima F 27 | 27 | 26 | 28

2006 | Directed by Clint Eastwood | With Ken Watanabe, Kazunari Ninomiya, Tsuyoshi Ihara | 141 minutes | Rated R

The "incomparable" Eastwood "brilliantly" bookends *Flags of Our Fathers* with this "eloquent" foreign-language epic, dubbed "one of the best WWII films ever" for its "humane" and ultimately "heartbreaking" depiction of the Japanese during their "doomed" final days on Iwo Jima; with the "fabulous" Watanabe leading an "outstanding" cast through "beautifully filmed" but "gruesome" battle scenes, this "remarkable achievement" dares to suggest that "we are all the same."

Letter to Three Wives, A ✉◑ 24 | 23 | 25 | 23

1949 | Directed by Joseph L. Mankiewicz | With Jeanne Crain, Linda Darnell, Ann Sothern, Kirk Douglas | 103 minutes | Not Rated

Three "country-club-set" women stuck on a boat trip "have an entire day to figure out" which one of their husbands "will be leaving town with the local seductress" in this "golden oldie" chick flick that "really takes you back"; Mankiewicz's "solid" script and direction both nabbed Academy Awards, leading some to label it the "witty precursor" to his later Oscar-winner, *All About Eve*.

	OVERALL	ACTING	STORY	PROD.

Lifeboat ◑ 25 | 26 | 25 | 22

1944 | Directed by Alfred Hitchcock | With Tallulah Bankhead, William Bendix, Walter Slezak | 96 minutes | Not Rated

"Can a one-set movie hold your attention?": this "fascinating Hitchcock" war-era thriller does, providing "more drama per square inch", since the "entire picture takes place in a small lifeboat"; among the "bickering crew of castaways", Bankhead is "superb, dahling", but blink and you'll miss the director's "inspired" cameo.

Life Is Beautiful ✉ F 27 | 27 | 27 | 25

1998 | Directed by Roberto Benigni | With Roberto Benigni, Nicoletta Braschi | 118 minutes | Rated PG-13

Simultaneously "heart-wrenching" and "uplifting", this story about an Italian family's attempt to shelter their son from the Holocaust is a "bittersweet fable about the triumph of the human spirit"; Oscar-winner Benigni provides an "emotional roller-coaster ride" with some "inspired comedic" touches, and though some "uncomfortable" viewers suggest a "trivialization" of a very serious subject, most agree "if you don't shed a tear, you're not human."

Life of Brian 23 | 21 | 23 | 20

1979 | Directed by Terry Jones | With Monty Python | 94 minutes | Rated R

"Profane, sacrilegious and really funny", this "hysterical" "cult classic" about a Holy Land sad sack mistaken for the Messiah is "as bitingly original a spoof as has ever been made" and "probably one of God's favorites"; only "Monty Python at their finest" could "get away with" the final scene that "sends you off singing 'Always Look on the Bright Side of Life.'"

Like Water for Chocolate F 25 | 24 | 25 | 25

1993 | Directed by Alfonso Arau | With Lumi Cavazos, Marco Leonardi | 123 minutes | Rated R

"Ahh, food and sex" make a "lip-smacking" combination in this "mouthwatering" Mexican "foodie classic" that serves up an "eccentric" love story that's "as pleasing to the eye as it is to the palate"; "deliciously true to the novel", it offers "magical realism at its best" and, "like a warm dessert", leaves one feeling so "content and hopeful" that many show up for "another helping."

Lili ∅ 24 | 24 | 23 | 24

1953 | Directed by Charles Walters | With Leslie Caron, Mel Ferrer, Jean-Pierre Aumont | 81 minutes | Rated G

Walking a tightrope between "deep whimsy" and "endearing" drama, this ringside look at an "innocent" orphan follows "ultimate waif" Caron as she joins the circus; enlivened by "one song" and some occasional dancing, the story is almost "too cute", but an "outstanding" cast ensures it will "turn on the tears every time."

Lilies of the Field ✉◑ 25 | 26 | 24 | 23

1963 | Directed by Ralph Nelson | With Sidney Poitier, Lilia Skala, Stanley Adams | 94 minutes | Not Rated

With his "flawless" performance in this "quiet, simple" tale about a handyman who helps refugee nuns build a chapel, Poitier became the first African-American to win a lead-role Oscar and also helped "open up racial dialogue" in the Civil Rights era; the film's many admirers hail a "sweet story" told with "heart and charm" that delivers a "lesson in dignity and trust."

Lilo & Stitch 23 | - | 22 | 24

2002 | Directed by Chris Sanders, Dean DeBlois | Animated | 85 minutes | Rated PG

"Different from the usual Disney stuff", this "adorable" animated tale features a "spunky" orphaned Hawaiian girl who adopts a "lovable" blue 'dog' that turns out to be a space alien; it's a "heartwarming story" with "great life lessons" about "love", the "meaning of family" and "finding your place in the world", as well as "laughs from beginning to end" and an Elvis-infused soundtrack; "beautiful watercolor backdrops" give the film its "distinctive look."

Limelight ◑ 24 | 25 | 22 | 23

1952 | Directed by Charlie Chaplin | With Charlie Chaplin, Claire Bloom, Buster Keaton, Nigel Bruce | 137 minutes | Rated G

"Chaplin's last great film", this "poignant" look at a British ballerina and a music hall clown draws mixed responses; foes call it "dated corn" and protest its "overstated" "self-indulgence", but fans counter it's "sensitive" stuff, and certainly worth watching to see "two giants of the silent film era [Charlie and Buster Keaton] on-screen together."

Lion in Winter, The ✉ 28 | 29 | 27 | 26

1968 | Directed by Anthony Harvey | With Peter O'Toole, Katharine Hepburn | 134 minutes | Rated PG

Hepburn and O'Toole give "performances so brilliant your eyes will hurt" as "two titans battling each other and history" in this "intelligent, delicious" drama that reigns as "one of the best historical films ever made"; indeed, this "masterful" look at Henry II and Eleanor of Aquitaine (the original "dysfunctional royal family") is so "superb" that it earned Kate her third Oscar, as well as statuettes for its "sparkling" screenplay and score.

Lion King, The 25 | - | 25 | 27

1994 | Directed by Roger Allers, Rob Minkoff | Animated | 89 minutes | Rated G

Hakuna Matata!: this "crowning achievement" garners roars of approval as one of "Disney's best" thanks to its "breakthrough animation techniques", "toe-tapping" music and "exceptional voice characterizations by Matthew Broderick and Jeremy Irons"; though this "heartwarming" tale about an exiled lion cub (sort of the "same story as *Bambi*") is "touching" and often "comedic", the film has some bona fide "scary moments" and "may be too intense" for smaller fry.

Little Big Man 24 | 25 | 24 | 23

1970 | Directed by Arthur Penn | With Dustin Hoffman, Faye Dunaway, Chief Dan George | 147 minutes | Rated PG

A "rousing" Wild West "saga", this "memorable period piece" concerns a "Forrest Gump-like" character with a knack for popping up at "famous historical moments"; plaudits go to its "engrossing blend of humor and drama" and "great" performances by George and Hoffman ("truly the man of 1,000 faces") - indeed, it's "one of the best looks at Native Americans" ever portrayed in moviedom.

OVERALL | ACTING | STORY | PROD.

Little Caesar ◑

24 | 26 | 23 | 22

1931 | Directed by Mervyn LeRoy | With Edward G. Robinson, Douglas Fairbanks Jr., Glenda Farrell | 79 minutes | Not Rated

"Crime doesn't pay" in this "seminal" gangster flicker, a "fictionalized" version of the Al Capone story starring "true Hollywood tough guy" Robinson, who brings some "Greek tragedy" to the role of a "moiderous bum" on the way up ("Tony Soprano, eat your heart out"); it's a "gritty", "fast-paced" ride that's best remembered for its immortal last line: "mother of mercy, is this the end of Rico?"

Little Children

24 | 27 | 23 | 23

2006 | Directed by Todd Field | With Kate Winslet, Patrick Wilson, Jennifer Connelly, Jackie Earle Haley | 130 minutes | Rated R

"Brilliant" Winslet and "easy-on-the-eyes" Wilson play "desperate" stay-at-home parents consumed by "forbidden attraction" in this "*American Beauty*"-esque study of suburban "infidelity" and "discontent"; though a "pedophilia" subplot adds a decidedly "dark" touch, Haley's "standout" supporting turn as a "creepy sex offender you actually feel bad for" drives home the picture's "powerful message about the consequences of your actions."

Little Foxes, The ◑

26 | 28 | 26 | 25

1941 | Directed by William Wyler | With Bette Davis, Herbert Marshall, Teresa Wright, Dan Duryea | 116 minutes | Not Rated

All the "power" of Lillian Hellman's "bitter little" stage drama is apparent in this "excellent" film adaptation via William Wyler, a showcase for "Bette at her bitchy best" as the mercenary missus in a shifty Southern family; the sly scheming and deadly betrayal make for such a bang-up "lesson in acting" that many wonder "why don't they make movies like this anymore."

Little Mermaid, The

24 | - | 23 | 25

1989 | Directed by Ron Clements, John Musker | Animated | 82 minutes | Rated G

This "first of the great second wave of Disney classics" manages to "hold its own against *Cinderella* and *Snow White*", what with its delightful cartoon "critters", "witty dialogue" and "upbeat", Oscar-winning music that "made animation sing again"; sure, feminists discern a "sexist message" ("why does the woman have to change for the man?"), but in the end "how could you not love this adorable red-headed mermaid?"

Little Miss Sunshine ✉

24 | 26 | 24 | 23

2006 | Directed by Jonathan Dayton, Valerie Faris | With Abigail Breslin, Greg Kinnear, Steve Carell, Toni Collette, Alan Arkin | 101 minutes | Rated R

"Wackiness" abounds when a "totally dysfunctional family" hops aboard a sputtering Volkswagen van en route to a beauty pageant in this "hilarious" but "dark"-edged road-trip comedy that's akin to an "indie version of *National Lampoon's Vacation*"; harnessing the talents of a "fine" ensemble cast – Carell is "fabulous", Breslin a "real find" and Arkin a "foul-mouthed treasure" – it's topped off with a "memorable" dance sequence that will "leave you squirming in your seat."

	OVERALL	ACTING	STORY	PROD.
Little Princess, A	24	22	25	25

1995 | Directed by Alfonso Cuarón | With Liesel Matthews, Eleanor Bron | 97 minutes | Rated G

"Shirley Temple's version has nothing on" this "sumptuous", "perfectly played" family fable of a "pampered" boarding-school lass with "mystical" leanings who goes from "riches to rags and back" after her dragoon dad is declared dead during WWI; though it attracts less than the "attention it deserves", loyalists label it a "top-flight tearjerker."

	OVERALL	ACTING	STORY	PROD.
Lives of Others, The	28	28	28	27

2007 | Directed by Florian Henckel von Donnersmarck | With Ulrich Mühe, Martina Gedeck, Sebastian Koch | 137 minutes | Rated R

A "fascinating yet chilling" peek "behind the Iron Curtain", this "near-perfect" drama exhibits the "stifling of artistic expression" in "pre-glasnost" East Germany, a "real-life police state" where "Big Brother" is always "listening in"; winner of the Oscar for Best Foreign Language Film, it features a "universally excellent" cast and its "suspenseful" script, highlighting the "best and worst of humanity", "keeps you guessing until the last scene."

	OVERALL	ACTING	STORY	PROD.
Local Hero	26	24	26	23

1983 | Directed by Bill Forsyth | With Burt Lancaster, Peter Riegert, Peter Capaldi | 111 minutes | Rated PG

"The little people triumph over the money people" in this "understated but brilliant" comedy contrasting the differences between a "quaint Scottish town" and the "corporate world"; its "engaging characters", "quirky" storyline and Mark Knopfler's "great soundtrack" make for such "bighearted", "whimsical" fun that many argue it "deserves a larger following."

	OVERALL	ACTING	STORY	PROD.
Lock, Stock and Two Smoking Barrels	23	22	25	23

1999 | Directed by Guy Ritchie | With Jason Flemyng, Dexter Fletcher, Nick Moran | 105 minutes | Rated R

"First-time director" Ritchie does a "brilliant job co-opting every gangster flick cliché" in this "violent but riveting" thriller that's a "Cockney" take on "*Pulp Fiction*"; agreed, it's "hard to understand the accents", but the "acting, setting and soundtrack are dead-on" and "super plot surprises" abound; all in all, this "fun romp with guns" is "lean", mean and "wonderfully produced."

	OVERALL	ACTING	STORY	PROD.
Lolita ◑	24	24	24	23

1962 | Directed by Stanley Kubrick | With James Mason, Sue Lyon, Shelley Winters, Peter Sellers | 152 minutes | Not Rated

Though this "fine adaptation of the Nabokov classic" might be somewhat "sanitized" ("it was made in 1962, after all"), it's still "slyly dirty" enough for its very adult subject, a middle-aged man's obsession with a barely teenaged girl; though ageists argue Lyon is "too old" for the title role, there still are plenty of "choice moments" supplied by an "extremely funny" Sellers and Winters, who "gives the performance of her life."

	OVERALL	ACTING	STORY	PROD.
Lone Star	25	25	25	22

1996 | Directed by John Sayles | With Kris Kristofferson, Matthew McConaughey, Chris Cooper | 135 minutes | Rated R

Director Sayles' "overlooked masterpiece" is a "flawless murder mystery that digs deep into the American psyche" and "takes a hard

	OVERALL	ACTING	STORY	PROD.

look at race relations"; following the discovery of a buried skeleton in a small Texas town, the plot goes through "more twists and turns than the Rio Grande" but still "works on multiple levels" as it "seamlessly interweaves multiple characters" – and that "ending will make your jaw drop."

Longest Day, The ◑ 24 | 20 | 25 | 26

1962 | Directed by Ken Annakin, Andrew Marton et al | With John Wayne, Rod Steiger | 180 minutes | Rated G

As far as "war-as-spectacle" epics go, this "sweeping" saga of the Normandy invasion sets the "standard by which all others are measured"; D-day devotees dig the "superb dedication to detail" and "all-star cast" that "really gets into their characters" thanks to a script that "includes the point of view of everyone involved"; still, foes snipe "too many cameos" turn it into a "cattle call."

Longtime Companion 23 | 25 | 25 | 21

1990 | Directed by Norman René | With Campbell Scott, Mary-Louise Parker, Bruce Davison | 100 minutes | Rated R

"Love and heartbreak" are the themes of this "groundbreaking" film that follows seven gay men throughout a "specific time and place": '80s Manhattan during the "first wave of AIDS"; "just as devastating today as when first released", it "gives legitimacy" to a former "forbidden subject" but "doesn't pander or trivialize the issues" thanks to the "heartfelt performances", notably the "standout" Davison and "up-and-coming" Parker.

Lord of the Flies ◑ 23 | 21 | 25 | 20

1963 | Directed by Peter Brook | With James Aubrey, Tom Chapin, Hugh Edwards | 90 minutes | Not Rated

The last word in youth gone wild, this "powerful" take on novelist William Golding's "modern classic" finds a pack of marooned British schoolboys slipping into "disturbing" behavior as barbarity overtakes breeding; the "realistic" style makes for an "unsettling" drama with bonus "social commentary buried within", though some savage the "incompetent acting" and sniff "read the book instead."

Lord of the Rings: The Fellowship of the Ring 27 | 25 | 27 | 29

2001 | Directed by Peter Jackson | With Elijah Wood, Ian McKellen, Viggo Mortensen, Sean Astin, Liv Tyler | 178 minutes | Rated PG-13

This "enthralling", "true-to-the-book" retelling of Tolkien's classic epic "transcends the genre" and "sets the benchmark for fantasy films to come" with its "lovingly crafted" visualization of Middle Earth; despite a somewhat "slow beginning", "three hours of brilliant bliss" ensue that are "exhilaratingly" perfect, "right down to the hairy Hobbit feet."

Lord of the Rings: The Return of the King ✉ 28 | 26 | 27 | 29

2003 | Directed by Peter Jackson | With Elijah Wood, Ian McKellen, Viggo Mortensen, Sean Astin, Liv Tyler | 201 minutes | Rated PG-13

Jackson "should be knighted" for this "history-making", Oscar-grabbing finale to the "superlative trilogy", a "paean to the goodness of good"

OVERALL	ACTING	STORY	PROD.

in the Fellowship's "united allegiance against evil"; it "lives up to the hoopla" from its two "faithfully rendered" predecessors thanks to "mythic sweep and grandeur" and a "cast obviously devoted to the picture"; in sum, this "masterpiece" is a "cinematic monument" to Tolkien's original fantasy, capped by a "long ending" that nonetheless draws a "big round of applause."

Lord of the Rings: The Two Towers 27 | 25 | 26 | 29

2002 | Directed by Peter Jackson | With Elijah Wood, Ian McKellen, Viggo Mortensen, Sean Astin, Liv Tyler | 179 minutes | Rated PG-13

There's "much less exposition" and much "more testosterone" in the second "gripping" installment of the Tolkien trilogy, which "starts right where the last one ended"; grab a "comfortable chair" and brace yourself for three hours of "flawless special effects" ("Gollum rocks"), "wonderful" acting by "hot guys", "epic battles the likes of which have never before been captured on celluloid" and an "amazing storyline" that really "does justice" to the book.

Lost Horizon ◑ 25 | 24 | 26 | 22

1937 | Directed by Frank Capra | With Ronald Colman, Jane Wyatt, Margo, Sam Jaffe | 138 minutes | Not Rated

A "nostalgic reminder of Hollywood's Golden Age", this "moving" adaptation of James Hilton's best-seller still "casts a spell" thanks to an "irresistible" conceit, the utopia known as "Shangri-la"; sure, this "fairy tale" of a picture may seem rather "quaint" and "dated" now, but Colman's performance is "as contemporary as if it were made today."

Lost Weekend, The 🖂◑ 25 | 27 | 24 | 22

1945 | Directed by Billy Wilder | With Ray Milland, Jane Wyman, Phillip Terry | 101 minutes | Not Rated

"Strong" stuff served neat, this "smart", sobering drama depicts the "terrifying inner world" of an alcoholic who "lives only" for the bottle, starring Milland in a "top-shelf", Oscar-winning turn as a barfly on a bender careening from double bourbons to detox to the d.t.'s; some maintain it "should be required viewing" at AA meetings – it's the "scariest movie of all time if you drink."

Love in the Afternoon ◑ 24 | 25 | 21 | 22

1957 | Directed by Billy Wilder | With Gary Cooper, Audrey Hepburn, Maurice Chevalier | 130 minutes | Not Rated

An "old-fashioned" romance set in "misty" Paree, this "witty" Wilder "treat" stars Coop as an "American playboy" who goes "mad with desire" for the much-younger Hepburn; if the "age difference" between the "odd couple" might seem "unspannable", the "bright cast" shows lots of "chemistry" – "isn't love grand?"

Love Is a Many-Splendored Thing 22 | 23 | 22 | 21

1955 | Directed by Henry King | With Jennifer Jones, William Holden | 102 minutes | Not Rated

"What drama! what heartbreak!" sigh admirers of this "classic" romantic "tearjerker", an "ahead-of-its-time" tale about an affair between a "liberated" Eurasian woman and a conflicted American war correspondent; ok, it's a little "soppy" and "Jones isn't believable as a Eurasian", but the "breathtaking" Hong Kong scenery and "memorable", Oscar-winning theme song "make the whole thing worth it."

	OVERALL	ACTING	STORY	PROD.
Lust for Life	23	25	23	23

1956 | Directed by Vincente Minnelli | With Kirk Douglas, Anthony Quinn, James Donald | 122 minutes | Rated PG

Kirk's "at his most tormented" as "revolutionary painter" Vincent van Gogh in this "powerful" biopic canvassing the "disturbed" Dutchman's "complex" life, along with his stormy friendship with Paul Gauguin (the Oscar-winning Quinn); a "colorful, vibrant" production filmed at many of the "original locations" where the master worked, it immortalizes a "genius" who was "never appreciated in his lifetime."

M ◑ F 26 | 26 | 26 | 23

1933 | Directed by Fritz Lang | With Peter Lorre, Ellen Widmann, Gustaf Gründgens | 99 minutes | Not Rated

Still "frightening seven decades later", this crime thriller features Lorre as a "nervous, sweaty little child killer" in a "riveting" performance that evokes "horror and pity at the same time"; set in "'30s Berlin" "plunging headlong into fascism", it's known for its "expressionistic" camerawork and montage sequences that "set the benchmark for film editing."

Magnificent Ambersons, The ◑ ∅ 25 | 26 | 22 | 24

1942 | Directed by Orson Welles | With Joseph Cotten, Dolores Costello, Anne Baxter, Agnes Moorehead | 88 minutes | Not Rated

"In the shadow of *Citizen Kane*" stands Welles' "visually brilliant" but oft-"overlooked" follow-up, this "turn-of-the-century" drama detailing the "downfall of an Indiana family" whose spoiled scion can't "keep up with the times"; some magnificence is lost due to the "damage done by the studio's re-editing", but admirers say this "90% masterpiece" is still "brilliant filmmaking."

Magnificent Seven, The 26 | 22 | 25 | 23

1960 | Directed by John Sturges | With Yul Brynner, Steve McQueen, Eli Wallach, Charles Bronson | 128 minutes | Not Rated

"Gunfighter cool" is alive and well in this "magnificent remake" of *The Seven Samurai* that "stands on its own" despite being "translated into a Western" and cast with "big stars of the '60s"; those who "never tire of watching it" "enjoy the adventure", "love the score" and attempt to "memorize the dialogue."

Malcolm X 23 | 26 | 23 | 23

1992 | Directed by Spike Lee | With Denzel Washington, Angela Bassett, Al Freeman Jr. | 194 minutes | Rated PG-13

In this "galvanizing" bio, the "transformation" of Malcolm X from "young hustler" to "outspoken" Civil Rights leader is portrayed by an "emotional" Washington in such a "bravura", "sympathetic" way that many say he was "robbed of an Oscar"; still, this "profound" film is a "time capsule of black American style" that resolutely "captivates and educates."

Maltese Falcon, The ◑ 28 | 27 | 27 | 25

1941 | Directed by John Huston | With Humphrey Bogart, Mary Astor, Peter Lorre | 101 minutes | Not Rated

The "stuff movies should be made of", this "vintage noir gem" boasts an "unforgettable Bogie" as the "hard-boiled detective" Sam Spade, plus a "blue-ribbon" supporting cast of "creeps and crooks", all searching for a mysterious "rara avis"; although its "taut script" that "runs like a Swiss watch" and "keeps you guessing to the end" is "often imitated", this "perfect rendering" of Dashiell Hammett's novel has been "never duplicated."

Man and a Woman, A ✉ F — 24 | 24 | 24 | 24

1966 | Directed by Claude Lelouch | With Anouk Aimée, Jean-Louis Trintignant | 102 minutes | Not Rated

For "romance par excellence", this "touching", "very French" '60s "classic" is served with "panache" and is "still worth seeing" today – indeed, the "music alone can make you fall in love"; detailing an affair between a widow and widower, it stars a "beautiful Aimée" opposite "Trintignant at his best"; "see it with someone special" and you may produce your own little sequel.

Manchurian Candidate, The ◑ — 27 | 26 | 28 | 25

1962 | Directed by John Frankenheimer | With Frank Sinatra, Laurence Harvey, Angela Lansbury | 126 minutes | Rated PG-13

As "perfectly paranoid" "Cold War" filmmaking, this provocative "conspiracy thriller" about Korean War–era "brainwashing" still packs a "wallop" due to a "twist"-laden script and a "take-your-breath-away" ending; Sinatra and Harvey are "electrifying", but the real revelation is Lansbury as an "evil", solitaire-playing mommy.

Man for All Seasons, A ✉ — 28 | 28 | 27 | 27

1966 | Directed by Fred Zinnemann | With Paul Scofield, Wendy Hiller, Robert Shaw | 120 minutes | Rated G

"Riveting in a quiet way", this "literate" historical drama about the "conflict between conscience and convenience" between Henry VIII and Sir Thomas More garnered six Oscars, including Best Actor for the "magnificent Scofield"; a "rare film about integrity", "loyalty and betrayal", it serves as a "reminder of the days when the movies enlightened."

Manhattan ◑ — 26 | 24 | 23 | 24

1979 | Directed by Woody Allen | With Woody Allen, Diane Keaton, Michael Murphy, Mariel Hemingway | 96 minutes | Rated R

"Even NYers get all mushy" about Woody Allen's "love letter to the Big Apple" filmed in "fantastic black and white" and set to a thrilling "Gershwin soundtrack"; a romance laced with "angst", it appeals to those who like their "philosophy mixed with a little comedy" and is "more fully realized than *Annie Hall*"; in short, "it can be fun to be depressive."

Man Who Came to Dinner, The ◑ — 26 | 27 | 26 | 24

1942 | Directed by William Keighley | With Bette Davis, Ann Sheridan, Monty Woolley | 112 minutes | Not Rated

Fans of "smart, hilarious" comedy relish the "unforgettable feast" in this screen treatment of Kaufman and Hart's stage play à clef, with Woolley "stealing the movie" as a "pompous radio personality" who visits a Midwestern household and "won't go home" after becoming wheelchair-bound; mixing "acid wit" with "fast-paced" dialogue, it's a "not-to-be-missed" "scream" from the "old school."

Man Who Knew Too Much, The — 24 | 24 | 25 | 24

1956 | Directed by Alfred Hitchcock | With James Stewart, Doris Day, Brenda de Banzie | 120 minutes | Rated PG

A "Hitchcock remake of an earlier Hitchcock" thriller, this "more commercial" version plays up the "amazing ordinariness" of its "everyman" stars as they seek their kidnapped son; for most, it's "very exciting" – especially the "unbearably suspenseful" scene in Royal Albert Hall – though a few "could do without" Day's "cornball" rendition of 'Que Sera, Sera' (which still snagged a Best Song Oscar).

Man Who Shot Liberty Valance, The ◑ 25 | 24 | 25 | 23

1962 | Directed by John Ford | With John Wayne, James Stewart, Vera Miles, Lee Marvin, Edmond O'Brien | 123 minutes | Not Rated

The formidable Ford's "darkest Western" is illuminated by a "star-studded" cast featuring "all-time bad guy" Lee Marvin in his "finest performance", with "dynamic" backup from Wayne and Stewart; though a bit "claustrophobic" (it was filmed "mostly on Hollywood soundstages"), this is still "mythic" moviemaking that "works like a huge, sprawling novel"; biggest surprise: "Wayne loses the girl."

Man Who Would Be King, The 25 | 26 | 26 | 25

1975 | Directed by John Huston | With Sean Connery, Michael Caine, Christopher Plummer | 129 minutes | Rated PG

Based on Kipling's "epic of friendship and heroism", this "classic adaptation" is a "ripsnorting", "good-time adventure" chronicling the perils of a pair of "opportunistic" "British rogues" on a "grand lark" in 19th-century colonial India; the combination of "sweeping vistas", "incandescent chemistry" between Connery and Caine and a "haunting ending" make for a "buddy flick that rises way above the genre."

Man with the Golden Arm, The ◑ 24 | 26 | 25 | 22

1955 | Directed by Otto Preminger | With Frank Sinatra, Eleanor Parker, Kim Novak | 119 minutes | Not Rated

Proof that "Sinatra was as good an actor as he was a singer", this "grim" look at one man's "drug problem" stars an "excellent" (Oscar-nominated) Frankie as a professional card dealer/"recovering heroin addict" who falls into a "downward spiral" after being discharged from rehab; some users find it rather "dated", but most warn it's a "harrowing", "fasten-your-seatbelts" ride.

Marathon Man 24 | 27 | 24 | 22

1976 | Directed by John Schlesinger | With Dustin Hoffman, Laurence Olivier, Roy Scheider | 125 minutes | Rated R

"Just when you thought it was safe to go back to the dentist" comes this "nasty" little thriller about a "totally mad", "tooth-drilling" "Nazi on the loose" hell-bent on retrieving ill-gotten loot; the "huffing, puffing" Hoffman is "superlative" as a man "drawn into something way beyond his control", while set pieces like the "whining drill" scene and the "diamond-swallowing" finale raise enough "goose bumps" to make most "swear off checkups for life."

Maria Full of Grace F 25 | 26 | 25 | 22

2004 | Directed by Joshua Marston | With Catalina Sandino Moreno, Yenny Paola Vega | 101 minutes | Rated R

The "horrific plight" of women desperate to "wean themselves from poverty" by becoming "pawns in the drug trade" is the "untold story" brought to light by this "raw", "impactful" indie; newcomer Moreno shows she's "full of talent" in the role of a Colombian cocaine mule, and while her near-"suicidal" mission "puts you through a wringer", it's worth it for the film's "unbleached message of hope."

	OVERALL	ACTING	STORY	PROD.

Mark of Zorro, The ◑

22	19	22	19

1940 | Directed by Rouben Mamoulian | With Tyrone Power, Linda Darnell, Basil Rathbone | 94 minutes | Not Rated

This "rousing adventure" tale of "double identity and romance" has "hardly dated" thanks to the "dashing", buckle-swashing Power's "sexy swordfighting"; "lady-in-distress" Darnell is "unbelievably lovely", "fop" Rathbone "as dastardly as ever" and a "marvelous" Alfred Newman score provides the cinematic coup de grace.

Marriage of Maria Braun, The F

25	25	24	23

1979 | Directed by Rainer Werner Fassbinder | With Hanna Schygulla, Klaus Löwitsch, Ivan Desny | 120 minutes | Rated R

This "scathing portrait" of "survival in postwar Germany" traces its gritty heroine's determined climb up the economic ladder with some "bitingly funny" scenes that demonstrate "you can't bury the past", no matter how hard you try to disguise it; "extraordinary" work from director Fassbinder and the "brilliant" Schygulla make up for that "letdown of an ending."

Marty ✉◑

25	27	24	21

1955 | Directed by Delbert Mann | With Ernest Borgnine, Betsy Blair, Esther Minciotti | 91 minutes | Not Rated

Ok, the story of a "sloppy butcher" who finds love with a "mousy clerk" might "never play", but this "poignant" Paddy Chayefsky drama proved naysayers wrong, garnering four Oscars (including Best Actor for Borgnine, who's "perfect" as an ordinary Brooklyn schmo); shot in black and white, its "realistic style" "never gets old" – but be prepared for a feeling of "hopelessness" throughout.

Mary Poppins ✉

27	24	25	27

1964 | Directed by Robert Stevenson | With Julie Andrews, Dick Van Dyke, David Tomlinson | 140 minutes | Rated G

Mix a "perky" Andrews (as an "odd" nanny with "magical powers") with a "cheeky" Van Dyke, "fantastic animation" and "catchy tunes", add a "spoonful of sugar" and the result is a "super-duper" Disney "treat"; a "technical marvel of its time", this "jolly" production "makes you feel good at any age" and serves as a dandy "introduction to musicals for kids."

MASH ✉

26	25	26	24

1970 | Directed by Robert Altman | With Donald Sutherland, Elliott Gould, Sally Kellerman | 116 minutes | Rated PG

"War is hell (and funny)" in this "groundbreaking" "black" satire about a dysfunctional Korean War medical unit that still "holds up" as "one of the smartest comedies ever written" – "once you get past all the blood", that is; maybe the "last third" goes "downhill" during the "lame" football game, but there's no doubt this is "Altman's breakthrough."

Master and Commander: The Far Side of the World

23	24	22	27

2003 | Directed by Peter Weir | With Russell Crowe, Paul Bettany | 138 minutes | Rated PG-13

For "textbook adventure filmmaking" sailing over the "bounding main", set your sights on this "visually extraordinary" nautical epic depicting "cat-and-mouse" high-sea games during the Napoleonic War;

the all-male cast includes the "great-as-usual" Crowe backed up by a "strong" Bettany, but despite "incredible battle scenes", "magnificent storms" and "stellar" special effects, mutineers say the "thin" storyline and "endless frigate jargon" simply "don't hold water"; other seafarers, however, "look forward to another installment."

Matrix, The 25 | 19 | 25 | 28

1999 | Directed by Andy Wachowski, Larry Wachowski | With Keanu Reeves, Laurence Fishburne, Carrie-Anne Moss | 136 minutes | Rated R

"Move over, *Star Wars*"; not even Reeves' "leaden" acting can sink this "mind-bending, reality-rocking" "new modern myth" of a movie that "raised the bar on special effects" and "revolutionized hand-to-hand combat in filmmaking"; even if its "intricate" plot (something about a computer hacker turned "humanity's last hope") verges on "incoherence", this "sci-fi shoot-'em-up for people with brains" just "gets better every time you see it."

McCabe & Mrs. Miller 23 | 23 | 23 | 24

1971 | Directed by Robert Altman | With Warren Beatty, Julie Christie, Shelley Duvall | 120 minutes | Rated R

Decidedly "not for conventional Western" fans, this "brilliantly directed", "postmodern deconstruction" of the genre "eliminates the clichés" and "faithfully re-creates what the West was really like": namely, "harsh, cruel and lacking true heroes"; despite one major drawback – "you can't understand what anyone is saying" – it's more than evident that the leads are "impossibly in love."

Meaning of Life, The 24 | 22 | 20 | 20

1983 | Directed by Terry Jones, Terry Gilliam | With Monty Python | 107 minutes | Rated R

"Lunacy abounds" in this "wonderfully outrageous" Monty Python flick rolling "music, comedy and philosophy" vignettes that attempt to answer life's big questions into one "screamingly funny" (if sometimes "retch-covered") package; marking the British troupe's "last spurt" of cinematic collaboration, it suffers the occasional "second-rate" segment but endures as a "classic" that "shines in comparison to what else is out there."

Mean Streets 24 | 27 | 23 | 22

1973 | Directed by Martin Scorsese | With Harvey Keitel, Robert De Niro | 110 minutes | Rated R

"Gritty and graphic before that became the norm", Scorsese's breakout drama of hoods in the 'hood "rings with truth" as a "definitive slice of NY", with Keitel out to "make it in the mob" in spite of "Catholic guilt" and ties to De Niro's "unforgettable" loose-cannon "loser"; it's a "grim" but "passionate" study of streetwise style, including some "pioneering" use of "oldies but goodies" on the soundtrack.

Meet John Doe ◑ 24 | 26 | 23 | 22

1941 | Directed by Frank Capra | With Gary Cooper, Barbara Stanwyck, Edward Arnold, Walter Brennan | 123 minutes | Not Rated

Cooper and Stanwyck are a "joy to watch" in this "classic" Capra fanfare for the "common man" that mixes some "social commentary" into its tale of an "honest" hobo who's recruited by a newspaper to "threaten suicide" in the name of America's "lost ideals" – and ends up capturing the nation's "attention and hearts"; despite the film's "heroic" intentions, "politics are still corrupt", but the "warm, fuzzy dream" that "things can be better" never looked so "convincing."

Meet Me in St. Louis

26 | 24 | 23 | 26

1944 | Directed by Vincente Minnelli | With Judy Garland, Margaret O'Brien, Mary Astor | 113 minutes | Not Rated

Clang, clang, clang, here comes Garland "at her radiant finest" as a girl who "adores the boy next door" in this musical "treasure" about a "turn-of-the-century" American family; fans laud its "sumptuous" Technicolor production and "unforgettable" tunes, while brainiacs hint it's "darker and deeper than its rep suggests."

Member of the Wedding, The ◑

25 | 27 | 26 | 25

1952 | Directed by Fred Zinnemann | With Ethel Waters, Julie Harris, Brandon De Wilde | 93 minutes | Not Rated

"One of the most touching films ever", this "sweet" slice of Americana adapted from (and "capturing the essence" of) Carson McCullers' play delineates a Southern household's "moving dynamic" between an alienated youngster, her black housekeeper and her soon-to-be-married brother; fans sing the praises of its "remarkable" cast, singling out the "soaring" Harris and the "remarkable" Waters, whose on-screen rendition of the hymn 'His Eye Is on the Sparrow' is "thankfully preserved forever."

Memento

26 | 25 | 27 | 25

2000 | Directed by Christopher Nolan | With Guy Pearce, Carrie-Anne Moss | 113 minutes | Rated R

"Bring your brain to the theater, you'll need it" for this "exquisitely existential" "mind-bender" about a man who loses his "short-term memory" following his wife's murder; it "turns traditional narrative on its head" by telling the story "in reverse" – so it may "require several viewings to get it all straight"; though there's applause for the "stunning" Pearce, befuddled folks "still trying to figure it out" wail it's too "gnisufnoc."

Metropolis ◑

27 | 22 | 24 | 28

1927 | Directed by Fritz Lang | With Alfred Abel, Gustav Froelich, Brigitte Helm | 153 minutes | Not Rated

A "visionary" film of "magnitude, imagination and depth", this "sci-fi social commentary" about "oppression and uprising" set in a "futuristic city" "still retains its visual impact" seven decades later; indeed, Lang's "man-versus-machine" story (embodied by a "fetishized woman robot") remains "revolutionary in every sense of the word" – this is a "movie everybody should watch at least once."

Michael Clayton

24 | 26 | 23 | 23

2007 | Directed by Tony Gilroy | With George Clooney, Tom Wilkinson, Tilda Swinton, Sydney Pollack | 119 minutes | Rated R

Clooney's "at his smoothest" playing a "law firm fixer" who's "expert at cleaning up messes" in this "thinking person's" legal thriller delineating the "world of corporate greed" and the extreme lengths taken to "kill a class-action lawsuit"; Swinton's Oscar-winning turn as an "ice queen" chief counsel is as "intense" as the rest of this "tight", "complex" film, but "pay close attention" – you "might not understand it all on the first viewing."

	OVERALL	ACTING	STORY	PROD.

Midnight Cowboy ✉

26	28	24	24

1969 | Directed by John Schlesinger | With Dustin Hoffman, Jon Voight, Sylvia Miles | 113 minutes | Rated R

"Still as gritty as ever", this "unvarnished look at NYC street life" is a "touching" if "depressing" depiction of a pair of "down-and-out" losers "spiraling downward" that turns the "buddy-flick concept" on its ear; the first "X-rated" film to take Best Picture honors (and since re-rated), it continues to wow with "inner beauty", "haunting music" and "brilliant" turns from Hoffman and Voight – and that "ending on the bus is unforgettable."

Midnight Express ✉

24	24	25	22

1978 | Directed by Alan Parker | With Brad Davis, Randy Quaid, John Hurt | 120 minutes | Rated R

This "frighteningly realistic" drama about a not-so-innocent American abroad imprisoned for smuggling hash "should be required viewing for teens and travelers", even though this "eye-opener" might "induce nightmares for years to come"; it probably "did more to stop kids from doing drugs" than all of "Nancy Reagan's efforts" combined.

Midnight Run

23	25	23	21

1988 | Directed by Martin Brest | With Robert De Niro, Charles Grodin, Yaphet Kotto | 126 minutes | Rated R

For a "quintessential" buddy flick, try this "wild", "witty" action comedy about a "white-collar crook" and the bounty hunter who "tries to bring him in alive" that runs strong on the "great chemistry" of "old pros" De Niro and Grodin, the "funniest odd couple since Oscar and Felix"; add in some "quirky" supporting players (a "fleet of FBI agents", "inept mobsters" and other "eccentrics"), and there's "never a dull moment."

Mighty Wind, A

23	26	21	23

2003 | Directed by Christopher Guest | With Bob Balaban, Christopher Guest, John Michael Higgins, Eugene Levy | 91 minutes | Rated PG-13

"You'll have almost as much fun as the cast" watching this "hysterical mockumentary" about the "'60s folk music scene" full of "priceless material", a "hilarious cast of characters" and "lots of hidden humor"; while "not as good as *Best in Show*", "anything by Guest is better than most everyone else's work."

Mildred Pierce ✉◑

26	25	25	24

1945 | Directed by Michael Curtiz | With Joan Crawford, Jack Carson, Ann Blyth, Eve Arden, Zachary Scott | 111 minutes | Not Rated

Oscar-winner Crawford is in "full weeper bloom" (with "shoulder pads for days" and "star lighting to make sure you get the point") in this noir "sudser" based on the James M. Cain novel about a "mother who sacrifices everything for her daughter"; "camp" followers crack up over Arden's "witty repartee" (which "would put any drag queen to shame") and "rent it as a double feature with *Mommie Dearest* for full impact."

Milk ✉

25	28	25	24

2008 | Directed by Gus Van Sant | With Sean Penn, James Franco, Emile Hirsch, Josh Brolin | 128 minutes | Rated R

An "important part of American history is brought to life" in this "moving" biopic about "gay rights activist" Harvey Milk, whose "charisma" and uncommon "courage" in the face of "bigotry" "broke barriers" in '70s San Francisco and beyond; Penn's Oscar-grabbing title turn pays "powerful" tribute to the "trailblazing" advocate for "equal rights", and despite the story's "tragic" end, it's still "inspirational."

Million Dollar Baby ✉ 27 | 28 | 25 | 26

2004 | Directed by Clint Eastwood | With Clint Eastwood, Hilary Swank, Morgan Freeman | 132 minutes | Rated PG-13

What begins as a boxing "Cinderella story" about a "guilt-racked coach" mentoring a "determined female fighter" takes a "sharp turn" and becomes a "profound" meditation on "significant moral dilemmas" in this "knockout" Oscar magnet from "powerhouse" actor/director Eastwood; a "flawless Swank" and "quietly brilliant" Freeman round out the cast in this "simple", "less-is-more" production, with a "surprise" ending that "leaves you breathless."

Miracle 24 | 23 | 26 | 24

2004 | Directed by Gavin O'Connor | With Kurt Russell, Patricia Clarkson | 135 minutes | Rated PG

Although most already "know the ending", this "feel-good" "insider's look" at the U.S. hockey team's quest for gold at the 1980 Olympics keeps athletic supporters "riveted" with its taut "they-shoot-they-score" script; indeed, Kurt's "commanding performance" and the "realistic moments on and off the ice" keep its "inspirational" themes resonating long afterwards – "way to go, team."

Miracle of Morgan's Creek, The ◑ 23 | 22 | 25 | 21

1944 | Directed by Preston Sturges | With Eddie Bracken, Betty Hutton, William Demarest | 99 minutes | Not Rated

From the "fabulous" Preston Sturges comes this "raucous farce" starring Betty Hutton as Trudy Kockenlocker, an "unwed mother-to-be who can't remember who the father is" ("they're still debating how the story got past the Hollywood production code"); admirers say this "crackerjack comedy" is all about the "tremendous dialogue" and only "grows richer with age" – capped by an "ending that should be enshrined in the Movie Hall of Fame."

Miracle on 34th Street ✉◑ 25 | 23 | 26 | 23

1947 | Directed by George Seaton | With Maureen O'Hara, Natalie Wood, Edmund Gwenn | 96 minutes | Not Rated

It "can't be Christmas" without a screening of this "schmaltzy", "charming fantasy" that embodies a "child's belief in Santa Claus" so well that it's become an enduring "seasonal favorite" for "every generation"; true believers say the Oscar-winning screenplay is the key behind this "perfect" "holiday classic" that puts the remakes to shame.

Miracle Worker, The ✉◑ 25 | 28 | 24 | 22

1962 | Directed by Arthur Penn | With Anne Bancroft, Patty Duke, Victor Jory, Inga Swenson | 106 minutes | Not Rated

"Beautifully transferred from stage to screen" by director Penn, this "moving" account of deaf-and-blind Helen Keller and her teacher Annie Sullivan garnered Oscars for both leads (who reprised their Broadway roles); while Duke is undeniably "superb", it's Bancroft who "dominates" this "fiercely acted", "exceptional" film; most memorable moment: at the water pump.

	OVERALL	ACTING	STORY	PROD.

Missing ✉ 24 | 26 | 25 | 22

1982 | Directed by Costa-Gavras | With Jack Lemmon, Sissy Spacek, John Shea | 122 minutes | Rated PG

Based on "actual events in South America", this fictionalized account of a U.S.-sanctioned military coup and its bloody aftermath is a "riveting" yet "moving" political thriller with a "devastating" message: "governments lie"; given "strong" performances by Lemmon and Spacek that "save it from being too preachy", many wonder why this Best Picture nominee is so "unheralded" and "overlooked" 25 years later.

Mission, The 24 | 24 | 22 | 25

1986 | Directed by Roland Joffé | With Robert De Niro, Jeremy Irons, Liam Neeson | 126 minutes | Rated PG

"Beautifully shot", Oscar-winning cinematography nearly steals the show in this "intriguing drama" about an 18th-century struggle between missionaries and mercenaries over the riches of South America; even though evangelist Irons and reformed slave trader De Niro turn out their usual "amazing" work, unfazed foes feel Ennio Morricone's "soundtrack is far better" than the picture itself.

Mississippi Burning 23 | 24 | 23 | 22

1988 | Directed by Alan Parker | With Gene Hackman, Willem Dafoe, Frances McDormand | 128 minutes | Rated R

A "story that needed to be told", this "powerful" depiction of '60s "racial unrest" focuses on an investigation of the murder of three Civil Rights workers; yet despite an "all-too-real glimpse of life in the Deep South", critics say it overemphasizes "white hate" to the point that there are few "speaking parts for black actors."

Mister Roberts 27 | 27 | 24 | 23

1955 | Directed by John Ford, Mervyn LeRoy | With Henry Fonda, James Cagney, Jack Lemmon | 123 minutes | Not Rated

A Broadway hit transposed to the big screen, this "heartfelt" story about the misadventures of a World War II supply ship crew delivers "wonderful acting all around", from the "unforgettable" Cagney to the "perfect" Fonda and "no-slouch" Lemmon; a "great wartime comedy with a serious side", it leaves even tough guys with a "lump in their throat."

Modern Times ◑ 28 | 26 | 26 | 25

1936 | Directed by Charlie Chaplin | With Charlie Chaplin, Paulette Goddard | 87 minutes | Not Rated

"Timelessly funny and resonant", this "man-vs.-machine" story runs on a "blend of slapstick and pathos" guaranteed to make you "smile . . . though your heart is breaking"; there's "little dialogue" (save for Chaplin's "singing waiter" "gibberish number"), but his "heartwarming" performance and sharp "swipes at the age of technology" transcend words; in short, this one's a "must-see in *these* times."

Monkey Business ◑ 26 | 24 | 21 | 22

1931 | Directed by Norman Z. McLeod | With the Marx Brothers, Thelma Todd | 77 minutes | Not Rated

This "early" Marx Brothers' "Hollywood vehicle" is both "solidly entertaining" and "suitably anarchic" as the sibs stow away on a luxury liner and much "hilarious" "shipboard mayhem" ensues; though maybe "not quite their best" work, this "could be their looniest" of all – especially Harpo's "Punch and Judy" riff.

26 | 25 | 22 | 23

Mon Oncle ✉ F

1958 | Directed by Jacques Tati | With Jacques Tati, Jean-Pierre Zola | 110 minutes | Not Rated

A trove of "very French" folly to "tickle your brain" and "set you giggling", this "delightful" comedy has Tati reprising his "sad-sack" Hulot act as he "bumbles through life" in a series of "superb gags and set pieces"; his "everyman-as-a-buffoon" shtick is a trusty "chuckle producer", while the underlying "commentary on modernity gone awry" is "really funny" too.

24 | 23 | 23 | 23

Monsoon Wedding F

2002 | Directed by Mira Nair | With Naseeruddin Shah, Lillete Dubey, Shefali Shetty, Vasundhara Das, Parvin Dabas | 114 minutes | Rated R

A "feast for the funny bone, eyes and mind", this "charming" dramedy about a "dysfunctional" Indian family and the wedding of their daughter "proves that all families are the same no matter the ethnicity"; it's "a bit slow", but the "colorful cinematography" and "fantastic music" will make you "want to see it again."

24 | 29 | 24 | 22

Monster ✉

2003 | Directed by Patty Jenkins | With Charlize Theron, Christina Ricci | 109 minutes | Rated R

"Frighteningly believable" and thus "tough to watch", this bio of serial murderess Aileen Wuornos "pushes all the emotional buttons" thanks to a "complete immersion" in the role by the Oscar-winning, "makeup"-slathered Theron (with ample backup from the "unsung" Ricci as her girlfriend); though "not as gruesome as it could have been", this "downer" does deliver enough imagery so "violent" that many vow to "never pick up a hitchhiker again."

26 | - | 25 | 28

Monsters, Inc.

2001 | Directed by Peter Docter, David Silverman, Lee Unkrich | Animated | 92 minutes | Rated G

"Pixar does it again" with this "innovative" "animation gem" that "shows kids that the monsters in their closets are really harmless"; this time around, the "*Toy Story*" tech team alloy an "original" plot, "amazing attention to detail" and "ugly" but "cute" characters to create an "endearing" entertainment that works "for adults" too; P.S. the "blow-you-away" "flying door" sequence has got "theme-park ride" written all over it.

26 | 22 | 23 | 21

Monty Python & the Holy Grail

1975 | Directed by Terry Gilliam, Terry Jones | With Monty Python | 91 minutes | Rated PG

By dint of "sheer tasteless genius", this "absurdly wacky" "burlesque of the King Arthur legend" turns "historic reverence" on its ear and rules among "true" Pythonettes as the "movie of a thousand quotes" ("bring out your dead!"); granted, it may be comprised of a series of "strung-together skits" involving "killer bunnies" and "knights who say 'ni'", but the array of "knee-slapping" characters provides enough "lunacy to last the ages."

	OVERALL	ACTING	STORY	PROD.

Moonstruck ✉ 24 | 25 | 24 | 22

1987 | Directed by Norman Jewison | With Cher, Nicolas Cage, Olympia Dukakis | 102 minutes | Rated PG

Both "Italians and wannabe Italians" fall for this "totally charming" "romp" that shows how "love can be found in the least likely places" – even Brooklyn; a "phenomenal" Cher and Cage (making *amore* at such "full throttle" that the "heat between them could peel wallpaper") combine with a "dead-on", "star-studded" ensemble to keep this "romance classic" shining bright; fave scene: the "snap-out-of-it" slap.

Motorcycle Diaries, The F 23 | 25 | 23 | 24

2004 | Directed by Walter Salles | With Gael García Bernal, Rodrigo de la Serna | 128 minutes | Rated R

Witness the "seeds of social conscience" sprouting in "young Che Guevara" in this "poetic" road picture set amid "breathtaking South American scenery"; "ogle"-icious Bernal's "marvelous" turn as the future "legendary figure" stokes the revolutionary fire despite hitting a raw nerve with a few *capitalistas* who claim this "saintly" depiction fosters too much "undeserved attention."

Moulin Rouge! 23 | 23 | 20 | 27

2001 | Directed by Baz Luhrmann | With Nicole Kidman, Ewan McGregor, Jim Broadbent | 127 minutes | Rated PG-13

This "dizzying, decadent" "fever dream of a musical" set in "bohemian Paris" earned a clutch of Oscar nominations and may have "single-handedly revived and re-created the genre" for the "new millennium"; the ever-"ravishing" Kidman "sheds her icy image" in a "kaleidoscopic" turn as a notorious "shady lady" smitten by a "naive poet", and it turns out "McGregor can sing", but naysayers call it a "confusing", "overedited" "mishmash" that's "all glitter, no substance."

Mouse That Roared, The 23 | 23 | 24 | 19

1959 | Directed by Jack Arnold | With Peter Sellers, Jean Seberg, David Kossoff | 83 minutes | Not Rated

"British humor has never been better" than in this "priceless" Cold War–era import about an impoverished nation that declares war on America, planning to lose in exchange for foreign aid; an "ingenious" satire that "pokes lots of holes" in a lot of targets, it's "worth seeing" for "Sellers' expert multiple performances alone."

Mr. Blandings Builds His Dream House ◑ 23 | 24 | 23 | 21

1948 | Directed by H.C. Potter | With Cary Grant, Myrna Loy, Melvyn Douglas | 94 minutes | Not Rated

"If you're thinking of building or remodeling your home", "there's no funnier movie" than this "timeless" "cautionary tale" that proves the "perils haven't changed in the last 50 years"; "fixer-uppers" laugh along with this amusing view of the "suburban dream gone askew", most notably "Myrna's painting-the-living-room" scene.

Mr. Deeds Goes to Town ✉◑ 25 | 26 | 24 | 23

1936 | Directed by Frank Capra | With Gary Cooper, Jean Arthur, George Bancroft, Lionel Stander | 115 minutes | Not Rated

With "all the heart and soul" (and "schmaltz") that you expect from director "Capra-corn", this "sweet" tale of a "pixilated" eccentric who inherits a fortune and then tries to give it away is one of the "great populist films" of the '30s; thanks to the "feel-good" mood, "heartwarming ending" and Cooper's "trademark underplaying", it's become a "standard."

Mr. Hulot's Holiday ◐ F
25 | 25 | 22 | 22

1954 | Directed by Jacques Tati | With Jacques Tati, Nathalie Pascaud | 86 minutes | Not Rated

Right "up there with Keaton and Chaplin", Tati's "irresistible" "comic masterpiece" is bound to "take away the worst blues" with some of the "best sight gags" delivered in "almost pure mime"; when its "hilariously" maladroit title character goes to a vacation retreat, whatever "could possibly go wrong does" and the payoff's a "quirky", "low-key" "laugh riot."

Mrs. Henderson Presents
23 | 27 | 22 | 23

2005 | Directed by Stephen Frears | With Judi Dench, Bob Hoskins, Kelly Reilly, Christopher Guest | 103 minutes | Rated R

"Dench didn't earn her reputation for nothing", as demonstrated by her "marvelous" performance in this British comedy about an "eccentric" theater owner whose "nude cuties" revue helps stiffen public resolve during WWII; co-star Hoskins is equally "wonderful" in support, and the pairing of "top-notch humor" with "poignant" meditations on "love and loss" strikes a "crowd-pleasing" balance.

Mrs. Miniver ✉ ◐
25 | 27 | 24 | 24

1942 | Directed by William Wyler | With Greer Garson, Walter Pidgeon, Teresa Wright | 134 minutes | Not Rated

For "WWII without the combat scenes", check out the "civilian side" in this "stirring" saga of Britain during the Blitz, starring Garson as a "stiff-upper-lipped" homemaker who stoically endures everything from "harrowing air raids" to "Nazi paratroopers" in the kitchen; while cynics say it seems "more propaganda than entertainment", the film was an Oscar magnet, taking home six statuettes, including Best Picture and Best Actress.

Mr. Smith Goes to Washington ◐
26 | 27 | 25 | 22

1939 | Directed by Frank Capra | With James Stewart, Jean Arthur, Claude Rains | 125 minutes | Not Rated

"As American as two slices of apple pie", Frank Capra's "rousing" "political fairy tale" about "one man's belief in goodness" and his eventual "triumph" "appeals to the idealist in each of us"; "corny", perhaps, but "you can't help but be moved" by Stewart waging the "filibuster to beat all filibusters" – and proving "you *can* beat City Hall."

Mulan
23 | - | 23 | 24

1998 | Directed by Tony Bancroft, Barry Cook | Animated | 88 minutes | Rated G

An "underrated" rarity, this "gorgeously realized" animated "Chinese folk tale" features a Disney heroine "who can carry a movie on her own"; its mix of "family honor" and "women power" make it "good for a girl's self-esteem", while "just the right balance of seriousness and humor" "sends its message without preaching."

Mummy, The ◐
24 | 20 | 22 | 23

1932 | Directed by Karl Freund | With Boris Karloff, Zita Johann | 72 minutes | Not Rated

Fresh out of his Frankenstein boots, "master" of fear Karloff wraps himself around the role of an ancient Egyptian priest who's revived when foolhardy explorers open his crypt in this "standout" horror flick; indeed, Boris is "so very creepy" that many say this "original" version of the oft-filmed tale is still the "best."

Munich 23 | 24 | 23 | 24

2005 | Directed by Steven Spielberg | With Eric Bana, Daniel Craig, Geoffrey Rush | 164 minutes | Rated R

The "spiritually corrosive effects of revenge" come under Steven Spielberg's "soul-searching" lens in this "provocative", "action-packed" thriller modeled on the "real events" that followed the 1972 "massacre of Israeli Olympic athletes" by Palestinian terrorists; treating the "very sensitive issue" of the Middle East conflict in a "balanced" manner, it suggests there are "no easy answers", frustrating foes who prefer a less "muddy" moral message.

Muppet Movie, The 24 | 23 | 23 | 25

1979 | Directed by James Frawley | With Charles Durning, Austin Pendleton | 97 minutes | Rated G

"You're never too old" to enjoy this "goofy" but "utterly delightful" romp that might unleash your "inner kid" thanks to some "wonderful puppetry" abetted by an array of star-studded cameos from everyone from Milton Berle to Steve Martin; fans say it's the "best" of the Muppet oeuvre, crediting the "genius" of "national treasure" Jim Henson.

Murder, My Sweet ◑ 24 | 24 | 24 | 22

1944 | Directed by Edward Dmytryk | With Dick Powell, Claire Trevor, Anne Shirley, Otto Kruger | 95 minutes | Not Rated

For "Dick Powell without Ruby Keeler", check out his "breakout" role as the "tough" private dick Philip Marlowe in this adaptation of Raymond Chandler's *Farewell, My Lovely*; it's a "quintessential" piece of "early noir", replete with a "perfect femme fatale", "unsurpassed" dialogue and a world-weary, "wisecracking" outlook on life.

Murder on the Orient Express 23 | 23 | 26 | 24

1974 | Directed by Sidney Lumet | With Albert Finney, Lauren Bacall, Ingrid Bergman | 128 minutes | Rated PG

"Agatha Christie hasn't been done better" than in this "fascinatingly complex" Hercule Poirot mystery set onboard the Orient Express; boasting a "crisply directed" "all-star" ensemble cast that "looks like they're having the time of their lives", this "luxuriously funny" "perfect thriller" certainly "won't bore you" – and "you'll never guess whodunit."

Muriel's Wedding 22 | 24 | 22 | 20

1995 | Directed by P.J. Hogan | With Toni Collette, Rachel Griffiths, Bill Hunter | 106 minutes | Rated R

Mating Aussie "quirkiness" to a "big heart", this "unique" romantic comedy gives the "dynamite" Collette her "breakthrough role" as a "nuptial-obsessed" small-town "wallflower" who "comes of age"; from the exuberant "ABBA-licious" soundtrack to its "poignant" undercurrent, devotees are wholly engaged and "left wanting more."

Music Man, The 25 | 24 | 25 | 26

1962 | Directed by Morton DaCosta | With Robert Preston, Shirley Jones, Buddy Hackett | 151 minutes | Rated G

Making an "exquisite, seamless transition from Broadway to the silver screen", this slice of "pure Americana" about a "traveling con man" let loose in River City, Iowa, hits "classic" notes with its "catchy" Meredith Willson score; thanks to a "tour-de-force" turn by a "mesmerizing" Preston, this "family treat" "never grows old."

Mutiny on the Bounty ✉◑ 25 | 25 | 25 | 23

1935 | Directed by Frank Lloyd | With Charles Laughton, Clark Gable, Franchot Tone | 132 minutes | Not Rated

Despite being "a bit creaky" after all these years, this original version of a legendary clash of egos on the high seas remains "the one and only" simply because "you don't get acting like this anymore": Laughton is darn "grand" as "definitive villain" Captain Bligh, and "Gable is, well, Gable" as Mr. Christian, his second-in-command.

Mutiny on the Bounty 22 | 24 | 24 | 22

1962 | Directed by Lewis Milestone | With Marlon Brando, Trevor Howard, Richard Harris | 178 minutes | Not Rated

Ultra-"fabulous scenery" that will surely make you "want to move to Tahiti" and a "cast of thousands" collide in this "big-budget" MGM remake about an uprising at sea; Brando turns in "one of his most controversial roles" as a "foppish" Fletcher Christian, even if foes harrumph "I'll take Gable."

My Beautiful Laundrette 23 | 24 | 23 | 19

1986 | Directed by Stephen Frears | With Daniel Day-Lewis, Gordon Warnecke | 98 minutes | Rated R

This "highly original" drama of "modern London" puts race and assimilation through a "wonderfully up-front" spin cycle in its story of "smart", "entrepreneurial" immigrants vs. the nativist "lower classes"; amid the many "honest" moments that come out in the wash is the "daring" bond between Warnecke's go-getting Pakistani and Day-Lewis' tough hooligan, resulting in some "steamy gay kissing."

My Big Fat Greek Wedding 23 | 22 | 23 | 21

2002 | Directed by Joel Zwick | With Nia Vardalos, John Corbett, Lainie Kazan | 96 minutes | Rated PG

It "doesn't matter whether you are Greek, Jewish, Italian or Albanian" – "we all see our crazy relatives up on the screen" in this "absolutely hilarious" "feel-good" look at Hellenic matrimony featuring a "likable cast of characters that you grow to love despite all their quirks"; critics claim "too much big fat hype", but they're outvoted by fans who "will never look at Windex the same way again."

My Brilliant Career 25 | 28 | 25 | 23

1980 | Directed by Gillian Armstrong | With Judy Davis, Sam Neill, Wendy Hughes | 100 minutes | Rated G

A "headstrong young woman" coming of age in 19th-century Australia must choose between a man or a career in this "wonderful" "feminist favorite" ("it changed my life"); in the "brilliant performance" that made her a star, "Davis rules", and abetted by "lovely photography and scenery", the film's an "absorbing" testimony to "girl power."

My Darling Clementine ◑ 25 | 27 | 23 | 24

1946 | Directed by John Ford | With Henry Fonda, Linda Darnell, Victor Mature, Walter Brennan | 97 minutes | Not Rated

"One of the all-time great Westerns", this "wonderfully humane" Ford oater strays from the "real history" behind the "shootout at the

O.K. Corral" to pose an "idealized" Wyatt Earp against a "rich" backdrop of a frontier "on the verge of change"; fortified with "romance", "moody characters" (Doc Holliday "reciting Shakespeare") and, you bet, lots of "gunplay", it's a "rewarding" ride that exemplifies the "definition of 'classic.'"

My Fair Lady ✉ 27 | 27 | 27 | 27

1964 | Directed by George Cukor | With Audrey Hepburn, Rex Harrison, Stanley Holloway | 170 minutes | Rated G

"Hollywood couldn't have done a better job" than this "grand, classy" version of Broadway's Lerner and Loewe musical "based on *Pygmalion*"; a "breathtaking" (but "dubbed") Hepburn is "incomparable" as the Cockney "guttersnipe turned into a lady", while Oscar-winner Harrison "at his tweedy best" plays her "superior yet vulnerable" teacher; "infectious" tunes and costumes that "leave you weak-kneed" ("those hats!") make this "luscious production" all the more "loverly."

My Favorite Year 22 | 25 | 22 | 20

1982 | Directed by Richard Benjamin | With Peter O'Toole, Mark Linn-Baker, Jessica Harper | 92 minutes | Rated PG

This "winning comedy" about the "early days of TV" involves a boozy matinee idol's appearance on a program that's a "great riff on the old Sid Caesar show"; although "O'Toole playing a drunk might not be a stretch", he "nails every nuance", turning this "affectionate period piece" into "one of the funniest movies no one has ever seen."

My Left Foot ✉ 25 | 28 | 25 | 23

1989 | Directed by Jim Sheridan | With Daniel Day-Lewis, Brenda Fricker, Hugh O'Conor | 98 minutes | Rated R

It "could have been sappy and overly sentimental", but this "stereotype-smashing" true account of an Irish man born with cerebral palsy is "handled with unvarnished dignity" thanks to the Oscar-winning Day-Lewis, who "maintains the contorted body and emotional scars" of his condition so adeptly that "you forget you're watching an actor"; "very moving", this film's a "beacon of light for all."

My Life As a Dog F 25 | 24 | 25 | 22

1987 | Directed by Lasse Hallström | With Anton Glanzelius, Melinda Kinnaman | 101 minutes | Rated PG-13

"For once, an adult really gets into a child's head" in this "enchanting" Swedish "coming-of-age" drama that devotees deem director "Hallström's best"; the "puckish" lead is both "complex" and "cute", his fellow villagers "wacky" and the story "heart-tugging" without a "single false note" – no wonder many say it's "goose bump-worthy."

My Little Chickadee ◑ 23 | 23 | 18 | 19

1940 | Directed by Edward F. Cline | With Mae West, W.C. Fields | 83 minutes | Not Rated

"Two comic pros" take on the Old West in this screwball oater about a fallen woman run out of town and the con man she weds; Mae's "priceless line delivery" works well against W.C.'s "vaudeville-era" gags – but since they "share very little screen time together" (interrupted by lengthy "pedestrian melodramatics"), some say the pairing of these screen legends "isn't as effective as one might hope."

	OVERALL	ACTING	STORY	PROD.
My Man Godfrey	25	25	23	21
Mystic River	26	28	25	25
Napoléon	28	24	26	28
Nashville	23	23	22	24
National Velvet	24	24	24	22
Natural, The	23	21	23	22

My Man Godfrey ◑

1936 | Directed by Gregory La Cava | With William Powell, Carole Lombard, Eugene Pallette | 94 minutes | Not Rated

As an "unconventional love-struck heiress", Lombard displays "impeccable timing" opposite the "masterful" Powell as the "hobo hired to be the family butler" in this "ultimate screwball comedy", the standard by which "all others are measured"; of course, the "fast-paced", fast-talking "plot is absurd" (that's "precisely the point"), but the "charming" principals "make it look convincing."

Mystic River ✉

2003 | Directed by Clint Eastwood | With Sean Penn, Tim Robbins, Kevin Bacon, Laurence Fishburne, Marcia Gay Harden, Laura Linney | 137 minutes | Rated R

"Lots of angst and anger" lie beneath this "bleak" tale of childhood buddies reunited as adults in the aftermath of a murder; it really "packs a wallop" thanks to a "pitch-perfect", "all-star" ensemble (with special kudos to Oscar winners Penn and Robbins for their "kick-in-the-gut" turns), not to mention Clint's "compelling" direction and "haunting score"; the only dissonant note is that "slightly off-the-mark" ending.

Napoléon ◑∅

1929 | Directed by Abel Gance | With Albert Dieudonné, Antonin Artaud | 235 minutes | Rated G

"Eye-popping even today", this bio of Napoléon Bonaparte from "audacious" director Gance is a "sweeping epic" from the silent era that had been truncated over time but then restored to its former glory; its "unsurpassed" camerawork includes shots made "from horseback" and on a "pendulum", but its "final triptych", predating widescreen photography, makes for a particularly "rousing" windup.

Nashville

1975 | Directed by Robert Altman | With Ronee Blakley, Keith Carradine, Lily Tomlin, Geraldine Chaplin, Karen Black, Shelley Duvall, Henry Gibson, Scott Glenn | 159 minutes | Rated R

It's the "wonderful ensemble" that makes this comic "portrait of '70s America" set in Nashville "richer and funnier with every viewing"; though some find it "frustrating" ("too many people talking at once"), "black humor" fans dub it "Altman's best", with enough "interesting characters" and "smart observations" to make it the "country cousin of *Gosford Park*."

National Velvet

1945 | Directed by Clarence Brown | With Elizabeth Taylor, Mickey Rooney, Anne Revere | 123 minutes | Rated G

The movie equivalent of "comfort food", this "classic" "coming-of-age story" about a "girl and her horse" stars a "dazzlingly young Taylor" and a "scene-stealing" Rooney; maybe it's "corny", but any young lady "who ever dreamed of having a pony" can't help but "gush" over that climatic steeplechase race.

Natural, The

1984 | Directed by Barry Levinson | With Robert Redford, Robert Duvall, Glenn Close | 134 minutes | Rated PG

"Every Little Leaguer's favorite flick", this mix of "magic" and "major league baseball" stars a "rugged Redford" as a "middle-aged rookie"

who hits a "chill"-inducing "home run into the lights"; though some sigh it's too "sentimental", fans cheer this "solid period drama" (and Randy Newman's "unforgettable score").

Network ✉ 24 | 25 | 24 | 22

1976 | Directed by Sidney Lumet | With Faye Dunaway, William Holden, Peter Finch, Beatrice Straight | 120 minutes | Rated R

Even 30 years later, newscaster Howard Beale's "fateful cry, 'I'm mad as hell, and I'm not going to take it anymore'" is still "relevant" to proponents of this "prophetic" dramedy about television's "battle between news and entertainment"; "expertly written" by Paddy Chayefsky and "brilliantly acted" by Finch, Dunaway and Straight (who all won Oscars), this "biting" dark comedy has surveyors citing "*Jerry Springer*" and sighing "it's all true now."

Neverending Story, The 23 | 19 | 24 | 24

1984 | Directed by Wolfgang Petersen | With Barret Oliver, Gerald McRaney, Noah Hathaway, Tami Stronach | 102 minutes | Rated PG

A "pre-*Harry Potter*" "escape from the mundane", this "visionary" fantasy combining live actors and animated creatures is an "enthralling" rendering of a "beautiful children's tale" about a lad who's "magically transported" by a storybook and finds he has the "power to save a far-off land"; despite "weak acting" and "'80s special effects", it still "holds up for family viewing after all these years"; P.S. "skip the sequels."

Never on Sunday ◑ 24 | 26 | 23 | 21

1960 | Directed by Jules Dassin | With Melina Mercouri, Jules Dassin | 91 minutes | Not Rated

A "sensuous" Mercouri became an international star after illuminating the screen in this "delightful" drama about an "earthy" Greek prostitute and an uptight American (played by director Dassin) who tries to pull a Pygmalion on her; although once "shocking" and now "delightfully dated", every-nighters could "watch it anytime – even on a Sunday."

Night at the Opera, A ◑ 26 | 25 | 22 | 22

1935 | Directed by Sam Wood | With the Marx Brothers, Kitty Carlisle, Margaret Dumont | 96 minutes | Not Rated

"Inspired insanity" meets "Marxist lunacy" in this "nutty" comedy (the "origin of the term 'laugh riot'") from the brothers Marx, wherein Groucho persuades a social-climbing Dumont to invest in an opera production; fans fast-forward through the "saccharine musical moments" in favor of the "verbal dazzle" of the "contract routine", the "baseball-in-the-orchestra-pit" bit and, of course, that "not-to-be-believed stateroom scene."

Nightmare Before Christmas, The 24 | - | 22 | 28

1993 | Directed by Henry Selick | Animated | 76 minutes | Rated PG

The "perfect antidote to the holidays" may well be this "magical", "macabre masterpiece" of stop-motion animation that ideally epitomizes the "bizarre genius" of producer Tim Burton; with a "cool story" – Halloween meets Christmas – "interesting characters" and "Danny Elfman's great score", it's a "must-see for kids of all ages."

	OVERALL	ACTING	STORY	PROD.

Night of the Hunter, The ◑ | 27 | 28 | 25 | 26

1955 | Directed by Charles Laughton | With Robert Mitchum, Shelley Winters, Lillian Gish | 93 minutes | Not Rated

Playing a "semi-psychotic preacher" "personifying pure evil", the "mesmerizing" Mitchum "terrorizes a bunch of kids" (and "invents tattooed knuckles") in this "strange" film noir frightfest; it's a "pity this was Laughton's only directorial" effort, given the "exquisite cinematography" and "unforgettable" performances.

Night of the Iguana, The ◑ | 23 | 26 | 22 | 22

1964 | Directed by John Huston | With Richard Burton, Ava Gardner, Deborah Kerr, Sue Lyon | 125 minutes | Not Rated

This "beautiful rendering" of Tennessee Williams' play concerns a defrocked clergyman turned south-of-the-border tour guide who lusts after three women, but is probably better known as the "movie that put Puerto Vallarta on the map as a tourist destination"; fans say the script is so "sultry" that you can almost "see the heat coming off the screen" – check out "Ava Gardner and those beach boys."

Nights of Cabiria ✉◑F | 27 | 28 | 25 | 24

1957 | Directed by Federico Fellini | With Giulietta Masina, François Périer | 117 minutes | Not Rated

"Post-WWII Italy" as seen "through the eyes of a streetwalker" is the premise of this "simple, heartfelt" drama that's one of Fellini's "most moving" (and least "bizarre") films; as the "lovable girl of the streets", the "radiant" Masina is nothing less than a "female Charlie Chaplin", rendering an "amazing" performance that "ranges from tragedy to transcendence to flat-out comedy."

Ninotchka ◑ | 25 | 27 | 24 | 23

1939 | Directed by Ernst Lubitsch | With Greta Garbo, Melvyn Douglas, Ina Claire | 110 minutes | Not Rated

This "great American comedy" depicts Soviet comrades seduced by capitalism, but is best known as the picture in which "Garbo laughs" for the first time on-screen; playing a "woman who follows her heart rather than the Communist manifesto", she's "smooth and sexy" spouting "incredibly funny dialogue" courtesy of a group of ace scenarists including Billy Wilder.

No Country for Old Men ✉ | 24 | 27 | 22 | 25

2007 | Directed by Joel Coen, Ethan Coen | With Tommy Lee Jones, Javier Bardem, Josh Brolin, Woody Harrelson | 122 minutes | Rated R

"Bone-chilling" is the word for this "bleak" "nightmare-maker" from the Coen brothers, a "Western horror film" about a "suitcase full of money" and the "bounty hunter" from hell out to get it (Bardem, who copped an Oscar as a "stone-faced" sociopath with a "scary" hairdo); provided "you can stomach the high body count" and "maddening ending", this "challenging" exercise in "pure nihilism" is "must-see" moviemaking, with a Best Picture statuette to prove it.

Norma Rae ✉ | 24 | 27 | 24 | 21

1979 | Directed by Martin Ritt | With Sally Field, Beau Bridges, Ron Leibman, Pat Hingle | 110 minutes | Rated PG

A "stirring tale about ordinary people", this "uplifting" drama "based on a true story" is a "painfully accurate look" at a "courageous" mill worker's "fight for justice" when caught between "unions and management"; in the title role, the "superb" Field really "earned her Oscar", and the "image of her holding up that sign" has become iconically "indelible."

North by Northwest 28 | 26 | 27 | 27

1959 | Directed by Alfred Hitchcock | With Cary Grant, Eva Marie Saint, James Mason, Martin Landau | 136 minutes | Not Rated

"James Bond, eat your heart out" – "no one is cooler than Cary Grant" in this "incredibly stylish" Hitchcock thriller, a "twisting story of mistaken identity" set "all over the country" involving a "cool blonde", a "smooth villain" and a "malevolent crop duster"; despite some "holes in the script", there's distraction via that "exhilarating" climb down Mount Rushmore and the "double entendre" scenario (e.g. the "train entering a tunnel" at the climax).

Nosferatu ◑ 26 | 22 | 24 | 24

1922 | Directed by F.W. Murnau | With Max Schreck, Gustav von Wangenheim, Greta Schroeder | 84 minutes | Not Rated

"Still creepy after all these years", this "important German horror film" (an "unauthorized version of *Dracula*") is "one spooky" silent flick that can "evoke terror" thanks to the "genuinely scary Schreck"; it's the "most poetic of vampire films" and the "standard that others are measured against – and usually found lacking."

Notebook, The 23 | 24 | 24 | 23

2004 | Directed by Nick Cassavetes | With Ryan Gosling, Rachel McAdams, James Garner, Gena Rowlands | 123 minutes | Rated PG-13

Sweet enough to "dissolve a tooth", this "hauntingly beautiful" sob-o-rama based on the Nicholas Sparks best-seller might be the "ultimate chick flick", a "testament to the awesome power of love" as it endures "through the ages"; naturally, the dry-eyed cry "corny", but even they credit the "genuinely sad Alzheimer's storyline" for addressing an issue that's "not often given attention."

Notes on a Scandal 24 | 28 | 23 | 23

2006 | Directed by Richard Eyre | With Judi Dench, Cate Blanchett, Bill Nighy | 92 minutes | Rated R

A "sad tale of obsessive love", this "disturbing" picture details "quite the touchy subject", a "pathetic spinster teacher" enamored with a younger colleague who "has a full life without her" – not to mention a "tawdry" secret of her own; it's "unsettling" stuff that's "adult in the best way", with "wonderful" performances that will "scare the hell out of you."

No Time for Sergeants ◑ 23 | 22 | 22 | 19

1958 | Directed by Mervyn LeRoy | With Andy Griffith, Myron McCornick, Nick Adams | 119 minutes | Not Rated

Managing to be "endearing without being annoying", Griffith "delivers the goods" in this "hilarious" comedy about a "dim hayseed who nearly destroys the U.S. Air Force"; the infamous "toilet-seat scene" is a "display of American ingenuity" at its finest.

Notorious ◑ 27 | 27 | 26 | 26

1946 | Directed by Alfred Hitchcock | With Cary Grant, Ingrid Bergman, Claude Rains | 101 minutes | Not Rated

"Fetching" Ingrid Bergman "goes under the sheets for her country and gets Cary Grant as a reward" in this "brilliantly subversive" Hitchcock spy thriller featuring equal parts of "suspicion", "hurt pride" and "Nazis too"; best remembered for the leads' "lingering, smoldering love scene", it also boasts "top-notch" supporting work from Rains, who has the best line: "mother, I'm married to an American agent."

Now, Voyager ◑

27 | 28 | 26 | 25

1942 | Directed by Irving Rapper | With Bette Davis, Paul Henreid, Claude Rains | 117 minutes | Not Rated

"Break out the hankies" – this "chick flick extraordinaire" features "the moon, the stars and Bette Davis", who effects an "appealing transformation" as an "old maid" defecting from a "demanding mother" to find kismet with a "perfect" Henreid; though the "two-cigarette scene" is decidedly un-PC today, it's become a "sacred" (and paradoxically "life-affirming") moment in this "classy" "mature love story."

Odd Couple, The

25 | 27 | 25 | 21

1968 | Directed by Gene Saks | With Jack Lemmon, Walter Matthau, John Fiedler | 105 minutes | Rated G

Lemmon and Matthau are "brilliant" in this "timeless" Neil Simon "classic" (which spawned a sequel and a TV series) that poses the question 'can two divorced men share an apartment without driving each other crazy?'; the ensuing dilemma makes for "unbeatable" comedy that'll make your "sides hurt from laughter."

Office Space

25 | 21 | 24 | 20

1999 | Directed by Mike Judge | With Ron Livingston, Jennifer Aniston, Gary Cole | 89 minutes | Rated R

"Required viewing for any cubicle dweller", this "instant classic" delivers a "spot-on skewering" of the "daily grind" in corporate America, "winning the hearts of the working class" with its "freaking hilarious" depiction of "disgruntled" desk jockeys; fans say there are "too many good lines to pick a favorite" in this "subversive" comedy, but "I think you have my stapler" and "it sounds like someone's got a case of the Mondays" are definite front runners.

Of Mice and Men ◑

26 | 27 | 27 | 23

1939 | Directed by Lewis Milestone | With Burgess Meredith, Lon Chaney Jr., Betty Field | 106 minutes | Not Rated

The "first and best screen adaptation" of John Steinbeck's acclaimed novel, this "moving" Depression-era portrait of two wandering farmhands – the diminutive George and his giant, feeble-minded companion Lenny – "sticks with you" thanks to the "fine performances" of Meredith and Chaney; an all-around "marvelous" production featuring an Oscar-nominated Aaron Copland score, it's an essential "classic" – and another reason why "1939 was the greatest year ever" in American film.

Oklahoma!

24 | 22 | 23 | 25

1955 | Directed by Fred Zinnemann | With Gordon MacRae, Shirley Jones, Gloria Grahame | 145 minutes | Rated G

"Every song" in this "sprawling" Rodgers and Hammerstein musical/Western "makes you want to sing along" with the "lovely" voices of Jones and MacRae, plus there are "rousing dance numbers"; though modernists malign it as a "little dated", for most it's a whole lot "more than O-K", it's a pure "C-L-A-S-S-I-C."

	OVERALL	ACTING	STORY	PROD.

Old Yeller 24 20 24 20

1957 | Directed by Robert Stevenson | With Dorothy McGuire, Fess Parker, Tommy Kirk | 83 minutes | Rated G

"You can't help but cry your eyes out" after watching this "outstanding" Disney "tearjerker" about a "boy and his big yellow dog"; if a few find the acting "formulaic" and the plot "sappy", most agree it's an "all-time" children's "standard" that even adults "never tire of watching" – despite that gosh-darned "sad ending."

Oliver! ✉ 24 23 24 26

1968 | Directed by Carol Reed | With Mark Lester, Ron Moody, Shani Wallis, Oliver Reed | 153 minutes | Rated G

Dickens' "bleak yet hopeful" novel is "lovingly brought to the screen" in this Oscar-winning adaptation of the "classic" stage musical; given the "incredible" production numbers, "wonderful" score and "just-about-perfect" cast, many "English orphan" wannabes beg 'please, sir can we watch it again?'

Oliver Twist ◑ 25 26 26 24

1951 | Directed by David Lean | With Robert Newton, Alec Guinness, John Howard Davies | 116 minutes | Not Rated

David Lean's "classic" take on Dickens' ageless novel "stands up over time" so well that many consider it the "best version of the book" put onto celluloid (indeed, it's "almost as good as *Great Expectations*"); admirers applaud Newton's "stunning", "tug-at-the-heartstrings" title turn and the "jolly good" Guinness, whose "controversial" performance as Fagin (deemed anti-Semitic by some) delayed the film's U.S. release.

Once 25 23 24 21

2007 | Directed by John Carney | With Glen Hansard, Markéta Irglová | 85 minutes | Rated R

"Love is the leitmotif" and "longing is the lyric" of this "sweet", "uplifting" little picture about two lonely souls connecting through the "joy of making music"; "great chemistry" between the leads, an Oscar-winning song and enough "sincere charm" to "melt an icy heart" is all "testament" to the "potential brilliance of low-budget filmmaking."

Once Upon a Time in America 24 26 24 24

1984 | Directed by Sergio Leone | With Robert De Niro, James Woods, Elizabeth McGovern | 227 minutes | Rated R

Some of De Niro's "most subtle and effective" acting is on display in this "unfairly neglected" crime epic spanning four decades, which hard-core cineasts hail as "truly remarkable" when "seen in the long [227-minute] director's cut"; but despite a "top-drawer cast" and "magnificent" direction, others are less enthused about the "flawed" end result that's awash in "too much blood."

Once Upon a Time in the West 25 24 23 25

1969 | Directed by Sergio Leone | With Henry Fonda, Claudia Cardinale, Charles Bronson | 165 minutes | Rated PG-13

This "ultimate Western" is "epic in every way", starting with its "big-name" cast, "long, long" running time and operatic plot about the desperate struggle for a piece of land; throw in Fonda as an "amazingly evil" villain, Ennio Morricone's "magical score" and "one of the coolest opening scenes ever", and it's easy to see why many consider this "high-water mark" to be director Leone's "definitive" work.

One Flew Over the Cuckoo's Nest ✉

27 29 27 25

1975 | Directed by Milos Forman | With Jack Nicholson, Louise Fletcher, Will Sampson | 133 minutes | Rated R

"Life in a mental ward" gets the "stand-up-for-your-rights" treatment in this "absorbing, disturbing" and "influential" drama starring "national treasure" Nicholson at his "ornery best", backed up by an "amazing" ensemble cast; no surprise, it took five major Oscars, made Nurse Ratched a household name and is "hard to top" – folks are just plain "nuts about it."

101 Dalmatians

24 - 22 24

1961 | Directed by Wolfgang Reitherman, Clyde Geronimi, Hamilton Luske | Animated | 79 minutes | Rated G

Puppy proponents put their paws together for Pongo, Perdita and their prolific progeny when watching this "fast, funny" piece of Disney animation; its "hugely entertaining" tale of a klatch of "cute" canines outrunning über-villainess Cruella De Vil appeals to the "little kid in everyone" and makes this one an "enduring winner."

One, Two, Three ◑

23 23 22 22

1961 | Directed by Billy Wilder | With James Cagney, Horst Buchholz, Pamela Tiffin | 108 minutes | Not Rated

"Billy Wilder scores in this Cold War comedy" set in Berlin, a "fast and furious farce" about a "harried Coca-Cola executive" whose "world is collapsing around him"; Cagney's "machine-gun delivery is a scream", though diehards say the picture's "underrated" and "overshadowed" by the director's better-known films.

On Golden Pond ✉

24 27 23 23

1981 | Directed by Mark Rydell | With Katharine Hepburn, Henry Fonda, Jane Fonda | 109 minutes | Rated PG

A "beautiful tale of growing old and looking back on life", this "brilliant" drama features the "stunning", Oscar-winning Hank and Kate "pulling out all the stops" as an elderly couple coming to terms with their child and each other over one golden summer; the "real-life tension" between the real-life father-and-daughter Fondas supplies some "electric" moments, while its timeless theme about the "strength of the human spirit" "will appeal to all."

Onion Field, The

24 26 25 23

1979 | Directed by Harold Becker | With John Savage, James Woods, Ted Danson, Franklyn Seales | 122 minutes | Rated R

A "disturbing" look at the "sad" side of police work, this "gritty crime drama" delineates a cop's gangland-style execution and its "depressing" aftermath; adapted from the Joseph Wambaugh book (itself based on an actual case), it's "more true to life than we want to believe" and features fine work from the "chilling" Woods and a "serious Danson."

On the Beach ◑

26 26 27 23

1959 | Directed by Stanley Kramer | With Gregory Peck, Ava Gardner, Fred Astaire, Anthony Perkins | 134 minutes | Not Rated

"Now dated, but still riveting", this "chilling" Cold War–era message picture details the "aftermath of a nuclear war", where the earth's sole survivors struggle to stay alive in Australia; it's an "intense" look at "how people spend their last days" that "isn't about explosions, but emotions", and many report "never listening to 'Waltzing Matilda' the same way again" after seeing it.

On the Town 23 | 23 | 21 | 25

1949 | Directed by Stanley Donen, Gene Kelly | With Gene Kelly, Frank Sinatra, Jules Munshin | 98 minutes | Not Rated

Despite "wonderful dancing by Kelly" and some "funny" bits from the ensemble cast, "NYC is the real star" of this "exuberant" musical "celebrating the American spirit in the '40s"; "filmed partially on location" and juiced up by a "great Leonard Bernstein score", it follows three sailors at liberty on the town, and although rather "silly", it effortlessly radiates the "pure joy" of simpler times.

On the Waterfront ✉◑ 28 | 29 | 26 | 26

1954 | Directed by Elia Kazan | With Marlon Brando, Karl Malden, Eva Marie Saint, Rod Steiger | 108 minutes | Not Rated

Most decidedly a "candidate for all-time greatest" film, this "gritty tale of corruption on the NJ docks" is a "movie to turn you onto movies", with Oscar wins by the "phenomenal Brando" (as a "washed-up", "Palookaville"-bound boxer) and a "knockout" Saint (in her screen debut); indeed, this "gutsy", "brutal masterwork" "rings so true" and is so "emotionally satisfying" that it's "nothing less than brilliant"; best line: "I coulda been a contender."

Ordinary People ✉ 25 | 27 | 25 | 23

1980 | Directed by Robert Redford | With Donald Sutherland, Mary Tyler Moore, Timothy Hutton | 124 minutes | Rated R

"Every parent's nightmare" – the death of a child – is dissected in this "devastating" drama that goes below the "veneer of an upper-middle-class family" to plumb the "dysfunction" below; Redford's "deserving" directorial debut copped a Best Picture Oscar, but it's Moore's "playing-against-type" role as a "classy" but "coldhearted" mom that "steals the movie."

Outlaw Josey Wales, The 25 | 23 | 24 | 23

1976 | Directed by Clint Eastwood | With Clint Eastwood, Sondra Locke, Chief Dan George | 135 minutes | Rated PG

Playing a renegade Confederate soldier seeking revenge after his wife and children are murdered, Eastwood is his "usual unreadable self" (though you "feel for his plight") in this "quirky" Western that's a "rural version of *Death Wish*"; fans rate it "better-than-usual Clint", given its "classic lines" and "profound issues."

Out of Africa ✉ 25 | 25 | 24 | 27

1985 | Directed by Sydney Pollack | With Meryl Streep, Robert Redford, Klaus Maria Brandauer | 150 minutes | Rated PG

Supporters are "spellbound" by this "splendiferous" "love story played out against the mysterious continent" starring a "radiant" Streep as Danish writer Karen Blixen (aka Isak Dinesen) and a "great-looking" Redford as her paramour; the "beauty" of Africa and "soaring score" help to "amplify the emotion", and even though there's no doubt that it's a "real tearjerker", most viewers eat up this "treat" "again and again."

OVERALL | ACTING | STORY | PROD.

Out of the Past ◑ 26 | 26 | 25 | 25

1947 | Directed by Jacques Tourneur | With Robert Mitchum, Jane Greer, Kirk Douglas | 97 minutes | Not Rated

The "*Citizen Kane* of film noir", this "fabled" picture "sets the standard" for the genre by pitting a "classic antihero" ("Mitchum at his laconic best") against the "ultimate femme fatale" (the "beautiful but deadly" Greer); the "insanely labyrinthine plot" with "twists in all directions" is equally "note perfect", and perfumed with a "whiff of French existentialism."

Over the Hedge 23 | - | 22 | 25

2006 | Directed by Tim Johnson, Karey Kirkpatrick | Animated | 83 minutes | Rated PG

Their habitat "dwindling as suburbia spreads", a gang of animals "tries to get food from humans" in this "clever" cartoon powered by "fantastic" animation and "excellent" celeb voicings ("Steve Carell's squirrel steals the show"); a "real crowd-pleaser", it boasts an "easy-to-follow" story for small fry plus "commentary about society" that goes over well with adults.

Ox-Bow Incident, The ◑ 27 | 27 | 26 | 23

1943 | Directed by William Wellman | With Henry Fonda, Dana Andrews | 75 minutes | Not Rated

"Decent, law-abiding folk never looked more pathetic" than in this message Western, a "gripping story of mob violence gone mad" that's a chilling indictment of American justice; there are no heroes in this dark "morality tale", though the "excellent ensemble" makes this "adaptation of the classic novel" come alive.

Painted Veil, The 23 | 25 | 23 | 26

2006 | Directed by John Curran | With Naomi Watts, Edward Norton, Liev Schreiber, Toby Jones | 125 minutes | Rated PG-13

Strains of "*The English Patient*" infect this "emotionally charged" W. Somerset Maugham adaptation starring Watts and Norton as "flawed" spouses who try to salvage their "fragile marriage" in the testy "political climate of 1920s China"; productionwise, the "gorgeous" cinematography shows off some "magnificent" Far East scenery – a "picturesque" palliative for what some call a "languid" drama.

Palm Beach Story, The ◑ 25 | 25 | 25 | 24

1942 | Directed by Preston Sturges | With Claudette Colbert, Joel McCrea, Mary Astor, Rudy Vallee | 88 minutes | Not Rated

Screwball comedies "don't get much better" than this "zany romp" about a married couple who separate over money troubles; the "smart" dialogue, "fast" pacing and "ridiculous" plot showcase director Sturges "at his wittiest and loopiest", and then there's the "irresistible" Colbert and "perfect" Rudy Vallee – "they don't write 'em like this anymore."

Pan's Labyrinth F 27 | 26 | 26 | 28

2006 | Directed by Guillermo del Toro | With Ivana Baquero, Sergi López, Maribel Verdú | 120 minutes | Rated R

Fantasy film fans faun over this "ethereal", "adult"-themed fairy tale – think a "grim" "*Alice in Wonderland*" – from "master" helmer del Toro, who corrals some "wild" visuals to depict the "nightmarish" imaginings of a "brilliant child" and the "harsh realities of Franco-era fas-

	OVERALL	ACTING	STORY	PROD.

cism" that spawn them; "enchanting" performances and spurts of "graphic violence" that "stay with you" should placate even the most "subtitle-leery" of onlookers.

Paper Chase, The 23 | 25 | 24 | 20

1973 | Directed by James Bridges | With Timothy Bottoms, Lindsay Wagner, John Houseman | 111 minutes | Rated PG

The "terrors and rigors of the first year of Harvard Law School" are revealed in this "seminal" '70s movie that re-creates the student "rat race" in an "entertaining" way; despite "outstanding performances by all", the Oscar-winning Houseman (as a "crusty professor") is the "main reason to see it."

Papillon 26 | 27 | 26 | 24

1973 | Directed by Franklin J. Schaffner | With Steve McQueen, Dustin Hoffman | 150 minutes | Rated R

It's hard to escape from this "powerful" tale of prisoners scheming to break out of Devil's Island, the French Guiana penal colony that makes "HBO's *Oz* look like Club Med"; a "consistently cool McQueen" and "heavyweight Hoffman" play "mistreated-but-not-defeated" inmates "determined to be free" in this "tight", taut drama that's all the more "scary" since it's "based on a true story."

Parallax View, The 24 | 23 | 25 | 21

1974 | Directed by Alan J. Pakula | With Warren Beatty, Paula Prentiss, William Daniels | 102 minutes | Rated R

"Conspiracy theorists" dig this "paranoid thriller" made in the "post-Kennedy assassination era" that's as "taut" and "frightening" as they come; playing a hotheaded young reporter who blunders into a perilous web of intrigue, a "young" Beatty "shows he can excel with serious material" and keep viewers on the "edge of their seats."

Parent Trap, The 23 | 21 | 23 | 21

1961 | Directed by David Swift | With Hayley Mills, Maureen O'Hara, Brian Keith | 129 minutes | Rated G

"Hayley Mills and Hayley Mills" star as "twins separated at birth plotting to bring their estranged parents together" in this "Disney classic", an "entertaining romp" that serves up "warmhearted family fare"; one of the "most remembered" movies in boomerdom, it's so "timeless" that most "stick to the original", having "no need for the remake."

Paris, Texas 22 | 24 | 21 | 20

1984 | Directed by Wim Wenders | With Harry Dean Stanton, Nastassja Kinski, Dean Stockwell | 147 minutes | Rated R

"Haunting landscapes" and "outstanding performances" are the hallmarks of this "unconventional" (verging on "totally bizarre") road movie about a lost soul rediscovering his wife and child; while there's praise for writer Sam Shepard's "spare dialogue" and composer Ry Cooder's "perfect soundtrack", many say the "drawn-out", "slow-moving" pace makes for "awfully strange" filmmaking.

Passage to India, A 25 | 26 | 23 | 26

1984 | Directed by David Lean | With Judy Davis, Victor Banerjee, Peggy Ashcroft, James Fox, Alec Guinness | 163 minutes | Rated PG

Lean's final opus, this "well-done epic" adapted from the E.M. Forster novel showcases the legendary director "at his very best", working as

OVERALL	ACTING	STORY	PROD.

one part "exotic travelogue" to "gorgeous" Indian locales and one part "gripping history piece" exploring the "tensions" between Britain and its colonial subjects in the 1920s; "expertly acted" performances from Davis and Ashcroft heighten the "ethereal" "sensory experience", even if a few travelers report a rather "slow-moving" journey.

Paths of Glory ◑ 28 | 27 | 28 | 26

1957 | Directed by Stanley Kubrick | With Kirk Douglas, Ralph Meeker, George Macready | 86 minutes | Not Rated

"All the hopelessness, folly and stupidity" of WWI is "dramatically" shown in Kubrick's "devastating" "anti-war" picture that "ruthlessly" depicts "corrupt" officers deploying "scapegoated enlisted men" as "cannon fodder"; even though this "grim" yet "moving" film is in black and white, the "story is full color", and it "really makes its point" and "stands the test of time."

Patton ✉ 27 | 28 | 26 | 27

1970 | Directed by Franklin J. Schaffner | With George C. Scott, Karl Malden | 170 minutes | Rated PG

Legions salute "one of the best biopics ever made", this "hauntingly mounted character study" of fabled WWII General Patton, who's "superbly fleshed out" as both "monstrous and human"; though there's "lots of drama" throughout, it "doesn't get much better than that opening speech" by "Old Blood and Guts", probably the most "memorable" scene; P.S. the "convincing" portrayal won Scott an Oscar, which he famously rejected.

Pawnbroker, The ◑ 26 | 28 | 24 | 22

1965 | Directed by Sidney Lumet | With Rod Steiger, Geraldine Fitzgerald | 116 minutes | Not Rated

This "disturbing", "depressing message picture", expertly rendered in "chilling black and white", shows the "horrors of the Holocaust" by focusing on one survivor, the owner of a Harlem pawnshop; in "one of the all-time great screen performances", Steiger is nothing short of "mesmerizing" in the title role – too bad it's been so "sadly neglected" over the years.

Persona ◑ F 27 | 28 | 25 | 26

1967 | Directed by Ingmar Bergman | With Bibi Andersson, Liv Ullmann | 81 minutes | Not Rated

Bergman's "plunge into the mysteries of the self" beguiles surveyors who say this "intense" film is the director's "best synthesis of symbolism and reality"; the story of a nurse and her patient (an actress who has gone mute) is "not rational but psychologically satisfying" as the two characters' identities "blend" together to make a "stunning" whole.

Peter Pan 25 | - | 25 | 25

1953 | Directed by Clyde Geronimi, Wilfred Jackson, Hamilton Luske | Animated | 76 minutes | Rated G

Lost boys and girls who "never want to grow up" fly to this "simple", pixie dust–peppered tale concerning the eternally youthful Peter's adventures in Neverland; a "true classic" of Disney animation from the days when "Walt was running the show", it remains enough of an "important childhood film" for latter-day critics to ask "why did they bother with a remake?"

	OVERALL	ACTING	STORY	PROD.

Philadelphia ✉ 24 | 27 | 25 | 23

1993 | Directed by Jonathan Demme | With Tom Hanks, Denzel Washington | 125 minutes | Rated PG-13

"Hollywood takes on AIDS" in this "extraordinarily powerful and poignant" drama that "puts a human face" on a "depressing" subject thanks to Hanks' "brave", Oscar-winning portrayal of a gay lawyer battling the "double-edged sword of discrimination and physical deterioration"; the final result resonates with "thought-provoking" issues, but don't forget to "bring the tissues – it's painful to watch."

Philadelphia Story, The ✉◑ 27 | 28 | 26 | 25

1940 | Directed by George Cukor | With Cary Grant, Katharine Hepburn, James Stewart | 112 minutes | Not Rated

For the "sheer joy" of "listening to fast, furious dialogue" that "doesn't insult your intelligence", this "laugh-out-loud" screwball "comedy of manners" provides a "wild ride"; "you'll need a scorecard to keep up" with the "banter and spark" between the "classy" Kate, "acerbic" Grant and "underplaying" Stewart, uttered in settings so "perfectly frothy" that many wish that "life was really like that."

Pianist, The ✉ 28 | 29 | 27 | 28

2002 | Directed by Roman Polanski | With Adrien Brody, Thomas Kretschmann | 150 minutes | Rated R

"Agonizing and beautiful all at once", this "haunting" true story about a concert pianist's struggle to survive in Nazi-occupied Warsaw receives raves as "Polanski's historic achievement", a "masterpiece of filmmaking" that "will stay in your mind"; Brody's "brilliant", "subdued performance" "conveys so much without hardly saying a word", while the "depiction of the horror" is "accurate and harrowing in its detail"; in sum, both the director and star "deserved to win those Oscars."

Pickup on South Street ◑ 23 | 24 | 24 | 22

1953 | Directed by Samuel Fuller | With Richard Widmark, Jean Peters, Thelma Ritter, Richard Kiley | 80 minutes | Not Rated

For "film noir at its best", check out this "knockout" flick about a pickpocket and a prostitute inadvertently mixed up with a "Communist spy" ring; it's an "old-school", Red-menace ride with fine work from the "consummate" Widmark and the overripe Peters, and if that's not enough for you, "there's Thelma Ritter too."

Picnic 24 | 24 | 24 | 24

1955 | Directed by Joshua Logan | With William Holden, Kim Novak, Rosalind Russell, Arthur O'Connell | 115 minutes | Not Rated

Darn "sexy for its time", this "star-crossed", "moonglow"-drenched romance relates the havoc that a "handsome drifter" wreaks upon a group of "small-town" gals; fans say it "retains its charm", since it "epitomizes the lush storytelling of the '50s", but admit it may be a "little too theatrical to appeal to today's audiences"; hottest scene, no contest: Novak and Holden's "sizzling dance on the bridge."

Picnic at Hanging Rock 24 | 23 | 24 | 24

1979 | Directed by Peter Weir | With Rachel Roberts, Anne-Louise Lambert, Helen Morse | 107 minutes | Rated PG

You "never really know what's going on" in this "enigmatic" drama from the "innovative" Peter Weir recounting the disappearance of three

	OVERALL	ACTING	STORY	PROD.

students from a "repressive girls' boarding school" in "Victorian Australia"; granted, the "slow" pacing is "not for short attention spans", but fans say its "unrelentingly atmospheric" cinematography and "unresolved ending" make for "hypnotic", "discussion"-worthy moviemaking.

Pink Floyd The Wall 23 | 17 | 18 | 24

1982 | Directed by Alan Parker | With Bob Geldof, Bob Hoskins | 95 minutes | Rated R

"Provocative and disturbing", this "psychedelic rock opera" about a musician's "all-encompassing depression" is "one crazy movie" but a "classic" just the same thanks to its "masterful blend" of "out-of-this-world" imagery combined with Pink Floyd's "incredible" soundtrack; "required viewing for stoned high school students", it's altogether an "awesome" cinematic "head trip" – "even when viewed sober."

Pink Panther, The 24 | 24 | 21 | 21

1964 | Directed by Blake Edwards | With Peter Sellers, David Niven, Robert Wagner | 113 minutes | Not Rated

"Hilarity abounds" – "starting with the opening credits" – in this "outlandish" caper, the first production by the "comedy dream team" of director Edwards and actor Sellers (in his "brilliant" debut as "bumbling Jacques Clouseau"); "funny to this day", it marked the start of a "sequel brigade" that marched along for years afterward.

Pinocchio 26 | - | 26 | 26

1940 | Directed by Hamilton Luske, Ben Sharpsteen | Animated | 88 minutes | Rated G

"Forget the wooden kid with the schnoz" (who's a bit "dull") – this "wonderful" animated fantasy is more memorable for its "classic" character, Jiminy Cricket, and its Oscar-winning song, 'When You Wish Upon a Star'; otherwise, this story of a puppet transformed into a boy still "combines some of the sweetest and scariest scenes" in all of Disneydom.

Pirates of the Caribbean: The Curse of the Black Pearl 24 | 25 | 22 | 27

2003 | Directed by Gore Verbinski | With Johnny Depp, Geoffrey Rush, Orlando Bloom, Keira Knightley | 143 minutes | Rated PG-13

"Eat your heart out, Errol Flynn" – Johnny Depp's a real "hoot" in this Disney high seas adventure, turning in an "over-the-top" performance as a pirate captain who's half "swashbuckling", half "swish" (think "Keith Richards with a cutlass"); though it "could have been fluff" given its "audio-animatronic", "theme-park-ride" origins, this "rollicking" romp keeps the violence "stylized" and rolls out enough "impressive" FX to provide lots of "salty fun."

Place in the Sun, A ✉◑ 27 | 27 | 27 | 24

1951 | Directed by George Stevens | With Montgomery Clift, Elizabeth Taylor, Shelley Winters | 122 minutes | Not Rated

This "classic American" love triangle from Oscar-winning director Stevens might be a "glamorized version of the Dreiser novel" but was still rather daring for its time given the unwed-mother subplot; while it's hard to miss the "radiant Clift and Taylor" (thanks to some swoon-worthy giant close-ups), "poor Shelley Winters" as the third wheel may well deliver the best performance; most famous line: Liz's smoldering "'tell mama all.'"

	OVERALL	ACTING	STORY	PROD.

Planet of the Apes 23 | 20 | 25 | 23

1968 | Directed by Franklin J. Schaffner | With Charlton Heston, Roddy McDowall, Kim Hunter | 112 minutes | Rated G

"Darwin would have loved" this "thought-provoking" stew of "science fiction and pop culture" about an American astronaut who crashes on a simian-ruled planet; Heston's "brawny", "over-the-top" performance brings equal parts "paranoid power" and "Republican campiness" to the leading role, while that "wallop" of an ending remains one of the "most talked-about ever."

Platoon ✉ 25 | 25 | 24 | 26

1986 | Directed by Oliver Stone | With Tom Berenger, Willem Dafoe, Charlie Sheen | 120 minutes | Rated R

"Disturbing" yet "unforgettable", this "almost-too-real" war picture offers a "raw" view of the Vietnam conflict as seen "through the eyes of a recruit just arrived in the jungle"; granted, it "fails to offer the slightest glimmer of hope", but it "captures the desperation" of battle "better than any other movie", with a clutch of Oscars (including Best Picture and Best Director) to prove it.

Player, The 23 | 23 | 23 | 22

1992 | Directed by Robert Altman | With Tim Robbins, Greta Scacchi, Fred Ward | 124 minutes | Rated R

"People who love movies about movies" love this "scathing satire" of "cutthroat" Hollywood, "perfectly directed" by "genius" Altman; cineasts cite the "excellent opening shot" (eight minutes "without a cut") and the "wonderful all-star cameo" appearances peppered throughout, but zero in on Robbins' "marvelous" portrayal of a "ne'er-do-well producer" as the real standout.

Play It Again, Sam 22 | 21 | 23 | 20

1972 | Directed by Herbert Ross | With Woody Allen, Diane Keaton, Tony Roberts | 85 minutes | Rated PG

Woody's "wonderful" in this "fine early comedy" adapted from his Broadway hit about a lovelorn film critic so enamored with *Casablanca* that he conjures up an imaginary Bogie for advice; though this spoof "works on every level" for "hard-core" Allen fans, purists protest there's one major problem: "he didn't direct it."

Poltergeist 22 | 20 | 23 | 24

1982 | Directed by Tobe Hooper | With JoBeth Williams, Craig T. Nelson, Beatrice Straight | 114 minutes | Rated PG

"Half social satire, half haunted-house tale", this "vivid" "roller-coaster ride" of a horror flick has a "pure Spielberg" premise: "affluent parents and cute children" living in a home "built over a graveyard" chock-full of "pesky ghosts"; the "strong story", "ahead-of-its-time special effects" and that "little voice" squeaking "they're he-ere" still startle boo-mers over "20 years later."

Postman Always Rings Twice, The ◑ 25 | 25 | 25 | 24

1946 | Directed by Tay Garnett | With John Garfield, Lana Turner, Cecil Kellaway | 113 minutes | Not Rated

Garfield and Turner "set off the smoke alarms" in this "steamy" slice of film noir, a "deliciously sinful" saga about a "married femme fatale", a "streetwise vagabond" and their simmering affair that "boils over into murderous passion"; though this "twisting" tale of "love, betrayal" and "homicide" is pretty "wonderful", one question remains: "didn't people know about divorce in those days?"

Potemkin ◑ 27 22 25 27

1926 | Directed by Sergei Eisenstein | With Aleksandr Antonov, Vladimir Barsky | 75 minutes | Not Rated

Over 80 years later, cineasts are still electrified by director Eisenstein's "influential" "triumph" that "put 'montage' into the filmmaking lexicon" and "forever set the standards for camerawork"; detailing the failed 1905 uprising against the Czar, it's best known for its "often copied baby-carriage-on-the-Odessa-steps sequence" that "paved the way for edit-happy MTV directors"; indeed, it's so "exciting" that many insist it "should be mandatory moviegoing."

Precious ✉ 24 27 24 24

2009 | Directed by Lee Daniels | With Gabourey Sidibe, Mo'Nique, Paula Patton, Mariah Carey | 109 minutes | Rated R

"Gut-wrenching" and "utterly believable", this "raw" drama of "ghetto life" is a "book-to-screen success" that "pushes the audience's boundaries" in its story of a "struggling, abused teen" coping with a "dead-end life" and a "scary monster" of a mother (Oscar-winner Mo'Nique); with "exceptional acting" from the "entire cast" - "even Mariah Carey" - it's "tough to watch", but "unforgettable."

Pretty Woman 23 22 22 22

1990 | Directed by Garry Marshall | With Richard Gere, Julia Roberts, Jason Alexander | 119 minutes | Rated R

Despite a premise somewhere between "Cinderella" and "Eliza Doolittle", this story of a "hooker with a heart of gold" who bags "Prince Charming" is a "happily-ever-after" romance that "put Julia (and her smile) on the map"; credit the "dizzying charisma" and "palpable chemistry between its stars" for its "believability", and though the "glamorization-of-prostitution" angle turns off bluenoses, "hopeless romantics" insist it will "steal your heart."

Pride and Prejudice ◑ 25 25 26 23

1940 | Directed by Robert Z. Leonard | With Greer Garson, Laurence Olivier, Mary Boland | 118 minutes | Not Rated

A "lovely, headstrong heroine and a handsome haughty hero" make "sparks fly" in this "lush", "true-to-the-book" adaptation of the Jane Austen classic; "fabulous period costumes and sets" in high MGM style contribute to the "splendid" feel, while "Garson and Olivier play off each other wonderfully" - now, "that's style."

Pride & Prejudice 23 24 25 25

2005 | Directed by Joe Wright | With Keira Knightley, Matthew Macfadyen, Donald Sutherland | 127 minutes | Rated PG

"New insights into an old classic" flow from this "pared-down" yet "delightful" translation of Jane Austen's novel featuring a "radiant" Knightley as the "headstrong" heroine who finds a "sparring partner and true love" in "brooding English Lord" Mr. Darcy; a "lavish production" featuring "breathtaking scenery", "intelligent" dialogue and an "alluring soundtrack", it maintains a modern "freshness" that tickles "silly romantic" types.

	OVERALL	ACTING	STORY	PROD.

Prime of Miss Jean Brodie, The ✉ | 25 | 28 | 24 | 23

1969 | Directed by Ronald Neame | With Maggie Smith, Robert Stephens, Pamela Franklin, Jane Carr | 116 minutes | Rated PG

Transposing "*Dead Poets Society*" to a '30s-era Scottish boarding school, this portrait of a "free-thinking teacher" is "worth revisiting" for Dame Maggie's "towering", Oscar-grabbing turn; it's a "coming-of-age classic" crafted with "impressionable girls" in mind, despite its "heartbreaker" message: "idealism can be bad for you."

Princess Bride, The | 27 | 23 | 27 | 24

1987 | Directed by Rob Reiner | With Cary Elwes, Mandy Patinkin, Robin Wright | 98 minutes | Rated PG

Despite the "chick-flick title", this "lighthearted" but "fractured fairy tale" defies any easy "categorization" and is admired by "even the most macho" guys for its "swordfights" and "verbal jousting"; thanks to an "intelligent" script, "masterful" direction by Reiner and an "incredibly talented" cast, "finding a better movie is inconceivable."

Producers, The ✉ | 26 | 26 | 26 | 23

1968 | Directed by Mel Brooks | With Zero Mostel, Gene Wilder, Kenneth Mars | 88 minutes | Rated PG

Flaunting "silly and shocking originality" long before the "Broadway hoopla", this "anarchic", "appallingly funny" comedy boasts Mostel and Wilder "at their best" as perps of a "Ponzi scheme" to produce an "unbelievably over-the-top" musical winningly titled *Springtime for Hitler* and cash in on its failure; it earns a standing ovation as "unrelenting", "inspired lunacy" from the "warped mind" of Mel Brooks that still "holds up" as a manic "masterpiece."

Professional, The | 25 | 25 | 24 | 23

1994 | Directed by Luc Besson | With Jean Reno, Gary Oldman, Natalie Portman | 110 minutes | Rated R

A "rare" example of a "well-executed" action flick, this "compelling" portrait of a hit man "with a heart of gold" who takes an orphan "under his wing" soars with its "unconventional" coupling of the "terrific" Reno with a "luminous" young Portman (in her feature film debut); count on "scary" Gary's "hyped-up bad cop" and some "wonderfully filmed" gunfight sequences to heighten the already "intense" mood.

Psycho ◑ | 28 | 26 | 27 | 27

1960 | Directed by Alfred Hitchcock | With Anthony Perkins, Vera Miles, John Gavin, Janet Leigh | 109 minutes | Rated R

"Generations of moviegoers started double-locking their bathroom doors" after one look at the "famous shower scene" in this "classic Hitchcock" "psycho-logical thriller" that was "quite a shocker in its day" and "still packs a wallop" - "without the gross violence of modern flicks"; standouts include Bernard Herrmann's "scariest film score ever" and Perkins' "twitchy", "tour-de-force" performance as the ultimate "mama's boy."

Public Enemy ◑ | 25 | 25 | 22 | 22

1931 | Directed by William Wellman | With James Cagney, Jean Harlow, Edward Woods, Mae Clarke | 84 minutes | Not Rated

"Cagney's spectacular" in this "classic '30s gangster flick" that made him a star in the role of a petty crook who evolves into a "dangerous" crime czar; the picture still delivers quite a punch, brimming with "energy", especially the famous scene in which the girlfriend gets it in the kisser with a grapefruit.

Pulp Fiction ✉ 26 | 26 | 25 | 25

1994 | Directed by Quentin Tarantino | With John Travolta, Samuel L. Jackson, Uma Thurman, Bruce Willis, Amanda Plummer, Tim Roth, Ving Rhames, Harvey Keitel | 154 minutes | Rated R

A "pioneer of plot shuffling" and "twisty chronology", this "propulsive", "in-your-face" thriller is a "true original" with an "unpredictable storyline" and "dialogue that's like a punch in the face"; recounting the affairs of some "charming hit men", it stars a "rogues' gallery of actors" in memorable bits ("Travolta's dancing", Uma's overdose, Plummer's "psychotic rant") played out with "dark humor", "intense violence" and "foul language"; not only did it "put Tarantino on the map", it's in a "genre all by itself."

Pursuit of Happyness, The 23 | 25 | 24 | 22

2006 | Directed by Gabriele Muccino | With Will Smith, Jaden Smith, Thandie Newton | 117 minutes | Rated PG-13

Open up and say "awww": this "heartstring-pulling" paean to the "American dream" will "grab you" with its "Alger"-esque plot and Will's "phenomenal" performance as a "dedicated father" who "never gives up" despite "life's hardships"; sure, "you know where it's going right from the beginning", but the fact that it's "based on a true story" keeps the "sappyness" in check.

Queen, The ✉ 26 | 29 | 23 | 25

2006 | Directed by Stephen Frears | With Helen Mirren, Michael Sheen, Helen McCrory, James Cromwell | 103 minutes | Rated PG-13

The "private side" of the British monarchy gets a public airing in this "wholly absorbing" look at the "royal response to the death of Diana", Princess of Wales; in the title role, Oscar-winner Mirren gives a "beautifully restrained" performance that goes "beyond the icy veneer" to "humanize" the "insulated" Queen and almost single-handedly crafts an "immensely entertaining" picture from "seemingly bland subject matter."

Quiet American, The 24 | 26 | 24 | 24

2002 | Directed by Phillip Noyce | With Michael Caine, Brendan Fraser | 101 minutes | Rated R

Delivering a "powerful performance", Caine demonstrates why he's "legendary" in this "highly underrated" adaptation of the Graham Greene novel about "America's involvement in the early stages of the Vietnam War"; a "terrific" Fraser, a "wonderful story" and a "lavish" re-creation of 1950s Saigon are more reasons why many say "it's a shame" this "sleeper wasn't promoted enough."

Quiet Man, The ✉ 27 | 25 | 25 | 27

1952 | Directed by John Ford | With John Wayne, Maureen O'Hara, Barry Fitzgerald | 129 minutes | Not Rated

"Every Irish cliché" is "alive and well" in this "romanticized" drama, starring the Duke as an American boxer who hangs up his gloves and settles in his Hibernian "ancestral home" only to be smitten by the "beautiful", "feisty" O'Hara; presenting a "postcard" Ireland populated by "enchanting townspeople", it's "witty" and - despite a wee bit o' "blarney" - judged "worthy of a yearly viewing."

Rabbit-Proof Fence 26 | 25 | 26 | 24

2002 | Directed by Phillip Noyce | With Everlyn Sampi, Tianna Sansbury, Laura Monaghan, Kenneth Branagh | 94 minutes | Rated PG

Young Aboriginal girls "escape forced slavery" and trek 1,500 miles across the Australian outback to return home in this "heart-wrenching true story" "acted wonderfully" by "three unknowns"; "don't expect special effects", and make sure to "watch the credits and you'll see the real children, now in their 80s."

Radio Days 23 | 23 | 23 | 23

1987 | Directed by Woody Allen | With Mia Farrow, Julie Kavner, Dianne Wiest | 85 minutes | Rated PG

Tune in for "fond memories" to this "charming" "family comedy", an "affectionate period piece" set in late-'30s Rockaway Beach, where "childhood innocence, neurotic relatives" and golden-age radio fill the airwaves in a series of "warm vignettes"; touted for "top-to-bottom acting excellence", it's a "funny", "free-form" sampler of "Allen at his sunniest" and "most enjoyable."

Raging Bull ✉◑ 26 | 28 | 24 | 26

1980 | Directed by Martin Scorsese | With Robert De Niro, Cathy Moriarty, Joe Pesci | 129 minutes | Rated R

Perhaps the "best boxing movie of all time", this "riveting" biopic charts the "rise and fall" of former middleweight champion Jake LaMotta, whose toughest opponents were his own "self-destructive tendencies"; shot in "beautiful black and white", it features a "primo De Niro", and though it can be "as painful as an open wound" to watch, most feel this is "knockout" filmmaking.

Raiders of the Lost Ark 28 | 24 | 27 | 28

1981 | Directed by Steven Spielberg | With Harrison Ford, Karen Allen, Paul Freeman, Denholm Elliott | 115 minutes | Rated PG

It doesn't get "more exciting" than this "benchmark" of "nonstop pulp-fiction action", Spielberg's "roller-coaster" homage to "Saturday matinee" serials that introduces the "rakish" Indiana Jones, a tweedy archaeologist with a "strapping-hero" alter ego who scraps with the Nazis over an "all-powerful artifact"; chock-full of "retro" delights like "tongue-in-cheek" humor, "improbable cliff-hanger escapes" and a "love interest" amid the "snakes, whips and guns", it's a "rousing blockbuster" that proves the "'80s weren't all bad."

Rain Man ✉ 25 | 27 | 24 | 23

1988 | Directed by Barry Levinson | With Dustin Hoffman, Tom Cruise, Valeria Golino | 133 minutes | Rated R

This Best Picture winner is an unconventional "brothers bonding" drama driven by an Oscar-winning performance from Hoffman, who's "nothing short of incredible" as a full-grown "autistic savant" blessed with an endless supply of "quirky mannerisms" and "memorable lines"; Cruise shows off his own "acting chops" as the "scheming" sibling angling for half his inheritance, bringing on showers of "insight" that clear up to let a "feel-good" resolution shine through.

	OVERALL	ACTING	STORY	PROD.
Raising Arizona	23	23	23	21

Raising Arizona

1987 | Directed by Joel Coen | With Nicolas Cage, Holly Hunter, John Goodman | 94 minutes | Rated PG-13

For a "completely original" and truly "bizarre" screwball comedy, check out this "hilarious white-trash" "cult classic" about a "childless", "criminal-class" couple (a policewoman married to a "failed convenience-store thief") that kidnaps a kid; Cage and Hunter are drolly "deadpan" delivering "dialogue that can't be beat", while the plot is typical Coen brothers: "goofy", "quirky" and gosh "darn funny."

26 | 28 | 26 | 23

Raisin in the Sun, A ◑

1961 | Directed by Daniel Petrie | With Sidney Poitier, Claudia McNeil, Ruby Dee, Diana Sands | 128 minutes | Not Rated

"Equal to" Lorraine Hansberry's award-winning Broadway play, this "groundbreaking" adaptation tells the story of a poor black family coping with a modest financial windfall; there's "emotional conflict" aplenty in its "dueling themes" of "racism, motherhood and manhood" and the "strong" cast is up to the challenge (particularly the "poignant Poitier"); pessimists say it's "sadly as applicable today as it was in the '60s."

27 | 25 | 27 | 29

Ran F

1985 | Directed by Akira Kurosawa | With Tatsuya Nakadai, Mieko Harada, Daisuke Ryu | 160 minutes | Rated R

"Big, bold and beautiful", Kurosawa's "swan song" shows his "deft touch" intact in this "expansive retelling of *King Lear*" transformed into a "riveting" samurai "epic" involving a Shogun warlord whose decision to sheath his sword leads to intra-clan "betrayals"; suitably "Shakespearean" in scale, with "stunning" depictions of "feudal society" and "incredible battle scenes", it's "slow"-running pacewise but most hail it as "brilliant almost beyond belief."

29 | 27 | 29 | 25

Rashomon ◑ F

1951 | Directed by Akira Kurosawa | With Toshiro Mifune, Machiko Kyo, Masayuki Mori | 88 minutes | Not Rated

Surely "truth is in the eye of the beholder", but most agree that Akira Kurosawa's "superb head-twister" of a Japanese drama should be "required viewing"; aided by "exquisite" camerawork, it's a "simple story" about an ambush in the forest told from "four different points of view", proving that "self-interest" amounts to "nine-tenths of everything"; in sum, this "seminal" tale has been tirelessly "copied but never equaled."

26 | - | 25 | 27

Ratatouille

2007 | Directed by Brad Bird, Jan Pinkava | Animated | 111 minutes | Rated G

In this animated "valentine to Paris and the art of cooking", an "unusual alliance" between a bus boy and a rodent "obsessed with haute cuisine" equals "another masterpiece cooked up by Pixar"; a "perfect recipe" for "broad audience appeal", it blends "visually stunning" animation with "loads of charm", adds "silly antics" for the kids and folds in some "smart dialogue" for adults; in sum, "*c'est magnifique!*"

26 | 29 | 25 | 26

Ray ✉

2004 | Directed by Taylor Hackford | With Jamie Foxx, Kerry Washington, Regina King | 152 minutes | Rated PG-13

"Foxx almost disappears into the person of Ray Charles" in this "phenomenal" bio-"tribute" to the "legendary musician", nabbing a "well-deserved" Oscar for his "foot-stomping", "heartrending" portrayal of the superstar that's so convincing you'll "forget who you're really watching"; fans agree the "uncompromising" look at the soul man's "boozing, drugs and womanizing" is right on key, with additional hoorays going out to that "marvelous soundtrack."

Reader, The ✉ 25 | 28 | 25 | 24

2008 | Directed by Stephen Daldry | With Kate Winslet, Ralph Fiennes, David Kross, Lena Olin, Bruno Ganz | 124 minutes | Rated R

Between its "controversial" depiction of the "sexual initiation" of a younger man by an older woman and its "provocative" look at post-war Germany facing its "monstrous" past, there's no shortage of "taboo subject matter" in this "compelling" Holocaust drama; owing to an "exceptional" cast led by the "fearless", Oscar-winning Winslet, the "challenging" material is conveyed with "compassion" and "insight."

Rear Window 28 | 27 | 28 | 27

1954 | Directed by Alfred Hitchcock | With James Stewart, Grace Kelly, Thelma Ritter, Raymond Burr | 112 minutes | Rated PG

"Voyeurism" meets "suspense" in this "snooper's dream" about a "wheelchair-bound" photographer "spying on his neighbors" and trying to "trap a killer" while fending off his girlfriend, who's tempting him into "another trap - marriage"; while the "crisp script" and "great NY set" draw huzzahs, fans tout its "perfectly cast" leads, the "solid" Stewart and "deeelicious" Kelly; so many find it "unsurpassed" that it was voted the top Hitchcock flick in this Survey.

Rebecca ✉◑ 27 | 27 | 27 | 25

1940 | Directed by Alfred Hitchcock | With Laurence Olivier, Joan Fontaine, Judith Anderson | 130 minutes | Not Rated

Based on Daphne du Maurier's "ultimate romance novel", "Hitchcock's first American film" is a "dark, moody" tale of a woman living in the shadow of her new husband's old wife; "haunting" and "eerily captivating", it showcases an "excellent" Olivier and a "gorgeous" Fontaine, but it's the "over-the-top" Anderson who's the real "hoot" here.

Rebel Without a Cause 24 | 24 | 21 | 22

1955 | Directed by Nicholas Ray | With James Dean, Natalie Wood, Sal Mineo | 111 minutes | Not Rated

A "lost generation lives on" in this "terse" depiction of "disaffected youth" and "family conflict", which elevated Dean to "icon" status as a "rebellious" juvenile delinquent who leads a "great cast" as they cope with "hope, fear and love" in the "inchoate LA" of the '50s; if all that acting out is a bit "dated", most maintain it "lives up to its rep" as the "ultimate" ode to "teen alienation."

Red River ◑ 26 | 25 | 25 | 27

1948 | Directed by Howard Hawks | With John Wayne, Montgomery Clift, Joanne Dru | 133 minutes | Not Rated

"Perhaps the grandest" Western of all, this cowpuncher "classic" breaks into a gallop when "lots of hunky men" saddle up for a dangerous cattle drive along the Chisholm Trail; Wayne "excels in an unsympathetic role" as a "stolid" rancher who turns against Monty, who "holds his own" as a buckaroo of "brooding sensitivity"; the result is a horn-lock that fans brand a grade-A prime "rewatcher."

	OVERALL	ACTING	STORY	PROD.
Red Shoes, The	26	24	24	26

1948 | Directed by Michael Powell, Emeric Pressburger | With Anton Walbrook, Moira Shearer | 133 minutes | Not Rated

With a tip of the slipper to Hans Christian Andersen, this "ageless" drama of "romance and ballet" "takes a fairy tale and creates magic" around the story of a young dancer who joins a celebrated troupe only to enter into a pas de deux with a composer; "sumptuous" staging and "dreamy choreography" make it a terpsichorean "benchmark", and fans "love every bit of it."

Red Violin, The F	24	23	24	24

1999 | Directed by François Girard | With Samuel L. Jackson, Greta Scacchi | 131 minutes | Rated R

A "symphony" recounting the "many tales of a violin's life", this "intricate" drama "follows the path" of a "fabulous instrument" from its creation in Renaissance Italy though various owners, countries and epochs, up to Jackson's encounter as a present-day appraiser; in spite of "art-house" airs, boosters bow to a "twisting" story that "keeps you guessing" - backed by a really "stunning" soundtrack featuring "real music by a real composer."

Remains of the Day, The	24	27	23	25

1993 | Directed by James Ivory | With Anthony Hopkins, Emma Thompson, Christopher Reeve | 138 minutes | Rated PG

"If you loved *Howards End*", you'll dig this "complex and entertaining" drama of "two fragile souls" on a British estate in the late '30s; "repressed" head butler Hopkins "puts duty above all else", even his yen for housekeeper Thompson, and both give "precise, controlled performances" filled with "gripping silences" to suit its "nuanced" story of "unfulfilled love", "class-system" bias and the "obtuseness of the upper crust" - just "don't expect action."

Requiem for a Heavyweight ◑	26	28	26	23

1962 | Directed by Ralph Nelson | With Anthony Quinn, Jackie Gleason, Mickey Rooney, Julie Harris | 95 minutes | Not Rated

Adapted from Rod Serling's Emmy-winning television play, this "knockout" drama is "one of the best fight films around", detailing a punch-drunk boxer's "gut-wrenching" decline; maybe it's turned "dated" and "preachy" over time, but for diversion there's always that "superb" ensemble cast, especially the "amazing" Quinn; P.S. look for cameos from real-life heavyweights Jack Dempsey and Muhammad Ali.

Rescuers, The	23	-	23	23

1977 | Directed by Wolfgang Reitherman, John Lounsbery, Art Stevens | Animated | 76 minutes | Rated G

A "must-see for every child", this animated feature stars a pair of "adorable" mice bent on rescuing a kidnapped kid; although maybe not at the top of the Mouse House pantheon, it's still "cute and fun" with memorable voicework from Bob Newhart, Eva Gabor and Geraldine Page.

Reservoir Dogs	24	25	24	22

1992 | Directed by Quentin Tarantino | With Harvey Keitel, Tim Roth, Michael Madsen, Steve Buscemi | 99 minutes | Rated R

The Tarantino "template" for a "new" style of crime thriller splices "hip, sharp" dialogue with "hard-core violence" as a "dream cast" sporting two-tone threads turns a jewel heist into a "riveting" "bloody spectacle"; the "clever" script relies on diced chronology, "sly riffs" on pop culture and "psychological twists" to lend heart to the "vicious" gang, though many howl the "nasty" bits ("ear removal", anyone?) are still "painful to watch."

Reversal of Fortune ✉ 23 | 26 | 23 | 21

1990 | Directed by Barbet Schroeder | With Jeremy Irons, Glenn Close, Ron Silver | 120 minutes | Rated R

"You can't make this stuff up" – Oscar-winner Irons is "totally mesmerizing" in his "smarmy" take on the real-life Claus von Bulow, the high-society ladies' man accused of sending his heiress wife into an irreversible coma; Close and Silver also deliver the goods in this "solid" picture whose only drawback is "not having the ending that you want."

Rifi ◑F 26 | 24 | 27 | 24

1956 | Directed by Jules Dassin | With Jean Servais, Carl Mohner, Robert Manuel | 115 minutes | Not Rated

Arguably the "first modern caper film", this "original" French take on film noir is loaded with "intrigue, gangsters and great scenes of Paris" as it details the plans to burgle a jewelry store; its "stunning" heist sequence – "totally silent for half an hour" – assures its "classic" status, and even if the "production quality seems dated now", ultimately it "still holds up after 50 years."

Right Stuff, The 26 | 24 | 26 | 26

1983 | Directed by Philip Kaufman | With Sam Shepard, Scott Glenn, Ed Harris | 193 minutes | Rated PG

"Exuberant", "involving" and "proud to be American", this "triumphant" drama "never flags" in launching Tom Wolfe's "snarky yet sincere" "epic of the space age" onto the big screen; a "retelling of true events" surrounding the evolution of test pilots into astronauts in the Mercury program, it takes "historical" stuff and pushes the envelope with "adventure, humor" and a cast that's "A-ok in every way."

Rio Bravo 24 | 22 | 21 | 22

1959 | Directed by Howard Hawks | With John Wayne, Dean Martin, Ricky Nelson | 141 minutes | Not Rated

"As Westerns go", this "entertaining" oater from the Hawks/Wayne team is an "expert reshuffling" of the plot elements of "*High Noon*", the story of a sheriff trying to hold a prisoner against a threatening mob virtually alone; though the picture was remade as *El Dorado* (and later as *Rio Lobo*), aficionados say the original is the "best version."

River Runs Through It, A 22 | 23 | 21 | 25

1992 | Directed by Robert Redford | With Brad Pitt, Craig Sheffer, Tom Skerritt | 123 minutes | Rated PG

Sounding "deep" waters with a "pastoral" tale of "life as we no longer know it", Redford's "elegiac" drama of "family bonds" takes a "moving", "candid" look at the sibling rivalry between two small-town minister's sons; the "smooth" pace is set by the stars' "subtle emotion" and "striking" cinematography that captures the "Montana wilderness" in all of its full "majesty", though some clock-watchers find the running time a bit "too slow."

OVERALL | ACTING | STORY | PROD.

Road to Perdition

23 | 26 | 22 | 25

2002 | Directed by Sam Mendes | With Tom Hanks, Paul Newman, Daniel Craig, Jude Law | 117 minutes | Rated R

"Hanks proves his versatility" in this "evocative period piece", playing a "cold-blooded hit man" for the Irish mafia during the Depression; the "intense journey" is "impeccably done", with Newman in "stellar form", Oscar-winning cinematography that will "take your breath away" (notably that "tommy gun scene in the rain") and "top-notch screenwriting" that "stays true to the novel."

Road Warrior, The

22 | 18 | 21 | 20

1982 | Directed by George Miller | With Mel Gibson, Bruce Spence, Mike Preston | 94 minutes | Rated R

"Road rage" kicks into overdrive in this "raw Aussie action flick", with "lean, mean" Gibson "at his baddest" as Mad Max, a "lone cowboy" cruising a "post-apocalyptic" wasteland and upholding his "own brand of justice"; set in a "nihilistic" near-future when barbaric gangs comb the desert pestering decent folk for petrol, its combo of an "intriguing" setup and "incredible car stunts" makes it a "visceral" "cult favorite"; gas up.

Rocky ✉

25 | 20 | 25 | 21

1976 | Directed by John G. Avildsen | With Sylvester Stallone, Talia Shire, Burt Young | 119 minutes | Rated PG

This "red-blooded" ring drama (and Oscar champ) "goes the distance" with an "underdog-makes-good" theme as "two-bit" boxer Sly "wins over everyone's heart" when he "gets his shot" at the title and "finds true love" along the way; though part "hokey" "Hollywood fantasy", it's also a "stirring confidence-booster" that packs an everlasting "wallop."

Roman Holiday ✉◑

27 | 26 | 25 | 25

1953 | Directed by William Wyler | With Gregory Peck, Audrey Hepburn, Eddie Albert | 118 minutes | Not Rated

A "date movie without equal", this "frothy", "witty romance" presents a "radiant" Hepburn as the "rebellious" "gamine princess" with a "pixie cut" who plays hooky in the Eternal City, escorted by "charming", "not-so-hard-boiled reporter" Peck; helped along by "wondrous Roman scenery", their "coy" exchanges lead things on their natural "exhilarating" course, making for a "captivating fantasy" that draws to a "bittersweet", "refreshingly realistic" ending ("awww!").

Romeo and Juliet

26 | 24 | 27 | 26

1968 | Directed by Franco Zeffirelli | With Olivia Hussey, Leonard Whiting | 138 minutes | Rated PG

"Achingly beautiful" and played with "youthful vigor", this "faithful Zeffirelli" reading renders the "grand" romance of star-crossed love so "accessible" that "even boys cry" at the end; the "classic" production stays "true to the Bard" with "so-cute" teenage actors, pleasing "purists" as the "definitive film version" and surviving as the odds-on favorite to be the Shakespeare everyone's "made to watch in school."

Room at the Top ✉◑

24 | 27 | 24 | 23

1959 | Directed by Jack Clayton | With Simone Signoret, Laurence Harvey, Heather Sears | 115 minutes | Not Rated

Britain's "class struggle" is the subject of this "powerful" "drama of ambition" starring an "excellent" Harvey as an angry young man bent on improving his lot in life by wooing a naive heiress; along the way, he has some "provocative" moments with the "smoky" Signoret, who steals the picture (and copped a Best Actress Oscar) as his "sultry, world-weary" playmate.

Room with a View, A ✉ 26 | 26 | 24 | 27

1986 | Directed by James Ivory | With Maggie Smith, Helena Bonham Carter, Denholm Elliott | 117 minutes | Not Rated

"Florence looks like heaven" in this "crisp" costume drama about a "proper Victorian girl's" sightseeing tour that's considerably perked up by "friendships that form in a pensione", leading to her "romantic awakening"; the "brilliant acting" brings "wit and energy" to a "sunny" "study of class and character" that finds all kinds of room for "superb fin de siècle" touches and "seductive" shots of the Italian landscape.

Rosemary's Baby 24 | 25 | 25 | 22

1968 | Directed by Roman Polanski | With Mia Farrow, John Cassavetes, Ruth Gordon | 136 minutes | Rated R

A "glamorous horror" flick about a "naive" housewife duped into bearing "Satan's child", this "gut-wrenching classic" still "scares the hell out" of nearly everybody; "pro-choice" types tout Farrow's "amazing" turn (and "faaabulous haircut") as well as Polanski's "very faithful adaptation" of Ira Levin's novel, but everyone says that the "devilishly good", Oscar-winning Gordon "steals the show."

Rudy 23 | 22 | 25 | 21

1993 | Directed by David Anspaugh | With Sean Astin, Jon Favreau, Ned Beatty | 116 minutes | Rated PG

"What *Hoosiers* is to basketball", this "inspiring" flick is to college football, "bringing grown men to tears" with its "sentimental" celebration of true-life "ultimate underdog" Rudy Ruettiger, an "undersized kid with an oversized heart" who famously tackled his "lifelong dream to play for Notre Dame"; fielding a stellar cast led by the "excellent" Astin, it will "have you chanting with the crowd" during the "feel-good" finale.

Ruling Class, The 23 | 26 | 22 | 21

1972 | Directed by Peter Medak | With Peter O'Toole, Alastair Sim, Arthur Lowe, Harry Andrews | 154 minutes | Rated PG

Alternately "funny and disturbing", this black "social satire" takes on "the British upper class" in its story of a "delusional" fellow who becomes "the 14th Earl of Gurney" after the death of his father; the "bizarre" plot includes some "absurd song-and-dance routines" but "moves like lightning", and as the "bonkers" nobleman, O'Toole's "totally over the top."

Run Lola Run F 23 | 21 | 24 | 24

1999 | Directed by Tom Tykwer | With Franka Potente, Moritz Bleibtreu, Herbert Knaup | 81 minutes | Rated R

There's "never a dull moment" in this "amped-up" German import involving the "sweat-dripping" effort of a fleet-footed fräulein to hustle a big pile of cash to save her boyfriend from a nasty mobster; "strongly driven" by an "adrenaline"-pumping "techno soundtrack" and "video-game" vibe, the "breathless" "nonlinear" narrative forges "different perspectives" and "time repeats" into a "pulse-pounding" "original" that's as "ultra-watchable" as it is "quirky."

	OVERALL	ACTING	STORY	PROD.

Rushmore 23 | 25 | 22 | 22

1998 | Directed by Wes Anderson | With Jason Schwartzman, Olivia Williams, Bill Murray | 93 minutes | Rated R

A monument of "quality quirkiness", this "unabashedly unusual" comedy stars Schwartzman as an "arrogant and clever" but "dysfunctional" scholarship student at an elite prep school whose "coming of age" takes many a "droll" twist when he befriends a rich alumnus and falls for a teacher; the "smart", "character-driven" script is "expertly acted", leading to high marks for a "winning gem" with "real heart" "beneath the smarminess" – and how about that "killer soundtrack"?

Saboteur ◑ 23 | 21 | 24 | 23

1942 | Directed by Alfred Hitchcock | With Robert Cummings, Priscilla Lane, Otto Kruger, Norman Lloyd | 108 minutes | Not Rated

"Cross-country intrigue" underlies this "effective" Hitchcock "romp across America", wherein an "innocent man" is "unwittingly involved in an espionage plot"; maybe it's a bit "cheesy by today's standards", but even "Bob Cummings' wooden performance" is blown away by that "unforgettable finale" atop the "torch of the Statue of Liberty."

Sabrina ◑ 25 | 25 | 25 | 23

1954 | Directed by Billy Wilder | With Humphrey Bogart, Audrey Hepburn, William Holden | 113 minutes | Not Rated

Like an order of "first-class everything", this "delicious" "rags-to-riches" romance sparkles with "wit and couture" as an "ethereal" Hepburn plays a "beguiling", love-struck chauffeur's daughter in a "little black dress"; the "modern Cinderella" scenario finds Bogie in a "comedic role" as an all-business heir determined to beat out his "younger playboy brother" for Audrey's affections; as for Harrison Ford's 1995 remake, loyalists "consider it blasphemy."

Sand Pebbles, The 24 | 26 | 25 | 24

1966 | Directed by Robert Wise | With Steve McQueen, Richard Crenna, Richard Attenborough, Candice Bergen | 179 minutes | Rated PG-13

An "epic of China" told from the point of view of Yank sailors knee-deep in the revolutionary turmoil of 1926, this "powerful, pertinent" war drama features "authentic hero" McQueen "smoldering in top form" as a "tough-guy" Navy mechanic "with a heart of gold", manning an American patrol boat; if the tale "meanders like the Yellow River", it's still a "must-see" for History Channel addicts.

Savages, The 23 | 28 | 22 | 22

2007 | Directed by Tamara Jenkins | With Laura Linney, Philip Seymour Hoffman, Philip Bosco | 113 minutes | Rated R

"Watching a parent's decline" is the "tough" theme of this "compassionate" indie tragicomedy about two "dysfunctional" siblings "dealing with their father's dementia" while "still grappling with their own childhood issues"; though it's oftentimes "too real for comfort", a "savagely smart script" makes the "tricky subject matter" work.

Saving Private Ryan ✉ 26 | 26 | 24 | 28

1998 | Directed by Steven Spielberg | With Tom Hanks, Tom Sizemore, Edward Burns | 170 minutes | Rated R

"As intense as it gets", Steven Spielberg's "celluloid monument" to WWII evokes the fear of war with "in-your-face" footage like the "devastating" opening, a "masterful" montage of "graphic" death and mayhem on a D-day beachhead; thereafter Hanks leads a "superbly" cast unit through no-man's-land on a "compelling" quest for a missing grunt, and despite sniping that "the story bogs down", it's a "wrenching" oh-"so-real" reminder that "war is hell."

Say Anything 23 | 22 | 22 | 20

1989 | Directed by Cameron Crowe | With John Cusack, Ione Skye, John Mahoney | 100 minutes | Rated PG-13

"Teenage love is beautiful" in this "quintessential" '80s romance that had a "serious impact on Gen-X women" by making them "fall in love with Cusack", the "geek who gets the popular girl" from a "different class of society"; though naysayers suggest the "dad drama" subplot "slows things down", overall this "youth-in-angst" story has become the "touchstone of a generation"; most memorable prop: the "boom box."

Scenes from a Marriage F 25 | 27 | 23 | 23

1974 | Directed by Ingmar Bergman | With Liv Ullmann, Erland Josephson, Bibi Andersson | 168 minutes | Rated PG

Originally a six-hour TV miniseries pared down to feature length, this still "powerful" portrayal of a "marriage breaking down" via Ingmar Bergman is a "real, poignant" tale told with such "rich execution" that it might "scare off all but the bravest from the altar"; though "hard to take for its intensity", this "talkathon" is worth seeing for its simply "astonishing performances."

Schindler's List ✉◑ 29 | 29 | 28 | 29

1993 | Directed by Steven Spielberg | With Liam Neeson, Ben Kingsley, Ralph Fiennes | 197 minutes | Rated R

Embarking on a "tour-de-force" "journey through a dark period", Spielberg's "direct", "painful" wartime drama "crystallizes the real-life horror" of the Holocaust in "stunning quasi-documentary" black-and-white, with Neeson as the man of "moral conscience" dealing with the Nazis in "shattering" circumstances; "beyond moving" and "tough to watch" in spite of its "understatement" and "touches of grace", it's a top Oscar honoree that's all-but-unanimously cited as "unforgettable required viewing."

Seabiscuit 25 | 25 | 25 | 26

2003 | Directed by Gary Ross | With Tobey Maguire, Jeff Bridges, Chris Cooper | 141 minutes | Rated PG-13

Set against the "backdrop of the Great Depression", this "winning" adaptation of Laura Hillenbrand's best-selling pony tale trots out an "old-fashioned" story about a "little horse that could"; "moving" turns from Maguire, Bridges and Cooper (as jockey, owner and trainer) and "beautifully photographed", "suspenseful" racing sequences evoke cheers, even if a few find this gelding's gait a tad "slow", saying "it misses greatness by a nose."

Searchers, The 27 | 25 | 27 | 27

1956 | Directed by John Ford | With John Wayne, Jeffrey Hunter, Vera Miles | 120 minutes | Not Rated

"Not just a shoot-'em-up", this "thinking person's" Western boasts "peak" work from Wayne, who delivers a "gripping" portrayal of a "brooding" Civil War vet obsessed with tracking down his niece, abducted by Comanches; with its "spectacular" backdrops and "controversial" handling of "kinship and racism", it's much praised as "Ford's masterpiece", "perhaps the finest in the genre."

Searching for Bobby Fischer

24 | 23 | 24 | 21

1993 | Directed by Steven Zaillian | With Max Pomeranc, Joe Mantegna, Ben Kingsley, Joan Allen | 110 minutes | Rated PG

The fraught dynamics between "parents and gifted children" underlie this "all-ages" drama featuring the "wonderful" Pomeranc as a chessboard "prodigy" who "learns about fair play" from a caring parent and a cutthroat grandmaster; even "without a lot of flash", it's "compelling" moviemaking – "who knew chess was this interesting?"

Secret of NIMH, The

24 | - | 25 | 24

1982 | Directed by Don Bluth | Animated | 82 minutes | Rated G

From the all-pro pens of "former Disney artists" comes this "freaky", oft-"forgotten" "alternative to sugar-coated" animation, a "beautifully drawn gem" of a barnyard yarn about a mama mouse desperately seeking a new nest for her brood; the "captivating" depiction of farm life comes with "character development" and an "interesting" story designed to appeal to the "adult" in everyone.

Secrets & Lies

24 | 27 | 24 | 22

1996 | Directed by Mike Leigh | With Brenda Blethyn, Marianne Jean-Baptiste | 136 minutes | Rated R

Bad boy Leigh turns "accessible" in this "smart", "solid British drama" of "long-lost" family ties concerning a young black Londoner who "searches out her biological mother" only to find out that mum may be a white woman; led by Blethyn's "pure, honest performance", the principals do a "terrific job" of making this tale "involving" and "heartbreaking."

Sense and Sensibility ✉

26 | 27 | 26 | 26

1995 | Directed by Ang Lee | With Emma Thompson, Alan Rickman, Kate Winslet, Hugh Grant | 136 minutes | Rated PG

"Jane Austen would have liked" this "bittersweet" story of two husband-hunting sisters that "captures the true flavor" of her novel "with wit and honesty" largely due to a "strong", Oscar-winning script from the "so-fine" Emma Thompson; sensitive types tout the "beautiful" scenery, director Lee's "brilliant" job and an ensemble cast that "rises to the occasion" - "this is what moviemaking should be."

Sergeant York ✉◑

25 | 25 | 24 | 22

1941 | Directed by Howard Hawks | With Gary Cooper, Walter Brennan, Joan Leslie | 134 minutes | Not Rated

A "true story that needs no amplification", this "satisfying" biopic stars an Oscar-winning Cooper as the pacifist who became WWI's most decorated soldier after single-handedly dismantling an enemy regiment; a "complex" piece of pro-war propaganda, it's also a "great depiction" of a man of "quiet inner strength."

Serpico

23 | 26 | 24 | 21

1973 | Directed by Sidney Lumet | With Al Pacino, John Randolph, Tony Roberts | 129 minutes | Rated R

Honesty "doesn't pay" in this "gritty" true story starring a "superb" Pacino as a whistle-blowing NYPD do-gooder who becomes a "man alone" when his exposure of "cop corruption" threatens to bring down the whole city; if all the "raw emotion" can grow "frustrating" and the milieu seems "a bit dated", it remains arresting as a "compelling commentary on the times."

Servant, The ◑ 25 | 27 | 25 | 23

1963 | Directed by Joseph Losey | With Dirk Bogarde, James Fox, Sarah Miles, Wendy Craig | 112 minutes | Not Rated

The "British class structure" gets the Harold Pinter treatment in this "dark", "nasty piece of work" detailing the "power struggle" between a "menacing butler" and his "decadent", weak-willed master; in the title role, the "peerless" Bogarde is so "appropriately creepy" that some consider "giving up their household staff."

Seven 23 | 23 | 24 | 23

1995 | Directed by David Fincher | With Brad Pitt, Morgan Freeman, Kevin Spacey | 123 minutes | Rated R

All the "elegant nastiness" of a "guided tour through hell" surfaces in this "macabre psychological thriller" about two big-city detectives on the trail of an "ingenious" serial killer who dreams up "genuinely disturbing" torments "based on the seven deadly sins"; an "unrelenting" dose of "creepy modern noir" at its "darkest", it's wickedly "riveting" and "impressive" but "hard-to-take" and "gruesome" – with "no happy ending."

Seven Beauties F 26 | 26 | 25 | 24

1976 | Directed by Lina Wertmüller | With Giancarlo Giannini, Fernando Rey, Shirley Stoler | 115 minutes | Rated R

Wertmüller's "extraordinary" exploration of "survival in WWII" stars Giannini as a Chaplin-esque romeo trying to stay alive in a German concentration camp; a "brilliant" "amalgam of comedy and drama", it's a "powerful introduction to foreign filmmaking."

Seven Brides for Seven Brothers 24 | 20 | 21 | 25

1954 | Directed by Stanley Donen | With Howard Keel, Jane Powell, Russ Tamblyn | 103 minutes | Rated G

Ok, it's "low on feasibility", but this "down-home" musical of "seven eligible backwoodsmen looking for love" with a septet of hillbilly "Sabine women" strikes "pure gold" with its "great Johnny Mercer" tunes and "extraordinary" choreography; fans dig its "exuberant" production numbers that "make dance macho", particularly that "barn-raising scene."

Seven Days in May ◑ 26 | 24 | 28 | 22

1964 | Directed by John Frankenheimer | With Burt Lancaster, Kirk Douglas, Fredric March | 118 minutes | Not Rated

"It could happen here", or so says this "riveting 'what-if' drama", a "scary" Cold War story about disgruntled Pentagon brass who lay plans for a "military takeover"; soldiering along with "well-plotted" plausibility and "Douglas and Lancaster turning up the star heat", it's a "powerful nail-biter" that "political junkies" consider – gulp – "as timely today as ever."

Seven Samurai, The ◑ F 29 | 27 | 28 | 27

1956 | Directed by Akira Kurosawa | With Toshiro Mifune, Takashi Shimura | 203 minutes | Not Rated

Credited with "defining its own genre", Kurosawa's "awesome", "pivotal" Japanese adventure introduces the "original magnificent seven" as old-time samurai "warrior-heroes" who rise to the defense of a village menaced by a "vicious band of marauders"; the "epic running time melts away" before the "exciting" display of "honor", "courage" and "classic swordplay", and though there are "countless" reworkings, connoisseurs claim this "way-cool prototype" is "far superior."

Seventh Seal, The ◑ F — 27 | 27 | 26 | 26

1958 | Directed by Ingmar Bergman | With Max von Sydow, Gunnar Björnstrand, Nils Poppe | 96 minutes | Not Rated

An utterly foreign flick and staple of "college days", Bergman's "challenging" drama is a "dark allegory" with von Sydow as a "knight returning from the Crusades to plague-swept Europe" only to hunker down for a high-stakes "chess game with Death"; as a "cerebral" meditation on the "meaning of existence", it seals the deal with "some of the greatest visuals ever" and a "symbolic story" that "makes everything else look like a game of checkers."

Seven Year Itch, The — 23 | 23 | 20 | 20

1955 | Directed by Billy Wilder | With Marilyn Monroe, Tom Ewell, Evelyn Keyes | 105 minutes | Not Rated

Marilyn's billowing-dress "subway-grate scene" is the iconic moment in this "enjoyable" comedy, which finds "ordinary guy" Ewell "on his own" when the wife and kiddies split for summer vacation simultaneous with the arrival of his new neighbor, a most "memorable" Monroe in full "innocent-sexpot" mode, who brings on a major "midlife crisis"; sure, the repartee seems "dated and stagy", but it can still tickle the "funny" bone.

Shadow of a Doubt ◑ — 26 | 26 | 26 | 25

1943 | Directed by Alfred Hitchcock | With Teresa Wright, Joseph Cotten, Macdonald Carey | 108 minutes | Not Rated

Hitchcock's "first truly American film" (and his "personal favorite"), this "dark" thriller is set in a "sunny", "Norman Rockwell"–esque town that's home to a "young girl and her mysterious yet appealing uncle" who's suspected of murder; the "is-he-or-isn't-he" plot works thanks to the "spot-on" Cotten, whose performance is "chilling" enough for you to consider "background checks on your own family."

Shakespeare in Love ✉ — 24 | 25 | 24 | 26

1998 | Directed by John Madden | With Gwyneth Paltrow, Geoffrey Rush, Joseph Fiennes, Judi Dench | 122 minutes | Rated R

"Whether it be true or not", this "lush, literate" romance is a "good-humored confection" that "lights up the screen" with "adorable" performances from Fiennes (an "ink-stained" Elizabethan scribe) whose "writer's block" is cleared by the "exquisitely attired" Paltrow (his not-so-secret admirer); a "rich" depiction of the age "laced with dialogue" from the plays, it's a "captivating", "rip-roaring" ride that's "accessible at any level."

Shall We Dance ◑ — 25 | 22 | 20 | 25

1937 | Directed by Mark Sandrich | With Fred Astaire, Ginger Rogers, Edward Everett Horton | 109 minutes | Not Rated

"Fred and Ginger" meet "George and Ira" (Gershwin) in this "champagne-bubbly" romance between a Russian ballet star and an American hoofer; maybe the "weak plot" is just another "variation on the

OVERALL	ACTING	STORY	PROD.

same storyline" from the series, but "who cares?" what with that "iconic" choreography and "great chemistry" between its "elegant" stars.

Shane

26	25	25	25

1953 | Directed by George Stevens | With Alan Ladd, Jean Arthur, Van Heflin | 118 minutes | Not Rated

There's "always a nuance to savor" in this "towering", "classic" Western, telling the "mythical American" tale of a "world-weary gunslinger forced out of retirement" when he sides with a homesteader family menaced by "ruthless cattle ranchers"; the "poignant" setup pays off with a "great finale" as Ladd walks tall in a showdown with "no-good" varmint Jack Palance, leading many oater voters to name it "best" in the West.

Shawshank Redemption, The

28	28	28	27

1994 | Directed by Frank Darabont | With Tim Robbins, Morgan Freeman, Bob Gunton | 142 minutes | Rated R

Finding the "stirring" in the stir and big hearts in the big house, this "first-rate" prison drama goes behind the walls of a "dismal" state pen to follow fellow lifers Robbins and Freeman on a "long, dark journey" that pits "friendship", "ingenuity and inner strength" against a "brutal, corrupt system"; besides the "marvelous acting", there's a last-reel "surprise" to add a "feel-good factor" and even some "hope."

She Wore a Yellow Ribbon

24	22	23	25

1949 | Directed by John Ford | With John Wayne, Joanne Dru, John Agar, Ben Johnson | 103 minutes | Not Rated

Ford's second bugle blast in his "cavalry trilogy" finds the director "at his best" in a tribute to the "honor and tradition" of horse soldiers posted to the ever-fleeting frontier; the Duke is typically "bigger than life" as a stiff-brimmed but sympathetic old man about to hang up his hat after a career in Injun territory, all portrayed against boundlessly "beautiful" big-sky scenery – "what else does a Western need?"

Shining, The

25	26	25	25

1980 | Directed by Stanley Kubrick | With Jack Nicholson, Shelley Duvall, Scatman Crothers | 146 minutes | Rated R

The "supernatural and psychotic" collide in this "revolutionary horror film", a "downright scary" story from the Stephen King novel about a "snowbound caretaker of an old hotel" running amok; though voters agree that the "elevator scene", "Diane Arbus twin girls" and "gloriously unhinged Nicholson" all shine, Duvall gets mixed marks: "intensely annoying" vs. "profoundly brilliant"; best line, no contest: "heeere's Johnny!"

Ship of Fools ◑

23	25	24	23

1965 | Directed by Stanley Kramer | With Vivien Leigh, Simone Signoret, José Ferrer, Lee Marvin, Oskar Werner, Elizabeth Ashley, George Segal, Michael Dunn | 149 minutes | Not Rated

A "touching but loaded adaptation" of the Katherine Anne Porter novel, this "clever" drama follows a clutch of characters "aboard an ocean liner" traveling from Mexico to Germany "on the eve of WWII"; while sinkers shrug it off as "hammy", "soap operatic" stuff (think *Grand Hotel* at sea), far more feel the "all-star" international cast is worth watching, notably the "memorable" Signoret, "standout" Werner and "heartbreaking" Leigh, who's "too convincing as a faded beauty."

	OVERALL	ACTING	STORY	PROD.

Shirley Valentine 24 24 23 20

1989 | Directed by Lewis Gilbert | With Pauline Collins, Tom Conti, Alison Steadman | 108 minutes | Rated R

A real "charmer" with a "Liverpudlian accent", this "spirited" comedy sends a "terrific message" with its "sweet midlife fantasy" of a "bored English housewife" who flees to the Aegean "looking for love" and nets Greek sailor Conti; adapted from the "superb" stage show, it "loses nothing in the translation" as a "wise" celebration of "independence and self-respect."

Shoot the Piano Player ◑ 🅵 25 24 23 22

1962 | Directed by François Truffaut | With Charles Aznavour, Marie Dubois, Nicole Berger | 84 minutes | Not Rated

Beside the "great title", Truffaut's "stylized" sophomore effort is a "slightly weird" combination of Gallic satire and American gangster picture that features a "not-so-romantic view of Paris"; its "unusual" story of a former concert pianist (the "sexy" Aznavour) mixed up with hooligans may be "for movie lovers only", but cineasts advise "see it with small expectations and you'll be rewarded."

Shop Around the Corner, The ◑ 24 25 25 23

1940 | Directed by Ernst Lubitsch | With Margaret Sullavan, James Stewart, Frank Morgan | 99 minutes | Not Rated

Lubitsch plies his signature touch to a "classic" romantic comedy template – "two people who don't like each other" falling in love – and cooks up this "tasteful but funny" production starring Stewart and Sullavan as "colleagues who spar at work" while sharing a passionate but "anonymous" postal correspondence on the side; like many "good old-fashioned" flicks, this one's been "remade and remade" (try "*You've Got Mail*"), but as usual, the imitators "can't beat" the original.

Shop on Main Street, The ✉ ◑ 🅵 27 27 26 24

1966 | Directed by Ján Kadár, Elmar Klos | With Ida Kaminska, Jozef Kroner | 125 minutes | Not Rated

A "classic" Czech import, this "delicate, heartrending" drama of "one man's moral struggle" is centered around an "elderly shopkeeper caught up in the beginning of the Holocaust"; winner of the Best Foreign Film Oscar, its "slow but powerful" narrative leaves one with the "long-lasting impression" reserved for "real art."

Shot in the Dark, A 23 22 20 20

1964 | Directed by Blake Edwards | With Peter Sellers, Elke Sommer, George Sanders | 102 minutes | Rated PG

Sort of a cub *Pink Panther,* this "laugh-aloud funny" comedy features a "brilliant" Sellers as the clueless Inspector Clouseau, bumbling his way through a "delicious red-herring salad" of a plot that finds him assigned to solve a murder pinned on a Parisian chambermaid; if the "charmingly quirky" setup has its "slow" moments, the "master" makes it watchable "for his accent alone."

Show Boat 23 20 24 25

1951 | Directed by George Sidney | With Kathryn Grayson, Ava Gardner, Howard Keel | 107 minutes | Not Rated

The "schmaltzy" but "fabulous" Broadway hit gets the "Technicolor" treatment in this "sterling MGM musical" about a showgirl's "sentimental" entanglement with a riverboat gambler; the big wheel paddles along to "unforgettable" songs, "solid production numbers" and hoofers who "dance up a storm", and if purists prefer 1936's "glory-days" version, most can't help lovin' dat "beautiful, melodic" spectacle.

Shrek 26 | - | 25 | 28

2001 | Directed by Andrew Adamson, Vicky Jenson | Animated | 90 minutes | Rated PG

They "added a category" on Oscar night to honor this "playfully creative original" that uses "exceptional" CGI animation and "great voicing" to rework a "hoary storyline" about an ogre saving a princess into "highly entertaining" fare; it challenges the "Disney fairy-tale formula" with adult-level "parody" and "inside jokes" underscored with a "positive message" for all.

Shrek 2 26 | - | 24 | 28

2004 | Directed by Andrew Adamson, Kelly Asbury, Conrad Vernon | Animated | 92 minutes | Rated PG

"Another ogre-achiever", this "worthy sequel" once again features "incredible animation so lifelike you forget it's animation", "star voice actors" (Mike Myers, Eddie Murphy, Cameron Diaz) and a "laugh-out-loud" love story that sends up classic fairy-tale films; the "sly" satire and "clever" dialogue are "as much fun for adults as for the kids", and new addition Antonio Banderas – "purrfect as Puss 'n' Boots" – nearly "steals the movie."

Sideways 23 | 26 | 22 | 22

2004 | Directed by Alexander Payne | With Paul Giamatti, Thomas Haden Church, Virginia Madsen, Sandra Oh | 123 minutes | Rated R

Oenophiles toast this "intoxicatingly hilarious" road tripper pitting Giamatti's "shlub" against Church's "crack-up" for a Bacchian weekend of "middle-aged angst"-inspired "debauchery" in "scenic California wine country"; the "literate", Oscar-winning script uncorks some "wonderfully painful" scenes that are "so real" it's "like watching a train wreck", though a few whine it's just a "mundane soaper" with as much depth as a "glass of merlot."

Silence of the Lambs, The ✉ 27 | 28 | 27 | 26

1991 | Directed by Jonathan Demme | With Jodie Foster, Anthony Hopkins, Scott Glenn | 118 minutes | Rated R

Every subsequent "psych-profiling" flick owes something to this "masterful", "profoundly creepy" thriller that combines "heart-thumping suspense" with "premier" performances as Foster, an FBI greenhorn on a serial-killer hunt, is drawn into "intense mind games" with the "soft-spoken" madman Hopkins; its "well-deserved Oscars" speak for its "twisted", "truly terrifying" achievement, though some say it "gives fava beans a bad name."

Silkwood 22 | 26 | 25 | 21

1983 | Directed by Mike Nichols | With Meryl Streep, Kurt Russell, Cher, Craig T. Nelson | 131 minutes | Rated R

This "somewhat forgotten" drama generates a "great deal of tension" telling the fact-based story of a whistle-blowing nuclear plant worker who comes to a "mysterious end" when she tries to go public with hazardous goings-on at the facility; lit up by "terrific acting" from "marvelous" Meryl and "eye-opener" Cher, it's a "moving" picture of blue-collar good guys vs. white-collar baddies.

Silverado

24 | 24 | 23 | 24

1985 | Directed by Lawrence Kasdan | With Kevin Kline, Scott Glenn, Kevin Costner | 127 minutes | Rated PG-13

Boys, the "fun Western" rides again in this "well-made" "modern horse opera", a "true homage" that "throws in all the clichés" and delivers some "slick sequences" and "great one-liners" of its own; a "tremendous" cast "manages to upstage the glorious scenery", though it's best appreciated on the "biggest screen you can find."

Singin' in the Rain

28 | 26 | 25 | 28

1952 | Directed by Stanley Donen, Gene Kelly | With Gene Kelly, Donald O'Connor, Debbie Reynolds | 103 minutes | Rated G

"Giddy", "wet and wonderful", this "timeless" musical brightens the worst day with an "exuberant" "something-for-everyone" blend of "quintessential" song and dance, "satire" and a "sappy, funny love story"; the "flawless" Kelly plays a silent movie star in a "sweet send-up" of Hollywood's early talkie days and effortlessly executes the puddle-hopping "title number", leaving fans "awed."

Sixth Sense, The

26 | 25 | 27 | 25

1999 | Directed by M. Night Shyamalan | With Bruce Willis, Haley Joel Osment, Toni Collette | 107 minutes | Rated PG-13

A "tricky" one, this mega-hit thriller "surprises even the most astute" with its "perfectly crafted story" of a troubled boy with an "unwelcome gift" who finds a friend in Willis, leading to "really spooky" plot developments; it's hailed as an "unpredictable" sensation that rewards with "white-knuckle jolts" and a "stunning" "O. Henry"-esque ending.

Sleeper

23 | 19 | 23 | 20

1973 | Directed by Woody Allen | With Woody Allen, Diane Keaton, John Beck | 89 minutes | Rated PG

Orwell's wake-up call has nothing on this "inspired sci-fi spoof", a "hilarious" comedy of a nebbishy NYer who's cryogenically preserved then "defrosted in the future"; "laced with fast-paced verbal" cracks, it's "vintage" Allen at his "goofiest" and "most slapsticky" in a romp that generates "nonstop laughs" – the "orgasmatron alone is worth the price of admission."

Sleeping Beauty

25 | - | 23 | 25

1959 | Directed by Clyde Geronimi | Animated | 75 minutes | Rated G

No snooze among the "old Disney greats", this "lushly animated" "princess movie" has a trio of good fairies protecting the titular knockout from an evil spell by zapping her into a sound nap, interrupted only after her true love battles it out with filmdom's most fearsome dragon lady; the very wicked witch may be "too scary for the little ones", but most say this "classic" only "gets better with age."

Sleuth

25 | 28 | 26 | 23

1972 | Directed by Joseph L. Mankiewicz | With Laurence Olivier, Michael Caine | 138 minutes | Rated PG

It's no mystery why this suspense thriller based on the Broadway smash adapts "wonderfully to film": "masters-at-work" Olivier and

Caine offer "witty", "subtle" work as a cuckolded writer and his rival engaged in a calculated confrontation in an English country manor; the "creative" story builds "numerous plot twists" that cross and double-cross, and "two of the greatest" muster up some of the liveliest back-and-forth volleys ever seen "outside of Wimbledon."

Sling Blade ✉ 25 | 27 | 25 | 22

1996 | Directed by Billy Bob Thornton | With Billy Bob Thornton, Dwight Yoakam, J.T. Walsh | 135 minutes | Rated R

"Too convincing" in the role that lands him "on the map", "creepy Billy Bob" is "brilliantly believable" in this "tragedy from the real world" playing a slow-witted country boy who's sprung from the state booby hatch and taken in by a single mom; a "unique, touching" drama of man trouble, it "earns every accolade" with "excellent acting" and an "unforgettable punch" at the climax.

Slumdog Millionaire ✉ 26 | 25 | 26 | 26

2008 | Directed by Danny Boyle | With Dev Patel, Freida Pinto, Anil Kapoor | 120 minutes | Rated R

"Heartbreaking yet wonderful", this "modern-day rags-to-riches" tale mixes "realism and fantasy" to "poignant" effect as it traces a young Indian man's "struggle to survive" in the slums of Mumbai and win the jackpot in a TV game show; the depictions of "poverty and cruelty" can be "hard to watch", but its "eye-opening" aspects are pleasingly offset by its "fabulous child actors" and "upbeat" touches like the famed "Bollywood dance sequence."

Smiles of a Summer Night ◑ F 26 | 26 | 25 | 26

1957 | Directed by Ingmar Bergman | With Ulla Jacobsson, Eva Dahlbeck, Gunnar Björnstrand | 108 minutes | Not Rated

For "Bergman without the angst", check out his "rare venture" into romantic comedy, this "sumptuous" tale of "what it means to be human" set in fin de siècle Sweden; probably the director's "most approachable" film, it was "most influential" to a generation of artists, and best known today as the inspiration for Sondheim's *A Little Night Music.*

Snake Pit, The ◑ 25 | 28 | 25 | 24

1948 | Directed by Anatole Litvak | With Olivia de Havilland, Mark Stevens, Leo Genn, Celeste Holm | 108 minutes | Not Rated

"Daring for its time", this "hair-raising" depiction of conditions inside a mental institution was made during the postwar "heyday of psychoanalytic films" and is "still frightening" today; in addition to de Havilland's "sensitive", Oscar-nominated performance, many say it's most "memorable" for that "bird's-eye view" of the asylum's psycho ward.

Snow White & the Seven Dwarfs 27 | - | 26 | 27

1937 | Directed by David Hand | Animated | 83 minutes | Rated G

The "one that started it all", this "true classic" is the "*Citizen Kane* of animation", the "first full-length feature" from the Disney drawing boards and "still the finest" of them all; this tale of a fair maiden hiding in the forest with a band of "cute little guys" to escape a "terrifying wicked queen" is a "masterpiece" of "charm, simplicity and beauty" that continues to "entertain generations" and leave 'em humming "hi ho, hi ho!"

	OVERALL	ACTING	STORY	PROD.

Soldier's Story, A 26 | 26 | 25 | 22

1984 | Directed by Norman Jewison | With Howard E. Rollins Jr., Adolph Caesar, Denzel Washington | 101 minutes | Rated PG

Partially a "mystery" chronicling an "investigation into the murder of an African-American soldier on an army base" in the segregated South, this "powerful" drama also functions as an "important morality play" dealing with the "class issues facing black men" under white rule; enhanced by the "riveting performances" of Rollins, Caesar and a "then-young" Denzel, it's a "gripping" exercise building up to a "great twist at the end."

Some Like It Hot ◑ 28 | 27 | 26 | 26

1959 | Directed by Billy Wilder | With Marilyn Monroe, Tony Curtis, Jack Lemmon, Joe E. Brown | 120 minutes | Rated PG

"Cross-dressing was never so hilarious" as in this "legendary" "laff riot" about "two patsies on the run from the mob" who don dresses and join an all-girl band as part of their escape plan; thanks to Wilder's "sure touch" and the "sidesplitting" script's "countless priceless scenes" ("Lemmon with the maracas", "Curtis' riff on Cary Grant", Monroe "running wild"), this is one hot contender for the "greatest comedy ever made" - with the "best closing line" in moviedom: "nobody's perfect."

Something's Gotta Give 23 | 26 | 22 | 23

2003 | Directed by Nancy Meyers | With Jack Nicholson, Diane Keaton, Keanu Reeves | 128 minutes | Rated PG-13

"People over 50 having sex" is the novel premise of this "middle-aged" romantic comedy positing that "growing old can be fun"; cynics nix the "lousy title" and "predictable", "sitcom-lite" plot, but the "*Architectural Digest*-worthy" settings and mighty "excellent chemistry" between Jack and Diane make it go down easy for "mature audiences"; just ignore the "lame", "too-bad-she-wound-up-with-the-wrong-guy" ending.

Song of Bernadette, The ✉◑ 22 | 24 | 22 | 21

1943 | Directed by Henry King | With Jennifer Jones, Charles Bickford, Gladys Cooper, Anne Revere | 156 minutes | Not Rated

This "uplifting", "inspirational" tale of a French peasant girl who claims to have seen a vision of the Virgin Mary features a "sympathetic", Oscar-winning performance by Jones that will make you "believe her, even if no one else in the film does"; overall, the picture's a relic of "less cynical" times and may be too "syrupy" for modern audiences, but "it can still touch your heart, if you let it."

Song of the South ∅ 23 | - | 22 | 26

1946 | Directed by Wilfred Jackson, Harve Foster | Animated | With Ruth Warrick, James Baskett | 94 minutes | Rated G

Yup, it's "corny and dated", but "Disney's version of the Uncle Remus stories" is "one of the earliest" to offer an "animation-live action mix" as a boy encounters Brers Rabbit, Fox and Bear; its "controversial" stereotyping of plantation life means it's "missing in action" on DVD, but music lovers say it will always be "tough to top 'Zip-A-Dee-Doo-Dah.'"

Sophie's Choice ✉ 26 | 28 | 26 | 24

1982 | Directed by Alan J. Pakula | With Meryl Streep, Kevin Kline, Peter MacNicol | 150 minutes | Rated R

A "luminous" Streep with a "faint Polish accent" "shows her stuff" in this "haunting", highly "emotional" drama, which draws its "powerful story" from William Styron's novel about an Auschwitz survivor; though "wrenching" at points, it's a "compelling tour de force" that many see as Oscar-winner Meryl's "finest" hour.

Sorry, Wrong Number ◑ 25 | 25 | 25 | 23

1948 | Directed by Anatole Litvak | With Barbara Stanwyck, Burt Lancaster | 89 minutes | Not Rated

This "real thriller" adapted from a famed radio play stars Stanwyck as an "invalid heiress" who overhears a murder plot over crossed telephone wires; it's "pretty much a one-woman show" that relies on flashbacks to keep in motion, and if some say the "static" story is "stretched too thin", many more report "enough twists" to keep your "spine tingling."

Sounder 26 | 27 | 26 | 25

1972 | Directed by Martin Ritt | With Cicely Tyson, Paul Winfield, Kevin Hooks | 105 minutes | Rated G

The "sadness and dignity" of life as a black sharecropper in the Depression-era South "still resonate" with those who grew up watching this "classic with a heart", a "beautifully crafted" story of "strength" over suffering highlighted by a boy's "poignant" odyssey to locate his imprisoned father; featuring the "wonderful", Oscar-nominated Winfield and Tyson – not to mention that "heartbreaking" dog – "it might be one of the best family films ever."

Sound of Music, The ✉ 28 | 25 | 27 | 28

1965 | Directed by Robert Wise | With Julie Andrews, Christopher Plummer, Eleanor Parker | 174 minutes | Rated G

Everyone has an Alp-size "soft spot" for this "schmaltzy" Rodgers and Hammerstein musical, wherein a "charming" governess marries into a "do-re-mi" singing family and "stands on principle" after the Huns invade; the only Best Picture winner to feature "nuns, Nazis" and "kids in lederhosen", it's "shamelessly saccharine" but loved for its "uplifting" story, "fantastic" songs and "lush" scenery.

South Pacific 24 | 22 | 24 | 25

1958 | Directed by Joshua Logan | With Mitzi Gaynor, Rossano Brazzi, John Kerr | 151 minutes | Not Rated

"Incomparable music" washes up in a "tropical paradise" in this Rodgers and Hammerstein songfest, which finds American sea dogs and dames living and loving and singing along to "beautiful orchestrations" on a WWII Pacific atoll; though a huge hit in its day owing to those "eternal" tunes, some say it "doesn't hold up" anymore, pointing to the "filtered camera gels" that drown meaningful moments in "gaudy Technicolor" tints.

Spartacus 26 | 24 | 25 | 26

1960 | Directed by Stanley Kubrick | With Kirk Douglas, Laurence Olivier, Jean Simmons | 184 minutes | Rated PG-13

"Elevated" by its "sweeping vision" and "superb all-star cast", Stanley Kubrick's "impressive" epic headlines Douglas in the title role as the "virile" leader of a "slave revolt against Rome"; pairing a "psychologically complex" story with plenty of "gory but good" action, it's an "exciting" box-office big-timer that's "matched by few" in the "classic" spectacle sweeps.

	OVERALL	ACTING	STORY	PROD.

Spellbound ◑ 24 | 25 | 23 | 24

1945 | Directed by Alfred Hitchcock | With Gregory Peck, Ingrid Bergman, Leo G. Carroll | 111 minutes | Not Rated

One of the first mainstream movies to tackle psychiatry, this "outstanding" Hitchcock thriller deals with unlocking a "repressed memory", and the "perfect Bergman" and "gorgeous Peck" are a "good match" as doctor and patient; but despite touches like the "ahead-of-its-time dream sequences" designed by Salvador Dali, some analysts dismiss it as "dated Freudian nonsense."

Spider-Man 2 22 | 20 | 21 | 26

2004 | Directed by Sam Raimi | With Tobey Maguire, Kirsten Dunst, Alfred Molina, James Franco | 127 minutes | Rated PG-13

"Spidey tries to hang up his tights" and "live his own life" only to be bugged by "super villain" Doc Ock in this comic-book movie follow-up that's "as good as the original"; expect the usual "jaw-dropping" FX plus a "deeper" exploration of the webslinger's struggles with "guilt, sacrifice" and "love", and get ready for "further sequels" 'cause this franchise has legs.

Spirited Away 27 | - | 25 | 28

2002 | Directed by Hayao Miyazaki | Animated | 125 minutes | Rated PG

"Master storyteller" Miyazaki's "inventive", "visually stunning" Japanese version of "*The Wizard of Oz*" meets "*Alice in Wonderland*" "transcends the animation genre", bringing viewers to an "enchanted" "spirit world" filled with "bizarre characters", "unexpected sights" and "fantastic artwork"; it's "a tad long" and "has some pretty scary moments in it", so it may be best for "those 10 and up" – "unless you want to spend money on therapy" for the kids later.

Splendor in the Grass 🖂 25 | 25 | 24 | 22

1961 | Directed by Elia Kazan | With Natalie Wood, Warren Beatty, Zohra Lampert | 124 minutes | Not Rated

There's "heartbreak" in the heartland as "yearning" breeds "teen angst" in this "bittersweet" romance set in pre-Depression Kansas; the very "young" and very "gorgeous" Wood and Beatty supply some "real acting" as a "modern Romeo and Juliet" driven to "wrenching" extremes in this drama of "stolen dreams" and "lost love" that makes some sob sisters "cry just thinking about it."

Spy Who Came in from the Cold, The ◑ 25 | 26 | 25 | 22

1965 | Directed by Martin Ritt | With Richard Burton, Claire Bloom, Oskar Werner | 112 minutes | Not Rated

"Spying isn't pretty" in this "very cold look at the Cold War" adapted from John Le Carré's "first major success"; Burton's "at his peak" as a "brooding" British secret agent who defects to East Germany, and his "brilliant" work is backed up by "taut direction" and a "stark", "realistic" screenplay – "James Bond, this is not."

Stagecoach ◑ 27 | 24 | 26 | 25

1939 | Directed by John Ford | With John Wayne, Claire Trevor, John Carradine | 96 minutes | Not Rated

"Wayne's grand entrance" alone immortalizes this "archetypal" Ford Western about a group of stock frontier types "traversing hostile Indian territory" by rickety stage; featuring the young Duke in his "breakthrough role" as a fugitive convict, it rolls along on "great dialogue" and "well-acted" ensemble work interrupted by "viscerally exciting" action scenes, making it the "classic source" of countless tumbleweed "clichés."

Stage Door ◑ 25 | 26 | 23 | 22

1937 | Directed by Gregory La Cava | With Katharine Hepburn, Ginger Rogers, Gail Patrick, Lucille Ball | 92 minutes | Not Rated

A "chick flick for the old guard", this "witty" dramedy is set in a boarding house occupied by "scrappy wannabe actresses" who "live and die for the theatuh"; its "nearly all-female" cast (a "who's who of stars" of the time) is "unusually cohesive", helped along by a "multifaceted screenplay" peppered with plenty of "snappy" patter; most legendary line: Kate's "the calla lilies are in bloom again . . ."

Stalag 17 ✉◑ 27 | 26 | 27 | 24

1953 | Directed by Billy Wilder | With William Holden, Don Taylor, Otto Preminger | 120 minutes | Not Rated

Wilder's "wonderful" adaptation of the stage drama supplies the "intrigue" of a "psychological thriller" with some comic relief in this story starring the "properly Oscarized" Holden as a "cynical prisoner" in a WWII POW camp who's "suspected of being a German spy"; thanks to "tremendous acting" and "tense" plotting that "keeps you guessing until the end", this study of military "camaraderie" and "mob judgment" is "not to be missed."

Stand by Me 24 | 23 | 25 | 23

1986 | Directed by Rob Reiner | With Wil Wheaton, River Phoenix, Corey Feldman | 89 minutes | Rated R

This "wholesome" "coming-of-ager" focuses on preadolescent "best buddies" in '50s Oregon who set out "in search of a missing boy", bonding in the face of various perils and learning about the "real stuff" along the way; a platform for "young talent", it carries a "strong message" about the "struggle to grow up."

Star Is Born, A 25 | 26 | 26 | 26

1954 | Directed by George Cukor | With Judy Garland, James Mason, Jack Carson | 181 minutes | Rated PG

"Forget the other versions": this "heartbreaking" musical drama revisits the Tinseltown parable of fickle celebrity fortunes with the "best Judy ever", showcasing her "true range" as the nobody whose rise to fame is paralleled by her big-name hubby's descent; whether laughing, singing or "turning on the waterworks", the "mesmerizing" Garland gives the "performance of her life", leaving loyalists to lament the Oscar "that got away."

Star Trek 26 | 23 | 24 | 27

2009 | Directed by J.J. Abrams | With Chris Pine, Zachary Quinto, Leonard Nimoy, Zoe Saldana | 127 minutes | Rated PG-13

The Star Trek franchise gets its "swagger" back with this "grand reboot", a "fantastic ride" that boldly goes back to the sci-fi saga's "beginnings" with help from a "capable new cast" and a blinged-out production with "great special effects"; maybe its "time-travel" story requires a "second viewing to understand fully", but "longtime fans" and newbies alike "approve" of the overall result - and "can't wait" for more.

	OVERALL	ACTING	STORY	PROD.
Star Trek II: The Wrath of Khan	23	19	24	24

1982 | Directed by Nicholas Meyer | With William Shatner, Leonard Nimoy, DeForest Kelley, Ricardo Montalban | 113 minutes | Rated PG

"Best villain + best story" = "best *Trek*": so say supporters of this "ripping" sci-fi sequel that hits warp speed when "scenery-chewing" outer-space outlaw Khan hijacks a starship and goes gunning for Admiral Kirk, back for yet one more mission with his familiar Starfleet crew; it offers all the "overblown acting" and "heart of the original", and the windup with Spock on the spot has enough "emotional punch" to "make a Trekkie out of anyone."

Star Wars 28 | 22 | 28 | 29

(aka Star Wars Episode IV: A New Hope)

1977 | Directed by George Lucas | With Mark Hamill, Harrison Ford, Carrie Fisher | 121 minutes | Rated PG

Lucas' "Force is strong" in this "visionary" blockbuster, the "quantum leap" that "redefined sci-fi" and established a "dynasty" by locating the "universal" in a "galaxy far, far away", where "original" "critters" and "futuristic samurais" side with a put-upon princess against an evil Empire; building to a "black hats/white hats" showdown, it's an "entertaining" mix of "modern myth" and "thrill-and-a-half" FX; subsequent space operas "can't touch" it.

Star Wars Episode III: Revenge of the Sith 23 | 16 | 23 | 28

2005 | Directed by George Lucas | With Hayden Christensen, Ewan McGregor, Ian McDiarmid | 140 minutes | Rated PG-13

"Even though you know" how it wraps up, seeing the "missing pieces of the puzzle" fall into place brings "closure" to a generation of fans who've waited "20-plus years" to learn how Jedi "badass" Anakin Skywalker falls from grace and "becomes Darth Vader" in this "very dark", "epic conclusion" to the beloved space saga; piling on more "dazzling" FX and "campy acting" than ever, it's the "stronger story" this time 'round ("it took Lucas three tries") that explains why it's widely considered "the best of the prequels."

Star Wars Episode V: The Empire Strikes Back 26 | 21 | 26 | 28

1980 | Directed by Irvin Kershner | With Mark Hamill, Harrison Ford, Carrie Fisher, Billy Dee Williams | 124 minutes | Rated PG

The "darkest of the *Star Wars* series", this "worthy" first sequel features more "depth" in its characterizations and the "best storyline so far", "revealing many important secrets" as the "cosmic struggle continues"; "blissfully free of wooden dialogue", it might be the "most adult" of the "original trilogy", while that open-ended "cliff-hanger" of a finale makes for a suitably "spectacular" windup.

Star Wars Episode VI: Return of the Jedi 24 | 20 | 23 | 28

1983 | Directed by Richard Marquand | With Mark Hamill, Harrison Ford, Carrie Fisher, Billy Dee Williams | 134 minutes | Rated PG

Either a "worthy sequel" or "leftovers", this "wrap-up" episode of the *Star Wars* original trilogy finds the now-classic cast "comfortable in their roles", mugging their way through a "patented good-wins-over-evil storyline" with ample space for "cool special effects" and an "amazing final battle"; loyalists say the force is with it, but skeptics see a "weak entry" overrun with "cute, furry Ewoks", foreshadowing "toy tie-ins" and the "beginnings of Jar Jar."

Steel Magnolias 24 | 25 | 24 | 23

1989 | Directed by Herbert Ross | With Sally Field, Dolly Parton, Shirley MacLaine, Daryl Hannah | 117 minutes | Rated PG

Break out the "Kleenex" for this "estrogen"-soaked drama, a "major tearjerker" smothered in "Southern-fried flavor", dashed with "laughs" and "memorable one-liners" and played "to the hilt and then some" by a "talented" bunch of "adorable" all-star "belles"; the story of "best girlfriends" in a Looziana beauty parlor bonding through "thick and thin", it's "captivating", "well-made" and "weepy" enough to qualify as the "ultimate chick flick."

Sting, The ✉ 27 | 26 | 27 | 26

1973 | Directed by George Roy Hill | With Paul Newman, Robert Redford, Robert Shaw | 129 minutes | Rated PG

"Deftly" charming its way to Best Picture honors, this "classy" comedy caper "succeeds in spades" as a "likable", "fast-paced" vehicle for Newman and Redford, radiating "great rapport" as a pair of grifters playing a gangster for a sucker in Depression-era Chicago; a "funny, intriguing" period piece set to "elegant" Joplin rags, it raises the "suspense" stakes with "masterful" plotting and a final "zinger" that saves the sharpest sting for last.

Story of Adele H., The F 24 | 26 | 24 | 24

1975 | Directed by François Truffaut | With Isabelle Adjani, Bruce Robinson | 96 minutes | Rated PG

"Unrequited love" turns into "single-minded obsession" and then to flat-out "stalking" in this "intense" psychological drama from François Truffaut, the story of a 19th-century woman (based on "Victor Hugo's actual daughter") infatuated with a "cruelly oblivious man"; in the Oscar-nominated performance that made her a star, Adjani is "near perfect", alternately "radiant, commanding and heartbreaking."

Straight Story, The 24 | 27 | 22 | 21

1999 | Directed by David Lynch | With Richard Farnsworth, Sissy Spacek, Jane Galloway | 111 minutes | Rated G

The "only G-rated" effort from malaise-meister Lynch goes straight for the heart in this "odd" but "compelling" drama of a septuagenarian "who rides his John Deere" power mower cross country to mend fences with his infirm brother; this "interesting" "character study" is polished into an "absolute gem" by "brilliant performances" and a "lovely" meditation on the "ending of the life cycle", but be warned that "travel by tractor" can be a "slow" ride.

Strangers on a Train ◑ 26 | 24 | 27 | 24

1951 | Directed by Alfred Hitchcock | With Farley Granger, Robert Walker, Ruth Roman | 101 minutes | Rated PG

Be careful "what you wish for" is the underlying theme of this "fascinating", "forward-thinking" Hitchcock thriller wherein a flippant "promise to exchange murders" spirals out of control into a "dark tale of unwanted bedfellows"; "spine-tingler" aficionados single out Walker's "chilling" turn as a "wacko" mama's boy, and among many "tense moments", the "carousel finale still amazes."

	OVERALL	ACTING	STORY	PROD.
Streetcar Named Desire, A ⊠◑	27	28	26	25

1951 | Directed by Elia Kazan | With Vivien Leigh, Marlon Brando, Kim Hunter, Karl Malden | 125 minutes | Rated PG

Destined to "hold great forever", this "brilliant interpretation" of Tennessee Williams' "overwrought classic" showcases the "amazing" Brando "exploding onto the scene" ("hey, *Stella!*") in the "legendary" role of a "rugged" slob who engages in "shattering" "psychological warfare" with his delicate sister-in-law (the "wonderful", "so-sad" Leigh); fans say it's worth watching if only for a look at the "virile" Marlon when he was "still acting."

Strictly Ballroom 23 | 21 | 23 | 22

1993 | Directed by Baz Luhrmann | With Paul Mercurio, Tara Morice, Bill Hunter | 94 minutes | Rated PG

This "quirky" dose of "flash and flamenco" is a surprise charmer of a romantic comedy pairing a "hot" Aussie hoofer with an "ugly duckling", who proceed to shake up a dance championship with the question "to tango or not to tango?"; a "delightful send-up" of the "viciousness of the competitive ballroom circuit", it amuses with "well-executed" moves, even if onlookers "kinda know" how the strictly by-the-numbers story will turn out.

Suddenly, Last Summer ◑ 24 | 26 | 23 | 22

1959 | Directed by Joseph L. Mankiewicz | With Elizabeth Taylor, Katharine Hepburn, Montgomery Clift | 114 minutes | Not Rated

Alright, this "sensational" Tennessee Williams "stunner" about a wealthy woman scheming to have her niece lobotomized in order to "silence her" is "a bit much" - and a little too "murky", "talky" and "icky" for the squeamish; but fans flip for its "baroque excess", Liz's "tight white bathing suit" and, most of all, that truly "shocking ending."

Sullivan's Travels ◑ 27 | 25 | 26 | 25

1941 | Directed by Preston Sturges | With Joel McCrea, Veronica Lake, William Demarest | 90 minutes | Not Rated

A Depression-era movie director suffering from a "mid-career crisis" "develops a conscience" and decides to shoot a truly "serious film" in this "profound comedy" from Preston Sturges; the result is a delightfully "inspirational" flick that not only has "something important to say about America", but also is one of the "best pictures ever made about Hollywood - even though it hardly takes place there."

Summertime 23 | 26 | 23 | 24

1955 | Directed by David Lean | With Katharine Hepburn, Rossano Brazzi | 100 minutes | Not Rated

"Venice is the star" of this "bittersweet" love story about an "aging spinster" who "experiences *amore*" while on holiday in "timeless" Italy; there's "not a false note" in Kate's "delicious" performance (though holdouts insist she's "too dynamic" to be an old maid), played against "stunning locales" and a "swooningly romantic score."

Sunday Bloody Sunday 24 | 26 | 24 | 22

1971 | Directed by John Schlesinger | With Peter Finch, Glenda Jackson, Murray Head | 110 minutes | Rated R

"Very adult for its time", this "complex" film about "a man, a woman and their shared male lover" is "still very adult", starting with its "unflinching look at homosexuality"; Oscar nominees Jackson and Finch are "unforgettable" as "lost souls in the modern world" on the opposite sides of this "love triangle", while a "literate" script and "flawless" direction make this "groundbreaking" work "as relevant today as it was then."

Sunset Boulevard ⊠◑ 28 | 28 | 27 | 27

1950 | Directed by Billy Wilder | With William Holden, Gloria Swanson, Erich von Stroheim | 110 minutes | Not Rated

"Some of the greatest dialogue ever" (most famously, "I'm ready for my close-up, Mr. DeMille") graces this hybrid of "Gothic" and "film noir", a "scabrous take on Hollywood" from the standpoint of a "struggling screenwriter" trying to "resurrect the career of a silent movie star" who's "not exactly in touch with reality"; given Wilder's "acerbic" direction, an "'in'-joke"-laced script and "pitch-perfect" performances from a "larger-than-life Swanson" and "hunky Holden", "who needs a musical version?"

Suspicion ⊠◑ 25 | 26 | 25 | 25

1941 | Directed by Alfred Hitchcock | With Joan Fontaine, Cary Grant, Cedric Hardwicke, Nigel Bruce | 99 minutes | Not Rated

A "poor little rich girl" hooks up with a "potential murderer" in this "top Hitchcock" thriller starring an appropriately "menacing" Grant and a "wimpy" (but Oscar-winning) Fontaine; if some find the picture "a bit tentative" for the master of suspense (who was famously forced to "change the ending"), everyone agrees on its most unforgettable prop, the "scariest looking glass of milk in cinema history."

Sweeney Todd: The Demon Barber of Fleet Street 23 | 26 | 23 | 26

2007 | Directed by Tim Burton | With Johnny Depp, Helena Bonham Carter, Alan Rickman, Sacha Baron Cohen | 116 minutes | Rated R

"Johnny sings" in this "bloody good" musical that "goes for the jugular" in its "gruesome" story of a "homicidal" Victorian-era barber whose victims are ground into "yummy meat pies"; Depp is "superb as always", Bonham Carter less so, and their singing is "good-enough-but-don't-quit-your-day-job" quality, while Burton gives a "Gothic-excess" spin to Sondheim's "Broadway classic"; still, hair-splitters say all that "blood flowing by the gallon" can be "difficult to digest."

Sweet Bird of Youth 24 | 28 | 24 | 23

1962 | Directed by Richard Brooks | With Paul Newman, Geraldine Page, Ed Begley, Shirley Knight | 120 minutes | Not Rated

A "young, gorgeous" Newman and "brilliant" Page ("what a combo!") reprise their stage roles in this cinematic adaptation of Tennessee Williams' play about a wannabe actor/gigolo and a faded, *Sunset Boulevard*–esque movie queen; sure, the story has been somewhat sanitized for the big screen, but most birdies still tweet "how sweet it is . . ."

Sweet Hereafter, The 24 | 25 | 23 | 23

1997 | Directed by Atom Egoyan | With Ian Holm, Sarah Polley, Bruce Greenwood | 112 minutes | Rated R

"Haunting" in a "somber" way, this adaptation of Russell Banks' novel is a "beautifully shot", "terribly moving" drama about the "after-

	OVERALL	ACTING	STORY	PROD.

math of a small-town tragedy" and the "dysfunction" it lays bare; the "terrific cast" led by Holm and Polley sees the burg's "delicate balance" upset when a group of children die in a bus crash, and the camera lends a "hypnotic" feel to material that's "smart" but "shrouded in sadness."

Sweet Smell of Success, The ◑ 27 | 28 | 26 | 26

1957 | Directed by Alexander Mackendrick | With Burt Lancaster, Tony Curtis, Martin Milner, Susan Harrison | 96 minutes | Not Rated

A "cookie full of arsenic" soaked in "hydrochloric acid", this extra-"tasty" morsel of "moody noir" unearths the "seamy side" of showbiz with its "cynical" "character study" of the "slimy" sorts working the "publicity end": a "superb" Lancaster as a "brutal", Winchell-esque columnist and the "unctuous Curtis" as his publicist toady; brace yourself for "crackling dialogue" and some "beyond beautiful" NYC "nighttime shots" in this "timeless" but never "more timely" picture.

Swept Away F 24 | 24 | 24 | 24

1975 | Directed by Lina Wertmüller | With Mariangela Melato, Giancarlo Giannini | 116 minutes | Rated R

Stranding strangers on a "sunbaked isle" long "before the arrival of *Survivor*", Wertmüller's "unforgettable" Italian comedy "steams up the screen" as a snobbish socialite and a coarsely "expressive" boatman develop a "passionate" "love/hate relationship" alone on a Mediterranean cay; the satire "speaks volumes" as a "comment on class" and the "battle of the sexes", though there's a strong undercurrent of "violence" running beneath the beautiful "scenery."

Swingers 23 | 22 | 23 | 20

1996 | Directed by Doug Liman | With Jon Favreau, Vince Vaughn, Heather Graham | 96 minutes | Rated R

"Hooking up in the '90s" gets a "hilarious" but "realistic" spin in this "hip, kinetic" buddy comedy-cum-"cultural phenomenon" about two single guys "finding their mojo" on the "Los Angeles dating scene"; it's "immensely funny", universally "accurate in defining a generation" and "'so money' that it spawned its very own vernacular."

Swing Time ◑ 26 | 23 | 20 | 26

1936 | Directed by George Stevens | With Fred Astaire, Ginger Rogers, Helen Broderick, Victor Moore | 103 minutes | Not Rated

The "easy grace" (and "winged feet") of Astaire and Rogers make for one "magical musical" in this "superb offering" that's voted "the best" of their pairings in this Survey; as usual, "there's not much of a story", but compensations include Fred's "sublime" 'Bojangles of Harlem' number and an "outstanding" Jerome Kern score, highlighted by the Oscar-winning 'The Way You Look Tonight.'

Swiss Family Robinson 23 | 20 | 24 | 23

1960 | Directed by Ken Annakin | With John Mills, Dorothy McGuire, James MacArthur, Tommy Kirk | 126 minutes | Rated G

"Action, romance, adventure and comedy" coexist amiably in this "absolute classic" from Walt Disney, a story of castaways shipwrecked on a tropical isle that "bears little resemblance to the novel"; an exercise in "good, clean fun", it's everything a "family movie should be", and that "terrific" treehouse set "still fascinates" smaller fry.

	OVERALL	ACTING	STORY	PROD.

Talk to Her ✉ F | 26 | 26 | 26 | 25

2002 | Directed by Pedro Almodóvar | With Javier Cámara, Darío Grandinetti, Leonor Watling | 112 minutes | Rated R

"Don't think about it too much and it will captivate you" advise fans of this "brilliant piece of art" by the "risk-taking" Almodóvar, a "haunting", "highly original" "drama, comedy and mystery all in one" about "two women who have fallen into comas and the men who love them"; a "wonderful cast" tackles a "provocative" "multilayered storyline" that "allows fantasy to play with reality" – "finally, a film for mature audiences!"

Tarzan | 22 | - | 21 | 24

1999 | Directed by Chris Buck, Kevin Lima | Animated | 88 minutes | Rated G

Some of "Disney's best work", this tale of man and monkey swinging through life features "phenomenally innovative" animation; a "fast-paced adventure" that takes time out for "character" but "keeps things relatively lighthearted", it adds some "thoughtful modern" angles and a "great score", including an Oscar-winning song from Phil Collins.

Taxi Driver | 27 | 29 | 25 | 25

1976 | Directed by Martin Scorsese | With Robert De Niro, Jodie Foster, Harvey Keitel, Cybill Shepherd | 113 minutes | Rated R

Confirming "non-NYers' greatest fears" about the "brutal underbelly" of "modern urban life", Scorsese's vividly "cerebral" thriller rolls through "sleazy" streets and "neon" nights charged by De Niro's "monumental performance" as a "creepy", insomniac hack – "you talking to me?" – whose live-wire issues build to "harrowing" magnum force in the "steam-filled" city; overall, its depiction of "urban decay, rage and alienation" is "top-class" but "lurid" and very "intense."

Ten Commandments, The | 24 | 21 | 25 | 27

1956 | Directed by Cecil B. DeMille | With Charlton Heston, Yul Brynner, Anne Baxter, Edward G. Robinson | 220 minutes | Rated G

"Let it be written" that DeMille's "over-the-top" biblical blockbuster is the "epic of all epics", a "Cliffs Notes" account of Exodus built on "Heston's finest" role as the "one and only Moses", performer of "monumental" miracles on land and Red Sea; though "fantastic sets" and Brynner's "badass" Egyptian king distract from the "kitschy" script and "overblown" production, it's "entertaining" enough to keep a "cast of thousands" in "constant circulation."

Tender Mercies ✉ | 24 | 26 | 22 | 22

1983 | Directed by Bruce Beresford | With Robert Duvall, Tess Harper, Betty Buckley, Ellen Barkin | 92 minutes | Rated PG

"Proving that less is more", Duvall delivers a "quiet yet unforgettable" portrait of a "has-been country singer" hiding out in a Texas motel, and transforms a "simple story" into something "truly great"; winner of two Oscars (for Best Actor and Screenplay), it also boasts a "rather good" soundtrack that lends the film its "haunting" air.

Terminator, The | 24 | 18 | 24 | 24

1984 | Directed by James Cameron | With Arnold Schwarzenegger, Michael Biehn, Linda Hamilton | 108 minutes | Rated R

Buckle up for Cameron's "unstoppable breakthrough", this sci-fi/action "genre-maker" about an "evil cyborg sent from the future" to

	OVERALL	ACTING	STORY	PROD.

wreak havoc on the past via Ah-nuld's "seriously scary presence" alone; it "doesn't disappoint" in dispensing "awesome" "violent" mayhem all over '80s LA, and its most famous line - "I'll be back" - was a harbinger of the sequels to come.

Terminator 2: Judgment Day 23 | 17 | 22 | 26

1991 | Directed by James Cameron | With Arnold Schwarzenegger, Linda Hamilton, Edward Furlong | 137 minutes | Rated R

The Terminator's "baaack" as a "kinder, gentler" cyborg in this "outsize thrill ride" that deftly embellishes the initial premise of murderous, "time-traveling" robots; fans say it's a "rare sequel that fulfills the promise of the original", citing the "whiz-bang", "ahead-of-their-time" FX, Hamilton's "buff", "kick-butt" heroine and the one-and-only Arnold, whose "mechanical" performance makes him the "perfect choice to play an android."

Terms of Endearment ✉ 25 | 26 | 24 | 22

1983 | Directed by James L. Brooks | With Shirley MacLaine, Debra Winger, Jack Nicholson, Jeff Daniels | 132 minutes | Rated PG

A "four-hanky tearjerker" "worth its weight in Kleenex", this "engrossing" "weepie with a spine" starts off comically enough depicting a "tangled mother-daughter relationship" but takes a "serious" turn in the second act when "life-and-death" issues arise; quite the Oscar magnet, it took home Best Picture honors as well as statuettes for the "amazing" MacLaine and Nicholson, who's a "hoot" as the former astronaut who lives next door.

Thank You for Smoking 23 | 23 | 23 | 21

2006 | Directed by Jason Reitman | With Aaron Eckhart, Maria Bello, Rob Lowe, Robert Duvall, William H. Macy, Katie Holmes | 92 minutes | Rated R

Eckhart's "killer" portrayal of a "smug" but "lovable" cigarette industry spin doctor has you "rooting for the bad guy" in this "hysterically sarcastic" send-up of "Big Tobacco" and the "art of lobbying"; packed with "intelligent commentary" and featuring a star-studded cast, it "throws some moral curveballs" that leave "plenty to talk about after the credits roll."

Thelma & Louise ✉ 23 | 25 | 23 | 21

1991 | Directed by Ridley Scott | With Susan Sarandon, Geena Davis, Brad Pitt, Harvey Keitel | 129 minutes | Rated R

A "high-powered" "girl-power" flick focusing on a "feminist crime spree", this "groundbreaking" display of "female macho" "rocks" as two everyday gals "finally get back" at the men who've wronged them by becoming "devil-may-care outlaws" on the lam; the "superb storyline" and "stellar performances" keep things "involving" right up to the "heartbreaking", "*Butch Cassidy*"-esque "bad ending."

There Will Be Blood ✉ 23 | 28 | 21 | 26

2007 | Directed by Paul Thomas Anderson | With Daniel Day-Lewis, Paul Dano, Kevin J. O'Connor, Ciarán Hinds | 158 minutes | Rated R

A "compelling portrait of a repellant man", this "booming, expansive epic" loosely based on an Upton Sinclair novel depicts the "rise of industrialization" and "everything that's wrong about capitalism" in its story of "greed, malice" and a "dark-as-coal" petroleum baron on the loose in turn-of-the-century California oilfields; Day-Lewis' "other-worldly" "gusher of a performance" deservedly won the Oscar, and despite "unlikable characters" and a "long" running time, this "companion piece to *Citizen Kane*" is widely considered an "instant classic"; already legendary line: "I drink your milkshake."

Thief of Bagdad, The ◑ 24 | 22 | 23 | 23

1924 | Directed by Raoul Walsh | With Douglas Fairbanks, Snitz Edwards, Julanne Johnston | 155 minutes | Not Rated

This Arabian Nights fantasy is a "definitive swashbuckler", featuring an "athletic" Douglas Fairbanks "at his best" as a charming rogue seeking a princess' hand; one of the most expensive silent movies ever made, it's a "lavish" spectacle with sets by William Cameron Menzies that are "still amazing by today's standards"; in short, it's simply "great."

Thing, The ◑ 23 | 19 | 25 | 19

(aka The Thing from Another World)

1951 | Directed by Christian Nyby | With Kenneth Tobey, Margaret Sheridan | 87 minutes | Not Rated

This "serious" '50s sci-fi suspenser "still holds up" as a "smart" "flying-saucer" shocker about a group of scientists driven to "creepy" extremes in a "claustrophobic, paranoid" encounter with a murderous alien found frozen in the Arctic ice; despite "skimpy" special effects, the "tight script" builds enough "tension" to frighten the "daylights" out of fans, who spurn the "gory remake" – there's nothing like "the real *Thing*."

Thing, The 23 | 19 | 23 | 23

1982 | Directed by John Carpenter | With Kurt Russell, Wilford Brimley, David Clennon | 109 minutes | Rated R

"Chills" abound in Carpenter's "excellent remake of the '51 classic", wherein the Antarctic's most "frigid science outpost" is beset by a "horrible alien" capable of disguising itself in human form; an "imaginative" contribution to the "sci-fi/horror pantheon", it supplies enough "true suspense" to keep the audience "guessing" as the "paranoia" mounts.

Thin Man, The ◑ 26 | 25 | 23 | 23

1934 | Directed by W.S. Van Dyke | With William Powell, Myrna Loy, Maureen O'Sullivan | 93 minutes | Not Rated

"Break out the martini glasses": "mystery meets screwball comedy" in this "snazzy" flicker featuring "cool detective" Nick Charles and his "classy wife", Nora, "drinking like fish" and "fluidly" spouting "snappy dialogue" ("double entendre, anyone?") as they investigate a murder; the "suave, sexy fun" is so "cosmopolitan" and "wonderfully evocative of the '30s" that it seems unsporting to point out that the "whodunit" plot is a bit thin.

Third Man, The ◑ 28 | 28 | 27 | 28

1949 | Directed by Carol Reed | With Joseph Cotten, Alida Valli, Orson Welles, Trevor Howard | 104 minutes | Not Rated

"Oh, that zither!"; this "masterful" piece of "postwar" noir simmers with shadowy "intrigue" as an "alienated" Cotten encounters "romance" and "betrayal" while searching "bombed-out" Vienna for a

OVERALL	ACTING	STORY	PROD.

"mysterious" black marketeer (played by Welles, who makes the most of a "small" role with an "arresting" entrance); graced with "expressionist" lensing, Graham Greene's "clever, dark script" and a "memorable" final fade, it's hailed as "all-around perfect."

39 Steps, The ◑ 27 | 25 | 27 | 24

1935 | Directed by Alfred Hitchcock | With Robert Donat, Madeleine Carroll, Lucie Mannheim | 86 minutes | Not Rated

"You can't go wrong" with this "classic" "British period" Hitchcock nail-biter, a "virtuoso" "thriller diller" wherein an "innocent man wrongly accused" of murder tries to clear his name amid "chase scenes, foreign spy intrigue and romance" (with a woman he winds up "handcuffed" to); sure, the "dated" special effects are on the low-tech side, but this "tense mystery" delivers enough suspense to "keep you on the edge of your seat.".

This Is Spinal Tap 26 | 24 | 25 | 22

1984 | Directed by Rob Reiner | With Christopher Guest, Michael McKean, Rob Reiner | 82 minutes | Rated R

"VH1's *Behind the Music*" pales before this "hysterical" "rock mockumentary", an "unbelievably authentic-feeling send-up" of the music industry and superstar "pretensions" that follows an "aging heavy-metal band" taking its act on the road; the "stellar cast" plays an "unforgettable" group of clueless musicians, simulating a "sidesplitting insider's view" that's alarmingly "like the real thing" - except "every single second is funny."

Thomas Crown Affair, The 23 | 23 | 24 | 22

1968 | Directed by Norman Jewison | With Steve McQueen, Faye Dunaway, Paul Burke | 102 minutes | Rated R

This "slick", "grown-up romance" offers a "cat-and-mouse" plot as millionaire McQueen engineers a bank heist for kicks until he encounters Dunaway, a "knockout" insurance sleuth in mad pursuit; their "smoldering", "high-tension" affair is a "stylish" standoff down to the final "checkmate" in that famed chess match, and as for the remake, "do not accept imitations."

Thousand Clowns, A ◑∅ 25 | 26 | 24 | 21

1965 | Directed by Fred Coe | With Jason Robards, Barbara Harris, Barry Gordon, Martin Balsam | 118 minutes | Not Rated

A "wonderful" cast including the "brilliant" Robards and Harris (and Oscar-winning Balsam) drives this "touching" but "unusual" comedy about a "nonconformist" whose disdain for the "daily grind" jeopardizes his guardianship of a beloved nephew; based on the Herb Gardner play, it's a "classic" example of the '60s "do-your-own-thing" ethic that nonetheless "has a lot of truth" in it.

Three Days of the Condor 24 | 24 | 25 | 22

1975 | Directed by Sydney Pollack | With Robert Redford, Faye Dunaway, Cliff Robertson | 117 minutes | Rated R

Filmed during the Watergate era, this "paranoid thriller" "still flies" today thanks to Redford's "absorbing" work as an "enigmatic", low-level CIA researcher "caught up in a conspiracy" and dodging an "impersonal assassin"; it's "absorbing", "expertly crafted" stuff, with a "twisty" plot that "puts the intelligence back into, um, intelligence."

	OVERALL	ACTING	STORY	PROD.

Three Faces of Eve, The ✉◑ | 24 | 27 | 24 | 20

1957 | Directed by Nunnally Johnson | With Joanne Woodward, David Wayne, Lee J. Cobb | 91 minutes | Not Rated

"Incredible" Oscar-winner Woodward delivers a "tour-de-force" turn in this "multiple-personality genre film", an "interesting drama" about a "woman tormented" by triple identities; switching from subdued homemaker to brazen party girl, Woodward does a "stellar" job of "bringing all three characters to life."

300 | 22 | 20 | 22 | 27

2007 | Directed by Zack Snyder | With Gerard Butler, Lena Headey, Dominic West, David Wenham | 117 minutes | Rated R

"Hunky" Hellenic he-men "wearing next to nothing" duke it out with the Persians at the Battle of Thermopylae in this "cool, stylish" and ultra-"gory" sword 'n' sandal epic adapted from Frank Miller's graphic novel; no question, the "balletic" action sequences and "top-notch" effects are a "treat for the eyes", but a phalanx of fence-sitters fret it's "all bang and no substance."

Three Musketeers, The | 22 | 22 | 22 | 23

1974 | Directed by Richard Lester | With Oliver Reed, Richard Chamberlain, Michael York | 105 minutes | Rated PG

A "rollicking rendition" of the Dumas classic, this "rousing" "old-fashioned" adventure "stays faithful" to the original tale but spices up the swordplay with "slapstick" and "bawdy" humor as a brave band of swashbucklers defends the queen's honor against that crooked cardinal; the "lavish" 17th-century sets and all-for-one "charm" of the "great cast" ensure its place as the "quintessential" version by which all others "shall be judged."

3:10 to Yuma | 23 | 25 | 22 | 24

2007 | Directed by James Mangold | With Russell Crowe, Christian Bale, Ben Foster, Peter Fonda | 122 minutes | Rated R

"John Wayne would have loved" this "solid" remake of the "classic oater" that "stands up well on its own" thanks to "solid" production values and "pitch-perfect performances" by Bale and Crowe, respectively playing a rancher and an outlaw engaged in an epic "battle of wits"; yee-haw, there's also "plenty of gun-fighting and explosions" along the way to its much-debated "surprise ending."

3 Women | 25 | 26 | 21 | 23

1977 | Directed by Robert Altman | With Shelley Duvall, Sissy Spacek, Janice Rule | 124 minutes | Rated PG

Altman is "at his trickiest" in this "dreamlike" drama about a downwardly mobile desert-town gal and her "ripe-for-the-picking" roommate who form an "eerie" triangle with a wronged spouse; though the "cryptic narrative" can be "easily dismissed as weird", it's still a "fascinating" exercise in feminine psychology with "super" acting – think "*Single White Female* for the arty set."

Thunderball | 22 | 21 | 21 | 23

1965 | Directed by Terence Young | With Sean Connery, Claudine Auger, Adolfo Celi | 130 minutes | Rated PG

Bringing the "basic Bond formula" to the Bahamas, this swimming entry in the superspy series has Connery breaking out his arsenal of "gadgets" and dry wisecracks against the "very real threat" of stolen nukes held for ransom; the "nonstop action" and "incredible underwater fight sequences" made it a thunderous success in its day, and if now "underappreciated", connoisseurs nevertheless rank it "near the top" of the 007 oeuvre.

Time After Time 23 23 25 21

1979 | Directed by Nicholas Meyer | With Malcolm McDowell, Mary Steenburgen, David Warner | 112 minutes | Rated PG

A "clever" bit of "brainy entertainment", this "charming" sci-fi thriller recounts "H.G. Wells chasing Jack the Ripper to modern-day San Francisco" via a "functioning time machine"; a "witty" romp expertly blending "romantic" interludes between McDowell and Steenburgen with "suspenseful" sequencing, it's "well worth seeing" for Warner's "helluva performance" alone.

Tin Drum, The ✉F 23 23 24 23

1980 | Directed by Volker Schlöndorff | With David Bennent, Mario Adorf, Angela Winkler | 142 minutes | Rated R

A "fine social commentary" about apathy and "life in Nazi Germany", this "disturbing" allegorical drama about a young boy who refuses to grow old "preserves the spirit of Günter Grass' novel" while charting the rise and fall of the Third Reich; the "well-deserved winner of the Best Foreign Film Oscar", it's a "surreal" work that remains "vivid and haunting" a generation later.

To Be or Not to Be ◑ 24 24 25 23

1942 | Directed by Ernst Lubitsch | With Carole Lombard, Jack Benny, Robert Stack | 99 minutes | Not Rated

"Life in Nazi-occupied Europe" becomes "exhilarating comedy" in this "funny but poignant" war story, an "oft-overlooked gem" via the ever "clever" Ernst Lubitsch; playing married actors, Benny and Lombard supply "barrels of laughs" – particularly when Jack "does to Shakespeare what the Germans are doing to Poland."

To Catch a Thief 25 25 24 25

1955 | Directed by Alfred Hitchcock | With Grace Kelly, Cary Grant, Jesse Royce Landis, Brigitte Auber | 106 minutes | Not Rated

"Slick, sophisticated and oh-so-cool", this romantic thriller may be "Hitchcock lite", but Grant and Kelly provide plenty of "dazzle" in an amusing trifle about a cat burglar prowling the south of France; maybe the "plot is secondary" to the "enjoyable scenery" and "fab clothes", but there's snappy patter aplenty, notably Grace's classic picnic query "would you prefer a leg or a breast?"

To Have and Have Not ◑ 26 27 24 24

1944 | Directed by Howard Hawks | With Humphrey Bogart, Lauren Bacall, Walter Brennan, Hoagy Carmichael | 100 minutes | Not Rated

Bacall (in her screen debut) teams with future real-life hubby Bogart to "define star chemistry" in this dramatization of the Hemingway novel about WWII resistance runners; Martinique supplies a sultry backdrop for the two stars to "smolder", especially when Lauren "steams up the screen" with her legendary question "you know how to whistle, don't you?"

	OVERALL	ACTING	STORY	PROD.
To Kill a Mockingbird ✉◑	29	29	29	26

1962 | Directed by Robert Mulligan | With Gregory Peck, Mary Badham, Robert Duvall | 129 minutes | Not Rated

"After all these years", this Southern courtroom drama about racism and prejudice "told from the point of view of a young girl" "still packs the same emotional punch"; kudos go to Oscar-winning screenwriter Horton Foote "for not having strayed" from Harper Lee's "original text", and to an "im-peck-able" Peck at his "peak" as the "dad we wish we had"; in short, "Hollywood got this one right."

	OVERALL	ACTING	STORY	PROD.
Tom Jones ✉	25	24	24	25

1963 | Directed by Tony Richardson | With Albert Finney, Susannah York, Hugh Griffith | 121 minutes | Not Rated

"Richly crafted and craftily acted" – with four Oscars to prove it – this hilariously "bawdy" "period piece par excellence" might be set in 18th-century England but moodwise is more like a "snapshot of the Swinging '60s"; devotees are ever smitten with its "clever script", "lively direction" and Finney's "lusty" title turn, while gourmands eat up that "sexy food-seduction scene."

	OVERALL	ACTING	STORY	PROD.
Tootsie	25	27	24	23

1982 | Directed by Sydney Pollack | With Dustin Hoffman, Jessica Lange, Bill Murray, Teri Garr, Charles Durning | 119 minutes | Rated PG

"Cross-dressing doesn't get much better" than this "brilliantly funny" comedy about a long-"struggling actor" who finally achieves success – "as an actress"; though Hoffman might be "one ugly" broad, his "sublime", "think-out-of-the-box" performance mixing "humor with humanity" is beautiful, while a "slick" but "unpredictable script" and an "outstanding" supporting cast make this one a "keeper, not a renter."

	OVERALL	ACTING	STORY	PROD.
Top Hat ◑	27	23	21	26

1935 | Directed by Mark Sandrich | With Fred Astaire, Ginger Rogers, Edward Everett Horton, Helen Broderick | 101 minutes | Not Rated

"Heaven, I'm in heaven" sigh fans of this "classic '30s musical" spotlighting the big-city charms of a "debonair Astaire" opposite a "feather"-gowned Rogers; sure, there's an "all-hit Irving Berlin score", "amazing production numbers" and a "witty French farce of a script", but in the end, it's "Fred and Ginger dancing cheek-to-cheek" that catapults it to "sublime"-ville.

	OVERALL	ACTING	STORY	PROD.
Topkapi	24	22	25	21

1964 | Directed by Jules Dassin | With Melina Mercouri, Peter Ustinov | 119 minutes | Not Rated

Director "Dassin's '60s caper holds up well", managing to "avoid clichés the same way" its jewel-thief cast "avoid traps" as they engineer a heist in Istanbul; owing to a "clever script" and some "beautifully drawn characters" (like the "sophisticated" Mercouri and "priceless", "Oscar-winning" Ustinov), this "taut" thriller/comedy is reminiscent of an erstwhile "*Mission: Impossible.*"

	OVERALL	ACTING	STORY	PROD.
Topsy-Turvy	23	25	23	26

1999 | Directed by Mike Leigh | With Jim Broadbent, Allan Corduner | 160 minutes | Rated R

This "finely observed story about the stormy partnership of Gilbert and Sullivan" provides a "window into the Victorian age" as well as a

Visit ZAGAT.com

"fascinating" glimpse into the "creative process" via a subplot about the first staging of *The Mikado*; "superb" acting (with an especially "grand Broadbent") and a "gorgeous production" make it a "joy to watch" for most, though a few yawn "boring."

Tora! Tora! Tora! 23 19 25 24

1970 | Directed by Richard Fleischer, Kinji Fukasaku, Toshio Masuda | With Martin Balsam, Jason Robards | 144 minutes | Rated G

Surveyors split on this "intricate" war chronicle of the "Japanese attack on Pearl Harbor": defenders say this "ultimate docudrama" is "well done historically", citing its "bilingual plotlines" and over-the-top "stunning" special effects, but curmudgeons counter it's a "comic-book" look at the tragedy.

Torch Song Trilogy 23 25 25 21

1988 | Directed by Paul Bogart | With Harvey Fierstein, Matthew Broderick, Anne Bancroft | 120 minutes | Rated R

A "faithful adaptation" of Fierstein's very "original" stage play, this "moving" account of a gay female impersonator's "need for family" was "very advanced for its time" and "still very entertaining" today; though a few feel it "doesn't translate well to the screen", there are kudos for the "boyish" Broderick and Bancroft's "outstanding" turn as an "archetypical Jewish mother."

Torn Curtain 23 24 23 22

1966 | Directed by Alfred Hitchcock | With Paul Newman, Julie Andrews, Lila Kedrova, Wolfgang Kieling | 128 minutes | Rated PG

This "compelling" Cold War spy thriller via Alfred Hitchcock concerns an American physicist who defects to East Germany, secretly bent on espionage; while it "isn't the greatest Newman or Andrews" effort by far, it still "has is moments", notably the 'silent murder' sequence and Lila Kedrova's "compelling" supporting role as a down-and-out countess.

To Sir, With Love 22 23 24 20

1967 | Directed by James Clavell | With Sidney Poitier, Judy Geeson, Christian Roberts | 105 minutes | Not Rated

The "always-excellent" Poitier stars in this "nice little piece of '60s" nostalgia as a "London high school teacher" passing on life lessons to "inner-city punks"; "sweet" and "timeless", it deals with "still-relevant" issues – "race, family conflicts, respect for authority" – in a "genuinely moving" fashion, and Lulu's smashing rendition of the title song "makes the movie."

Touch of Evil ◑ 26 24 25 26

1958 | Directed by Orson Welles | With Charlton Heston, Janet Leigh, Orson Welles, Akim Tamiroff | 95 minutes | Rated PG-13

"Proof that Welles was more than a one-hit wonder", this "rococo" "pinnacle of film noir" stars the director as a "bloated" Texas border town cop feuding with his south-of-the-border counterpart (Heston in "Mexican blackface"); among its many memorable touches are the "sweeping" opening sequence and the "effortless scene-stealing" by Marlene Dietrich, who has the picture's best line: "lay off the candy bars"; P.S. the "restored version" is "much better" than the original release.

	OVERALL	ACTING	STORY	PROD.
Toy Story	27	-	25	28

1995 | Directed by John Lasseter | Animated | 81 minutes | Rated G
Ushering in a "new era of animation" with "breakthrough" computer-generated effects, this Pixar-produced "instant classic" is a bona fide "technical wonder"; its "humorous" storyline, "lovable characters" and the "great concept" of walking, talking toys add up to a picture that's not only "equally entertaining for adults and kids" but also "deserving of the franchise it started."

	OVERALL	ACTING	STORY	PROD.
Toy Story 2	26	-	24	28

1999 | Directed by John Lasseter, Ash Brannon, Lee Unkrich | Animated | 92 minutes | Rated G
"Not just another wind-up sequel", this "worthy successor" is a "marvel" in its own right, this time following the misadventures of Woody, a toy cowboy who's been "stolen by a greedy collector to be sold to the highest bidder"; Pixar's "wonderfully creative" CGI renderings work their usual magic so well that parents report "you almost don't mind watching it the 8,000 times that your kids request."

	OVERALL	ACTING	STORY	PROD.
Trading Places	23	22	23	20

1983 | Directed by John Landis | With Dan Aykroyd, Eddie Murphy, Jamie Lee Curtis, Ralph Bellamy | 118 minutes | Rated R
This "hysterical" treatment of the "classic" "rags-to-riches" "switcheroo" has "pauper" Murphy turned into "prince" Aykroyd and vice-versa; "quickly paced and never boring", it's memorable for "early vintage" Eddie moments and some "funny" business from Dan.

	OVERALL	ACTING	STORY	PROD.
Traffic ✉	23	24	23	25

2000 | Directed by Steven Soderbergh | With Michael Douglas, Benicio Del Toro, Catherine Zeta-Jones | 147 minutes | Rated R
Maybe "more realistic than you want", this "eye-opening portrait of the drug wars" is "poignant" and "troubling", using "multiple storylines" to create a "stunning" hybrid of "thriller" and "cautionary tale"; the "amazing use of color", "documentary-like handheld" camerawork and Del Toro's deft, Oscar-winning turn all get the green light, though the highest praise is reserved for its "absolutely brilliant" director.

	OVERALL	ACTING	STORY	PROD.
TransAmerica	24	28	23	22

2005 | Directed by Duncan Tucker | With Felicity Huffman, Kevin Zegers, Fionnula Flanagan | 103 minutes | Rated R
Huffman's "fearless", "dead-on" portrayal of an "uptight" male-to-female transsexual who "learns she has a son" provides this "original" gender-bender dramedy with plenty of "hilarious", "seat-squirming" moments mixed with "compelling", "raw emotion"; ok, it may "drag" in places, but at least its pro-"acceptance" message "pulls no punches."

	OVERALL	ACTING	STORY	PROD.
Treasure of the Sierra Madre, The ✉◑	27	27	26	24

1948 | Directed by John Huston | With Humphrey Bogart, Walter Huston, Tim Holt | 126 minutes | Not Rated
"Human nature poisoned by greed" is the theme of this "old-fashioned" "treasure hunt", a "wonderful adventure" that won Oscars for the father-and-son Hustons; Bogart exudes "masculine energy" showing "what gold will do to a man" in an "unforgettably powerful" performance that devolves into "paranoia" – and as for the "stunning" black-and-white photography, purists say "we don't need no stinkin' color."

	OVERALL	ACTING	STORY	PROD.
Triplets of Belleville, The F	24	-	23	26

2003 | Directed by Sylvain Chomet | Animated | 80 minutes | Rated PG-13

"Trippy and funny in a way that American animation isn't", this "art house" French cartoon sure "ain't Disney" with its "surreal" plot, "stylized" illustration and "nearly dialogue-free" soundtrack; having something to do with a kidnapped bicyclist rescued by his "grandmère", an "amazing" dog and the "wacky" Triplets of Belleville, it's both "innovative" and "offbeat", and probably more "for adults" than small fry.

Trip to Bountiful, The ✉	24	26	23	21

1985 | Directed by Peter Masterson | With Geraldine Page, John Heard, Carlin Glynn, Rebecca De Mornay | 108 minutes | Rated PG

An "elderly lady's wish" to relive her past by visiting her Texas hometown frames this "poignant" stage-to-screen adaptation, a journey through "memory and reality" featuring Page in an "exquisite", Oscar-grabbing turn; the "parable"-esque plot manages to strike "spiritual" chords, but it's the heroine's "suffocating situation" – an "all too common" dilemma for those "in their later years" – that will "haunt" you.

True Grit ✉	22	23	21	22

1969 | Directed by Henry Hathaway | With John Wayne, Glen Campbell, Kim Darby | 128 minutes | Rated G

"Another Western for your library", this "classic" oater is made "especially for Wayne fans" because the Duke took home his first (and only) Oscar here; otherwise, it's standard stuff about a vengeful lawman, though early-in-their-career performances by Dennis Hopper and Robert Duvall keep things lively.

True Romance	24	23	24	22

1993 | Directed by Tony Scott | With Christian Slater, Patricia Arquette, Dennis Hopper, Christopher Walken | 120 minutes | Rated R

Brace yourself for some "big-time gore" in this "ultraviolent" "true cult classic" about newlyweds on the run, scripted by a "pre-*Pulp Fiction* Quentin Tarantino" and featuring an "all-star" ensemble (including bits by Brad Pitt, Samuel L. Jackson and James Gandolfini "when they were little known"); sticklers note it "steals heartily from *Badlands*", but ultimately, it's "kinetic", "edgy", "weird" and just plain "cool"; best scene: the "showdown between Hopper and Walken."

Truly Madly Deeply	23	25	23	22

1991 | Directed by Anthony Minghella | With Juliet Stevenson, Alan Rickman | 106 minutes | Rated PG

A "better British version of *Ghost*", this "deeply affecting" romance stars "sadly radiant" Stevenson as a Londoner who's "codependent with her husband" Rickman – even though he's recently deceased and "sticking around for unfinished business"; truly "stellar performances" transform the "odd" story into a "moving", sometimes "funny" meditation on the "nature of love" and "letting go."

Turning Point, The	23	25	22	23

1977 | Directed by Herbert Ross | With Shirley MacLaine, Anne Bancroft, Mikhail Baryshnikov | 119 minutes | Rated PG

Ascend to "chick-flick heaven" via this "moving" drama that sets the oft-told story of "women choosing between marriage and a career" in a "world-renowned ballet company"; as "longtime friends who took different paths" in life, Bancroft and MacLaine are "brilliant" (especially during that climactic "classic catfight" at Lincoln Center), though balletomanes only have eyes for "Baryshnikov's spectacular dance scenes."

12 Angry Men ◑ 28 | 28 | 27 | 23

1957 | Directed by Sidney Lumet | With Henry Fonda, Martin Balsam, Lee J. Cobb, E.G. Marshall | 96 minutes | Not Rated

"Human nature at its best and worst" is on display in this "brilliant courtroom drama" depicting the "hidden agendas" of jurors deciding the fate of a murder defendant; thanks to its "taut" script and an "unforgettable Fonda", this "study of American democracy" is alternately "suspenseful and compelling."

Twelve Monkeys 22 | 23 | 24 | 23

1995 | Directed by Terry Gilliam | With Bruce Willis, Madeleine Stowe, Brad Pitt | 129 minutes | Rated R

Gilliam's "master-of-the-bizarre" status is reinforced by this "complex", "super-ingenious" time-travel tale about the "release of a deadly virus" followed by a "post-apocalyptic" attempt to "save the world"; the sets are "dazzling", Brad 'n' Bruce prove they can "actually act" and if the "*Terminator*-meets-*Brazil*" sci-fi storyline is "confusing", it's "wonderfully" so.

Twelve O'Clock High ◑ 26 | 25 | 26 | 23

1949 | Directed by Henry King | With Gregory Peck, Hugh Marlowe, Dean Jagger | 132 minutes | Not Rated

"Peck is marvelous" as a WWII Brigadier General "placing terrible pressure on young American pilots" in this "accurate" depiction of the "burdens of command" and the "human side of war"; a "perfect screenplay" "rooted in historical reality" "manipulates the tension" right up to the compelling climax.

21 Grams 22 | 27 | 21 | 21

2003 | Directed by Alejandro González Iñárritu | With Sean Penn, Naomi Watts, Benicio Del Toro | 124 minutes | Rated R

"Not an easy watch", this "disturbing take on love and loss" details the lives of three people who meet as the result of a deadly accident; its "nonlinear storyline" told via "flashbacks and flashforwards" (à la "*Memento*" and "*Pulp Fiction*") might be "intriguing" to some and "confusing" to others, but the "stellar" ensemble supplies enough "brain candy" to make for "compelling" viewing; in sum, be ready for an "emotionally draining downer" that's "moving, intelligent" and guaranteed to "keep you guessing."

Two for the Road 24 | 27 | 24 | 24

1967 | Directed by Stanley Donen | With Albert Finney, Audrey Hepburn | 111 minutes | Not Rated

"Love isn't always easy" in this "bittersweet travelogue of the ups and downs of a married couple" that "jumps back and forth in time" as they "find, lose and rekindle" their relationship; Audrey's at her "most charming" and "marvelous together" with Finney amid all that "unmatched European scenery"; meanwhile, the "mesmerizing, melodious" Mancini music "sustains the mood."

	OVERALL	ACTING	STORY	PROD.
2001: A Space Odyssey	26	19	24	27

1968 | Directed by Stanley Kubrick | With Keir Dullea, Gary Lockwood, William Sylvester | 139 minutes | Rated G

The "*Citizen Kane* of science-fiction films", this "era-defining" Kubrick interpretation of an Arthur C. Clarke story "changed movies forever" with its "haunting view" of a future world of "machine domination"; sure, some modernists find it "slow" and "ponderous", but even those who have "no clue what it all means" say this "coldly magnificent" epic is "undeniably influential" – and add "you'll never hear Strauss' 'Blue Danube Waltz' the same way again"; P.S. "don't bother trying to figure out the ending."

Two Women ✉ ◐ F — 25 | 28 | 25 | 24

1961 | Directed by Vittorio De Sica | With Sophia Loren, Eleanora Brown, Raf Vallone | 99 minutes | Not Rated

The "horror of war" from a "woman's viewpoint" is delineated in this "heartbreaking" Italian drama where a "protective mother and her daughter" bond after being "brutally raped" by a gang of soldiers; best remembered for Sophia's "riveting" performance, it's a "very emotional" film that's "seldom seen these days."

Umbrellas of Cherbourg, The F — 24 | 22 | 21 | 26

1964 | Directed by Jacques Demy | With Catherine Deneuve, Nino Castelnuovo | 87 minutes | Not Rated

Ultra-"bright Technicolor" and "captivating" music from Michel Legrand provide the uplift in this "sad story" of love in vain, an idiosyncratic French bonbon that's "entirely sung" (a "risky" proposition that ultimately "works"); starring a "fetching young Deneuve", it has the "courage" to turn a potentially "cheesy" premise into "inspiring" filmmaking.

Unforgiven ✉ — 26 | 26 | 24 | 25

1992 | Directed by Clint Eastwood | With Clint Eastwood, Gene Hackman, Morgan Freeman | 131 minutes | Rated R

"Clint directs, Clint scores, Clint wins" a Best Picture statuette with this "grim" "anti-Western" that manages to "revise every convention and cliché of the genre" with a "superb script" and cast of "unforgivable", "unforgettable" characters; indeed, it's so "powerful" and "dark", you'll find "no white hats here."

Up — 27 | - | 26 | 28

2009 | Directed by Pete Docter, Bob Peterson | Animated | 96 minutes | Rated PG

"Maybe Pixar's most moving film", this "animated wonder" sets the "emotional" tone at the outset with a "remarkable" "story-of-a-marriage" montage that will "have you in tears", followed by a "balloon"-assisted adventure involving a "curmudgeon" and his "pudgy sidekick"; whether enjoyed as a "deep" meditation on "love, loss" and "embracing life" or "just plain escapist fun", it's "totally absorbing."

Up in the Air — 23 | 25 | 23 | 23

2009 | Directed by Jason Reitman | With George Clooney, Vera Farmiga, Anna Kendrick, Sam Elliott | 108 minutes | Rated R

"Timely and topical", this "smart" dramedy stars Clooney as a "callow" professional downsizer who "makes his living firing people across the country" while becoming romantically involved with "fellow millionmiler" Farmiga; "acting chops" and a "pitch-perfect" script make for a "grown-up parable" laced with "humor and irony", even if the "up-in-the-air" ending is "kind of a downer."

Usual Suspects, The ✉ 27 | 28 | 28 | 25

1995 | Directed by Bryan Singer | With Gabriel Byrne, Kevin Spacey, Benicio Del Toro, Stephen Baldwin | 106 minutes | Rated R

"Don't blink" or you'll risk missing one of the many "imaginative" twists in this "tricky-as-hell" "instant classic" that may be one of the finest "whodunit" "thrill rides" ever made; fans "watch it at least twice" to absorb the "brilliant" story, admire the "flawless" Spacey and figure out what the heck "Benicio's saying"; as for that "unpredictable finale", you'll "never see it coming."

Vera Drake 24 | 28 | 25 | 23

2004 | Directed by Mike Leigh | With Imelda Staunton | 125 minutes | Rated R

Wherever you stand on Roe vs. Wade, it's "hard not to be moved" by this "devastating portrait" of a "well-meaning abortionist who runs afoul of the law" in '50s London; "delicate" direction by Leigh keeps the "polarizing" material in check, while "flawless" performances by a "magnificent" ensemble (particularly Staunton's "unforgettable" title turn) ensure there's "never a false moment."

Verdict, The 23 | 25 | 23 | 20

1982 | Directed by Sidney Lumet | With Paul Newman, Charlotte Rampling, Jack Warden | 129 minutes | Rated R

A "David-vs.-Goliath" legal struggle is the underpinning of this "underrated" courtroom drama about a "burned-out lawyer trying one last case to keep from going under"; Newman's "intense", "tour-de-force" turn is one of his "greatest" roles (leaving many "stunned" that the Oscar eluded him), while the "mesmerizing" Rampling "excels" as the love interest.

Vertigo 27 | 26 | 27 | 26

1958 | Directed by Alfred Hitchcock | With James Stewart, Kim Novak, Barbara Bel Geddes | 128 minutes | Rated PG

"Don't look down": this "dizzyingly complex" thriller offers lots of "twists and turns" as it details the "haunting" tale of an "obsessive" man who "tries to mold a woman into a vision of his lost love"; many call it "Hitchcock's crowning achievement" thanks to a Bernard Herrmann score that's "like perfume" as well as "spellbinding" work from a "bewitching Novak" and "Stewart at his darkest"; as for that "fever dream" of a plot, "it's not supposed to make sense."

Victor/Victoria 23 | 24 | 23 | 23

1982 | Directed by Blake Edwards | With Julie Andrews, James Garner, Robert Preston, Lesley Ann Warren | 132 minutes | Rated PG

"What a hoot!" holler fans who "never tire of watching" this "hilarious" musical farce about Parisian nightlife denizens in the '30s; "Andrews lights up the screen" as the titular double-crossed cross-dresser, while Leslie Ann Warren's fabulous floozie is deliciously "over-the-top"; in sum, this "fast-paced", "madcap" tale of "jazz-age gender bending" is "just plain fun."

	OVERALL	ACTING	STORY	PROD.

Viva Zapata! ◑

23	24	22	21

1952 | Directed by Elia Kazan | With Marlon Brando, Jean Peters, Anthony Quinn | 113 minutes | Not Rated

Elia Kazan directs a John Steinbeck screenplay in this "passionate" profile of Emiliano Zapata, the revolutionary hero who led a rebellion against Mexican dictator Porfirio Diaz; featuring an "unusual but expert turn" by Brando in the title role (as well as an Oscar-winning turn by Quinn), it's "historical" cinema "at its best" and, given the climate of its 1952 release, an "important political drama."

Volver F

24	26	23	23

2006 | Directed by Pedro Almodóvar | With Penélope Cruz, Carmen Maura, Lola Dueñas | 121 minutes | Rated R

Spanish "master" Almodóvar "just gets better and better", coaxing a "luminously beautiful" performance from "luscious" "muse" Cruz ("no one writes for women the way Pedro does") in this "spellbinding" mother-daughter "family drama"; mixing "tragedy and laughter in the right amounts" with a splash of "Hitchcock", this "sentimental, emotional" concoction "has it all" for fans of cinema "*maravillosa.*"

Wages of Fear ◑F

27	26	27	24

1955 | Directed by Henri-Georges Clouzot | With Yves Montand, Charles Vanel | 148 minutes | Not Rated

"Fasten your seatbelts for a bumpy" ride via this "nerve-racking" "nail-biter" about "down-and-outers" racing a "nitroglycerine-loaded truck" across the mountains of South America; Clouzot's knack for "oh-my-God" suspense and "social commentary" makes it one of the "best art-house action" flicks around.

Waiting for Guffman

25	26	24	23

1996 | Directed by Christopher Guest | With Christopher Guest, Eugene Levy, Fred Willard, Catherine O'Hara | 84 minutes | Rated R

"Anyone who loves the theater and loves to laugh" shouldn't miss this "hilarious" mockumentary about "community theater in the boonies" courtesy of "comic genius" Guest and his "usual incredibly talented ensemble"; it's a "laugh riot from the first frame to the last", with "classic" scenes you'll "quote lines from" – "I'm still searching for *My Dinner with Andre* action figures."

Waitress

24	26	23	23

2007 | Directed by Adrienne Shelly | With Keri Russell, Jeremy Sisto, Nathan Fillion, Andy Griffith | 107 minutes | Rated PG-13

With a "nod to *Alice Doesn't Live Here Anymore*", this "sweet-natured" comic confection about a "small-town" diner waitress "caught in a loveless marriage" has enough ingredients to "steal your heart", including an "outstanding" Russell, the "consummate" Griffith and, of course, those "delicious"-looking pies; indeed, many call this "uplifting" "little jewel" a "rallying cry for women everywhere."

Wait Until Dark

25	26	27	23

1967 | Directed by Terence Young | With Audrey Hepburn, Alan Arkin, Richard Crenna, Efrem Zimbalist Jr. | 107 minutes | Not Rated

This "unforgettable" thriller posits a "simple, nerve-shattering premise": a blind woman, alone in her apartment, in a "game of cat-and-mouse" with a "brutal psychopath"; gird yourself for an "eerie Henry Mancini

score" and a "twists-and-turns"-laden scenario with "one particularly electrifying moment" that's guaranteed to "have you out of your seat."

Walk the Line ✉ 25 | 28 | 23 | 25

2005 | Directed by James Mangold | With Joaquin Phoenix, Reese Witherspoon, Ginnifer Goodwin | 136 minutes | Rated PG-13

The "Man in Black" walks again courtesy of this "evocative", "behind-the-music" biopic that pays "touching tribute" to country "legend" Johnny Cash and his "true love", June Carter, the "good woman" who "saved him" from a life of "drugs and temptation"; both Phoenix and Witherspoon are "phenomenal" (yep, "they do their own singing"), and the "foot-stomping" tunes "ain't bad", either.

Wallace & Gromit in the Curse of the Were-Rabbit 24 | - | 22 | 27

2005 | Directed by Steve Box, Nick Park | Animated | 85 minutes | Rated G

Appearing in their first feature-length flick, "goofy" gadgeteer Wallace and his silently "expressive" pooch Gromit come to the neighborhood's rescue when a "mutated rabbit terrorizes its gardens" in this "jolly good", "for-all-ages" claymation comedy brimming with "Brit wit" and "inventive" visual spectacle; fans beg series creator Nick Park "please sir, may we have some more?"

WALL-E 26 | - | 25 | 27

2008 | Directed by Andrew Stanton | Animated | 98 minutes | Rated G

"Wow-E!" is the response to this Pixar "winner", a "visually stunning" animated flick channeling "Charlie Chaplin" via its nearly dialogue-free tale of a "robot with a heart" cleaning the debris cluttering up a "depopulated Earth"; not only will you "laugh and cry", you'll also think about "our world as it could become", which might scream "environmentalist agenda" were it not for the "tremendous creativity" evident.

War of the Worlds, The 23 | 16 | 24 | 23

1953 | Directed by Byron Haskin | With Gene Barry, Ann Robinson, Les Tremayne | 85 minutes | Rated G

Although the "Orson Welles radio broadcast" is "more famous", this "faithful" filming of the H.G. Wells "sci-fi classic" still clearly telegraphs its "frightening premise" of Martians run amok on Planet Earth; ok, it may be a bit "overstated" and "unintentionally funny today", but boob-tubers tune in "every time it's on television."

Warriors, The 23 | 16 | 22 | 18

1979 | Directed by Walter Hill | With Michael Beck, James Remar, David Patrick Kelly | 93 minutes | Rated R

The "seedy cesspool that was NYC in the '70s" serves as the "dystopian" backdrop for this "intriguing" "gangland warfare" flick following a Coney Island crew pegged "for a murder they didn't commit"; boasting "great action", "fabulous production design" and even its own "video game", this movie has long enjoyed "cult classic" status - "can you dig it?"

Way We Were, The 24 | 25 | 25 | 23

1973 | Directed by Sydney Pollack | With Barbra Streisand, Robert Redford, Bradford Dillman | 118 minutes | Rated PG

"Still a tearjerker after all these years", this "improbable romance" pits a "brainy" Jewish girl opposite a "golden Wasp boy" and "tugs every heartstring available" in its "realistic" depiction of their "ill-fated" affair; Streisand and Redford "at their peak" are "beyond delicious" together, though the most indelible "memories" involve the "famous final scene" at the "Plaza Hotel" with that "sad", Oscar-winning song playing in the background.

Wedding Banquet, The F 22 | 21 | 25 | 21

1993 | Directed by Ang Lee | With Winston Chao, May Chin, Mitchell Lichtenstein | 106 minutes | Rated R

"Family dynamics" get a "touching" twist in this "gently told" Taiwanese tale about a "marriage of convenience" between a "gay man" hoping to make his parents happy and his green card–seeking bride; this "funny charade" comes to a climax at the titular feast, where "unconditional love" comes "out of the closet" in a "warmhearted", "bittersweet finale."

West Side Story ✉ 27 | 24 | 27 | 27

1961 | Directed by Robert Wise, Jerome Robbins | With Natalie Wood, Richard Beymer, Rita Moreno, George Chakiris | 151 minutes | Not Rated

Starting with that "opening bird's-eye view of Manhattan", this "remarkable musical" that transposes "*Romeo and Juliet*" to "urban" turf is "sheer perfection" thanks to "fiery acting", Robbins' "superb" streetwise choreography and the "dynamic" Leonard Bernstein/Stephen Sondheim score; sure, Beymer might be "miscast" and it's "too bad they wouldn't let Natalie sing", but otherwise this Oscar magnet – 10 statuettes including Best Picture – is "forever fabulous."

Whale Rider 25 | 26 | 24 | 24

2003 | Directed by Niki Caro | With Keisha Castle-Hughes, Rawiri Paratene, Vicki Haughton | 101 minutes | Rated PG-13

Featuring "no stars, no explosions and no CGI effects", this nonetheless "powerful" film tells the "captivating" story of a Maori girl's struggle to help her tribe balance "tradition and the 21st century"; a "refreshing", family-friendly slice of "edutainment" complete with "beautiful" New Zealand vistas and "phenomenal" work by "up-and-comer" Castle-Hughes, this "achingly sad" story will "leave your soul touched."

When Harry Met Sally . . . 26 | 25 | 25 | 24

1989 | Directed by Rob Reiner | With Billy Crystal, Meg Ryan, Carrie Fisher, Bruno Kirby | 96 minutes | Rated R

"Can a man and a woman be just friends?"; this romantic comedy – the "king of all date movies" – attempts to answer that question as it details a "terrific take on relationships" that "rings true for many"; written by Nora Ephron as an "ode to Manhattan", it stars an "adorable", "pre-pixie cut" Ryan opposite a "perfect" Crystal, both "forever remembered" for the "infamous orgasm scene" in Katz's Deli that inspired one of the best lines in moviedom: "I'll have what she's having."

Where's Poppa? 23 | 25 | 23 | 21

1970 | Directed by Carl Reiner | With George Segal, Ruth Gordon, Trish Van Devere, Ron Leibman | 82 minutes | Rated R

This "twisted" black comedy from Carl Reiner examines the "sick relationship" between a "senile" mom living with her "dutiful (up-to-a-point)" son; "painfully funny", it's acquired "cult" status over the years for set pieces like the "ape suit scene" and the "tush-biting" sequence; P.S. the original ending, an extra on the DVD, is truly "insane."

	OVERALL	ACTING	STORY	PROD.

White Christmas

25	21	22	24

1954 | Directed by Michael Curtiz | With Bing Crosby, Danny Kaye, Rosemary Clooney | 120 minutes | Not Rated

"It wouldn't be Christmas" without a peek at this "sentimental" favorite, a virtual holiday "requirement" with "all the trimmings": "wonderful dance numbers", "essential" Irving Berlin tunes and "Der Bingle" crooning "kringle jingles"; in short, this "classic" is so "charming", it's almost "un-American not to love it"; P.S. sticklers note that Bing originally "made the title song famous in *Holiday Inn*."

White Heat ◑

25	28	24	23

1949 | Directed by Raoul Walsh | With James Cagney, Virginia Mayo, Edmond O'Brien | 114 minutes | Not Rated

One part "descent into madness", one part "valentine to mom", this schizophrenic, noirish thriller represents the "classic gangster film refined to the nth degree"; as a "homicidal nut job" "mama's boy", Cagney turns in one of his "greatest performances", though the flick's most remembered for the "best last line in movie history": 'made it, ma! top of the world!'

Who Framed Roger Rabbit

24	-	23	27

1988 | Directed by Robert Zemeckis | Animated | With Bob Hoskins, Christopher Lloyd | 103 minutes | Rated PG

This "one-of-a-kind treat" featuring a "glorious mix of live action and animation" boasts an all-star cartoon cast, with appearances by every 'toon from Mickey to Woody (though the "seductive" Jessica Rabbit runs away with the picture); set in the Hollywood of yore, the "classic" noir plot has Hoskins investigating a murder case, with "wonderfully entertaining" results.

Who's Afraid of Virginia Woolf? ✉◑

25	27	25	23

1966 | Directed by Mike Nichols | With Elizabeth Taylor, Richard Burton, George Segal, Sandy Dennis | 134 minutes | Not Rated

Maybe "Liz made up to look frumpy is a laugh", but otherwise this "scalding adaptation" of Edward Albee's "masterpiece" about an "unraveling marriage" is pretty serious stuff, "brilliantly acted" and "brutally honest"; it's "funny and mean and sad" all at once – "never has a play been converted into a movie" with such "power."

Wild Bunch, The

27	26	25	27

1969 | Directed by Sam Peckinpah | With William Holden, Ernest Borgnine, Robert Ryan, Ben Johnson | 134 minutes | Rated R

Not for the faint of heart, this "blood-and-guts" Peckinpah "epic" is a "Western to end all Westerns" that "transcends the genre" with an "in-your-face style" that turns "violence into poetry"; starring Holden as the leader of a band of "honorable outlaws", it depicts a "changing world" at the "end of an era" in "unsentimental" terms and manages to be both "noble and perverse at the same time."

Wild Strawberries ◑F

26	26	24	25

1959 | Directed by Ingmar Bergman | With Victor Sjöström, Bibi Andersson, Ingrid Thulin | 91 minutes | Not Rated

"Essential Bergman" that's not just for art movie mavens, this "elegiac" "road film about life, death and redemption" "continues to hold up well"; a "bittersweet" story of an "elderly doctor who learns how to love at

	OVERALL	ACTING	STORY	PROD.

the last minute of his life", it's ultimately "cathartic and hopeful", even if it occasionally displays the director's signature "depressive" streak.

Willy Wonka and the Chocolate Factory 26 | 22 | 26 | 26

1971 | Directed by Mel Stuart | With Gene Wilder, Jack Albertson, Peter Ostrum | 100 minutes | Rated G

Chocoholics cheer this "delicious family classic" adeptly adapted from the "brilliant Roald Dahl book" about an "underdog" kid who gets a "once-in-a-lifetime" chance to tour a "curious candy factory"; it's such a "blast to watch" (thanks to "psychedelic" sets, "imaginative" vignettes and "great songs") that it's almost become a "rite of passage" for the stroller set.

Wind and the Lion, The 24 | 25 | 24 | 24

1975 | Directed by John Milius | With Sean Connery, Candice Bergen, Brian Keith | 119 minutes | Rated PG

This "old-fashioned, character-driven adventure" about an Arab chieftain's abduction of an American widow is loosely "based on a real incident during Teddy Roosevelt's presidency"; despite the "wonderful desert romance" that blooms between the "charismatic" Connery and "watchable" Bergen, there's "still enough action for the guys" in this "obscure history lesson."

Wings of Desire ◑ F 24 | 24 | 22 | 25

1988 | Directed by Wim Wenders | With Bruno Ganz, Solveig Dommartin | 127 minutes | Rated PG-13

A "charming meditation" about the "angels who watch over us", "longing to be human", this "haunting" German film "celebrates the human condition"; "dreamy cinematography" and an "amazing" cast elevate it to "pure poetry" – but don't "judge it by its self-conscious remake", Hollywood's "unfortunate" *City of Angels.*

Witness ✉ 23 | 24 | 23 | 22

1985 | Directed by Peter Weir | With Harrison Ford, Kelly McGillis, Lukas Haas | 112 minutes | Rated R

"One of Weir's finest", this "quiet" film offers a "sensitive portrayal" of a "small Amish community" that "collides with the violent outside world" in the aftermath of a murder; the actors have "perfect pitch" (particularly the "workmanlike" Ford, who "sizzles" against the "luminous McGillis"), and even if the story's somewhat "improbable", its overall "excellence sneaks up on you."

Witness for the Prosecution ◑ 27 | 28 | 28 | 25

1957 | Directed by Billy Wilder | With Tyrone Power, Marlene Dietrich, Charles Laughton | 116 minutes | Not Rated

Perhaps the "best murder mystery ever", this "Agatha Christie puzzler" is one of "Wilder's wiliest", featuring "two legends" – an "incredible" Laughton and an "outstanding" Dietrich – along with a courtroom-full of "compelling characterizations"; the dialogue "crackles" and the "plot twists and double twists" right up to the "still shocking ending."

Wizard of Oz, The 28 | 26 | 28 | 29

1939 | Directed by Victor Fleming | With Judy Garland, Ray Bolger, Jack Haley, Bert Lahr | 101 minutes | Rated G

A "star is born" – the "iconic" "Judy, Judy, Judy" – in this "timeless", "transporting" musical about a Kansas girl "off to see the Wizard" that's been "adored for decades" thanks to its "tremendous" cast, "glorious", "rainbow"-hued score and "inspired" moments involving a pair of "ruby slippers", a pack of "scary flying monkeys" and that "magical", "hello-Technicolor" transition; in Toto, this "landmark in family entertainment" is the ultimate proof that "there's no place like home."

Woman of the Year ✉◑ 27 | 28 | 26 | 26

1942 | Directed by George Stevens | With Katharine Hepburn, Spencer Tracy, Fay Bainter | 114 minutes | Not Rated

The "war between the sexes was never more fun" than in this first matchup of legendary duo Hepburn and Tracy in what some call the "best" of their eight films together; its Oscar-winning script pits the "right-on" Kate as an "ahead-of-her-time" foreign correspondent against Spence's laid-back sportswriter, but the hands-down winner in this battle of wills is clearly the audience.

Woman Under the Influence, A 24 | 27 | 22 | 21

1974 | Directed by John Cassavetes | With Peter Falk, Gena Rowlands | 155 minutes | Rated R

"Raw, naturalistic performances" lie at the core of this "stunning", "hyper-real" drama about a "housewife's sad decline" into mental illness; a "heartbreaking" Rowlands plays the title role "like a Stradivarius", and even though some "overlong, meandering" scenes can be "difficult to watch", ultimately it's a "tender", "uncompromising" look at the "beautiful mess that is marriage."

Women, The ◑ 26 | 26 | 24 | 25

1939 | Directed by George Cukor | With Norma Shearer, Joan Crawford, Rosalind Russell, Paulette Goddard | 133 minutes | Not Rated

"*Meow!*": a "wonderful wallow" in "bitchy backstabbing", this "marvelous" MGM adaptation of Clare Boothe Luce's "snappy" stage play about high-society divorcées boasts an all-star, all-gal cast rattling off "extraordinary fast-paced" dialogue; though the constant "cattiness" can be a turnoff, it's still "required viewing" for "chick flick" and camp followers – "long live Jungle Red!"

Women in Love ✉ 23 | 26 | 24 | 23

1970 | Directed by Ken Russell | With Alan Bates, Oliver Reed, Glenda Jackson, Jennie Linden | 131 minutes | Rated R

Ken Russell's "visually amazing", "erotically charged" take on the D.H. Lawrence novel "deals frankly" with two couples' struggle to conform to the marital and sexual conventions of 1920s England; it's a "sensual", "memorable" picture that's most renowned for Jackson's "strong", Oscar-winning turn and that notorious "nude male wrestling scene."

Women on the Verge of a Nervous Breakdown F 24 | 24 | 23 | 22

1988 | Directed by Pedro Almodóvar | With Carmen Maura, Antonio Banderas | 90 minutes | Rated R

Forget the "depressing" title: this "campy", "door-slamming farce" "put director Almodóvar on the map" and is one of the "funniest foreign films" ever made; a "wacky" story of "neurotic characters with different agendas", it also introduced "eye-candy Banderas to the Western world."

Wuthering Heights ◑

OVERALL	ACTING	STORY	PROD.
27	27	27	24

1939 | Directed by William Wyler | With Laurence Olivier, Merle Oberon, David Niven | 103 minutes | Not Rated

This "Gothic romance" is a "charter" member of the "pantheon" of silver screen weepies and the "ultimate" adaptation of the Brontë tale; Olivier's "soulful brooding" as a spurned, lower-caste lover is so "brilliantly intense" that it's inspired generations of maidens to "waste away from heartbreak on the moors" ever after.

X2: X-Men United

OVERALL	ACTING	STORY	PROD.
24	21	22	27

2003 | Directed by Bryan Singer | With Patrick Stewart, Hugh Jackman, Ian McKellen, Halle Berry, Brian Cox | 133 minutes | Rated PG-13

"Finally, a sequel to sink your claws into": this "X-cellent" follow-up "tops the mediocre original" "in just about every way" – a "better storyline", "intriguing new characters", a "deservedly bigger role" for the "buff", "brooding" Jackman and "mega-cool special effects"... "what a bigger budget will do for a movie"; "can't wait for the next one – and there *will* be a next one."

Yankee Doodle Dandy ✉◑

OVERALL	ACTING	STORY	PROD.
25	25	23	25

1942 | Directed by Michael Curtiz | With James Cagney, Joan Leslie, Walter Huston | 126 minutes | Not Rated

"Flag-waving", "red-white-and-blue" musical bio of the "all-American" showman George M. Cohan, starring Cagney in full "hoofer" bloom; the story's "whitewashed", but after a few bars of its "patriotic tunes" you'll understand why the "4th of July wouldn't be the same without it."

Year of Living Dangerously, The

OVERALL	ACTING	STORY	PROD.
24	25	25	24

1983 | Directed by Peter Weir | With Mel Gibson, Sigourney Weaver, Linda Hunt | 117 minutes | Rated PG

An outbreak of "civil war" during the "Sukarno regime" in '60s Indonesia comes alive in this "captivating" "political" drama following a journalist who's covering the conflict; though the "compelling" Gibson and Weaver cast "steamy sparks", Hunt took home an Oscar for her "tour-de-force", "gender-bending role" in this "tense" thriller.

Yojimbo ◑F

OVERALL	ACTING	STORY	PROD.
28	27	26	26

1961 | Directed by Akira Kurosawa | With Toshiro Mifune, Tatsuya Nakadai | 110 minutes | Not Rated

"Kurosawa's classic samurai film" stars Mifune as the "ultimate anti-hero" who "plays both sides" of a village feud between a silk merchant and a sake merchant, and then watches as the depraved "warring factions" destroy each other; the "inspiration" for myriad remakes (*A Fistful of Dollars, Last Man Standing,* etc.), this "far superior" original clearly "shows how great this director really is."

Young Frankenstein ◑

OVERALL	ACTING	STORY	PROD.
27	26	25	25

1974 | Directed by Mel Brooks | With Gene Wilder, Peter Boyle, Marty Feldman, Madeline Kahn, Cloris Leachman | 108 minutes | Rated PG

"Frankenstein Sr. would be proud" of this "insanely hysterical" "spoof of the Mary Shelley" horror classic that's Mel Brooks' "high-water mark" ("who else would have the monster" perform 'Puttin' on the Ritz' wearing a tuxedo?); Wilder is "pure genius" in the title role backed up by an "endlessly amusing" cast of characters spouting some of the "most quoted" dialogue in movie history; best line: a toss-up between "walk this way", "what knockers" and "hump? what hump?"; best song: Kahn's rendition of 'Ah! Sweet Mystery of Life', no contest.

Y Tu Mamá También F 24 | 24 | 23 | 21

2002 | Directed by Alfonso Cuarón | With Maribel Verdu, Gael García Bernal, Diego Luna, Diana Bracho | 105 minutes | Rated R

Two "upper-middle-class Mexican boys" "learn the facts of life" and then some from a "sexy older woman" during a road trip "that takes some unexpected turns" in this *muy caliente* "coming-of-age" character study; some say "everything takes a back seat (no pun intended)" to the "very explicit sex scenes" – whew! –but more cerebral types see it more as a "passionate film about life, youth and love" that's "far greater than the sum of its parts."

Z ✉ F 26 | 25 | 26 | 24

1969 | Directed by Costa-Gavras | With Yves Montand, Irene Papas, Jean-Louis Trintignant, Jacques Perrin | 127 minutes | Rated PG

Unfortunately all "too true", this fact-based account of the assassination of a left-leaning scientist in a right-wing country is a crackerjack "political thriller" that's "deeply affecting" and "not easy to watch"; Montand is "nothing less than superb" in the title role, while director Costa-Gavras makes this "documentary-like" "exposé" of corruption "captivating from the first scene."

Ziegfeld Follies 24 | 21 | - | 26

1946 | Directed by Vincente Minnelli et al | With Fred Astaire, Gene Kelly, Lena Horne, Judy Garland, Lucille Ball | 110 minutes | Not Rated

"Nearly every great star at MGM" is showcased in this "episodic" musical revue featuring "memorable" song-and-dance routines (like Fred Astaire and Gene Kelly in their only appearance together) interspersed with "dated comedy skits"; overall, it may be a "mixed bag", but aficionados swoon over the "lavishly ridiculous" highlights: a "breathtaking" Judy Garland number, "rare footage of Fanny Brice" and "Lucille Ball as a glamour girl with a whip."

Zorba the Greek ◑ 25 | 27 | 25 | 23

1964 | Directed by Michael Cacoyannis | With Anthony Quinn, Alan Bates, Irene Papas, Lila Kedrova | 142 minutes | Not Rated

There's ex-zorba-tant praise for this "still-fresh" drama about an Englishman visiting Crete on an existential quest, only to fall under the spell of a "person full of passion", the "flamboyant" Zorba; Quinn's "breakout" performance, plus some "memorable" theme music and dancing, keep this "feel-good" "affirmation of life" so "exciting and entertaining" that repeaters faithfully "see it every year."

Zulu 24 | 24 | 25 | 24

1964 | Directed by Cy Endfield | With Stanley Baker, Jack Hawkins, Michael Caine | 138 minutes | Not Rated

The "true story of valor in the face of incredible odds", this "epic treatment of a 19th-century British military disaster" is played out against the "broad canvas of Africa" and features an "unknown Caine" in his "first big film"; "visually and viscerally stunning", it's "historically accurate without sacrificing dramatic appeal", and the "tension's unrelenting."

INDEXES

By Year 212
Genres/Special Features 223

Years

Listings include Overall ratings.

1910s/1920s

Birth of a Nation | 1915 25
Cabinet of Dr. Caligari | 1921 26
Cocoanuts, The | 1929 24
General, The | 1927 28
Gold Rush | 1925 28
Metropolis | 1927 27
Napoléon | 1929 28
Nosferatu | 1922 26
Potemkin | 1926 27
Thief of Bagdad | 1924 24

1930

All Quiet on Western Front 28
Animal Crackers 26
Blue Angel 25

1931

City Lights 28
Dracula 24
Frankenstein 25
Front Page 24
Little Caesar 24
Monkey Business 26
Public Enemy 25

1932

Freaks 23
Grand Hotel 25
Horse Feathers 24
Mummy, The 24

1933

Dinner at Eight 27
Duck Soup 27
Flying Down to Rio 23
Footlight Parade 23
42nd Street 24
Gold Diggers of 1933 25
I'm No Angel 23
Invisible Man 22
King Kong 25
M 26

1934

Gay Divorcee 25
It Happened One Night 28
Thin Man 26

1935

Anna Karenina 26
Bride of Frankenstein 25
Captain Blood 23
Mutiny on the Bounty (1935) 25
Night at the Opera 26
39 Steps 27
Top Hat 27

1936

Modern Times 28
Mr. Deeds Goes to Town 25
My Man Godfrey 25
Swing Time 26

1937

Awful Truth 25
Camille 26
Captains Courageous 25
Day at the Races 24
Lost Horizon 25
Shall We Dance 25
Snow White 27
Stage Door 25

1938

Adventures of Robin Hood 25
Angels with Dirty Faces 24
Bringing Up Baby 27
Grand Illusion 28
Holiday 27
Jezebel 25
Lady Vanishes 25

1939

Alexander Nevsky 26
Beau Geste 25
Dark Victory 25
Destry Rides Again 25
Gone with the Wind 28
Goodbye, Mr. Chips 25
Gunga Din 25
Hound of the Baskervilles 22
Hunchback/Notre Dame 26
Mr. Smith Goes to Washington 26
Ninotchka 25
Of Mice and Men 26
Stagecoach 27
Wizard of Oz 28
Women, The 26
Wuthering Heights 27

1940

All This, and Heaven Too 26
Fantasia 28

Title	Rating
Foreign Correspondent	24
Grapes of Wrath	28
Great Dictator	26
His Girl Friday	26
Mark of Zorro	22
My Little Chickadee	23
Philadelphia Story	27
Pinocchio	26
Pride and Prejudice (1940)	25
Rebecca	27
Shop Around the Corner	24

1941

Title	Rating
Ball of Fire	26
Citizen Kane	28
Dumbo	24
High Sierra	25
How Green Was My Valley	27
Lady Eve	28
Little Foxes	26
Maltese Falcon	28
Meet John Doe	24
Sergeant York	25
Sullivan's Travels	27
Suspicion	25

1942

Title	Rating
Bambi	26
Casablanca	29
Cat People	23
Holiday Inn	23
Jungle Book (1942)	24
Magnificent Ambersons	25
Man Who Came to Dinner	26
Mrs. Miniver	25
Now, Voyager	27
Palm Beach Story	25
Saboteur	23
To Be or Not to Be	24
Woman of the Year	27
Yankee Doodle Dandy	25

1943

Title	Rating
Cabin in the Sky	24
For Whom the Bell Tolls	25
Heaven Can Wait	24
Ox-Bow Incident	27
Shadow of a Doubt	26
Song of Bernadette	22

1944

Title	Rating
Arsenic and Old Lace	26
Double Indemnity	28
Gaslight	26
Going My Way	24
Jane Eyre	25
Laura	27
Lifeboat	25
Meet Me in St. Louis	26
Miracle of Morgan's Creek	23
Murder, My Sweet	24
To Have and Have Not	26

1945

Title	Rating
Bells of St. Mary's	24
Lost Weekend	25
Mildred Pierce	26
National Velvet	24
Spellbound	24

1946

Title	Rating
Best Years of Our Lives	28
Big Sleep	27
Brief Encounter	27
Children of Paradise	28
Duel in the Sun	23
Gilda	24
It's a Wonderful Life	27
Killers, The	25
My Darling Clementine	25
Notorious	27
Postman Always Rings . . .	25
Song of the South	23
Ziegfeld Follies	24

1947

Title	Rating
Beauty/Beast (1947)	28
Bishop's Wife	24
Body and Soul	25
Gentleman's Agreement	26
Ghost and Mrs. Muir	24
Great Expectations	27
Kiss of Death	23
Miracle on 34th Street	25
Out of the Past	26

1948

Title	Rating
Big Clock	25
Call Northside 777	25
Easter Parade	22
Fort Apache	23
Hamlet (1948)	27
Key Largo	26
Lady from Shanghai	25
Mr. Blandings	23
Red River	26
Red Shoes	26
Snake Pit	25
Sorry, Wrong Number	25
Treasure of the Sierra Madre	27

1949

Adam's Rib	26
All the King's Men	25
Bicycle Thief	27
Fountainhead, The	22
Gun Crazy	27
Heiress, The	27
Letter to Three Wives	24
On the Town	23
She Wore a Yellow Ribbon	24
Third Man	28
Twelve O'Clock High	26
White Heat	25

1950

All About Eve	28
Asphalt Jungle	24
Born Yesterday	26
Cinderella	26
Father of the Bride	23
Harvey	26
Kind Hearts and Coronets	26
Sunset Boulevard	28

1951

Ace in the Hole	26
African Queen	28
Alice in Wonderland	24
American in Paris	26
Christmas Carol	27
Day the Earth Stood Still	25
Lavender Hill Mob	25
Oliver Twist	25
Place in the Sun	27
Rashomon	29
Show Boat	23
Strangers on a Train	26
Streetcar Named Desire	27
Thing, The (1951)	23

1952

Bad and the Beautiful	24
High Noon	28
Limelight	24
Member of the Wedding	25
Quiet Man	27
Singin' in the Rain	28
Viva Zapata!	23

1953

Band Wagon	26
Big Heat	25
From Here to Eternity	26
Gentlemen Prefer Blondes	23
Kiss Me Kate	24
Lili	24
Peter Pan	25
Pickup on South Street	23
Roman Holiday	27
Shane	26
Stalag 17	27
War of the Worlds	23

1954

Barefoot Contessa	24
Brigadoon	24
Caine Mutiny	27
Carmen Jones	23
Country Girl	24
Dial M for Murder	25
Mr. Hulot's Holiday	25
On the Waterfront	28
Rear Window	28
Sabrina	25
Seven Brides/Seven Brothers	24
Star Is Born	25
White Christmas	25

1955

Bad Day at Black Rock	24
Blackboard Jungle	23
Court Jester, The	24
Diabolique	26
East of Eden	24
Guys and Dolls	24
Kiss Me Deadly	24
Lady and the Tramp	26
Love Is Many-Splendored . . .	22
Man with the Golden Arm	24
Marty	25
Mister Roberts	27
Night of the Hunter	27
Oklahoma!	24
Picnic	24
Rebel Without a Cause	24
Seven Year Itch	23
Summertime	23
To Catch a Thief	25
Wages of Fear	27

1956

Anastasia	23
Bad Seed	22
Carousel	24
Forbidden Planet	25
Friendly Persuasion	24
Giant	24
High Society	23
Invasion/Body Snatchers	24
Killing, The	25
King and I	27

La Strada 27
Lust for Life 23
Man Who Knew Too Much 24
Rififi 26
Searchers, The 27
Seven Samurai 29
Ten Commandments 24

1957

Affair to Remember 26
Bridge on the River Kwai 28
Desk Set 25
Face in the Crowd 26
Funny Face 24
Love in the Afternoon 24
Nights of Cabiria 27
Old Yeller 24
Paths of Glory 28
Smiles of a Summer Night 26
Sweet Smell of Success 27
Three Faces of Eve 24
12 Angry Men 28
Witness for the Prosecution 27

1958

Auntie Mame 25
Cat on a Hot Tin Roof 25
Damn Yankees 24
Gigi 24
I Want to Live! 24
Mon Oncle 26
No Time for Sergeants 23
Seventh Seal 27
South Pacific 24
Touch of Evil 26
Vertigo 27

1959

Anatomy of a Murder 26
Ben-Hur 26
Black Orpheus 26
Diary of Anne Frank 23
400 Blows 27
Mouse That Roared 23
North by Northwest 28
On the Beach 26
Rio Bravo 24
Room at the Top 24
Sleeping Beauty 25
Some Like It Hot 28
Suddenly, Last Summer 24
Wild Strawberries 26

1960

Apartment, The 25
Bells Are Ringing 24
Butterfield 8 23
Elmer Gantry 25
Exodus 23
Hiroshima, Mon Amour 25
Inherit the Wind 26
Magnificent Seven 26
Never on Sunday 24
Psycho 28
Spartacus 26
Swiss Family Robinson 23

1961

Breakfast at Tiffany's 26
Breathless 25
Children's Hour 24
Guns of Navarone 23
Hustler, The 25
Judgment at Nuremberg 26
La Dolce Vita 25
L'Avventura 24
101 Dalmatians 24
One, Two, Three 23
Parent Trap 23
Raisin in the Sun 26
Splendor in the Grass 25
Two Women 25
West Side Story 27
Yojimbo 28

1962

Advise & Consent 27
Cape Fear 25
Counterfeit Traitor 25
Days of Wine and Roses 27
Divorce Italian Style 24
Experiment in Terror 25
Jules and Jim 24
Lawrence of Arabia 29
Lolita 24
Longest Day 24
Manchurian Candidate 27
Man Who Shot Liberty Valance 25
Miracle Worker 25
Music Man 25
Mutiny on the Bounty (1962) 22
Requiem for a Heavyweight 26
Shoot the Piano Player 25
Sweet Bird of Youth 24
To Kill a Mockingbird 29

1963

Birds, The 24
Charade 26
Dr. No 23
8½ 26

YEARS

Great Escape 27
How the West Was Won 23
Hud 26
It's a Mad Mad Mad World 24
Knife in the Water 24
Leopard, The 25
Lilies of the Field 25
Lord of the Flies 23
Servant, The 25
Tom Jones 25

1964

Americanization of Emily 24
Becket 26
Contempt 25
Dr. Strangelove 28
Fail-Safe 24
From Russia With Love 23
Goldfinger 26
Hard Day's Night 24
Hush . . . Hush, Sweet Charlotte 24
Mary Poppins 27
My Fair Lady 27
Night of the Iguana 23
Pink Panther 24
Seven Days in May 26
Shot in the Dark 23
Topkapi 24
Umbrellas of Cherbourg 24
Zorba the Greek 25
Zulu 24

1965

Agony and the Ecstasy 23
Cincinnati Kid 24
Collector, The 23
Darling 22
Doctor Zhivago 27
Flight of the Phoenix 25
Ipcress File 24
Juliet of the Spirits 25
Pawnbroker, The 26
Ship of Fools 23
Sound of Music 28
Spy Who Came in from Cold 25
Thousand Clowns 25
Thunderball 22

1966

Blowup 26
Born Free 24
Fortune Cookie 23
Georgy Girl 23
Man and a Woman 24
Man for All Seasons 28
Sand Pebbles 24
Shop on Main Street 27
Torn Curtain 23
Who's Afraid of V. Woolf? 25

1967

Barefoot in the Park 23
Battle of Algiers 28
Bonnie and Clyde 25
Cool Hand Luke 26
Far from the Madding Crowd 23
For a Few Dollars More 23
Good, the Bad and the Ugly 24
Graduate, The 27
Guess Who's Coming . . . 25
In Cold Blood 25
In the Heat of the Night 24
Jungle Book (1967) 23
King of Hearts 26
Persona 27
To Sir, With Love 22
Two for the Road 24
Wait Until Dark 25

1968

Belle de Jour 24
Funny Girl 26
Heart Is a Lonely Hunter 25
Lion in Winter 28
Odd Couple 25
Oliver! 24
Planet of the Apes 23
Producers, The 26
Romeo and Juliet 26
Rosemary's Baby 24
Thomas Crown Affair 23
2001: A Space Odyssey 26

1969

Anne of the Thousand Days 26
Butch Cassidy 26
Damned, The 23
Easy Rider 23
Midnight Cowboy 26
Once Upon a Time/West 25
Prime of Miss Jean Brodie 25
True Grit 22
Wild Bunch 27
Z 26

1970

Catch-22 25
Five Easy Pieces 24
Great White Hope 25
I Never Sang for My Father 27

Little Big Man	24
MASH	26
Patton	27
Tora! Tora! Tora!	23
Where's Poppa?	23
Women in Love	23

1971

Bananas	23
Claire's Knee	23
Clockwork Orange	25
Conformist, The	26
Death in Venice	24
Fiddler on the Roof	26
French Connection	25
Garden of the Finzi-Continis	25
Last Picture Show	23
McCabe & Mrs. Miller	23
Sunday Bloody Sunday	24
Willy Wonka	26

1972

Cabaret	26
Cries and Whispers	26
Deliverance	25
Discreet Charm	24
Getaway, The	22
Godfather, The	29
Harold and Maude	25
Jeremiah Johnson	23
Play It Again, Sam	22
Ruling Class	23
Sleuth	25
Sounder	26

1973

American Graffiti	24
Badlands	25
Bang the Drum Slowly	23
Day for Night	27
Day of the Jackal	25
Don't Look Now	24
Enter the Dragon	23
Exorcist, The	25
Mean Streets	24
Paper Chase	23
Papillon	26
Serpico	23
Sleeper	23
Sting, The	27
Way We Were	24

1974

Alice Doesn't Live Here	24
Blazing Saddles	25
Chinatown	27
Conversation, The	25
Godfather Part II	29
Lenny	24
Murder on the Orient Express	23
Parallax View	24
Scenes from a Marriage	25
Three Musketeers	22
Woman Under the Influence	24
Young Frankenstein	27

1975

Amarcord	26
Dog Day Afternoon	24
Jaws	26
Man Who Would Be King	25
Monty Python/Holy Grail	26
Nashville	23
One Flew Over Cuckoo's . . .	27
Story of Adele H.	24
Swept Away	24
Three Days of the Condor	24
Wind and the Lion	24

1976

All the President's Men	25
Front, The	23
Marathon Man	24
Network	24
Outlaw Josey Wales	25
Rocky	25
Seven Beauties	26
Taxi Driver	27

1977

Aguirre: The Wrath of God	25
Annie Hall	27
Close Encounters	24
Julia	25
Rescuers, The	23
Star Wars	28
3 Women	25
Turning Point	23

1978

Animal House	24
Boys from Brazil	24
Coming Home	23
Days of Heaven	23
Deer Hunter	26
Dona Flor/Her Two Husbands	24
Grease	23
Halloween	22
Interiors	23
Midnight Express	24

YEARS

1979

Alien	25
All That Jazz	24
And Justice for All	23
Apocalypse Now	27
Being There	26
Black Stallion	24
Breaking Away	24
Escape from Alcatraz	23
In-Laws, The	24
Kramer vs. Kramer	23
La Cage aux Folles	24
Life of Brian	23
Manhattan	26
Marriage of Maria Braun	25
Muppet Movie	24
Norma Rae	24
Onion Field	24
Picnic at Hanging Rock	24
Time After Time	23
Warriors, The	23

1980

Airplane!	24
Atlantic City	24
Breaker Morant	27
Caddyshack	24
Coal Miner's Daughter	24
Elephant Man	24
My Brilliant Career	25
Ordinary People	25
Raging Bull	26
Shining, The	25
Star Wars V/Empire Strikes	26
Tin Drum	23

1981

Body Heat	24
Chariots of Fire	26
Eye of the Needle	23
Eyewitness	23
Gallipoli	25
Last Metro	24
On Golden Pond	24
Raiders of the Lost Ark	28

1982

Blade Runner	26
Dark Crystal	24
Das Boot	28
Diner	25
Diva	24
E.T.	26
Fitzcarraldo	27
Frances	23
Gandhi	27
Missing	24
My Favorite Year	22
Pink Floyd The Wall	23
Poltergeist	22
Road Warrior	22
Secret of NIMH	24
Sophie's Choice	26
Star Trek II	23
Thing, The (1982)	23
Tootsie	25
Verdict, The	23
Victor/Victoria	23

1983

Big Chill	23
Christmas Story	26
Fanny and Alexander	26
King of Comedy	23
Local Hero	26
Meaning of Life	24
Right Stuff	26
Silkwood	22
Star Wars VI/Return of Jedi	24
Tender Mercies	24
Terms of Endearment	25
Trading Places	23
Year of Living Dangerously	24

1984

Amadeus	26
Birdy	23
Brother from Another Planet	23
Killing Fields	26
Natural, The	23
Neverending Story	23
Once Upon a Time/America	24
Paris, Texas	22
Passage to India	25
Soldier's Story	26
Terminator, The	24
This Is Spinal Tap	26

1985

Back to the Future	23
Blood Simple	24
Brazil	24
Color Purple	26
Goonies, The	23
Out of Africa	25
Ran	27
Silverado	24
Trip to Bountiful	24
Witness	23

1986

Aliens	23
Children of a Lesser God	23
Down by Law	24
Ferris Bueller's Day Off	23
Hannah and Her Sisters	24
Hoosiers	23
Mission, The	24
My Beautiful Laundrette	23
Platoon	25
Room with a View	26
Stand by Me	24

1987

Au Revoir Les Enfants	27
Broadcast News	23
Dead, The	24
Empire of the Sun	25
Full Metal Jacket	24
Hope and Glory	26
House of Games	24
Jean de Florette	27
Last Emperor	26
Moonstruck	24
My Life As a Dog	25
Princess Bride	27
Radio Days	23
Raising Arizona	23

1988

Accused, The	23
Babette's Feast	26
Beaches	22
Big	23
Crossing Delancey	23
Dangerous Liaisons	24
Die Hard	23
Eight Men Out	24
Fish Called Wanda	23
Midnight Run	23
Mississippi Burning	23
Rain Man	25
Torch Song Trilogy	23
Who Framed Roger Rabbit	24
Wings of Desire	24
Women on the Verge	24

1989

Crimes and Misdemeanors	26
Dead Poets Society	24
Do the Right Thing	23
Driving Miss Daisy	24
Glory	25
Henry V	26
Indiana Jones/Last Crusade	24
Little Mermaid	24
My Left Foot	25
Say Anything	23
Shirley Valentine	24
Steel Magnolias	24
When Harry Met Sally . . .	26

1990

Akira	23
Avalon	24
Cinema Paradiso	26
Dances with Wolves	23
Goodfellas	27
Hunt for Red October	24
Longtime Companion	23
Pretty Woman	23
Reversal of Fortune	23

1991

Beauty/Beast (1991)	26
Boyz N the Hood	23
Commitments, The	24
Dead Again	22
Fried Green Tomatoes	23
La Femme Nikita	23
Silence of the Lambs	27
Terminator 2: Judgment Day	23
Thelma & Louise	23
Truly Madly Deeply	23

1992

Aladdin	24
Delicatessen	26
Enchanted April	24
Few Good Men	23
Glengarry Glen Ross	23
Indochine	23
Last of the Mohicans	22
Malcolm X	23
Player, The	23
Reservoir Dogs	24
River Runs Through It	22
Unforgiven	26

1993

Army of Darkness	23
Carlito's Way	22
Farewell My Concubine	25
Fugitive, The	23
Gettysburg	25
In the Name of the Father	23
Joy Luck Club	25
Like Water for Chocolate	25
Nightmare Before Christmas	24
Philadelphia	24

Remains of the Day	24
Rudy	23
Schindler's List	29
Searching for Bobby Fischer	24
Strictly Ballroom	23
True Romance	24
Wedding Banquet	22

1994

Adventures of Priscilla	23
Clerks	23
Eat Drink Man Woman	25
Forrest Gump	24
Heavenly Creatures	24
Last Seduction	22
Lion King	25
Professional, The	25
Pulp Fiction	26
Shawshank Redemption	28

1995

Apollo 13	24
Babe	25
Before Sunrise	23
Braveheart	26
Dead Man Walking	23
Il Postino	24
Little Princess	24
Muriel's Wedding	22
Sense and Sensibility	26
Seven	23
Toy Story	27
Twelve Monkeys	22
Usual Suspects	27

1996

Antonia's Line	25
Big Night	24
Breaking the Waves	23
Fargo	25
Hamlet (1996)	24
Lone Star	25
Secrets & Lies	24
Sling Blade	25
Swingers	23
Waiting for Guffman	25

1997

Good Will Hunting	24
L.A. Confidential	26
Sweet Hereafter	24

1998

American History X	25
Bug's Life	24
Central Station	26
Elizabeth	24
Gods and Monsters	23
Happiness	23
Life Is Beautiful	27
Mulan	23
Rushmore	23
Saving Private Ryan	26
Shakespeare in Love	24

1999

All About My Mother	25
American Beauty	24
Being John Malkovich	22
Boys Don't Cry	23
Fantasia 2000	24
Fight Club	23
Green Mile	23
Insider, The	25
Iron Giant	24
Lock, Stock and Two . . .	23
Matrix, The	25
Office Space	25
Red Violin	24
Run Lola Run	23
Sixth Sense	26
Straight Story	24
Tarzan	22
Topsy-Turvy	23
Toy Story 2	26

2000

Almost Famous	23
Best in Show	24
Billy Elliot	25
Chicken Run	23
Chocolat	22
Crouching Tiger	24
Gladiator	23
Memento	26
Traffic	23

2001

Amélie	26
Beautiful Mind	26
Black Hawk Down	23
Donnie Darko	22
Gosford Park	23
Harry Potter/Sorcerer's	24
Lord of Rings/Fellowship	27
Monsters, Inc.	26
Moulin Rouge!	23
Shrek	26

2002

Antwone Fisher	23
Catch Me If You Can	23

Chicago	27
Far From Heaven	24
Frida	25
Harry Potter/Chamber	24
Hours, The	25
Ice Age	23
Lilo & Stitch	23
Lord of Rings/Two Towers	27
Monsoon Wedding	24
My Big Fat Greek Wedding	23
Pianist, The	28
Quiet American	24
Rabbit-Proof Fence	26
Road to Perdition	23
Spirited Away	27
Talk to Her	26
Y Tu Mamá También	24

2003

American Splendor	23
Bend It Like Beckham	26
Calendar Girls	23
Cold Mountain	22
Dirty Pretty Things	23
Finding Nemo	28
House of Sand and Fog	23
In America	26
Kill Bill Vol. 1	23
Last Samurai	23
Lord of Rings/Return	28
Master and Commander	23
Mighty Wind	23
Monster	24
Mystic River	26
Pirates Caribbean/The Curse	24
Seabiscuit	25
Something's Gotta Give	23
Triplets of Belleville	24
21 Grams	22
Whale Rider	25
X2: X-Men United	24

2004

Aviator, The	23
Bad Education	23
Being Julia	23
Eternal Sunshine	23
Finding Neverland	25
Harry Potter/Prisoner	24
Hero	25
Hotel Rwanda	28
House of Flying Daggers	24
Incredibles, The	26
Kill Bill Vol. 2	25
Maria Full of Grace	25
Million Dollar Baby	27
Miracle	24
Motorcycle Diaries	23
Notebook, The	23
Ray	26
Shrek 2	26
Sideways	23
Spider-Man 2	22
Vera Drake	24

2005

Batman Begins	23
Brokeback Mountain	24
Capote	26
Chronicles of Narnia/Lion	23
Cinderella Man	25
Constant Gardener	23
Crash	26
Good Night, and Good Luck	25
Harry Potter/Goblet of Fire	24
Hustle & Flow	23
Kung Fu Hustle	23
Mrs. Henderson Presents	23
Munich	23
Pride & Prejudice (2005)	23
Star Wars III/Revenge of Sith	23
TransAmerica	24
Walk the Line	25
Wallace & Gromit	24

2006

Blood Diamond	25
Cars	24
Casino Royale	23
Charlotte's Web	23
Departed, The	26
Dreamgirls	23
Flags of Our Fathers	23
Illusionist, The	23
Inside Man	23
Last King of Scotland	25
Letters from Iwo Jima	27
Little Children	24
Little Miss Sunshine	24
Notes on a Scandal	24
Over the Hedge	23
Painted Veil	23
Pan's Labyrinth	27
Pursuit of Happyness	23
Queen, The	26
Thank You for Smoking	23
Volver	24

2007

American Gangster	23
Before the Devil Knows . . .	23
Bourne Ultimatum	25
Breach	23
Diving Bell & the Butterfly	26
Eastern Promises	24
Enchanted	23
Gone Baby Gone	24
Great Debaters	25
Harry Potter/Order of Phoenix	24
In the Valley of Elah	22
Into the Wild	23
Juno	25
Kite Runner	24
La Vie en Rose	25
Lives of Others	28
Michael Clayton	24
No Country for Old Men	24
Once	25
Ratatouille	26
Savages, The	23
Sweeney Todd	23
There Will Be Blood	23
300	22
3:10 to Yuma	23
Waitress	24

2008

Boy in the Striped Pajamas	26
Changeling	23
Chronicles of Narnia/Prince	23
Curious Case of Benjamin Button	23
Dark Knight	26
Doubt	25
Frost/Nixon	25
Gran Torino	26
Iron Man	26
Milk	25
Reader, The	25
Slumdog Millionaire	26
WALL-E	26

2009

Avatar	26
Blind Side	26
Coraline	23
Crazy Heart	25
District 9	22
Education, An	25
(500) Days of Summer	22
Hangover, The	22
Harry Potter/Half-Blood Prince	25
Hurt Locker	26
Inglourious Basterds	25
Invictus	24
It's Complicated	22
Julie & Julia	24
Precious	24
Star Trek	26
Up	27
Up in the Air	23

Genres/Special Features

Listings include Overall ratings.

ACTION/ADVENTURE

Adventures of Robin Hood	25
Aguirre: The Wrath of God	25
Batman Begins	23
Black Stallion	24
Blood Diamond	25
Bourne Ultimatum	25
Captain Blood	23
Captains Courageous	25
Catch Me If You Can	23
Chronicles of Narnia/Prince	23
Chronicles of Narnia/Lion	23
Crouching Tiger	24
Dark Knight	26
Deliverance	25
Die Hard	23
Easy Rider	23
Enter the Dragon	23
Fitzcarraldo	27
Flight of the Phoenix	25
Getaway, The	22
Gladiator	23
Goonies, The	23
Great Escape	27
Hero	25
House of Flying Daggers	24
Indiana Jones/Last Crusade	24
Inglourious Basterds	25
Iron Man	26
Kill Bill Vol. 1	23
Kill Bill Vol. 2	25
King Kong	25
Kung Fu Hustle	23
Last Samurai	23
Lawrence of Arabia	29
Lord of Rings/Fellowship	27
Lord of Rings/Return	28
Lord of Rings/Two Towers	27
Magnificent Seven	26
Man Who Would Be King	25
Mark of Zorro	22
Master and Commander	23
Matrix, The	25
Midnight Run	23
Mission, The	24
Mutiny on the Bounty (1935)	25
Mutiny on the Bounty (1962)	22
Papillon	26
Pirates Caribbean/The Curse	24
Planet of the Apes	23
Professional, The	25
Raiders of the Lost Ark	28
Rio Bravo	24
Road Warrior	22
Rocky	25
Seven Samurai	29
Spartacus	26
Spider-Man 2	22
Star Trek	26
Star Trek II	23
Star Wars	28
Star Wars III/Revenge of Sith	23
Star Wars V/Empire Strikes	26
Star Wars VI/Return of Jedi	24
Swiss Family Robinson	23
Terminator, The	24
Terminator 2: Judgment Day	23
Thief of Bagdad	24
Three Musketeers	22
Topkapi	24
Treasure of the Sierra Madre	27
Wages of Fear	27
War of the Worlds	23
Warriors, The	23
Wind and the Lion	24
X2: X-Men United	24
Yojimbo	28
Zulu	24

AMERICANA

All the King's Men	25
American Graffiti	24
Badlands	25
Best Years of Our Lives	28
Christmas Story	26
Dances with Wolves	23
Days of Heaven	23
East of Eden	24
Far From Heaven	24
Forrest Gump	24
Friendly Persuasion	24
Giant	24
Grapes of Wrath	28
It's a Wonderful Life	27
Last Picture Show	23
Meet Me in St. Louis	26
Member of the Wedding	25
Miracle of Morgan's Creek	23
Mr. Deeds Goes to Town	25
Mr. Smith Goes to Washington	26

Music Man	25
Nashville	23
Natural, The	23
Oklahoma!	24
Old Yeller	24
Picnic	24
Radio Days	23
Seabiscuit	25
Shadow of a Doubt	26
Stand by Me	24
Straight Story	24
To Kill a Mockingbird	29
Trip to Bountiful	24
Yankee Doodle Dandy	25

ANIMATED

(* Not for children)

Akira*	23
Aladdin	24
Alice in Wonderland	24
Bambi	26
Beauty/Beast (1991)	26
Bug's Life	24
Cars	24
Chicken Run	23
Cinderella	26
Coraline	23
Dumbo	24
Fantasia	28
Fantasia 2000	24
Finding Nemo	28
Ice Age	23
Incredibles, The	26
Iron Giant	24
Jungle Book (1967)	23
Lady and the Tramp	26
Lilo & Stitch	23
Lion King	25
Little Mermaid	24
Monsters, Inc.	26
Mulan	23
Nightmare Before Christmas	24
101 Dalmatians	24
Over the Hedge	23
Peter Pan	25
Pinocchio	26
Ratatouille	26
Rescuers, The	23
Secret of NIMH	24
Shrek	26
Shrek 2	26
Sleeping Beauty	25
Snow White	27
Song of the South	23
Spirited Away	27
Tarzan	22
Toy Story	27
Toy Story 2	26
Triplets of Belleville*	24
Up	27
Wallace & Gromit	24
WALL-E	26
Who Framed Roger Rabbit	24

BIOGRAPHIES

Agony and the Ecstasy	23
Alexander Nevsky	26
Amadeus	26
American Splendor	23
Anastasia	23
Anne of the Thousand Days	26
Antwone Fisher	23
Aviator, The	23
Becket	26
Bonnie and Clyde	25
Born Free	24
Capote	26
Cinderella Man	25
Coal Miner's Daughter	24
Diary of Anne Frank	23
Elephant Man	24
Elizabeth	24
Finding Neverland	25
Frances	23
Frida	25
Frost/Nixon	25
Funny Girl	26
Gandhi	27
Gods and Monsters	23
Great White Hope	25
Invictus	24
Julia	25
Julie & Julia	24
Last Emperor	26
Last King of Scotland	25
La Vie en Rose	25
Lawrence of Arabia	29
Lenny	24
Lust for Life	23
Malcolm X	23
Man for All Seasons	28
Milk	25
Miracle Worker	25
Napoléon	28
Patton	27
Queen, The	26
Raging Bull	26
Ray	26

Sergeant York	25
Song of Bernadette	22
Viva Zapata!	23
Walk the Line	25
Yankee Doodle Dandy	25

BLACK COMEDIES

Arsenic and Old Lace	26
Being John Malkovich	22
Being There	26
Brazil	24
Catch-22	25
Clerks	23
Delicatessen	26
Discreet Charm	24
Divorce Italian Style	24
Dr. Strangelove	28
Fortune Cookie	23
Front, The	23
Happiness	23
Harold and Maude	25
Kind Hearts and Coronets	26
King of Comedy	23
Life of Brian	23
Lolita	24
MASH	26
Meaning of Life	24
Monty Python/Holy Grail	26
Producers, The	26
Ruling Class	23
Where's Poppa?	23

BLOCKBUSTERS

(Annual highest grossing movies with year of release)

Aladdin | 1992	24
Avatar | 2009	26
Back to the Future | 1985	23
Bambi | 1942	26
Bells of St. Mary's | 1945	24
Ben-Hur | 1959	26
Best Years of Our Lives | 1946	28
Birth of a Nation | 1915	25
Blazing Saddles | 1974	25
Bridge on the River Kwai | 1957	28
Butch Cassidy | 1969	26
Dark Knight | 2008	26
E.T. | 1982	26
Exorcist, The | 1973	25
Forrest Gump | 1994	24
French Connection | 1971	25
Funny Girl | 1968	26
Godfather, The | 1972	29
Going My Way | 1944	24
Gone with the Wind | 1939	28
Graduate, The | 1967	27
Grease | 1978	23
Harry Potter/Sorcerer's | 2001	24
Jaws | 1975	26
King Kong | 1933	25
Kramer vs. Kramer | 1979	23
Lawrence of Arabia | 1962	29
Lord of Rings/Return | 2003	28
Mary Poppins | 1964	27
Mister Roberts | 1955	27
Mrs. Miniver | 1942	25
Night at the Opera | 1935	26
Raiders of the Lost Ark | 1981	28
Rain Man | 1988	25
Red River | 1948	26
Rocky | 1976	25
Saving Private Ryan | 1998	26
Sergeant York | 1941	25
Shrek 2 | 2004	26
Snow White | 1937	27
Sound of Music | 1965	28
South Pacific | 1958	24
Spartacus | 1960	26
Star Wars | 1977	28
Star Wars III/Revenge of Sith | 2005	23
Star Wars V/Empire Strikes | 1980	26
Star Wars VI/Return of Jedi | 1983	24
Ten Commandments | 1956	24
Terminator 2: Judgment Day | 1991	23
Thin Man | 1934	26
Toy Story | 1995	27
West Side Story | 1961	27
White Christmas | 1954	25

BUDDY FILMS

Breaking Away	24
Brokeback Mountain	24
Butch Cassidy	26
Down by Law	24
Easy Rider	23
Gunga Din	25
Hangover, The	22
Man Who Would Be King	25
Mean Streets	24
Midnight Cowboy	26
Midnight Run	23
Motorcycle Diaries	23
Odd Couple	25
Swingers	23
Thelma & Louise	23

CAMP CLASSICS

Adventures of Priscilla 23
Auntie Mame 25
Bride of Frankenstein 25
Duel in the Sun 23
Gentlemen Prefer Blondes 23
Hush . . . Hush, Sweet Charlotte 24
I'm No Angel 23
I Want to Live! 24
La Cage aux Folles 24
Mildred Pierce 26
Women, The 26
Women on the Verge 24

CAPERS

Asphalt Jungle 24
Catch Me If You Can 23
Fish Called Wanda 23
Getaway, The 22
Inside Man 23
Killing, The 25
Lavender Hill Mob 25
Lock, Stock and Two . . . 23
Pink Panther 24
Reservoir Dogs 24
Rififi 26
Sting, The 27
Thomas Crown Affair 23
Topkapi 24

CHICK FLICKS

(See also Romance)

Affair to Remember 26
Amélie 26
Beaches 22
Breakfast at Tiffany's 26
Calendar Girls 23
Enchanted April 24
Fried Green Tomatoes 23
Funny Face 24
Joy Luck Club 25
Julie & Julia 24
Letter to Three Wives 24
Love Is Many-Splendored . . . 22
Muriel's Wedding 22
Notebook, The 23
Now, Voyager 27
Out of Africa 25
Pretty Woman 23
Pride and Prejudice (1940) 25
Roman Holiday 27
Sense and Sensibility 26
Shakespeare in Love 24
Something's Gotta Give 23
Splendor in the Grass 25
Stage Door 25
Steel Magnolias 24
Terms of Endearment 25
Thelma & Louise 23
Turning Point 23
Way We Were 24
When Harry Met Sally . . . 26
Women, The 26

CHILDREN/FAMILY

(See also Animated)

Babe 25
Bells of St. Mary's 24
Big 23
Black Stallion 24
Born Free 24
Charlotte's Web 23
Christmas Carol 27
Christmas Story 26
Dark Crystal 24
Enchanted 23
E.T. 26
Father of the Bride 23
Goonies, The 23
Harry Potter/Chamber 24
Harry Potter/Goblet of Fire 24
Harry Potter/Half-Blood Prince 25
Harry Potter/Order of Phoenix 24
Harry Potter/Prisoner 24
Harry Potter/Sorcerer's 24
It's a Wonderful Life 27
Jungle Book (1942) 24
Lili 24
Little Princess 24
Mary Poppins 27
National Velvet 24
Neverending Story 23
Old Yeller 24
Oliver! 24
Parent Trap 23
Princess Bride 27
Sounder 26
Sound of Music 28
Swiss Family Robinson 23
Whale Rider 25
Willy Wonka 26
Wizard of Oz 28

CITY SETTINGS

LA

Bad and the Beautiful 24
Big Sleep 27
Blade Runner 26

Boyz N the Hood	23
Chinatown	27
Crash	26
Gods and Monsters	23
L.A. Confidential	26
Player, The	23
Pretty Woman	23
Reservoir Dogs	24
Singin' in the Rain	28
Sunset Boulevard	28
Swingers	23

LONDON

Blowup	26
Education, An	25
Elephant Man	24
Fish Called Wanda	23
Gaslight	26
Georgy Girl	23
Ipcress File	24
Lock, Stock and Two . . .	23
Man Who Knew Too Much	24
Mary Poppins	27
My Fair Lady	27
Oliver!	24
Secrets & Lies	24

NEW YORK

Affair to Remember	26
All About Eve	28
All That Jazz	24
Angels with Dirty Faces	24
Annie Hall	27
Apartment, The	25
Barefoot in the Park	23
Bells Are Ringing	24
Big	23
Breakfast at Tiffany's	26
Carlito's Way	22
Crimes and Misdemeanors	26
Dog Day Afternoon	24
Do the Right Thing	23
Eyewitness	23
42nd Street	24
French Connection	25
Godfather, The	29
Godfather Part II	29
Guys and Dolls	24
Hannah and Her Sisters	24
Hustler, The	25
Inside Man	23
King Kong	25
King of Comedy	23
Manhattan	26
Marathon Man	24
Marty	25
Mean Streets	24
Midnight Cowboy	26
Miracle on 34th Street	25
Moonstruck	24
My Favorite Year	22
Network	24
Odd Couple	25
Once Upon a Time/America	24
On the Town	23
On the Waterfront	28
Pawnbroker, The	26
Precious	24
Radio Days	23
Rear Window	28
Rosemary's Baby	24
Serpico	23
Spider-Man 2	22
Sweet Smell of Success	27
Taxi Driver	27
Tootsie	25
Warriors, The	23
West Side Story	27
When Harry Met Sally . . .	26

PARIS

Amélie	26
American in Paris	26
Belle de Jour	24
Breathless	25
Charade	26
Children of Paradise	28
Diva	24
400 Blows	27
Funny Face	24
Gigi	24
Hunchback/Notre Dame	26
Love in the Afternoon	24
Moulin Rouge!	23
Ratatouille	26
Rififi	26
Shoot the Piano Player	25
Victor/Victoria	23

ROME

Ben-Hur	26
Bicycle Thief	27
Gladiator	23
La Dolce Vita	25
Roman Holiday	27
Spartacus	26

SAN FRANCISCO

Birds, The	24
Conversation, The	25
Dead Man Walking	23

Experiment in Terror	25
Milk	25
Pursuit of Happyness	23
Time After Time	23
Vertigo	27

COMEDIES

(See also Black Comedies, Dramedies, Screwball Comedies)

Adam's Rib	26
Adventures of Priscilla	23
Airplane!	24
Amarcord	26
Animal House	24
Annie Hall	27
Auntie Mame	25
Bananas	23
Barefoot in the Park	23
Best in Show	24
Big	23
Bishop's Wife	24
Blazing Saddles	25
Brother from Another Planet	23
Caddyshack	24
Court Jester, The	24
Crossing Delancey	23
Desk Set	25
Dona Flor/Her Two Husbands	24
Eat Drink Man Woman	25
Father of the Bride	23
Ferris Bueller's Day Off	23
Fish Called Wanda	23
General, The	28
Gold Rush	28
Graduate, The	27
Great Dictator	26
Hangover, The	22
Harvey	26
Heaven Can Wait	24
I'm No Angel	23
In-Laws, The	24
It's a Mad Mad Mad World	24
It's Complicated	22
Jungle Book (1967)	23
Kung Fu Hustle	23
La Cage aux Folles	24
Lavender Hill Mob	25
Little Big Man	24
Local Hero	26
Manhattan	26
Man Who Came to Dinner	26
Midnight Run	23
Mighty Wind	23
Mister Roberts	27
Modern Times	28
Monkey Business	26
Mon Oncle	26
Mouse That Roared	23
Mr. Blandings	23
Mr. Deeds Goes to Town	25
Mr. Hulot's Holiday	25
Muppet Movie	24
Muriel's Wedding	22
My Big Fat Greek Wedding	23
My Favorite Year	22
My Little Chickadee	23
No Time for Sergeants	23
Odd Couple	25
Office Space	25
One, Two, Three	23
Parent Trap	23
Pink Panther	24
Play It Again, Sam	22
Pretty Woman	23
Radio Days	23
Seven Year Itch	23
Shirley Valentine	24
Shot in the Dark	23
Sleeper	23
Smiles of a Summer Night	26
Some Like It Hot	28
Something's Gotta Give	23
Strictly Ballroom	23
Swingers	23
Thank You for Smoking	23
This Is Spinal Tap	26
Thousand Clowns	25
Tom Jones	25
Tootsie	25
Topkapi	24
Trading Places	23
Two for the Road	24
Waiting for Guffman	25
Waitress	24
Wedding Banquet	22
When Harry Met Sally . . .	26
Woman of the Year	27
Young Frankenstein	27
Ziegfeld Follies	24

COMIC BOOK ADAPTATIONS

Akira	23
American Splendor	23
Batman Begins	23
Dark Knight	26
Iron Man	26
Road to Perdition	23

Visit ZAGAT.com

Title	Rating
Spider-Man 2	22
300	22
X2: X-Men United	24

COMING OF AGE

Title	Rating
Almost Famous	23
Bambi	26
Billy Elliot	25
Boy in the Striped Pajamas	26
Breaking Away	24
Coming Home	23
Education, An	25
Empire of the Sun	25
400 Blows	27
Graduate, The	27
Into the Wild	23
Juno	25
Last Picture Show	23
Muriel's Wedding	22
My Brilliant Career	25
My Life As a Dog	25
National Velvet	24
Precious	24
Prime of Miss Jean Brodie	25
Rushmore	23
Stand by Me	24
Y Tu Mamá También	24

CRIME

(See also Film Noir)

Title	Rating
American Gangster	23
Anatomy of a Murder	26
Angels with Dirty Faces	24
Arsenic and Old Lace	26
Badlands	25
Before the Devil Knows . . .	23
Bonnie and Clyde	25
Boyz N the Hood	23
Capote	26
Carlito's Way	22
Chicago	27
Clockwork Orange	25
Departed, The	26
Diabolique	26
Dial M for Murder	25
Dirty Pretty Things	23
Dog Day Afternoon	24
Eastern Promises	24
Experiment in Terror	25
French Connection	25
Getaway, The	22
Godfather, The	29
Godfather Part II	29
Gone Baby Gone	24
Goodfellas	27
Heavenly Creatures	24
Hustle & Flow	23
In Cold Blood	25
Inside Man	23
In the Heat of the Night	24
I Want to Live!	24
Lavender Hill Mob	25
Little Caesar	24
Lock, Stock and Two . . .	23
M	26
Mean Streets	24
Monster	24
Mystic River	26
No Country for Old Men	24
Once Upon a Time/America	24
Onion Field	24
On the Waterfront	28
Public Enemy	25
Pulp Fiction	26
Rear Window	28
Reservoir Dogs	24
Road to Perdition	23
Serpico	23
Shoot the Piano Player	25
Sting, The	27
Sweeney Todd	23
To Catch a Thief	25
Traffic	23
True Romance	24
Usual Suspects	27

CULT FILMS

Title	Rating
Adventures of Priscilla	23
Akira	23
All About Eve	28
American Splendor	23
Army of Darkness	23
Being John Malkovich	22
Blade Runner	26
Brazil	24
Breakfast at Tiffany's	26
Brother from Another Planet	23
Children of Paradise	28
Clerks	23
Clockwork Orange	25
Donnie Darko	22
Down by Law	24
Dr. Strangelove	28
8½	26
Enter the Dragon	23
Eternal Sunshine	23
Fantasia	28
Ferris Bueller's Day Off	23
Fight Club	23

Forbidden Planet	25
Freaks	23
Grease	23
Gun Crazy	27
Harold and Maude	25
It's a Wonderful Life	27
Kill Bill Vol. 1	23
Kill Bill Vol. 2	25
King of Hearts	26
Life of Brian	23
Manchurian Candidate	27
Meaning of Life	24
Monty Python/Holy Grail	26
Office Space	25
Pink Floyd The Wall	23
Princess Bride	27
Raising Arizona	23
Red Shoes	26
Road Warrior	22
Ruling Class	23
Rushmore	23
Shawshank Redemption	28
Sound of Music	28
Star Wars	28
True Romance	24
Waiting for Guffman	25
Warriors, The	23
Where's Poppa?	23
Willy Wonka	26
Wizard of Oz	28

DATE FLICKS

Amélie	26
Annie Hall	27
Barefoot in the Park	23
Before Sunrise	23
Big Chill	23
Casablanca	29
Chocolat	22
Education, An	25
Eternal Sunshine	23
(500) Days of Summer	22
Georgy Girl	23
It's Complicated	22
Man and a Woman	24
Moonstruck	24
My Big Fat Greek Wedding	23
Once	25
Pretty Woman	23
Roman Holiday	27
Romeo and Juliet	26
Say Anything	23
Shakespeare in Love	24
Sideways	23
Something's Gotta Give	23
Strictly Ballroom	23
Truly Madly Deeply	23
Up in the Air	23
Way We Were	24
When Harry Met Sally . . .	26

DRAMAS

(Best of many; see also Crime, Dramedies, Film Noir)

Advise & Consent	27
All This, and Heaven Too	26
Anna Karenina	26
Au Revoir Les Enfants	27
Babette's Feast	26
Beautiful Mind	26
Best Years of Our Lives	28
Bicycle Thief	27
Black Orpheus	26
Blind Side	26
Blowup	26
Boy in the Striped Pajamas	26
Breaker Morant	27
Caine Mutiny	27
Central Station	26
Chariots of Fire	26
Cinema Paradiso	26
Citizen Kane	28
Color Purple	26
Conformist, The	26
Crash	26
Cries and Whispers	26
Day for Night	27
Days of Wine and Roses	27
Deer Hunter	26
Diving Bell & the Butterfly	26
8½	26
Face in the Crowd	26
Fanny and Alexander	26
400 Blows	27
From Here to Eternity	26
Gentleman's Agreement	26
Grand Illusion	28
Gran Torino	26
Grapes of Wrath	28
Great Expectations	27
Hamlet (1948)	27
Heiress, The	27
Henry V	26
High Noon	28
Hotel Rwanda	28
How Green Was My Valley	27
Hunchback/Notre Dame	26
Hurt Locker	26

In America 26
I Never Sang for My Father 27
Inherit the Wind 26
Jean de Florette 27
Judgment at Nuremberg 26
La Strada 27
Lion in Winter 28
Little Foxes 26
Lives of Others 28
Midnight Cowboy 26
Million Dollar Baby 27
Nights of Cabiria 27
Now, Voyager 27
Of Mice and Men 26
Ox-Bow Incident 27
Paths of Glory 28
Pawnbroker, The 26
Persona 27
Pianist, The 28
Place in the Sun 27
Quiet Man 27
Rabbit-Proof Fence 26
Raisin in the Sun 26
Rashomon 29
Ray 26
Red Shoes 26
Requiem for a Heavyweight 26
Right Stuff 26
Romeo and Juliet 26
Room with a View 26
Schindler's List 29
Seven Days in May 26
Seventh Seal 27
Shawshank Redemption 28
Shop on Main Street 27
Slumdog Millionaire 26
Soldier's Story 26
Sophie's Choice 26
Streetcar Named Desire 27
Talk to Her 26
Taxi Driver 27
To Have and Have Not 26
To Kill a Mockingbird 29
12 Angry Men 28
Wild Strawberries 26
Witness for the Prosecution 27
Wuthering Heights 27
Yojimbo 28

DRAMEDIES

(Part comedy, part drama)

African Queen 28
All About Eve 28
All About My Mother 25
Almost Famous 23
American Beauty 24
American Graffiti 24
Americanization of Emily 24
American Splendor 23
Apartment, The 25
Beaches 22
Being Julia 23
Bend It Like Beckham 26
Big Chill 23
Big Night 24
Breakfast at Tiffany's 26
Broadcast News 23
Calendar Girls 23
Charade 26
City Lights 28
Cool Hand Luke 26
Crimes and Misdemeanors 26
Diner 25
Dinner at Eight 27
Do the Right Thing 23
Down by Law 24
Fargo 25
Fight Club 23
Five Easy Pieces 24
(500) Days of Summer 22
Forrest Gump 24
Fried Green Tomatoes 23
Front Page 24
Georgy Girl 23
Going My Way 24
Good Will Hunting 24
Gosford Park 23
Guess Who's Coming . . . 25
Hannah and Her Sisters 24
It's a Wonderful Life 27
Julie & Julia 24
Juliet of the Spirits 25
Juno 25
King of Comedy 23
King of Hearts 26
Lady Vanishes 25
Letter to Three Wives 24
Life Is Beautiful 27
Limelight 24
Little Miss Sunshine 24
Love in the Afternoon 24
Meet John Doe 24
Monsoon Wedding 24
Moonstruck 24
Mrs. Henderson Presents 23
Mr. Smith Goes to Washington 26
Nashville 23
Network 24

Ninotchka 25
One Flew Over Cuckoo's . . . 27
Paper Chase 23
Player, The 23
Pride and Prejudice (1940) 25
Rushmore 23
Sabrina 25
Savages, The 23
Sense and Sensibility 26
Seven Beauties 26
Shakespeare in Love 24
Sideways 23
Stage Door 25
Stalag 17 27
Steel Magnolias 24
Sting, The 27
Sullivan's Travels 27
Swept Away 24
Terms of Endearment 25
Three Musketeers 22
To Be or Not to Be 24
Torch Song Trilogy 23
TransAmerica 24
Triplets of Belleville 24
Volver 24
Women, The 26
Y Tu Mamá También 24

DVD NOT AVAILABLE

I Never Sang for My Father 27
Lili 24
Magnificent Ambersons 25
Napoléon 28
Song of the South 23
Thousand Clowns 25

END OF THE WORLD

Dr. Strangelove 28
Matrix, The 25
On the Beach 26
Planet of the Apes 23
Road Warrior 22
Terminator, The 24
Terminator 2: Judgment Day 23
War of the Worlds 23

EPICS

Alexander Nevsky 26
Ben-Hur 26
Birth of a Nation 25
Braveheart 26
Bridge on the River Kwai 28
Dances with Wolves 23
Doctor Zhivago 27
Duel in the Sun 23
Empire of the Sun 25
Exodus 23
Gandhi 27
Giant 24
Gladiator 23
Gone with the Wind 28
Gunga Din 25
Hamlet (1996) 24
How the West Was Won 23
It's a Mad Mad Mad World 24
Last Emperor 26
Last Samurai 23
Lawrence of Arabia 29
Leopard, The 25
Longest Day 24
Master and Commander 23
Mutiny on the Bounty (1935) 25
Mutiny on the Bounty (1962) 22
Napoléon 28
Once Upon a Time/America 24
Once Upon a Time/West 25
Passage to India 25
Ran 27
Sand Pebbles 24
Seven Samurai 29
Spartacus 26
Ten Commandments 24
There Will Be Blood 23
300 22
Tora! Tora! Tora! 23
2001: A Space Odyssey 26
Zulu 24

FANTASY

Alice in Wonderland 24
Alice in Wonderland 23
Back to the Future 23
Beauty/Beast (1947) 28
Being John Malkovich 22
Brazil 24
Brigadoon 24
Charlotte's Web 23
Christmas Carol 27
Chronicles of Narnia/Prince 23
Chronicles of Narnia/Lion 23
Crouching Tiger 24
Curious Case of Benjamin Button 23
Dark Crystal 24
Dona Flor/Her Two Husbands 24
Donnie Darko 22
Enchanted 23
Eternal Sunshine 23
Ghost and Mrs. Muir 24

Harry Potter/Chamber 24
Harry Potter/Goblet of Fire 24
Harry Potter/Half-Blood Prince 25
Harry Potter/Order of Phoenix 24
Harry Potter/Prisoner 24
Harry Potter/Sorcerer's 24
Harvey 26
Juliet of the Spirits 25
King Kong 25
Little Princess 24
Lord of Rings/Fellowship 27
Lord of Rings/Return 28
Lord of Rings/Two Towers 27
Lost Horizon 25
Mary Poppins 27
Miracle on 34th Street 25
Neverending Story 23
Pan's Labyrinth 27
Princess Bride 27
Raiders of the Lost Ark 28
Truly Madly Deeply 23
Willy Wonka 26
Wings of Desire 24
Wizard of Oz 28

FILM NOIR

Ace in the Hole 26
Asphalt Jungle 24
Big Clock 25
Big Heat 25
Big Sleep 27
Blade Runner 26
Blood Simple 24
Body and Soul 25
Body Heat 24
Call Northside 777 25
Cape Fear 25
Chinatown 27
Dead Again 22
Double Indemnity 28
Fargo 25
Gilda 24
Gun Crazy 27
High Sierra 25
Key Largo 26
Killers, The 25
Killing, The 25
Kiss Me Deadly 24
Kiss of Death 23
L.A. Confidential 26
Lady from Shanghai 25
Last Seduction 22
Laura 27
Maltese Falcon 28
Memento 26
Mildred Pierce 26
Murder, My Sweet 24
Night of the Hunter 27
Out of the Past 26
Pickup on South Street 23
Postman Always Rings . . . 25
Rififi 26
Seven 23
Sorry, Wrong Number 25
Strangers on a Train 26
Sunset Boulevard 28
Sweet Smell of Success 27
Third Man 28
Touch of Evil 26
White Heat 25
Who Framed Roger Rabbit 24

FOOD-THEMED

Babette's Feast 26
Big Night 24
Chocolat 22
Delicatessen 26
Diner 25
Dinner at Eight 27
Discreet Charm 24
Eat Drink Man Woman 25
Fried Green Tomatoes 23
Julie & Julia 24
Like Water for Chocolate 25
My Big Fat Greek Wedding 23
Ratatouille 26
Sweeney Todd 23
Tom Jones 25
Waitress 24
Wedding Banquet 22

FOREIGN FILMS

AUSTRALIAN

Adventures of Priscilla 23
Babe 25
Breaker Morant 27
Gallipoli 25
Muriel's Wedding 22
My Brilliant Career 25
Picnic at Hanging Rock 24
Rabbit-Proof Fence 26
Road Warrior 22
Strictly Ballroom 23
Year of Living Dangerously 24

BRAZILIAN

Central Station 26
Dona Flor/Her Two Husbands 24
Motorcycle Diaries 23

BRITISH

Anne of the Thousand Days 26
Becket 26
Bend It Like Beckham 26
Billy Elliot 25
Blowup 26
Born Free 24
Boy in the Striped Pajamas 26
Brazil 24
Bridge on the River Kwai 28
Brief Encounter 27
Calendar Girls 23
Chariots of Fire 26
Christmas Carol 27
Clockwork Orange 25
Constant Gardener 23
Darling 22
Day of the Jackal 25
Dirty Pretty Things 23
Don't Look Now 24
Dr. No 23
Education, An 25
Elizabeth 24
Enchanted April 24
Eye of the Needle 23
Far from the Madding Crowd 23
From Russia With Love 23
Gandhi 27
Georgy Girl 23
Goodbye, Mr. Chips 25
Great Expectations 27
Hamlet (1948) 27
Hamlet (1996) 24
Hard Day's Night 24
Henry V 26
Hope and Glory 26
Ipcress File 24
Killing Fields 26
Kind Hearts and Coronets 26
Lady Vanishes 25
Last Emperor 26
Last King of Scotland 25
Lavender Hill Mob 25
Lawrence of Arabia 29
Life of Brian 23
Lion in Winter 28
Local Hero 26
Lock, Stock and Two . . . 23
Lord of the Flies 23
Man for All Seasons 28
Meaning of Life 24
Mission, The 24
Monty Python/Holy Grail 26
Mouse That Roared 23
Mrs. Henderson Presents 23
Murder on the Orient Express 23
My Beautiful Laundrette 23
Notes on a Scandal 24
Oliver! 24
Oliver Twist 25
Passage to India 25
Pink Floyd The Wall 23
Pride & Prejudice (2005) 23
Prime of Miss Jean Brodie 25
Queen, The 26
Red Shoes 26
Remains of the Day 24
Romeo and Juliet 26
Room at the Top 24
Room with a View 26
Ruling Class 23
Secrets & Lies 24
Sense and Sensibility 26
Servant, The 25
Slumdog Millionaire 26
Spy Who Came in from Cold 25
Sunday Bloody Sunday 24
Third Man 28
39 Steps 27
Tom Jones 25
Topsy-Turvy 23
To Sir, With Love 22
Truly Madly Deeply 23
Vera Drake 24
Wallace & Gromit 24
Women in Love 23
Zulu 24

CANADIAN

Red Violin 24
Sweet Hereafter 24

CHINESE

Crouching Tiger 24
Farewell My Concubine 25
Hero 25
House of Flying Daggers 24
Kung Fu Hustle 23

CZECHOSLOVAKIAN

Shop on Main Street 27

DANISH

Babette's Feast 26
Breaking the Waves 23

DUTCH

Antonia's Line 25

FRENCH

Amélie 26
Au Revoir Les Enfants 27

Title	Rating
Beauty/Beast (1947)	28
Belle de Jour	24
Black Orpheus	26
Breathless	25
Children of Paradise	28
Claire's Knee	23
Contempt	25
Day for Night	27
Delicatessen	26
Diabolique	26
Discreet Charm	24
Diva	24
Diving Bell & the Butterfly	26
400 Blows	27
Grand Illusion	28
Hiroshima, Mon Amour	25
Indochine	23
Jean de Florette	27
Jules and Jim	24
King of Hearts	26
La Cage aux Folles	24
La Femme Nikita	23
Last Metro	24
La Vie en Rose	25
Man and a Woman	24
Mon Oncle	26
Mr. Hulot's Holiday	25
Napoléon	28
Paris, Texas	22
Pianist, The	28
Professional, The	25
Rififi	26
Shoot the Piano Player	25
Story of Adele H.	24
Triplets of Belleville	24
Umbrellas of Cherbourg	24
Wages of Fear	27
Z	26

GERMAN

Title	Rating
Aguirre: The Wrath of God	25
Blue Angel	25
Cabinet of Dr. Caligari	26
Das Boot	28
Fitzcarraldo	27
Lives of Others	28
M	26
Marriage of Maria Braun	25
Metropolis	27
Neverending Story	23
Nosferatu	26
Run Lola Run	23
Tin Drum	23
Wings of Desire	24

GREEK

Title	Rating
Never on Sunday	24
Zorba the Greek	25

INDIAN

Title	Rating
Monsoon Wedding	24

IRISH

Title	Rating
Commitments, The	24
In America	26
In the Name of the Father	23
My Left Foot	25
Once	25

ITALIAN

Title	Rating
Amarcord	26
Battle of Algiers	28
Bicycle Thief	27
Cinema Paradiso	26
Conformist, The	26
Damned, The	23
Death in Venice	24
Divorce Italian Style	24
8½	26
For a Few Dollars More	23
Garden of the Finzi-Continis	25
Good, the Bad and the Ugly	24
Il Postino	24
Juliet of the Spirits	25
La Dolce Vita	25
La Strada	27
L'Avventura	24
Leopard, The	25
Life Is Beautiful	27
Nights of Cabiria	27
Once Upon a Time/West	25
Seven Beauties	26
Swept Away	24
Two Women	25

JAPANESE

Title	Rating
Akira	23
Ran	27
Rashomon	29
Seven Samurai	29
Spirited Away	27
Yojimbo	28

MEXICAN

Title	Rating
Like Water for Chocolate	25
Y Tu Mamá También	24

NEW ZEALAND

Title	Rating
District 9	22
Whale Rider	25

RUSSIAN

Title	Rating
Alexander Nevsky	26
Potemkin	27

SPANISH

All About My Mother 25
Bad Education 23
Pan's Labyrinth 27
Talk to Her 26
Volver 24
Women on the Verge 24

SWEDISH

Casablanca 29
Cries and Whispers 26
Fanny and Alexander 26
My Life As a Dog 25
Persona 27
Scenes from a Marriage 25
Seventh Seal 27
Smiles of a Summer Night 26
Wild Strawberries 26

TAIWANESE

Eat Drink Man Woman 25
Wedding Banquet 22

GAY-THEMED

Adventures of Priscilla 23
Brokeback Mountain 24
Children's Hour 24
Gods and Monsters 23
La Cage aux Folles 24
Longtime Companion 23
Milk 25
Notes on a Scandal 24
Philadelphia 24
Sunday Bloody Sunday 24
Torch Song Trilogy 23
Wedding Banquet 22

HIGH SCHOOL

American Graffiti 24
Blackboard Jungle 23
Dead Poets Society 24
Donnie Darko 22
Ferris Bueller's Day Off 23
Grease 23
Rushmore 23
Say Anything 23

HORROR

Army of Darkness 23
Bride of Frankenstein 25
Cabinet of Dr. Caligari 26
Cat People 23
Dracula 24
Exorcist, The 25
Frankenstein 25
Freaks 23
Halloween 22
Hush . . . Hush, Sweet Charlotte 24
Invasion/Body Snatchers 24
Invisible Man 22
Mummy, The 24
Nosferatu 26
Poltergeist 22
Rosemary's Baby 24
Shining, The 25
Thing, The (1951) 23
Thing, The (1982) 23
Young Frankenstein 27

INDIES

American Splendor 23
Before the Devil Knows . . . 23
Being John Malkovich 22
Being Julia 23
Big Night 24
Blood Simple 24
Brokeback Mountain 24
Brother from Another Planet 23
Capote 26
Clerks 23
Crash 26
Donnie Darko 22
Down by Law 24
Eastern Promises 24
Far From Heaven 24
(500) Days of Summer 22
Frida 25
Gods and Monsters 23
Good Night, and Good Luck 25
Happiness 23
Henry V 26
Hurt Locker 26
Hustle & Flow 23
Illusionist, The 23
Juno 25
Little Miss Sunshine 24
Longtime Companion 23
Monster 24
Monty Python/Holy Grail 26
My Beautiful Laundrette 23
My Big Fat Greek Wedding 23
Painted Veil 23
Reservoir Dogs 24
Room with a View 26
Savages, The 23
Sideways 23
Swingers 23
This Is Spinal Tap 26
Torch Song Trilogy 23
TransAmerica 24

Trip to Bountiful 24
21 Grams 22
Waitress 24
Whale Rider 25
Woman Under the Influence 24

JAMES BOND

Casino Royale 23
Dr. No 23
From Russia With Love 23
Goldfinger 26
Thunderball 22

LITERARY ADAPTATIONS

(Best of many)

Adventures of Robin Hood 25
Advise & Consent 27
All Quiet on Western Front 28
All the King's Men 25
All the President's Men 25
Anna Karenina 26
Babette's Feast 26
Beau Geste 25
Beautiful Mind 26
Beauty/Beast (1947) 28
Being There 26
Ben-Hur 26
Big Sleep 27
Blade Runner 26
Blind Side 26
Bourne Ultimatum 25
Breakfast at Tiffany's 26
Bridge on the River Kwai 28
Caine Mutiny 27
Camille 26
Captains Courageous 25
Catch-22 25
Christmas Carol 27
Christmas Story 26
Clockwork Orange 25
Color Purple 26
Day of the Jackal 25
Deliverance 25
Diving Bell & the Butterfly 26
Doctor Zhivago 27
Elmer Gantry 25
Empire of the Sun 25
Exorcist, The 25
Forbidden Planet 25
For Whom the Bell Tolls 25
Frankenstein 25
From Here to Eternity 26
Gentleman's Agreement 26
Godfather, The 29
Goldfinger 26
Gone with the Wind 28
Goodbye, Mr. Chips 25
Graduate, The 27
Grand Hotel 25
Grapes of Wrath 28
Great Expectations 27
Gunga Din 25
Hamlet (1948) 27
Harry Potter/Half-Blood Prince 25
Heart Is a Lonely Hunter 25
Henry V 26
High Sierra 25
Hours, The 25
Hud 26
Hunchback/Notre Dame 26
In Cold Blood 25
Jane Eyre 25
Jaws 26
Jean de Florette 27
Joy Luck Club 25
Julia 25
Killers, The 25
Lady Vanishes 25
Last King of Scotland 25
Laura 27
Like Water for Chocolate 25
Lord of Rings/Fellowship 27
Lord of Rings/Return 28
Lord of Rings/Two Towers 27
Lost Horizon 25
Lost Weekend 25
Maltese Falcon 28
Manchurian Candidate 27
Man Who Would Be King 25
Mary Poppins 27
Mildred Pierce 26
Mutiny on the Bounty (1935) 25
Mystic River 26
Night of the Hunter 27
Nosferatu 26
Of Mice and Men 26
Oliver Twist 25
One Flew Over Cuckoo's . . . 27
Ordinary People 25
Out of Africa 25
Ox-Bow Incident 27
Papillon 26
Passage to India 25
Pianist, The 28
Place in the Sun 27
Postman Always Rings . . . 25
Pride and Prejudice (1940) 25
Prime of Miss Jean Brodie 25

GENRES/FEATURES

Rabbit-Proof Fence 26
Reader, The 25
Rebecca 27
Right Stuff 26
Room with a View 26
Sense and Sensibility 26
Seven Days in May 26
Shawshank Redemption 28
Shining, The 25
Silence of the Lambs 27
Sophie's Choice 26
Sounder 26
Spy Who Came in from Cold 25
Strangers on a Train 26
Terms of Endearment 25
Thin Man 26
To Have and Have Not 26
To Kill a Mockingbird 29
Tom Jones 25
Treasure of the Sierra Madre 27
2001: A Space Odyssey 26
Two Women 25
Whale Rider 25
Willy Wonka 26
Wizard of Oz 28
Wuthering Heights 27

MARTIAL ARTS

Crouching Tiger 24
Enter the Dragon 23
Hero 25
House of Flying Daggers 24
Kill Bill Vol. 1 23
Kill Bill Vol. 2 25
Kung Fu Hustle 23
Last Samurai 23
Magnificent Seven 26
Matrix, The 25
Ran 27
Seven Samurai 29
Yojimbo 28

MOVIES ABOUT MOVIES

Aviator, The 23
Bad and the Beautiful 24
Bad Education 23
Barefoot Contessa 24
Cinema Paradiso 26
Contempt 25
Day for Night 27
8½ 26
Frances 23
Player, The 23
Singin' in the Rain 28
Star Is Born 25
Sullivan's Travels 27
Sunset Boulevard 28

MUSICALS

All That Jazz 24
American in Paris 26
Band Wagon 26
Bells Are Ringing 24
Brigadoon 24
Cabaret 26
Cabin in the Sky 24
Carmen Jones 23
Carousel 24
Chicago 27
Commitments, The 24
Court Jester, The 24
Crazy Heart 25
Damn Yankees 24
Dreamgirls 23
Easter Parade 22
Enchanted 23
Fiddler on the Roof 26
Footlight Parade 23
42nd Street 24
Funny Face 24
Funny Girl 26
Gay Divorcee 25
Gentlemen Prefer Blondes 23
Gigi 24
Gold Diggers of 1933 25
Grease 23
Guys and Dolls 24
Hard Day's Night 24
High Society 23
Holiday Inn 23
King and I 27
Kiss Me Kate 24
Mary Poppins 27
Meet Me in St. Louis 26
Moulin Rouge! 23
Music Man 25
My Fair Lady 27
Oklahoma! 24
Oliver! 24
Once 25
On the Town 23
Pink Floyd The Wall 23
Seven Brides/Seven Brothers 24
Shall We Dance 25
Show Boat 23
Singin' in the Rain 28
Sound of Music 28

South Pacific 24
Sweeney Todd 23
Swing Time 26
Top Hat 27
Umbrellas of Cherbourg 24
Victor/Victoria 23
West Side Story 27
White Christmas 25
Wizard of Oz 28
Yankee Doodle Dandy 25
Ziegfeld Follies 24

OCCUPATIONS

DOCTORS

Dark Victory 25
Elephant Man 24
Last King of Scotland 25
Marathon Man 24
MASH 26
One Flew Over Cuckoo's . . . 27
Spellbound 24
Three Faces of Eve 24

JOURNALISTS

Ace in the Hole 26
All the President's Men 25
Almost Famous 23
Broadcast News 23
Call Northside 777 25
Capote 26
Chicago 27
Citizen Kane 28
Foreign Correspondent 24
Front Page 24
Frost/Nixon 25
Gentleman's Agreement 26
Good Night, and Good Luck 25
His Girl Friday 26
Insider, The 25
It Happened One Night 28
Killing Fields 26
La Dolce Vita 25
Love Is Many-Splendored . . . 22
Nashville 23
Network 24
Parallax View 24
Philadelphia Story 27
Quiet American 24
Roman Holiday 27
Sweet Smell of Success 27
Talk to Her 26
Woman of the Year 27
Year of Living Dangerously 24

LAWYERS

Accused, The 23
Anatomy of a Murder 26
And Justice for All 23
Body Heat 24
Breaker Morant 27
Caine Mutiny 27
Chicago 27
Few Good Men 23
Fortune Cookie 23
Inherit the Wind 26
Judgment at Nuremberg 26
Kramer vs. Kramer 23
Man for All Seasons 28
Michael Clayton 24
Paper Chase 23
Philadelphia 24
Reversal of Fortune 23
To Kill a Mockingbird 29
12 Angry Men 28
Verdict, The 23
Witness for the Prosecution 27

POLITICIANS

Advise & Consent 27
All the King's Men 25
All the President's Men 25
Being There 26
Face in the Crowd 26
Frost/Nixon 25
Gandhi 27
Good Night, and Good Luck 25
Great Dictator 26
Malcolm X 23
Manchurian Candidate 27
Mississippi Burning 23
Mr. Smith Goes to Washington 26
Nashville 23
Parallax View 24
Seven Days in May 26
Taxi Driver 27
Z 26

PROSTITUTES

Belle de Jour 24
Butterfield 8 23
Camille 26
8½ 26
Elmer Gantry 25
Farewell My Concubine 25
McCabe & Mrs. Miller 23
Midnight Cowboy 26
Monster 24
Never on Sunday 24
Nights of Cabiria 27

Pretty Woman 23
Taxi Driver 27
Trading Places 23

SPIES
(See also James Bond)
Bourne Ultimatum 25
Breach 23
Conversation, The 25
Counterfeit Traitor 25
Eye of the Needle 23
Foreign Correspondent 24
General, The 28
Hunt for Red October 24
Ipcress File 24
La Femme Nikita 23
Man Who Knew Too Much 24
Notorious 27
Spy Who Came in from Cold 25
39 Steps 27
Torn Curtain 23

TEACHERS
Au Revoir Les Enfants 27
Ball of Fire 26
Beautiful Mind 26
Billy Elliot 25
Blackboard Jungle 23
Blue Angel 25
Children of a Lesser God 23
Children's Hour 24
Dead Poets Society 24
Diabolique 26
Goodbye, Mr. Chips 25
Great Debaters 25
Harry Potter/Chamber 24
Harry Potter/Goblet of Fire 24
Harry Potter/Half-Blood Prince 25
Harry Potter/Order of Phoenix 24
Harry Potter/Prisoner 24
Harry Potter/Sorcerer's 24
Inherit the Wind 26
King and I 27
Miracle Worker 25
My Fair Lady 27
Notes on a Scandal 24
Oliver! 24
Paper Chase 23
Prime of Miss Jean Brodie 25
Red Shoes 26
Rushmore 23
To Sir, With Love 22

OFFICE POLITICS

Apartment, The 25
Broadcast News 23
Desk Set 25
Front Page 24
Glengarry Glen Ross 23
His Girl Friday 26
Michael Clayton 24
Network 24
Office Space 25

OSCAR WINNERS

BEST PICTURE
All About Eve | 1950 28
All Quiet on Western Front | 1930 28
All the King's Men | 1949 25
Amadeus | 1984 26
American Beauty | 1999 24
American in Paris | 1951 26
Annie Hall | 1977 27
Apartment, The | 1960 25
Beautiful Mind | 2001 26
Ben-Hur | 1959 26
Best Years of Our Lives | 1946 28
Braveheart | 1995 26
Bridge on the River Kwai | 1957 28
Casablanca | 1943 29
Chariots of Fire | 1981 26
Chicago | 2002 27
Crash | 2005 26
Dances with Wolves | 1990 23
Deer Hunter | 1978 26
Departed, The | 2006 26
Driving Miss Daisy | 1989 24
Forrest Gump | 1994 24
French Connection | 1971 25
From Here to Eternity | 1953 26
Gandhi | 1982 27
Gentleman's Agreement | 1947 26
Gigi | 1958 24
Gladiator | 2000 23
Godfather, The | 1972 29
Godfather Part II | 1974 29
Going My Way | 1944 24
Gone with the Wind | 1939 28
Grand Hotel | 1932 25
Hamlet (1948) | 1948 27
How Green Was My Valley | 1941 27
Hurt Locker | 2009 26
In the Heat of the Night | 1967 24
It Happened One Night | 1934 28
Kramer vs. Kramer | 1979 23
Last Emperor | 1987 26
Lawrence of Arabia | 1962 29
Lord of Rings/Return | 2003 28

Lost Weekend | 1945	25
Man for All Seasons | 1966	28
Marty | 1955	25
Midnight Cowboy | 1969	26
Million Dollar Baby | 2004	27
Mrs. Miniver | 1942	25
Mutiny on the Bounty (1935) | 1935	25
My Fair Lady | 1964	27
No Country for Old Men | 2007	24
Oliver! | 1968	24
One Flew Over Cuckoo's . . . | 1975	27
On the Waterfront | 1954	28
Ordinary People | 1980	25
Out of Africa | 1985	25
Patton | 1970	27
Platoon | 1986	25
Rain Man | 1988	25
Rebecca | 1940	27
Rocky | 1976	25
Schindler's List | 1993	29
Shakespeare in Love | 1998	24
Silence of the Lambs | 1991	27
Slumdog Millionaire | 2008	26
Sound of Music | 1965	28
Sting, The | 1973	27
Terms of Endearment | 1983	25
Tom Jones | 1963	25
Unforgiven | 1992	26
West Side Story | 1961	27

BEST ACTOR

F. Murray Abraham	
Amadeus	26
Roberto Benigni	
Life Is Beautiful	27
Humphrey Bogart	
African Queen	28
Ernest Borgnine	
Marty	25
Marlon Brando	
Godfather, The	29
On the Waterfront	28
Adrien Brody	
Pianist, The	28
Yul Brynner	
King and I	27
James Cagney	
Yankee Doodle Dandy	25
Gary Cooper	
High Noon	28
Sergeant York	25
Broderick Crawford	
All the King's Men	25
Bing Crosby	
Going My Way	24
Russell Crowe	
Gladiator	23
Daniel Day-Lewis	
My Left Foot	25
There Will Be Blood	23
Robert De Niro	
Raging Bull	26
Robert Donat	
Goodbye, Mr. Chips	25
Robert Duvall	
Tender Mercies	24
Peter Finch	
Network	24
Henry Fonda	
On Golden Pond	24
Jamie Foxx	
Ray	26
Clark Gable	
It Happened One Night	28
Alec Guinness	
Bridge on the River Kwai	28
Gene Hackman	
French Connection	25
Tom Hanks	
Forrest Gump	24
Philadelphia	24
Rex Harrison	
My Fair Lady	27
Charlton Heston	
Ben-Hur	26
Dustin Hoffman	
Kramer vs. Kramer	23
Rain Man	25
Philip Seymour Hoffman	
Capote	26
William Holden	
Stalag 17	27
Anthony Hopkins	
Silence of the Lambs	27
Jeremy Irons	
Reversal of Fortune	23
Jeff Bridges	
Crazy Heart	25
Ben Kingsley	
Gandhi	27
Burt Lancaster	
Elmer Gantry	25
Fredric March	
Best Years of Our Lives	28
Ray Milland	
Lost Weekend	25

Jack Nicholson
One Flew Over Cuckoo's . . . 27
Laurence Olivier
Hamlet (1948) 27
Gregory Peck
To Kill a Mockingbird 29
Sean Penn
Milk 25
Mystic River 26
Sidney Poitier
Lilies of the Field 25
Paul Scofield
Man for All Seasons 28
George C. Scott
Patton 27
Kevin Spacey
American Beauty 24
Rod Steiger
In the Heat of the Night 24
James Stewart
Philadelphia Story 27
Spencer Tracy
Captains Courageous 25
Jon Voight
Coming Home 23
John Wayne
True Grit 22
Forest Whitaker
Last King of Scotland 25

BEST ACTRESS

Julie Andrews
Mary Poppins 27
Anne Bancroft
Miracle Worker 25
Ingrid Bergman
Anastasia 23
Gaslight 26
Ellen Burstyn
Alice Doesn't Live Here 24
Cher
Moonstruck 24
Julie Christie
Darling 22
Claudette Colbert
It Happened One Night 28
Marion Cotillard
La Vie en Rose 25
Joan Crawford
Mildred Pierce 26
Bette Davis
Jezebel 25
Faye Dunaway
Network 24
Sally Field
Norma Rae 24
Louise Fletcher
One Flew Over Cuckoo's . . . 27
Jane Fonda
Coming Home 23
Joan Fontaine
Suspicion 25
Jodie Foster
Accused, The 23
Silence of the Lambs 27
Greer Garson
Mrs. Miniver 25
Olivia de Havilland
Heiress, The 27
Susan Hayward
I Want to Live! 24
Audrey Hepburn
Roman Holiday 27
Katharine Hepburn
Guess Who's Coming . . . 25
Lion in Winter 28
On Golden Pond 24
Judy Holliday
Born Yesterday 26
Glenda Jackson
Women in Love 23
Jennifer Jones
Song of Bernadette 22
Kate Winslet
Reader, The 25
Diane Keaton
Annie Hall 27
Grace Kelly
Country Girl 24
Nicole Kidman
Hours, The 25
Vivien Leigh
Gone with the Wind 28
Streetcar Named Desire 27
Sophia Loren
Two Women 25
Shirley MacLaine
Terms of Endearment 25
Marlee Matlin
Children of a Lesser God 23
Frances McDormand
Fargo 25
Liza Minnelli
Cabaret 26
Helen Mirren
Queen, The 26

Visit ZAGAT.com

Patricia Neal
- Hud 26

Geraldine Page
- Trip to Bountiful 24

Gwyneth Paltrow
- Shakespeare in Love 24

Sandra Bullock
- Blind Side 26

Susan Sarandon
- Dead Man Walking 23

Simone Signoret
- Room at the Top 24

Maggie Smith
- Prime of Miss Jean Brodie 25

Sissy Spacek
- Coal Miner's Daughter 24

Meryl Streep
- Sophie's Choice 26

Barbra Streisand
- Funny Girl 26

Hilary Swank
- Boys Don't Cry 23
- Million Dollar Baby 27

Jessica Tandy
- Driving Miss Daisy 24

Elizabeth Taylor
- Butterfield 8 23
- Who's Afraid of V. Woolf? 25

Charlize Theron
- Monster 24

Reese Witherspoon
- Walk the Line 25

Joanne Woodward
- Three Faces of Eve 24

BEST DIRECTOR

All About Eve 28
All Quiet on Western Front 28
Amadeus 26
American Beauty 24
Annie Hall 27
Apartment, The 25
Awful Truth 25
Beautiful Mind 26
Ben-Hur 26
Best Years of Our Lives 28
Braveheart 26
Bridge on the River Kwai 28
Brokeback Mountain 24
Cabaret 26
Casablanca 29
Dances with Wolves 23
Deer Hunter 26
Departed, The 26
Forrest Gump 24
French Connection 25
From Here to Eternity 26
Gandhi 27
Gentleman's Agreement 26
Giant 24
Gigi 24
Godfather Part II 29
Going My Way 24
Gone with the Wind 28
Graduate, The 27
Grapes of Wrath 28
How Green Was My Valley 27
Hurt Locker 26
It Happened One Night 28
Kramer vs. Kramer 23
Last Emperor 26
Lawrence of Arabia 29
Letter to Three Wives 24
Lord of Rings/Return 28
Lost Weekend 25
Man for All Seasons 28
Marty 25
Midnight Cowboy 26
Million Dollar Baby 27
Mr. Deeds Goes to Town 25
Mrs. Miniver 25
My Fair Lady 27
No Country for Old Men 24
Oliver! 24
One Flew Over Cuckoo's . . . 27
On the Waterfront 28
Ordinary People 25
Out of Africa 25
Patton 27
Pianist, The 28
Place in the Sun 27
Platoon 25
Quiet Man 27
Rain Man 25
Rocky 25
Saving Private Ryan 26
Schindler's List 29
Silence of the Lambs 27
Slumdog Millionaire 26
Sound of Music 28
Sting, The 27
Terms of Endearment 25
Tom Jones 25
Traffic 23
Treasure of the Sierra Madre 27
Unforgiven 26
West Side Story 27

BEST FOREIGN LANGUAGE FILM

Title	Rating
All About My Mother	25
Amarcord	26
Antonia's Line	25
Babette's Feast	26
Bicycle Thief	27
Black Orpheus	26
Cinema Paradiso	26
Crouching Tiger	24
Day for Night	27
Discreet Charm	24
8½	26
Fanny and Alexander	26
Garden of the Finzi-Continis	25
Indochine	23
La Strada	27
Life Is Beautiful	27
Lives of Others	28
Man and a Woman	24
Mon Oncle	26
Nights of Cabiria	27
Shop on Main Street	27
Tin Drum	23
Z	26

BEST SCREENPLAY

Title	Rating
All About Eve	28
Almost Famous	23
Amadeus	26
American Beauty	24
American in Paris	26
Annie Hall	27
Apartment, The	25
Bad and the Beautiful	24
Beautiful Mind	26
Becket	26
Best Years of Our Lives	28
Breaking Away	24
Bridge on the River Kwai	28
Brokeback Mountain	24
Butch Cassidy	26
Casablanca	29
Chariots of Fire	26
Chinatown	27
Citizen Kane	28
Coming Home	23
Country Girl	24
Crash	26
Dances with Wolves	23
Dangerous Liaisons	24
Darling	22
Dead Poets Society	24
Departed, The	26
Divorce Italian Style	24
Doctor Zhivago	27
Dog Day Afternoon	24
Driving Miss Daisy	24
Elmer Gantry	25
Exorcist, The	25
Fargo	25
Forrest Gump	24
French Connection	25
From Here to Eternity	26
Gandhi	27
Gigi	24
Godfather, The	29
Godfather Part II	29
Gods and Monsters	23
Going My Way	24
Gone with the Wind	28
Good Will Hunting	24
Gosford Park	23
Guess Who's Coming . . .	25
Hannah and Her Sisters	24
How the West Was Won	23
Hurt Locker	26
In the Heat of the Night	24
It Happened One Night	28
Judgment at Nuremberg	26
Julia	25
Juno	25
Kramer vs. Kramer	23
L.A. Confidential	26
Last Emperor	26
Lavender Hill Mob	25
Letter to Three Wives	24
Lion in Winter	28
Little Miss Sunshine	24
Lord of Rings/Return	28
Lost Weekend	25
Man and a Woman	24
Man for All Seasons	28
Marty	25
MASH	26
Midnight Cowboy	26
Midnight Express	24
Milk	25
Miracle on 34th Street	25
Missing	24
Moonstruck	24
Mrs. Miniver	25
Network	24
No Country for Old Men	24
One Flew Over Cuckoo's . . .	27
On Golden Pond	24
On the Waterfront	28
Ordinary People	25
Out of Africa	25
Patton	27

Philadelphia Story 27
Place in the Sun 27
Precious 24
Producers, The 26
Pulp Fiction 26
Rain Man 25
Roman Holiday 27
Room at the Top 24
Room with a View 26
Schindler's List 29
Sense and Sensibility 26
Shakespeare in Love 24
Silence of the Lambs 27
Sling Blade 25
Slumdog Millionaire 26
Splendor in the Grass 25
Sting, The 27
Sunset Boulevard 28
Talk to Her 26
Tender Mercies 24
Terms of Endearment 25
Thelma & Louise 23
To Kill a Mockingbird 29
Tom Jones 25
Traffic 23
Treasure of the Sierra Madre 27
Usual Suspects 27
Witness 23
Woman of the Year 27

RELIGION

Agony and the Ecstasy 23
Bells of St. Mary's 24
Ben-Hur 26
Boy in the Striped Pajamas 26
Chronicles of Narnia/Lion 23
Doubt 25
Elmer Gantry 25
Exorcist, The 25
Going My Way 24
Hunchback/Notre Dame 26
Life of Brian 23
Song of Bernadette 22
Ten Commandments 24

ROAD MOVIES

Adventures of Priscilla 23
Central Station 26
Crazy Heart 25
Easy Rider 23
Little Miss Sunshine 24
Midnight Run 23
Motorcycle Diaries 23
Paris, Texas 22
Straight Story 24
Thelma & Louise 23
TransAmerica 24
Up in the Air 23
Y Tu Mamá También 24

ROCK 'N' ROLL

Almost Famous 23
Blackboard Jungle 23
Commitments, The 24
Grease 23
Hard Day's Night 24
Pink Floyd The Wall 23
This Is Spinal Tap 26

ROMANCE

(See also Chick Flicks)

Adventures of Robin Hood 25
African Queen 28
All This, and Heaven Too 26
Almost Famous 23
American in Paris 26
Annie Hall 27
Apartment, The 25
Awful Truth 25
Ball of Fire 26
Barefoot in the Park 23
Before Sunrise 23
Bishop's Wife 24
Breaking the Waves 23
Brief Encounter 27
Bringing Up Baby 27
Broadcast News 23
Brokeback Mountain 24
Camille 26
Carousel 24
Casablanca 29
Charade 26
Children of a Lesser God 23
Children of Paradise 28
Chocolat 22
Claire's Knee 23
Cold Mountain 22
Crossing Delancey 23
Curious Case of Benjamin Button 23
Dangerous Liaisons 24
Dark Victory 25
Days of Heaven 23
Desk Set 25
Doctor Zhivago 27
Easter Parade 22
Education, An 25
Enchanted 23
Eternal Sunshine 23

Title	Rating
Farewell My Concubine	25
Far From Heaven	24
Far from the Madding Crowd	23
(500) Days of Summer	22
Flying Down to Rio	23
For Whom the Bell Tolls	25
Fountainhead, The	22
From Here to Eternity	26
Gay Divorcee	25
Georgy Girl	23
Ghost and Mrs. Muir	24
Gigi	24
Gone with the Wind	28
Graduate, The	27
Hannah and Her Sisters	24
Harold and Maude	25
His Girl Friday	26
Holiday	27
Holiday Inn	23
House of Flying Daggers	24
How Green Was My Valley	27
Indochine	23
It Happened One Night	28
It's Complicated	22
Jane Eyre	25
Jezebel	25
Jules and Jim	24
Kiss Me Kate	24
Lady and the Tramp	26
Lady Eve	28
Laura	27
Like Water for Chocolate	25
Lili	24
Little Children	24
Lost Horizon	25
Love in the Afternoon	24
Man and a Woman	24
Manhattan	26
Marty	25
Moonstruck	24
Moulin Rouge!	23
My Big Fat Greek Wedding	23
My Brilliant Career	25
My Fair Lady	27
Ninotchka	25
Notorious	27
Once	25
Painted Veil	23
Philadelphia Story	27
Picnic	24
Place in the Sun	27
Play It Again, Sam	22
Pride & Prejudice (2005)	23
Quiet Man	27
Reader, The	25
Rebecca	27
Red Shoes	26
Remains of the Day	24
Romeo and Juliet	26
Room with a View	26
Sabrina	25
Say Anything	23
Shall We Dance	25
Shop Around the Corner	24
Slumdog Millionaire	26
Smiles of a Summer Night	26
South Pacific	24
Spellbound	24
Story of Adele H.	24
Strictly Ballroom	23
Summertime	23
Swing Time	26
Talk to Her	26
Thomas Crown Affair	23
To Catch a Thief	25
To Have and Have Not	26
Tootsie	25
Top Hat	27
Truly Madly Deeply	23
Two for the Road	24
Umbrellas of Cherbourg	24
Up in the Air	23
Vertigo	27
Waitress	24
Walk the Line	25
West Side Story	27
White Christmas	25
Witness	23
Women in Love	23
Wuthering Heights	27

SCI-FI

Title	Rating
Akira	23
Alien	25
Aliens	23
Avatar	26
Back to the Future	23
Blade Runner	26
Brother from Another Planet	23
Close Encounters	24
Day the Earth Stood Still	25
District 9	22
Donnie Darko	22
E.T.	26
Forbidden Planet	25
Invasion/Body Snatchers	24
Iron Man	26
Matrix, The	25

Metropolis	27
On the Beach	26
Planet of the Apes	23
Sleeper	23
Star Trek	26
Star Trek II	23
Star Wars	28
Star Wars III/Revenge of Sith	23
Star Wars V/Empire Strikes	26
Star Wars VI/Return of Jedi	24
Terminator, The	24
Terminator 2: Judgment Day	23
Thing, The (1951)	23
Thing, The (1982)	23
Time After Time	23
Twelve Monkeys	22
2001: A Space Odyssey	26
War of the Worlds	23
X2: X-Men United	24

SCREWBALL COMEDIES

Animal Crackers	26
Awful Truth	25
Ball of Fire	26
Born Yesterday	26
Bringing Up Baby	27
Cocoanuts, The	24
Day at the Races	24
Duck Soup	27
His Girl Friday	26
Horse Feathers	24
It Happened One Night	28
Lady Eve	28
Miracle of Morgan's Creek	23
My Man Godfrey	25
Night at the Opera	26
Palm Beach Story	25
Philadelphia Story	27
Raising Arizona	23
Thin Man	26
Women on the Verge	24

SILENT

Birth of a Nation	25
Cabinet of Dr. Caligari	26
City Lights	28
General, The	28
Gold Rush	28
Metropolis	27
Modern Times	28
Napoléon	28
Nosferatu	26
Potemkin	27
Thief of Bagdad	24

SOUNDTRACKS

(See also Musicals;
* Best Score Oscar winner)

Adventures of Robin Hood*	25
Aladdin*	24
Alexander Nevsky	26
All That Jazz*	24
Almost Famous	23
Amadeus	26
Amarcord	26
American Beauty	24
American Graffiti	24
American in Paris*	26
Anatomy of a Murder	26
Beauty/Beast (1991)*	26
Bells Are Ringing	24
Ben-Hur*	26
Big Chill	23
Blackboard Jungle	23
Black Orpheus	26
Born Free*	24
Braveheart	26
Breakfast at Tiffany's*	26
Bridge on the River Kwai*	28
Brief Encounter	27
Brokeback Mountain*	24
Butch Cassidy*	26
Cabaret*	26
Charade	26
Chariots of Fire*	26
Chinatown	27
Cinema Paradiso	26
Clockwork Orange	25
Cold Mountain	22
Commitments, The	24
Crazy Heart	25
Crouching Tiger*	24
Damn Yankees	24
Dances with Wolves*	23
Days of Heaven	23
Days of Wine and Roses	27
Death in Venice	24
Diner	25
Diva	24
Doctor Zhivago*	27
Donnie Darko	22
Down by Law	24
Dracula	24
Dreamgirls	23
Dumbo*	24
Easter Parade*	22
Easy Rider	23
8½	26
Empire of the Sun	25

GENRES/FEATURES

E.T.* 26
Exodus* 23
Fantasia 28
Fantasia 2000 24
Far From Heaven 24
Fiddler on the Roof* 26
Fight Club 23
Forbidden Planet 25
Forrest Gump 24
Frida* 25
Gigi* 24
Gladiator 23
Godfather, The 29
Godfather Part II* 29
Gold Diggers of 1933 25
Goldfinger 26
Gone with the Wind 28
Good, the Bad and the Ugly 24
Graduate, The 27
Great Escape 27
Hard Day's Night 24
Harold and Maude 25
Harry Potter/Sorcerer's 24
High Noon* 28
Hustle & Flow 23
Il Postino* 24
In Cold Blood 25
I Want to Live! 24
Jaws* 26
Jungle Book (1967) 23
King and I* 27
Last Emperor* 26
Last of the Mohicans 22
La Strada 27
La Vie en Rose 25
Lawrence of Arabia* 29
Life Is Beautiful* 27
Lili* 24
Limelight* 24
Lion in Winter* 28
Lion King* 25
Little Mermaid* 24
Local Hero 26
Lock, Stock and Two . . . 23
Lord of Rings/Fellowship* 27
Lord of Rings/Return* 28
Lord of Rings/Two Towers 27
Love Is Many-Splendored . . .* 22
Magnificent Seven 26
Man and a Woman 24
Man Who Knew Too Much 24
Man with the Golden Arm 24
Mark of Zorro 22
Mary Poppins* 27
Mean Streets 24
Midnight Cowboy 26
Midnight Express* 24
Mighty Wind 23
Mission, The 24
Muriel's Wedding 22
Music Man* 25
My Fair Lady* 27
Nashville 23
Natural, The 23
Nightmare Before Christmas 24
Night of the Hunter 27
North by Northwest 28
Now, Voyager* 27
Oklahoma!* 24
Oliver!* 24
Once* 25
Once Upon a Time/West 25
On the Town* 23
Out of Africa* 25
Pink Floyd The Wall 23
Pink Panther 24
Place in the Sun* 27
Princess Bride 27
Psycho 28
Pulp Fiction 26
Raiders of the Lost Ark 28
Ray 26
Red Shoes* 26
Red Violin* 24
Rescuers, The 23
Right Stuff* 26
Rocky 25
Romeo and Juliet 26
Room with a View 26
Run Lola Run 23
Rushmore 23
Say Anything 23
Schindler's List* 29
Seven Brides/Seven Brothers* 24
Shakespeare in Love* 24
Shall We Dance 25
Shrek 26
Slumdog Millionaire* 26
Snow White 27
Song of Bernadette 22
Sound of Music* 28
Spartacus 26
Spellbound* 24
Stagecoach* 27
Stand by Me 24
Star Trek II 23
Star Wars* 28
Star Wars V/Empire Strikes 26

Star Wars VI/Return of Jedi 24
Sting, The* 27
Strictly Ballroom 23
Sunset Boulevard* 28
Sweet Smell of Success 27
Talk to Her 26
Tarzan 22
Taxi Driver 27
Third Man 28
This Is Spinal Tap 26
Thunderball 22
To Kill a Mockingbird 29
Tom Jones* 25
To Sir, With Love 22
Touch of Evil 26
Two for the Road 24
2001: A Space Odyssey 26
Vertigo 27
Victor/Victoria* 23
Wait Until Dark 25
Walk the Line 25
Way We Were* 24
West Side Story* 27
When Harry Met Sally . . . 26
Wild Bunch 27
Willy Wonka 26
Wind and the Lion 24
Wizard of Oz* 28
Yankee Doodle Dandy* 25
Young Frankenstein 27
Zorba the Greek 25
Zulu 24

SPORTS

BASEBALL

Bang the Drum Slowly 23
Damn Yankees 24
Eight Men Out 24
Natural, The 23

BASKETBALL

Hoosiers 23

BOXING

Body and Soul 25
Cinderella Man 25
Great White Hope 25
Million Dollar Baby 27
On the Waterfront 28
Raging Bull 26
Requiem for a Heavyweight 26
Rocky 25

FOOTBALL

Blind Side 26
Fortune Cookie 23
Rudy 23

HOCKEY

Miracle 24

OTHER

Bend It Like Beckham 26
Chariots of Fire 26
Hustler, The 25
Invictus 24
Seabiscuit 25

STAGE ADAPTATIONS

Amadeus 26
Animal Crackers 26
Anne of the Thousand Days 26
Arsenic and Old Lace 26
Auntie Mame 25
Awful Truth 25
Bad Seed 22
Barefoot in the Park 23
Becket 26
Bells Are Ringing 24
Born Yesterday 26
Brief Encounter 27
Brigadoon 24
Cabaret 26
Cabin in the Sky 24
Carmen Jones 23
Carousel 24
Cat on a Hot Tin Roof 25
Chicago 27
Children of a Lesser God 23
Children's Hour 24
Cocoanuts, The 24
Country Girl 24
Damn Yankees 24
Desk Set 25
Dial M for Murder 25
Diary of Anne Frank 23
Dinner at Eight 27
Doubt 25
Dreamgirls 23
Driving Miss Daisy 24
Elephant Man 24
Fiddler on the Roof 26
Front Page 24
Frost/Nixon 25
Funny Girl 26
Gaslight 26
Gay Divorcee 25
Glengarry Glen Ross 23
Grease 23
Great White Hope 25
Guys and Dolls 24
Hamlet (1948) 27

GENRES/FEATURES

Title	Rating
Hamlet (1996)	24
Harvey	26
Heaven Can Wait	24
Heiress, The	27
Henry V	26
High Society	23
His Girl Friday	26
Holiday	27
I Never Sang for My Father	27
Inherit the Wind	26
Jezebel	25
Key Largo	26
King and I	27
Kiss Me Kate	24
La Cage aux Folles	24
Lion in Winter	28
Little Foxes	26
Man for All Seasons	28
Man Who Came to Dinner	26
Member of the Wedding	25
Miracle Worker	25
Mister Roberts	27
Music Man	25
My Fair Lady	27
Night of the Iguana	23
Odd Couple	25
Oklahoma!	24
Oliver!	24
One, Two, Three	23
On Golden Pond	24
On the Town	23
Peter Pan	25
Philadelphia Story	27
Picnic	24
Play It Again, Sam	22
Raisin in the Sun	26
Romeo and Juliet	26
Ruling Class	23
Seven Year Itch	23
Shirley Valentine	24
Shop Around the Corner	24
Show Boat	23
Sleuth	25
Soldier's Story	26
Sound of Music	28
South Pacific	24
Stage Door	25
Stalag 17	27
Steel Magnolias	24
Streetcar Named Desire	27
Suddenly, Last Summer	24
Summertime	23
Sweeney Todd	23
Sweet Bird of Youth	24
Thousand Clowns	25
Torch Song Trilogy	23
Trip to Bountiful	24
Wait Until Dark	25
West Side Story	27
Who's Afraid of V. Woolf?	25
Witness for the Prosecution	27
Women, The	26

SWASHBUCKLERS

Title	Rating
Adventures of Robin Hood	25
Captain Blood	23
Court Jester, The	24
Mark of Zorro	22
Master and Commander	23
Mutiny on the Bounty (1935)	25
Mutiny on the Bounty (1962)	22
Pirates Caribbean/The Curse	24
Thief of Bagdad	24
Three Musketeers	22

THRILLERS

(See also James Bond)

Title	Rating
Accused, The	23
Alien	25
Aliens	23
Apollo 13	24
Bad Day at Black Rock	24
Bad Seed	22
Birds, The	24
Blood Simple	24
Body Heat	24
Bourne Ultimatum	25
Boys from Brazil	24
Breach	23
Cape Fear	25
Changeling	23
Collector, The	23
Constant Gardener	23
Counterfeit Traitor	25
Day of the Jackal	25
Dead Again	22
Diabolique	26
Dial M for Murder	25
Dirty Pretty Things	23
District 9	22
Diva	24
Dog Day Afternoon	24
Don't Look Now	24
Eastern Promises	24
Escape from Alcatraz	23
Experiment in Terror	25
Eye of the Needle	23
Eyewitness	23
Fail-Safe	24

Forbidden Planet 25
Foreign Correspondent 24
Fugitive, The 23
Gaslight 26
Hound of the Baskervilles 22
Hunt for Red October 24
Illusionist, The 23
Inside Man 23
Insider, The 25
In the Valley of Elah 22
Invasion/Body Snatchers 24
Ipcress File 24
Jaws 26
Kiss Me Deadly 24
Lady Vanishes 25
La Femme Nikita 23
Last Seduction 22
Lifeboat 25
Manchurian Candidate 27
Man Who Knew Too Much 24
Marathon Man 24
Memento 26
Midnight Express 24
Munich 23
Murder on the Orient Express 23
Night of the Hunter 27
North by Northwest 28
Notorious 27
Parallax View 24
Poltergeist 22
Psycho 28
Pulp Fiction 26
Rear Window 28
Rosemary's Baby 24
Run Lola Run 23
Saboteur 23
Seven 23
Seven Days in May 26
Shadow of a Doubt 26
Silence of the Lambs 27
Sixth Sense 26
Sleuth 25
Spellbound 24
Spy Who Came in from Cold 25
Strangers on a Train 26
Suspicion 25
Taxi Driver 27
Third Man 28
39 Steps 27
Three Days of the Condor 24
Time After Time 23
To Catch a Thief 25
Torn Curtain 23
Twelve Monkeys 22
Vertigo 27
Wages of Fear 27
Wait Until Dark 25
Z 26

WAR

CIVIL WAR

Cold Mountain 22
Dances with Wolves 23
Friendly Persuasion 24
Gettysburg 25
Glory 25
Gone with the Wind 28
Good, the Bad and the Ugly 24

IRAQ WAR

Hurt Locker 26

KOREAN WAR

Manchurian Candidate 27
MASH 26

OTHER

Alexander Nevsky 26
Battle of Algiers 28
Beau Geste 25
Black Hawk Down 23
Braveheart 26
For Whom the Bell Tolls 25
Gunga Din 25
Henry V 26
Last of the Mohicans 22
Master and Commander 23
Napoléon 28
Ran 27
Sand Pebbles 24
300 22

VIETNAM WAR

Apocalypse Now 27
Coming Home 23
Deer Hunter 26
Full Metal Jacket 24
Killing Fields 26
Platoon 25
Quiet American 24

WWI

All Quiet on Western Front 28
Gallipoli 25
Grand Illusion 28
Lawrence of Arabia 29
Paths of Glory 28
Sergeant York 25

WWII

Americanization of Emily 24
Best Years of Our Lives 28

Boy in the Striped Pajamas	26
Bridge on the River Kwai	28
Caine Mutiny	27
Casablanca	29
Catch-22	25
Counterfeit Traitor	25
Damned, The	23
Das Boot	28
Diary of Anne Frank	23
Empire of the Sun	25
Eye of the Needle	23
Flags of Our Fathers	23
Garden of the Finzi-Continis	25
Great Escape	27
Guns of Navarone	23
Hope and Glory	26
Inglourious Basterds	25
Letters from Iwo Jima	27
Longest Day	24
Mister Roberts	27
Mrs. Henderson Presents	23
Mrs. Miniver	25
Patton	27
Pianist, The	28
Saving Private Ryan	26
Schindler's List	29
Seven Beauties	26
Shop on Main Street	27
South Pacific	24
Stalag 17	27
Tin Drum	23
To Have and Have Not	26
Tora! Tora! Tora!	23
Twelve O'Clock High	26
Two Women	25

WEDDINGS

Father of the Bride	23
Godfather, The	29
In-Laws, The	24
Monsoon Wedding	24
Muriel's Wedding	22
My Big Fat Greek Wedding	23
Philadelphia Story	27
Wedding Banquet	22

WESTERNS

Blazing Saddles	25
Butch Cassidy	26
Dances with Wolves	23
Destry Rides Again	25
Duel in the Sun	23
For a Few Dollars More	23
Fort Apache	23
Good, the Bad and the Ugly	24
High Noon	28
How the West Was Won	23
Hud	26
Jeremiah Johnson	23
Little Big Man	24
Magnificent Seven	26
Man Who Shot Liberty Valance	25
McCabe & Mrs. Miller	23
My Darling Clementine	25
My Little Chickadee	23
No Country for Old Men	24
Oklahoma!	24
Once Upon a Time/West	25
Outlaw Josey Wales	25
Ox-Bow Incident	27
Red River	26
Rio Bravo	24
Searchers, The	27
Shane	26
She Wore a Yellow Ribbon	24
Silverado	24
Stagecoach	27
3:10 to Yuma	23
True Grit	22
Unforgiven	26
Viva Zapata!	23
Wild Bunch	27

ZAGATWINE™

Presents

12 BLOCKBUSTER WINES for ONLY $69.99

HOLLYWOOD

Starring CULT WASHINGTON CABERNET, GOLD-MEDAL MALBEC, SUMPTUOUS BORDEAUX, COOL CALIFORNIA CHARDONNAY and more.

Also featuring FOUR FREE WINE GLASSES.

Order at **zagatwine.com/2161024**

or call 1-800-892-4427 quote code 2161024

You must be at least 21 years old to order. All wine orders will be processed and fulfilled by a licensed retailer in the industry and applicable taxes are paid. Offer may vary. Void where prohibited by law. **Please visit our website for complete list of shipping states, terms and conditions.**

Take us with you.
ZAGATMobile

You choose the phone and we'll help you choose the place. Access Zagat dining & travel content on your **iPhone, BlackBerry, Android, Windows Mobile** and **Palm smartphones.**

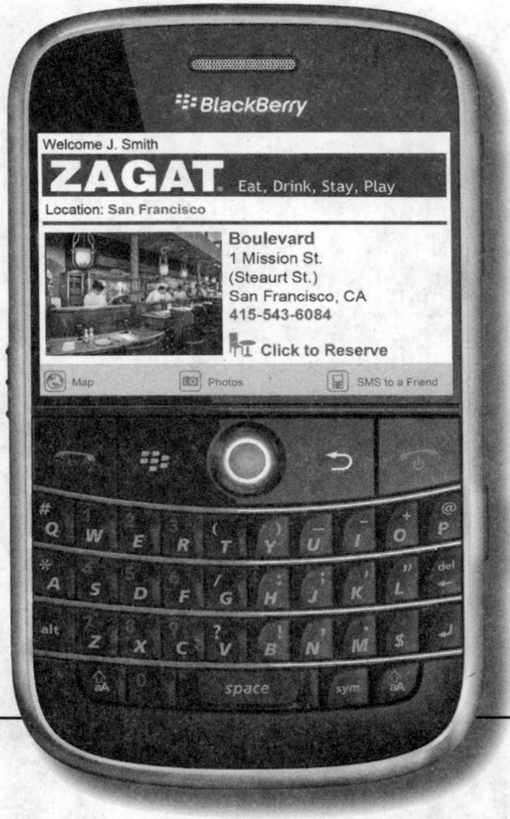

Text **EAT to 78247** for more information or visit us online at **www.zagat.com/mobile**